**5-7, rue de l'Ecole-Polytechnique, 75005 Paris**

http://www.harmattan.fr
diffusion.harmattan@wanadoo.fr
harmattan1@wanadoo.fr

ISBN : 978-2-343-07969-1
EAN : 9782343079691

**Ambash Affair**
**L'Affaire Ambash**
משפט אמבש

**Quête du sens**

*Collection dirigée par Georges-Elia Sarfati*

« Quête du sens » participe d'une réévaluation de l'éthique et de l'accomplissement des fins humaines, considérant que l'émancipation des sujets est indissociable des luttes pour l'émancipation collective. Fondée en référence à la pensée de Viktor Frankl, philosophe et pionner de la thérapie existentielle, cette collection accueille des textes narratifs, des essais critiques, des entretiens, des collectifs dont les auteurs sont soucieux de témoigner de la recherche du sensé, et de l'affirmation persistante de l'action et de la liberté humaines dans une histoire en proie aux conflits des significations. Ses perspectives questionnent la condition humaine – compte tenu de ses dimensions tragiques : souffrance, culpabilité, finitude- dans les trois registres de la création, de l'expérience et de l'attitude. Ses contributions – de la clinique à la politique- ouvrent sur la possibilité d'un remaniement discret des idées reçues, comprises comme des héritages actifs du conformisme et des totalitarismes, privilégiant ainsi l'expression de l'expérience immédiate et concrète d'une pensée de rupture avec l'air du temps.

Dernières parutions

Léo Michel Abrami, *La recherche du sens en analyse existentielle et logothérapie*, 2015.
Mohamed Yahya Ould Ciré, *La Mauritanie, Entre l'esclavage et le racisme,* 2014.
Sarah Bensaïd, *Bénéfices secondaires*, 2013.

AMBASH
Préface d'Emmanuel Athanasiou
Introduction de Georges-Elia Sarfati

# Ambash Affair
# L'Affaire Ambash
# משפט אמבש

L'Harmattan

# PREFACE

> "Everyone shall be entitled to a fair and public hearing by a competent, independent and impartial tribunal established by law."
>
> Article 14 of the International Covenant on Civil and Political Rights (ICCPR)[1]

The right to a fair hearing, the right to due process of law is the corner stone of democracy. It is the basic pillar of a modern State respecting, protecting and promoting human rights. What many have the tendency to forget is that this particular right, consecrated by international human rights law has a major purpose: to protect the liberty and the security of the person, under any circumstances. Indeed, it is the right to due process of law that guarantees people their right to live freely, to exercise other liberties and rights freely, not to

---

[1] International Covenant on Civil and Political Rights, UN General Assembly resolution 2200A (XXI), December 16, 1966, entered into force March 23, 1976 [hereinafter ICCPR]. The Article 14 states *inter alia*: "1. *All persons shall be equal before the courts and tribunals. In the determination of any criminal charge against him, or of his rights and obligations in a suit at law, everyone shall be entitled to a fair and public hearing by a competent, independent and impartial tribunal established by law. The press and the public may be excluded from all or part of a trial for reasons of morals, public order (ordre public) or national security in a democratic society, or when the interest of the private lives of the parties so requires, or to the extent strictly necessary in the opinion of the court in special circumstances where publicity would prejudice the interests of justice; but any judgement rendered in a criminal case or in a suit at law shall be made public except where the interest of juvenile persons otherwise requires or the proceedings concern matrimonial disputes or the guardianship of children.*
*2. Everyone charged with a criminal offence shall have the right to be presumed innocent until proved guilty according to law*".

be afraid of human rights violations such as arbitrary detention, police violence, such as confession under torture, and many other types of violations that we have observed across the world.

The fundamental importance of this particular right was recognized under international human rights instruments adopted not only at the global level of the United Nations but also in many regional human rights treaties like the European Convention for the Protection of Human Rights and Fundamental Freedoms (article 6), adopted in the framework of the Council of Europe or the American Convention on Human Rights (article 8) adopted by the Organization of American States. At the international level, the major role of this particular right to a fair trial or due process of law was highlighted by its inclusion as a non-derogable right provided for in Article 4(2) of the ICCPR[2]. That means that this special category of rights is considered so crucial that they cannot be taken away or compromised under any circumstances, not even when a State is at war or facing internal conflict or social unrest.

The right to a fair trial can be violated in many ways, but as a general principle it must always be kept in mind that the accused person must at all times be given a genuine opportunity to answer the charges, challenge evidence and cross-examine witnesses, and to do so in a dignified atmosphere. Needless to say, that all information gathered during my own independent investigation on this landmark case, which became a media experiment and a barometer of social attitude, showed clearly that in spite of the grave accusations and extremely serious character of the case, the Israeli judicial system did not guarantee the right to due process of law in a dignified way. Media and judges behaved as if the accused was already guilty of all the

---

[2] Article 4. 1: *In time of public emergency which threatens the life of the nation and the existence of which is officially proclaimed, the States Parties to the present Covenant may take measures derogating from their obligations under the present Covenant to the extent strictly required by the exigencies of the situation, provided that such measures are not inconsistent with their other obligations under international law and do not involve discrimination solely on the ground of race, color, sex, language, religion or social origin.*
*2. No derogation from articles 6, 7, 8 (paragraphs I and 2), 11, 15, 16 and 18 may be made under this provision.*

charges. Taking into account that the major charge was slavery, one of the worst human rights violations and a major criminal offence, one would expect of the Israeli police and judicial system to deal with such case with the utmost professionalism. This was clearly not the case, as proved during the trial several times and stated even in the judgement, from the very first paragraphs. Except if one considers that the loss of investigation videos, threatening the accused and witnesses, promising gifts or exercising physical and verbal violence are part of normal professional police conduct in a modern State. Interrogations taking place in hotel rooms and coercing or torturing persons under investigation is what we call "miscarriage of justice".

The guidelines of the Office of the United Nations High Commissioner for Human Rights (OHCHR) clearly underline: "Failures and shortcomings at the stage of the criminal investigation may seriously jeopardize the right to fair trial proceedings and thereby also prejudice the right to be presumed innocent"[3]. In the mini – ratio (reasoning) part of the judgement of Daniel Ambash, the 3 judges of the Jerusalem District Court state clearly that "*some of the investigations were not documented, but these are negligible, especially at the beginning of the investigation, often due to error and sometimes due to a lack of care and attention. Though they were some investigation failures or violence, they are not significant and cannot cause us to discard the nature of the investigation and its results.*" This is quite a surprising appreciation, to say the least as regards legal analysis, when a Court of justice, composed of 3 judges, passes so rapidly from clearly demarked red lines regarding police misconduct in such an important case – well documented misconduct and relevant violations, so shocking that in any other legal system of a modern so-called "democratic State" there would have been an institutional response – to admit the police failures not only at the stage of investigation but also with respect to all the other parts of the legal proceedings. As a human rights activist and lawyer, I was extremely surprised, even before coming to Israel and meeting different actors involved in this case that a court simply dismissed, in one phrase, violations that would have invalidated the process in any other

[3] http://search.ohchr.org/results.aspx?k=right%20to%20a%20fair%20trial.

country, or at least any other democratic country with independent and impartial institutions.

It is the role of the judges to remind to Prosecutor of the Guidelines on the Role of Prosecutors, in particular Guideline 16: "*When prosecutors come into possession of evidence against suspects that they know or believe on reasonable grounds was obtained through recourse to unlawful methods, which constitute a grave violation of the suspect's human rights, especially involving torture or cruel, inhuman or degrading treatment or punishment, or other abuses of human rights, they shall refuse to use such evidence against anyone other than those who used such methods, or inform the Court accordingly, and shall take all necessary steps to ensure that those responsible for using such methods are brought to justice.*" Is it possible that the Prosecutor was not aware of the multiple and repeated violations and shameless behavior of police agents throughout this process? Even if that was so, should he not have changed his attitude when the defense lawyers of Daniel Ambash brought those shocking elements before the court? I shall refer to another fundamental principle: the prohibition on the use of evidence obtained through unlawful means, in other words: the right of an accused not to be compelled to testify against himself or herself remains valid throughout the trial proceedings. It means that "*there must be an absence of both direct and indirect physical or psychological pressure from the investigating authorities for the purposes of obtaining a confession. An accused who has confessed guilt after such undue pressure must bring the matter before the competent authorities, including the judge(s) in the trial court, failing which he or she runs the risk of not having this undue compulsion considered in connection with the determination of the criminal charge.*[4]" That is exactly what happened in the case of Daniel Ambash. It is not a simple assumption, it is a matter of fact, of truth, of evidence, simply ignored by the judges and the prosecutor whose role in all this remains a big mystery.

The police behavior from the beginning and even several months after the sentencing of the accused, is not only problematic but illegal.

---

[4] Op. idem.

Their acts, in the framework of a legal process amount to torture. Allow me to remind you of some basic rules of international law regarding torture, especially in the framework of a legal process: article 7 of the ICCPR[5] prohibits torture or cruel, inhuman or degrading treatment or punishment and is a norm of customary international law that also belongs to the category of *jus cogens*. In practical terms that means that this rule is applicable to all States, regardless if they have signed and/or ratified the international instrument on torture. This is a universal principle of law applied in all circumstances. The numerous testimonies regarding physical violence, threats, verbal abuse, mental intimidation (the list goes on and on) the unprofessional and illegal methods that police agents, in other words State agents used against several members of the Ambash family should shock the judges and journalists and Israeli society as a whole. It should not be treated like a minor detail of the case, it should be regarded as proof that State agents breached the law. I personally contacted Mahash, Israel's Police Investigation Unit to ask where the internal investigations stands following complaints of many members of the Ambash family. I saw with my own eyes the video of the adolescent girls, Haya 16 years old, with traces of police violence on her face and body. Until today, this process has not moved forward leaving serious doubts whether the Police of the Police does, indeed, take seriously into account civil complains.

It is even more shocking that the same women, the Ambash partners (who are considered by the judicial system of Israel as victims of slavery, sexual exploitation, violence etc.), are also victims of institutional violence from several fronts: police, justice, social workers, etc. What kind of system judicial, legal and institutional would treat victims of slavery in this manner? What kind of society or

---

[5] Art 1(1): ... "*the term "torture" means any act by which severe pain or suffering, whether physical or mental, is intention ally inflicted on a person for such purposes as obtaining from him or a third person information or a confession, punishing him for an act he or a third person has committed or is suspected of having committed, or intimidating or coercing him or a third person, or for any reason based on discrimination of any kind, when such pain or suffering is inflicted by or at the instigation of or with the consent or acquiescence of a public official or other person acting in an official capacity*".

enlightened individual would not ask any questions regarding the handling of this case? How is it that the prosecution had such unlimited access to the media, when the Ambash companions did not have any? How can a modern, civilized and open society, as the Israeli society aspires to be, exercise its lawful right to information, criticism, institutional control, when there is such a biased interpretation of the law, supposed to protect the victims, when the victims themselves do not have the right to express themselves? That is a perverted interpretation of the law and the reality is that today, many of the members of the so called "sect" are in such a bad situation – as seen with my own eyes – that one should ask himself or herself: "has something gone wrong here" or "has justice played its role to protect society from a danger"? When I say danger, I am not referring to the defendants, by referring to their situation I am definitely not implying that the responsibility lies upon Daniel Ambash. The responsibility lies primarily on the system which treats those women in an unspeakable manner and marginalizes them increasingly throughout the years. Personally, I was totally surprised that the judges decided whether and how those 4 women, were under the mental control of Daniel Ambash without a proper psychological or psychiatric expert assessment, without inviting reputable psychiatrists to examine them and to submit report in proper and due form. I consider, that after all those years, it is quite obvious that the intense and non-stop struggle of the 4 women, to support the plea of their companion is the best proof that obviously the judges are not psychiatrists and obviously "the monster" cannot exercise his control over the women while in prison. These are quite evident questions. I am quite dismayed by the attitude of the legal system towards the Ambash family. Ignorance? Bad faith? Marginalization? Punishment? Limiting the scope of an open society?

I will not enter into the details of the case, currently pending before the Appeal Court of Jerusalem. I will not express in public my doubts regarding the guilt or innocence of Daniel Ambash, I will not criticize the judgement of the District Court as I was not present during the trial. However, what I can definitely state is that there are so many doubts over this case, there are so many lives broken, so many children abused by the social workers, women being harassed by police officers, that the State agents and representatives exercise such power without any control, that it is obvious that misconduct by State actors and miscarriages of justice exist. In the end, the members of the Ambash family were not protected by the law, the Akiva case demonstrates that in the most evident manner, and his story could well be that of a horror movie. His shocking letter should be a wakeup call to the entire political, social and judicial system of the State of Israel. His testimony, the allegations included in his letter, are of paramount importance not only for the right to due process of law but for the most fundamental right to liberty and security of a person, of a fellow human being. When I met him at his grandmother's house, the amazing artist Nina Mayo, the mother of Daniel, who was living just across the ancient walls of the historic Jerusalem, in the neighborhood of the artists, as it is called, I was wondering while listening carefully to their stories, whether there is an institutional policy of impunity in Israel or if one day the persons responsible for the tragedy that this child lived and experienced during his adolescence will be brought to justice. After reading the letter of Israel, we should exercise at least a minimum level of intellectual honesty and admit that the system did to this child exactly what the State accused his father of doing: torturing him in every possible way. The forced isolation into a psychiatric institution in combination with forced medical psychiatric treatment reminds us of the criminal methods used by other types of authoritarian regimes. The way this child was treated is a dark page in a modern history of Israeli justice. It is a total shame.

It is now up to the Appeal Court, part of the Supreme Court, to examine all these problematic elements and to show Israeli society that Justice is above all, even security considerations, social stereotypes or State power. Justice is a cornerstone of Democracy and democracy does not allow even one tiny doubt, not a single misbehavior from State agents or representatives, regarding the way its citizens are treated. As the Nobel Peace Prize Laureate from South Africa, the Archbishop Desmond Tutu once said: "*If you are neutral in situations of injustice, you have chosen the side of the oppressor.*"

*Emmanouil Athanasiou*

Note of the Editor: Internationally recognized human rights activist and lawyer, Emmanouil Athanasiou has served in several Inter-Governmental Organizations (United Nations, EU and OSCE) as well as Non-Governmental Organizations (MEF, FIDH, ECPM, FEMED). He was a founding member and coordinator of the international campaign for the 2010 Nobel Peace Prize Laureate Liu Xaobo. He is considered to be one of the most outspoken human rights advocates.

# PRÉFACE

> « Toute personne a droit à ce que sa cause soit entendue équitablement et publiquement par un tribunal compétent, indépendant et impartial, établi par la loi »[6]
>
> Article 14 du Pacte international relatif aux droits civils et politique.

Le droit à une audition équitable, le droit à un procès équitable est une des pierres d'angle de la démocratie. Il constitue le pilier fondamental d'un Etat moderne qui respecte, protège et promeut les droits de l'homme. Ce que beaucoup ont tendance à oublier c'est que ce droit particulier, consacré par le droit international vise un objectif majeur : protéger la liberté et la sécurité de la personne, en toutes circonstances. En effet, c'est le droit à un procès équitable qui garantit

[6] Adopté et ouvert à la signature, à la ratification et à l'adhésion par l'Assemblée générale dans sa résolution 2200 A (XXI) du 16 décembre 1966. L'article 14 1. Tous sont égaux devant les tribunaux et les cours de justice. Toute personne a droit à ce que sa cause soit entendue équitablement et publiquement par un tribunal compétent, indépendant et impartial, établi par la loi, qui décidera soit du bien-fondé de toute accusation en matière pénale dirigée contre elle, soit des contestations sur ses droits et obligations de caractère civil. Le huis clos peut être prononcé pendant la totalité ou une partie du procès soit dans l'intérêt des bonnes moeurs, de l'ordre public ou de la sécurité nationale dans une société démocratique, soit lorsque l'intérêt de la vie privée des parties en cause l'exige, soit encore dans la mesure où le tribunal l'estimera absolument nécessaire lorsqu'en raison des circonstances particulières de l'affaire la publicité nuirait aux intérêts de la justice ; cependant, tout jugement rendu en matière pénale ou civile sera public, sauf si l'intérêt de mineurs exige qu'il en soit autrement ou si le procès porte sur des différends matrimoniaux ou sur la tutelle des enfants.

2. Toute personne accusée d'une infraction pénale est présumée innocente jusqu'à ce que sa culpabilité ait été légalement établie.

aux citoyens leur droit de vivre librement, d'exercer leurs autres libertés et leurs autres droits librement, de créer, de progresser, de vivre en sécurité, de ne pas avoir à craindre les violations des droits tels que la détention arbitraire, la violence policière, tels que l'aveu obtenu sous la torture, et plusieurs autres violations que nous avons constatées dans le monde.

L'importance fondamentale de ce droit particulier a été reconnue par le droit international des droits de l'homme élaboré non seulement au niveau global dans le cadre des Nations Unies, mais aussi dans plusieurs traités régionaux des droits de l'homme, tels que la Convention Européenne pour la Sauvegarde des Droits de l'Homme et les Libertés Fondamentales (article 6), adoptée dans le cadre du Conseil de l'Europe ou la Convention Américaine des Droits de l'Homme (article 8) adoptée par l'Organisation des Etats d'Amérique. Au niveau international, le rôle majeur de ce droit particulier à un procès équitable (ou à une instruction judiciaire équitable) a été reconnu par son inclusion comme un droit non-dérogable par l'Article 42 (2) de l'ICCPR[7]. Cela signifie que cette catégorie spéciale de droits est considérée comme tellement cruciale qu'ils ne peuvent être ni supprimés ni restreints quelles que soient les circonstances, pas même lorsqu'un Etat est en guerre ou qu'il fait face à un conflit international ou une crise sociale majeure.

Le droit à un procès équitable peut être violé de différentes manières, mais en tant que principe général nous devons toujours garder à l'esprit que l'accusé(e) doit, à tout moment, avoir la possibilité de répondre aux accusations, d'examiner ou mettre en doute une preuve ou un témoin, et de le faire dans une atmosphère qui respecte sa dignité. Il est inutile de dire que toute information

---

[7] Article 4. 1. Dans le cas où un danger public exceptionnel menace l'existence de la nation et est proclamé par un acte officiel, les Etats parties au présent Pacte peuvent prendre, dans la stricte mesure où la situation l'exige, des mesures dérogeant aux obligations prévues dans le présent Pacte, sous réserve que ces mesures ne soient pas incompatibles avec les autres obligations que leur impose le droit international et qu'elles n'entraînent pas une discrimination fondée uniquement sur la race, la couleur, le sexe, la langue, la religion ou l'origine sociale.
2. La disposition précédente n'autorise aucune dérogation aux articles 6, 7, 8 (par. 1 et 2), 11, 15, 16 et 18.

recueillie au cours de mon enquête indépendante sur ce dossier choquant, qui est devenu un révélateur médiatique ainsi qu'un baromètre de l'attitude sociale, a clairement montré qu'en dépit des graves accusations et du caractère très sérieux du dossier, la justice israélienne n'a garanti a aucun des accusés le droit à un procès digne et équitable. Les médias et les juges se sont comportés comme si l'accusé était déjà coupable de toutes les charges retenues contre lui. Prenant en considération que l'accusation principale était l'esclavage, l'une des pires violations des droits de l'Homme et un crime majeur, on aurait attendu de la police et du système pénal israélien qu'ils traitent ce dossier avec le plus grand professionnalisme. De toute évidence, ce ne fut nullement le cas, comme cela fut démontré plusieurs fois tout au long du procès et même affirmé dans le jugement, dès les premiers paragraphes. Sauf si l'on considère que le fait de perdre les vidéos des interrogatoires, de menacer l'accusé et les témoins, de promettre des cadeaux ou d'user de violence verbale et physique constitue une conduite normale de la police professionnelle d'un Etat moderne. Les interrogatoires menés dans des chambres d'hôtel et le fait d'exercer des pressions ou de torturer les personnes impliquées, tout cela définit ce que l'on appelle en droit international un déni de justice ou une mauvaise administration de la justice.

Les lignes directrices du Bureau du Haut-Commissariat des Nations unies pour les Droits de l'Homme (HCDH) stipule explicitement : « Les échecs et les raccourcis au stade de l'enquête criminelle sont susceptibles de menacer sérieusement le droit à un procès équitable et portent par conséquent préjudice au droit à la présomption d'innocence »[8]. Dans l'introduction même du jugement de Daniel Ambash, les trois juges du Tribunal du District de Jérusalem déclarent clairement que « certains interrogatoires et parties de l'enquête n'étaient pas documentées, mais ceci est négligeable, particulièrement au début de l'enquête, ce qui est souvent dû à une erreur et quelquefois à un manque d'attention. Même si certaines erreurs d'enquête ou certaines violences ont été commises, celles-ci ne sont pas significatives et ne sont pas de nature à nous inciter à remettre en cause l'enquête ni ses résultats ». Il s'agit d'une appréciation assez

[8] http://search.ohchr.org/results.aspx?k=right%20to20a%20fair%20trial.

surprenante, c'est le moins que l'on puisse dire, s'agissant d'une analyse légale, lorsqu'une Cour de justice, composée de trois juges, franchit aussi rapidement la ligne rouge qui devrait être clairement établie sur les inconduites de la police dans un dossier aussi important – une inconduite et des violations bien documentées, qui sont tellement choquantes que dans n'importe quel autre système légal d'un soi-disant « Etat démocratique » moderne il y aurait eu une réponse et une réaction institutionnelle aux erreurs de la police, avec un impact non seulement sur l'enquête mais également sur toutes les autres étapes du processus judiciaire. En tant qu'avocat et militant des droits de l'homme, j'ai été extrêmement surpris, même avant de venir en Israël et de rencontrer les différents acteurs de ce dossier, qu'un Tribunal balaye purement et simplement d'une phrase les violations qui aurait invalidé le procès dans n'importe quel autre pays, ou au moins dans n'importe quel autre pays démocratique doté d'institutions indépendantes et impartiales.

Il incombe aux juges de rappeler au procureur les principes qui définissent la fonction des Procureurs, en particulier la Règle 16 : « Lorsque les procureurs entrent en possession d'une preuve à charge contre l'accusé, mais qu'ils savent ou suspectent, sur des bases raisonnables, que cette preuve a été obtenue par des méthodes illégales, qui constituent une grave violation des droits humains, particulièrement s'il s'agit de torture ou de traitement cruel, inhumain ou dégradant, ou encore d'humiliation, ou d'autres entraves aux droits humains, ils devront refuser d'utiliser une telle preuve contre quiconque, à part ceux qui ont recouru à de telles méthodes ; ou bien, ils en informeront la Cour, compte tenu de la situation, et prendront toutes les mesures pour s'assurer que les responsables de ces violations soient traduits en justice ». Est-il possible que le Procureur n'ait pas été au courant des violations, nombreuses et répétées, ni du comportement éhonté des fonctionnaires de police tout au long de cette affaire ? Même s'il en était ainsi, n'aurait-il pas dû changer d'attitude lorsque les avocats de la défense de Daniel Ambash ont présenté devant la Cour ces informations choquantes ? Je dois rappeler un autre principe fondamental : l'interdiction qui frappe l'usage de la preuve obtenue par des méthodes illégales, en d'autres termes : le droit de l'accusé(e) de ne pas être contraint de témoigner contre lui-même ou elle-même, demeure entier tout au long du procès. Cela signifie que « qu'il ne doit y avoir aucun recours ni à des pressions physique ou psychologique, directes ou indirectes, de la part des autorités, afin d'obtenir des aveux. Un accusé qui a avoué après avoir subi ce genre de pression doit le faire savoir aux autorités compétentes, y compris le(s) juge(s) du tribunal, prenant le risque de ne pas voir sa déclaration prise en considération dans la détermination de l'accusation criminelle.[9] » C'est exactement ce qui s'est produit dans l'affaire de Daniel Ambash. Ce n'est pas une simple supposition, c'est un état de fait, une vérité, une preuve, purement et simplement ignorés par les juges ainsi qu'un procureur dont le rôle dans tout cela demeure un mystère.

Le comportement de la police depuis le début, et même plusieurs mois après la condamnation de l'accusé, n'est pas seulement problématique, mais illégale. Leurs actes, dans le cadre d'une instruction légale confine à la torture. Permettez-moi de vous rappeler quelques règles fondamentales de la législation internationale concernant la torture, particulièrement dans le cadre d'une instruction légale : l'article 7 du PIDCP[10] interdit la torture ou tout traitement cruel, dégradant ou toute punition, et ceci constitue la norme du droit coutumier international qui tombe aussi dans la catégorie du *jus cogens*. Cela signifie pratiquement que cette règle s'applique à tous les Etats, indépendamment du fait qu'ils aient ou non signé et/ou ratifié la législation internationale concernant la torture. C'est un principe universel du droit à respecter en toutes circonstances. Les nombreux

---

[9] Op.idem.

[10] Art. 1. 1 : le terme "torture" désigne tout acte par lequel une douleur ou des souffrances aiguës, physiques ou mentales, sont intentionnellement infligées à une personne aux fins notamment d'obtenir d'elle ou d'une tierce personne des renseignements ou des aveux, de la punir d'un acte qu'elle ou une tierce personne a commis ou est soupçonnée d'avoir commis, de l'intimider ou de faire pression sur elle ou d'intimider ou de faire pression sur une tierce personne, ou pour tout autre motif fondé sur une forme de discrimination quelle qu'elle soit, lorsqu'une telle douleur ou de telles souffrances sont infligées par un agent de la fonction publique ou toute autre personne agissant à titre officiel ou à son instigation ou avec son consentement exprès ou tacite.

témoignages concernant le recours à la violence, aux menaces, à l'agression verbale, l'intimidation (la liste est longue), la conduite à la fois non-professionnelle et illégale dont les fonctionnaires de police ont fait preuve, en d'autres termes les moyens utilisés par des agents de l'Etat à l'encontre de plusieurs membres de la famille Ambash devraient choquer les juges, les journalistes et la société israélienne dans son ensemble. Ceci ne devrait pas être considéré comme un détail dans le traitement de ce dossier, mais au contraire comme une preuve que les représentants de l'Etat ont méprisé la loi. J'ai personnellement pris contact avec Mahash, l'Unité d'enquête spéciale de la police – la police des polices comme on l'appele – pour demander où en était l'enquête interne, suite aux plaintes des membres, de nombreux membres de la famille Ambash. J'ai vu de mes propres yeux la vidéo d'une jeune adolescente, H, âgée de 16 ans, qui portait sur son visage et sur son corps les traces de la violence policière. Jusqu'à ce jour, aucune enquête n'a progressé, ce qui laisse subsister de sérieux doutes sur la question de savoir si la Police des Polices prend effectivement au sérieux les plaintes des citoyens.

Il est encore plus choquant que ces mêmes femmes, les compagnes de Daniel Ambash, que la justice israélienne considère comme victimes d'esclavage, d'exploitation sexuelle, de violence, etc., soient les principales victimes d'une violence institutionnelle sur plusieurs fronts : la police, la justice, les assistants sociaux, etc. Quelle sorte de système juridique, légal et institutionnel traiterait de cette manière des victimes d'esclavage ? Quelle sorte de société ou de citoyens éclairés se priveraient de poser la moindre question, la moindre critique sur la manière dont ce dossier a été traité? Comment se fait-il que le ministère public ait un accès illimité aux médias, alors que les compagnes de Daniel Ambash n'en ont aucun ? Comment une société moderne, civilisée et ouverte, telle que l'est ou prétend l'être la société israélienne, peut exercer son droit légal à l'information, à la critique, son devoir démocratique de contrôle des institutions, quand existe une interprétation biaisée de la loi, censée protéger les victimes, alors que les victimes elles-mêmes n'ont pas le droit de s'exprimer ? Il s'agit là d'une interprétation perverse de la loi, et la situation est telle aujourd'hui que de nombreux membres de la soi-disant « secte » sont dans un si mauvais état – je l'ai constaté de mes propres yeux – que chacun devrait se demander : « ici, n'a-t-on pas commis une erreur ?», ou bien : « Est-ce que la justice a vraiment rempli son rôle pour protéger la société d'un danger ?» Lorsque je dis danger, je ne parle pas des accusés, en faisant référence à leur situation, je ne dis absolument pas que la responsabilité en incombe à Daniel Ambash. La responsabilité incombe en premier lieu au système qui a traité ces femmes d'une façon inqualifiable et qui les a marginalisées davantage, année après année. Personnellement, j'ai été très étonné de constater la manière dont les juges ont tranché la question de savoir si et comment ces 4 femmes étaient sous l'emprise psychologique de Daniel Ambash, sans s'appuyer sur la moindre expertise psychologique ou psychiatrique, sans inviter des psychiatres de renom à les examiner puis à remettre un rapport en bonne et due forme. Je considère qu'après toutes ces années, il est évident que le combat intense et incessant de ces quatre femmes, pour plaider en faveur de leur compagnon est la meilleure preuve que de toute évidence les juges n'ont pas la compétence de psychiatres et que de toute évidence aussi le « monstre » ne saurait exercer son pouvoir d'emprise sur les femmes, alors qu'il est en prison. Dès lors certaines questions simples se posent. Je suis assez consterné par l'attitude du système judiciaire à l'égard du groupe Ambash. Ignorance ? Mauvaise foi ? Marginalisation ? Punition ? Volonté de restreindre la portée de ce qu'est une société ouverte ?

Je n'entrerai pas dans les détails du dossier, qui est en attente de l'appel devant la Cour d'Appel de Jérusalem. Je ne ferai pas publiquement part de mes doutes concernant la culpabilité ou l'innocence de Daniel Ambash, et je ne disqualifierai pas le jugement du Tribunal de Première Instance, car je n'étais pas présent pendant le procès. Cependant, je peux affirmer sans hésiter que tant de doutes entourent ce dossier, tant de vies ont été brisées, tant d'enfants ont été malmenés par les services sociaux, et les femmes harcelées par les fonctionnaires de la police, que les agents et les représentants de l'Etat exercent un tel pouvoir sans aucun contrôle, qu'il est évident que les acteurs de l'Etat se sont comportés comme des voyous et qu'il y a là une mauvaise administration de la justice. Les membres de la famille

Ambash n'ont finalement pas été protégés par la loi ; le cas d'Israël le démontre de la façon la plus évidente, et son histoire pourrait bien être celle d'un film d'horreur. Sa lettre très choquante devrait sonner l'éveil de tout le système politique, social et judiciaire de l'Etat d'Israël. Son témoignage, les allégations que comporte cette lettre, sont d'une importance capitale, non seulement pour le droit à un procès équitable, mais pour le droit à la liberté et à la sécurité de la personne, le droit le plus fondamental d'un être humain. Lorsque je l'ai rencontré dans la maison de sa grand-mère –la très impressionnante artiste Nina Mayo – mère de Daniel, qui habitait tout près des murailles de la cité historique de Jérusalem, dans un quartier d'artistes, je me demandais, en écoutant attentivement toutes leurs histoires, s'il existe une politique d'impunité en Israël, et si un jour les gens responsables de la tragédie que cet enfant a vécu et subi au cours de son adolescence seront traduits en justice. Après avoir lu la lettre d'Israël, nous devrons avoir un minimum d'honnêteté intellectuelle et admettre que le système a infligé à cet enfant exactement ce dont l'Etat accuse son père : il l'a torturé de toutes les manières possibles. L'isolement forcé dans une institution psychiatrique, combiné avec l'administration forcée d'un traitement médical psychiatrique nous rappelle les méthodes criminelles des régimes autoritaires. La façon dont cet enfant a été traité constitue une page noire de l'histoire moderne de la justice israélienne. C'est une honte totale.

A présent, il incombe à la Cour d'Appel, qui fait partie de la Cour Suprême, d'examiner tous ces éléments problématiques et de montrer à la société israélienne que la Justice prime sur tout, y compris sur les considérations de sécurité, les stéréotypes sociaux ou le pouvoir d'Etat. La justice est la pierre angulaire de la Démocratie, et la démocratie ne permet pas le moindre doute, pas même le plus petit manquement de la part des agents et des représentants de l'Etat, s'agissant de la façon dont sont traités ses citoyens. Comme l'a dit un jour l'Archevêque Desmond Tutu, Lauréat Sud-Africain du Prix Nobel de la Paix : « Si vous restez neutres dans une situation d'injustice, vous prenez le parti de l'oppresseur ».

Emmanouil Athanasiou

Note de l'éditeur : Emmanouil Athanasiou est un avocat et un militant des droits de l'homme internationalement reconnu. Il a travaillé pour plusieurs Organisations Inter-Gouvernementales (Nations Unies, Union Européenne et OSCE) ainsi que pour des Organisations Non-Gouvernementales (MEF, FIDH, ECPM, FEMED). Il a été membre fondateur et coordinateur de la campagne internationale en faveur du Lauréat du Prix Nobel de la Paix 2010, le Chinois, Liu Xaobo. Il est considéré comme l'un des défenseurs les plus fermes des droits de l'homme.

# INTRODUCTION

In the modern state of Israel, an exemplary democracy, even too liberal on account of the wide freedom of expression that it provides to its adversaries as well as to its domestic ideological enemies, the Ambash Affair has been in the news for several years. It would be more correct to say that the *vox populi* has heard so much about it and has had its fill of it, that this case is now considered to be an understood matter, suitable for enriching the judicial annals with a precedent unique in the history of this young society.

Let's recall the facts. In 2013, after two years of preventive detention, which formed the first violation of the norms of criminal law, Daniel Ambash was condemned by the Jerusalem District Court to a prison sentence of 26 years, at the end of a rushed trial with considerable media attention. The indictment against the defendant contained no less than 18 charges, going from enslaving to regular maltreatment and acts of aggravated violence committed against six women and their children, within the community that he formed with them for more than twenty years.

Daniel Ambash, now sixty years old, has devoted himself since childhood to art – choreography, music, and design. He and his sister were members for several years running of Maurice Béjart's troupe, *Les Ballets du XXè siècle* and of the *Bat Dor* troupe. In 1978, he founded his own company, *Le Ballet-Théâtre de l'Arche,* with Maguy Marin, his first wife, whom he divorced in 1985. After a career crowned with success and marked by productions one more original and demanding than the next – the audio-visual archives attest to that—this artist decided in 1988 to settle down in Jerusalem. Daniel was born a Jew and his parents were themselves artists. He spent his youth in France and his show tours took him throughout all of Europe. In 1985, he wished to reorient his life by coming close to the sources of his original culture, by adopting the spiritual way of life of the Hassidim[11].

Daniel's parents, Nina and Arie Ambash, who had come from Bulgaria and Russia, were both pioneers of animated motion pictures, but also were, respectively, a talented painter and poet. In love with Paris, they first settled there with their children, leading a bohemian life style, concerned to transmit the spirit of freedom and creativity that had been at the origin of their coming together.

After getting married in Paris, at the synagogue on the Rue Pavé, to Ilana – a Jewish young woman, champion of Kung Fu in France – Daniel, shortly before the age of thirty-five, settled down in the Jerusalem region with his young wife. Their way of life little by little bloomed in the direction of a choice of communal living, marked by generosity and their very broad openmindedness towards all those, men and women, who found a welcome as well as comfort in their home. I had known Daniel in Paris, but the geographic distance had detached me from him. I still remember the feeling of sympathy that I felt when seeing their home on a hillside on the way out of Jerusalem, every time that I entered or left the city, on the occasion of my regular trips.

The years passed, the warm community that had developed around Daniel and Ilana became enriched by the presence of other friends, men and women, in couples or as singles, while the children multiplied. A born artist, having moved away from a great classic career, which promised recognition and public glory, Daniel had kept since his youth his taste for spectacles, then by mixing into his early education that which he was gradually giving himself, in contact with the masters of Jewish tradition, he had changed his life's ambition. He was now raising his own children according to the principles of generosity, of the tradition of welcoming and of hospitality, broadly open to society. While walking through the streets of Jerusalem, the passersby recognize Daniel's family, with their performances of

[11] Le lecteur se reportera au site consacré à Daniel Ambash : www.danielambash.info

dancing and singing, full of enthousiasm and devotion. Over the years, the original couple formed by Daniel and Ilana had undergone significant rearrangements, entered into by common accord, so much and so well that five new women companions had joined them. By the same impetus, this model of respectful polygamy, based on love and consent among adults, matched by a collective way of life oriented towards their spiritual ideals and the spreading of the books of Rabbi Nachman of Bratslav and his pupil, Rav Israel Ber Odesser, master of a marginal branch of Bratslaver [Breslover] Hassidism, who lived for more than a century (he died in Jerusalem in 1994). The expanded family devoted itself entirely to spreading the lessons for life of this great mystic.

Obviously, this mode of living together, which hardly conformed to contemporary norms, earned this group as much sympathy on the part of their friends than suspicion and hostility on the part of religious and secular circles, hardly inclined to tolerate a frank deviation from the conventions of the day: from a family based on polygamy (however, without these being officially sanctioned marriages by virtue of the legal prohibitions), children raised outside the current educational system, the activities of street artists based on sometimes rowdy performances, naïvely proselytizing conduct connected with the traditional quest for contributions, to the sale of books and disks or the free distribution of brochures with the image of their Rabbi.

All that went through a progress and an end that are recounted by the book written by four hands that the reader is going to read.

*

Daniel Ambash has shared for four years the lot of common criminals, whose everyday living regime, as we perceive it from outside, or during visits, as to what the free citizen can know of it, says a great deal about the violence of life in jail. We know, after Deleuze and Foucault, that despite the juridical safeguards of the system of justice, beyond their walls, prisons often constitute lawless zones, where a specific order reigns, an order based on relations of strength, as well as tacit or clandestine solidarity, and this reign is reenforced by the arbitrary, by the ruse and by legitimized brutality.

The practical treatment of the common criminal prisoner is constraint of the body at all times. But outside, nothing that reaches us disturbs the general indifference. Whereas what happens to the least of the prisoners ought to be the concern of every citizen. What diverts the free citizen from looking at the secret crannies of the social order, comes from the fact that he ordinarily places confidence in his leaders or, in the worst case, he is kept in his cruel indifference by a vengeful state of mind according to which the legal sequestration that prison represents is a deserved punishment, sometimes too soft for what the prisoners have committed. In short, they must ''pay for what they have done''.

Let's linger for an instant over what it costs to live in prison, in the modern State of Israel.

When a prisoner has to answer the summons of a court, the convoys of the prison administration make a tour of the prisons in every region according to each sector, gathering the prisoners one by one. Long chains are put on their ankles and wrists. They are closed up in a metal box that is narrow, hermetically closed, without a window, with just enough space to stay seated, enclosed among three thin partitions that do not communicate between them. The partition that takes the place of a door and that only opens from the outside, opens onto the very narrow corridor of the cell van, it too in metal, distinguished by an opaque window with wire netting. The prisoners are pushed in one by one, sometimes after midnight, and stay there until dawn, since it takes several hours starting from early morning to arrive at the district court. Confined in these coffins for men condemned, they always roll along still in chains, in the silence and the calculated oppression of the van. In summer, they are not given anything to drink. Often, drivers and guards, during the stops, leave this motorized dungeon in the hot sun. In winter, the steam and the frost darken the inside of every cell even more. They are enclosed there for hours, having eaten nothing before getting on board, kept that way almost immobile, without being able to budge, without food and without water. There is neither an air vent nor heating, just a hole under their feet for urinating.

When they get out, with the few family members who wait for them, it is pitiful to see these men and women, looking out for human warmth, searching for a friendly face, raising themselves above the rampart that their guards form around them to perceive the movement of daily life. An unwholesome atmosphere reigns over the passage of the troop that encircles them. This staged show of public power is in these moments a detail marking the violence of the state.

During the hearing, which in the Ambash affair was held behind closed doors, the prisoners live as at rest for the instant of grace when they are no longer so constrained, but they are so exhausted by the trip, by fatigue and by anxiety that they don't have the strength needed to assert a presence that they are denied, to freely utter an audible word. Most often, their remarks are cut off and they are ordered to stop talking. After the court proceeding which took place in front of them as if it had nothing to do with them, they get back on once more, for the same long trip of deprivation : of water, bread, air, light and speech.

Returning to jail twenty-two hours later : once again chained and convoyed in their mobile cage, in the same conditions as during the previous night, the prisoners traverse the anonymous corridors to find their walls once again. The cell is a compartment of about eight square meters, where six men live together. Once the door is shut, they live for hours in very close proximity. The room where Daniel Ambash is confined has no other opening, there is no window, not even a porthole. In summer, the atmosphère is boiling, preventing sleep, in winter the nights are icy. Everything is planned to produce suffering.

The common hall of the prison is the only everyday horizon : noisy, supervised, without any space for being alone. There is no walking outside. You never see the sky, not even from an enclosed courtyard that might open on an open area.

It is best to stay in good health. It is best to avoid falling ill. There is a complete absence of care. Only prisoners injured in a brawl are brought to the infirmary, or those already dead from an illness without having been helped. The security measures : call for help, opening the safety passages, waiting time, verification procedure – are so slow, so exhaustive, that you have enough time to die before having seen a physician hardly concerned about your fate.

The rhythm, as well as the duration of visits, despite the rules, remains at the discretion of the establishment's director. It is not rare that after a suicide or attempted suicide, a brawl among prisoners, or a protest movement, the director decrees an indefinite closure for the total population of the wing. The last time that I visited Daniel, it was over after thirty minutes. The new director was asserting his style by reducing by half the duration of meetings in the visiting room, and by diminishing visits to one every two weeks. Up till then, visits took place every week and lasted one hour.

Flying in the face of all legal provisions and regulations, Daniel Ambash was not authorized to meet any of his female partners, from the beginning of his imprisonment in July 2011. He was subjected to an exceptional regime, which constituted an offense against his most elementary rights. But as with all the others, his telephone remains his only link with them. « If they and you were not there », he confided to me, « I would have killed myself ».

By comparison, the fate of political prisoners in jail for terrorist acts and murders is more enviable than that of common criminals. The first are better treated : They can engage in sports, receive conjugal visits and until recently, they had the same right to receive the salary, stemming from their enrollment, from political organizations of which they were militant members! The murderers, those who cut the throats of women or children, animated by fanatic hatred of Israel, have a greater chance of getting out, because the State of Israel may have some interest in freeing them some day in exchange for the remains of a dead soldier, or in exchange for a captive. That is what happened in 2011, when Gilad Shalit, after five years in the hands of Hamas in the cellars of Gaza, « came home », in exchange for the release of 3000 terrorists, some of whom became recidivists.

Prisoners such as Daniel Ambash do not have the same horizon, they cannot hope to be part of any exchange. Daniel's female partners : Ilana (with whom he has ten children), Azamra (with whom he has one child), Adéret and Shiran are forbidden to visit, under the pretext that they themselves have been in prison. According to the indictment, they violated the obligation imposed on them to not meet each other or speak to each other. Having failed to comply with this injunction, they were thrown in prison, mistreated, threatened, and spent one year in borderline situations of destitution and psychological and physical violence.

Through the quite peculiar prism of the Jerusalem district court, Daniel's partners were his first victims : he supposedly raped them, made them into slaves constantly subject to humiliating treatment; they and their children. Neither the defense, nor the judges, no one, considered that the word of these four partners – who love each other like sisters – was admissible, under the pretext that mentally subjugated slaves do not have healthy judggment nor can they testify validly.

However, any experienced expert – psychiatrist, psycholoqist, physician or psychotherapist – could eassily establish that nothing in the conduct of Ilana, Azamra, Aderet or Shiran attested to a state of post-traumatic shock. Curiously, no expert opinion was ordered. Unlike victims, they do not consider Daniel to be an agressor, neither against an adult, nor a child. He has no reason to be in prison.

One question now must be asked however. Since the court holds them to be victims, why did it not order that they be protected? Why did it imprison them for one year? Why did Society not indemnify them for all the damage that Daniel had supposedly inflicted on them? The State of Israel had destroyed their family.

*

For its part, the Diaspora lulls itself with a sweet dream of the Promised Land, while often maintaining an idyllic tie with the State of Israel, its cherished child, born in a forceps birth through the torments of History, after an exile of 2000 years. The Diaspora does not want to see, nor know what happens there since it means opening one's eyes to the flagrant imperfections of the judicial institutions. If the Diaspora only knew ! The Israeli jails are full of poor folk, alone, isolated, out of luck, mistakenly thrown into the abyss, as the outcome of botched investigations and hearings; lacking means. They do not have the ability to provide themselves with a defense worthy of the name.

Lawyer's fees are crippling. Most prominent lawyers behave like cynical chief executives in business, concerned above all by the profit margin of their firms. Israel registers among the highest scores of judicial errors in the free world.

What does this penal justice resemble? What does its ordinary functioning consist of ? As the authors of the account that you are going to read point out, the good conduct of justice rests on the ''good cooperation'' of the police, social welfare workers, investigators, the prosecutor's office and the judges. Only very normal, even desirable, at least in appearance. Everything is as if normal, in a modern, complex society, the fragmentation of responsibilities and the transmission of information, through successive levels.

But in a country at war, which is the case of the State of Israel, since its foundation, an ideology of security, partially justified by the legitimate struggle against the terrorism of irredentists or fundamentalists, constitutes over time a factor of corruption of democratic life. Most likely in a stronger manner than anywhere else in the Western sphere, the judicial bodies obliged to presume innocence, and respect the ethics attached to the right of the defense, place little value on these prerequisites. A certain moral corruption – perhaps naïve – reigns without opposition. The esprit de corps within the police, in the milieu of investigators, social welfare workers, in short among all those players suffused with a sense of duty, has the incidental result of basing the procedures on legally and morally unjustified practices, and finally of introducing severe motives for dysfunctioning into the judicial system.

This systemic dysfunctioning – it is not seldom that it culminates in systematic dysfunctioning – first involves the degree of intimate conviction that motivates the behavior and manner of judging on the part of the several judicial bodies involved on all levels of the judicial hierarchy.

Each body sets to work according to the procedures that characterize its functions. The police investigates starting on the basis of a bundle of indications and material proofs that support its suspicions (complaints, records, line up of witnesses) but is capable of aiding the truth to break out by concealing information or proofs that might introduce doubt, by corrupting or forcing witnesses to help them lock up a dangerous guilty individual[12]. The investigators exercised pressure on the children, suggesting false memories to them by requiring that they confirm them in writing[13] ! The welfare services, « haRevahha », have full authority to remove minors from a milieu that they view as dangerous and the welfare services get 17 000 NIS per month for each child placed in an institution or in a foster family. The journalists who get wind of a scandalous affair exploit the elements that they have available and make a lot of noise ; the prosecutor's office follows the normal route which is to work on compiling evidence against the accused; the judges, most of them former prosecutors, come into play in the last stage, with the elements of a synthesis that the bodies in the previous stages have furnished them. They do their work, interrogate, evaluate, form an opinion, decide and state the law.

This book tells how the Jerusalem police heedlessly launched themselves into fabricating a file of incriminating evidence based on false accusations, and how, in order to win credibility, they did not hesitate to use violence, blackmail, and threats, in order to extort testimonies or signed confessions by these means, that the interested parties (adults or children at the time of the events) subsequently contradicted, while explaining under what circumstances they had 'testified' or 'admitted'.

This book also tells how the country's social services, firm in their conviction that they must « dismantle a sadistic sect », separated the children from their mothers, imposing on the mothers prohibiting measures, or measures restricting their prerogatives, and about the pressures the children had to undergo in the various institutions where

[12] Prof Boaz Sangero, a respected prof of Israeli penal law, says it explicitly. He compares the Israeli police to horses wearing blinkers.

[13] Obscene suggestions are not rare, with children of 8 and 10 years of age, at the time of the events. Once a child has ''confirmed'' and ''confessed'', under the threat of complicity if he does not acknowledge it. He hears that : « Your father is a monster who has made you into a marginal person. It is not your fault. Now we are going to protect you''. This conclusion is supposed to remove the child's guilt. Except that today these children have sunk into drug addiction, and in some cases, a suicidal state.

they were placed. In the case which we are dealing with, the religious children, talented and happy to be alive, were metamorphosed into cyncial adolescents or young adults, disoriented, severely disturbed, drug-addicted or suicidal, avid for revenge, marked like their father with the sign of infamy, perhaps irrecoverable. That is probably what the social sevices in the modern State of Israel think is successful « normalization ».

This book also tells what ruses were used by some reporting journalists, more concerned about ratings and scandal than accuracy, to carry out a campaign of defamation against Daniel Ambash and his family, before he was even arrested, committing a media lynch which one wishes were the only example in Israel.

Further, this book tells how the prosecutor's office was determined to find suborned witnesses in order to aggravate the weight of the false accusations against Daniel Ambash, without the least concern for verifying the facts.

Finally this book tells in what routine manner, and basically hardly in conformity with the criteria of enlightened justice, certain judges of the Jerusalem district were able to pronounce, under the pressure of the media, but also by placing confidence in their various associates, a sentence which confirmed what organized condemnation had decided.

This book especially shows how the harmful actions of a mafia-like association – which adorns itself supposedly in the principle of the defense of the common good and poses as the guarantor of the purity of family morality – having gained in power and influence in the Land of Israel, can orient the course of ordinary justice, and induce the subversion of the whole system.

Added to all that at each stage, is the motive of professional zeal and personal profit, in each case rewarded by a promotion or by an increase in prestige. This process is first that of marginality.

*

The Hebraic tradition did not have to wait for the great Cesare Beccaria in order to codify the domain of penal justice, to rule on the need for a rational inquiry, to confer the value of proof on several corroborating testimonies, obtained without constraint, to arm oneself against false witnesses, and to require from judges a sense of proportion, clarity of reasoning and the most perfect sense of equity and fairness. All of these provisions were stated in *Deuteronomy*, and developed in detail in several tractates of the Talmud[14]. However, in the State of Israel, modern to be sure but an heir to Ottoman law, British law, and certain traits of rabbinic law, the time is still far off when the ordinary citizen will be able to take pride in living in a country where justice is just.

All that leads us to ask ourselves about the manner in which the investigation was conducted, but also about the meaning of the punishment. From a historical point of view, three conceptions prevail : the punishment must be punitive and repressive, educational or reparative. Most Western nations tend, at least in theory, to adopt the principle of reparative/corrective punishment, at best, that of educational punishment. They both must open onto a virtuous circle of rehabilitation and reinsertion into society. Repressive and punitive punishment is more and more considered the major trait of archaic legislation. The same necessarily goes for the conduct of the investigation since, in principle, as in law as well, the practice of torture and bad treatment tend to cede to scientific investigation. In regard to the manner in which the indictment, the trial and the verdict of the Ambash Affair were organized, it appears that – perhaps due to the fact of the war mentality – the State of Israel stagnates laboriously in the archaic character of common law based on inflicting grossly punitive punishments : the deprivation of freedom that prison represents in principle, to which is added the amoral and vicious practice of violent manipulation of prisoners as well as of witnesses, and the constant humiliation of the prisoner, and the very great inadequacy of possibilities of appeal. To these gaps which continue, is added the administration of useless suffering characterized by mental cruelty unworthy of contemporary ethical norms. This parameter, absolutely deplorable, is in our eyes even worse in the case of Israel, which can, on the other hand, in comparison with the history of other nations, take pride in a very carefully worked out ethical tradition based on study and example more than on habit.

---

[14] Notably, the tractates *Sanhédrin* and *Makot*.

Starting with the imprisonment flowing from the sentence pronounced against Daniel, this affair had very grave consequences. Arié Ambash did not survive the arrest of his son. He died in November 2011, four months after his imprisonment. At the end of 2014, Daniel's sister, the mother of three children, developed cancer of the esophagus. After eight months of struggle against the disease, she died in the Hadassah Hospital, Ein Kerem, in Jerusalem, on 5/18/2015. Overwhelmed by the fate offered to her son, exhausted by grief after the deaths of her husband and daughter, Nina Ambash, Daniel's mother, died in Jerusalem, two months after her daughter on 7/29/2015.

The prison administration did not allow Daniel Ambash to be present at the burial of his father nor of his sister nor of his mother. Just one week after the burial of his father, he was able to go to the cemetery, under heavy guard, handcuffed, in chains, kept at a distance by eight armed guards, and not authorized to take part in prayers.

The true guilty parties in the facts that could be established during Daniel's trial are still at liberty, and enjoy the protection of the authorities. The dispersed family, condemned, is the object of constant harassment.

*

What is a modern state, presumably democratic, in principle the guarantor of the rights of persons, in which there are policemen, social welfare workers, journalists, suborned witnesses, officials of associations, prosecutors and unworthy judges who ought to be behind bars instead of those whom they have unjustly discriminated against and arbitrarily condemned? Neither more nor less than a sham Republic, the usurper of the symbols of the historic tradition of the people that it claims to represent, and adorning itself with the illusory finery of grand principles.

The degree of development of a state is not judged by its ideal Constitution, nor by its enchanting Basic Laws –as those which in Israel regulate life among its citizens : On the contrary, it is the fate that this state imposes on its outsiders, on its marginalized, and first of all on those that it sentences in court.

Wake up, citizens of the world, and citizens of Israel : In the 21st century, certain zones of the free world, those that escape your glance, certain zones have not finished with either the aberrations or the cruelties of the Middle Ages !

Furthermore, Israeli is distinguished among all societies in the free world as one of the most given to making rules. It is difficult to define oneself without being gently summoned to attach oneself to a group, to a milieu. The endemic state of war is not favorable to individualizing oneself, nor to freedom of thought. Criticism is paradoxical in Israel : full licence is afforded to anti-Zionism. A stale, wooden discourse against minorities is doing well. Xenophobia is not absent. With the advance of free market capitalism, the gaps in economic condition are deepening without being given attention. If the social fabric is still resistant, and relatively stable, it is because the values of solidarity and humanity of the Jewish tradition, are still hardy and holding on among most of Israel's inhabitants.

Criticism is free but it muzzles itself out of fear of adding to the accusations of Israel's worst enemies. It is not good to attack the institutions of the State. The Jewish people has suffered too much to finally have the right to reconstitute a sovereign nation on its ancestral soil to offer itself the luxury of challenging its authorities. So much wariness, with profound affective roots, ends up by devitalizing the critical function. If is commonplace to let loose one's tongue against the State of Israel, including in the Israeli paper most read outside of Israel – we mean the daily *Ha'aretz*, very obliging towards the themes of post-Zionist post-modernism – on the other hand, the fact of expressing one's disagreement with the those in charge of the state's security is viewed with disfavor. Most adopt a posture marked by blind confidence –quite sentimental confidence in those who « guard our gates » – because criticizing the institutions of the State of Israel in the name of the values of Judaism or Zionism is felt as a form of transgression, or of moral treason. That is because people keep silent, or cover their faces, because the worst may come, and in fact the worst is taking place. Israel is a blindly conformist society, which is not surprising when one considers the acuity of the talmudic mentality.

In order to explain certain events of great magnitude – like the Shoah for example – the historians tend to divide up among two schools: those who think that the genocide was the result of an absolutely intentional process, and those who think that it was the consequence of a combination of initiatives, which ended up in a functioning overall operation. The first school are called intentionalists, the second school are called functionalists.

The trial of Daniel Ambash, in view of the miserable manner in which the investigation had been conducted, and the crudeness of the conclusions which underlay the verdict, we might raise an analogous question : Was this enormous judicial error the fruit of an entirely intentional process, ordered by a master hand at every stage of its development? Or was it the result of a combination of small random events, proceeding according to their own logic, and converging finally in this immense national failure?

I say ''national failure'' because the very manner in which this affair was sewn up, spread by the media and settled, essentially accuses all the parties that played a role in it, either closely or from afar. A national failure finally because preparing public opinion for it attained no less considerable effects than those obtained by the propaganda of the worst dictatorships. A country's justice is too serious a matter to be abandoned to the experts alone.

This book, written by Daniel Ambash's four companions, attests to the interior of the history of their family and to the manner in which – in a highly murky police, media, and judicial context – the state put a sudden, destructive stop to the way of life that they had chosen for themselves together. This is an essential document that tries to bring to public knowledge a truth that has been buried. It would be to the honor of the artisans of iniquity that it might strike them into recognizing that they went astray by sending an innocent man to prison. Beyond their own situation, their testimony warns us against the arbitrary act that might, one day or another, knock at our own door.

The witnesses who were forced into silence, like the citizens of the country or the world who are concerned about what are the true values of democracy are the only investigators and the only judges who should prevail in the face of so much stupidity, manipulation and arbitrary violence, of moralism, of criminal conformism and of a blind will to do right. They have the right to be angry as I am, and to ask for an accounting as I do. They have the right and even the duty to demand the truth.

Whoever is concerned about closely examining the Israeli penal justice system – and all the spheres that in principle are at its service – will see first of all that its norms have little to do with Biblical norms. This is the first point of disillusion for the Diaspora. Jewish thought however did not wait for Beccaria to elaborate rules for the conditions of testimony, the obligation that witnesses be honest, the fairness of the investigators, the gravity of a false accusation, the corruption or integrity of the judges. Suffused with nostalgia after the occupation of the Land of Israel by the pagan empires, the daily prayer of Judaism – the *Shemoneh essreh*[15] – requests of God : « Restore our judges as of old ».

Georges-Elia Sarfati
*University Professor*
*Former associate professor at the Universit y of Tel Aviv*
*Member of the Elie Wiesel Institute (Paris)*
*Supervisor of instruction (psycho-traumatology) at the Faculty of Medicine of Paris,*
*And at the Sigmund Freud University (Vienna).*
*Director of the French School of Existential*
*Analysis and Therapy (logotherapy) V. Frankl*

[15] Literally the « Eighteen » (blessings).

should prevail in the face of seemingly simplistic, petrification and secondary violence, [illegible] of cardinal conceptions and in a blind way to [illegible] the right [illegible] and to act [illegible] as I do, [illegible] have the right and [illegible] command the [illegible]

[illegible]

# INTRODUCTION

Dans l'Etat moderne d'Israël, démocratie exemplaire, voire licencieuse par la latitude d'expression qu'elle accorde à ses opposants autant qu'à ses ennemis idéologiques de l'intérieur, l'Affaire Ambash défraye la chronique depuis plusieurs années. Il serait plus juste de dire, que la *vox populi* s'en est tant et si bien repue, que ce dossier est aujourd'hui tenu pour une affaire entendue, juste bonne à enrichir les annales judiciaires d'un précédent unique dans l'histoire de cette jeune société.

Rappelons les faits. En 2013, après deux ans de détention préventive, ce qui constitue la première entorse aux normes du droit pénal, Daniel Ambash a été condamné, par la Cour du district de Jérusalem, à une peine d'emprisonnement de 26 ans, au terme d'un procès expéditif, fortement médiatisé. L'instruction a retenu contre le prévenu pas moins de 18 chefs d'accusations, allant de la mise en esclavage, à des maltraitances régulières et violences aggravées, commises sur six femmes et leurs enfants, au sein de la communauté qu'il formait avec eux depuis plus de vingt ans.

Daniel Ambash, aujourd'hui âgé de soixante ans, s'est consacré dès son enfance à l'art – chorégraphie, musique, dessin. Avec sa sœur, ils ont été membres, plusieurs années consécutives, de la troupe *Les Ballets du XXè siècle* de Maurice Béjart, de la troupe *Bat Dor.* En 1978, il fonde sa propre compagnie *Le Ballet-Théâtre de l'Arche* avec Maguy Marin qui fut sa première épouse et dont il divorça en 1985. Après une carrière couronnée de succès et jalonnée de réalisations plus originales et exigeantes les unes que les autres – des archives audio-visuelles en témoignent – cet artiste a décidé, en 1988, de s'établir à Jérusalem. Né juif, de parents eux-mêmes artistes, Daniel

Ambash a passé sa jeunesse en France et en voyage de représentations dans toute l'Europe. En 1985, il a souhaité orienter sa vie autrement, en se rapprochant des sources de sa culture d'origine, en adoptant le mode de vie spirituel des Hassidim[16].

Les parents de Daniel, Nina et Arié Ambash, originaires de Bulgarie et de Russie, ont été tous deux des pionniers du cinéma d'animation, mais aussi respectivement peintre et poète de talent. Amoureux de Paris, ils s'y sont d'abord fixés avec leurs enfants, menant une vie de bohême, soucieux de transmettre l'esprit de liberté et de créativité qui avait été au principe de leur rencontre.

Après s'être marié à Paris, à la synagogue de la rue Pavé, avec Ilana – une jeune fille juive et championne de France de Kung Fu – Daniel, un peu avant ses trente cinq ans, s'est fixé dans la région de Jérusalem avec sa jeune épouse. Leur mode de vie s'est peu à peu épanoui dans le sens d'un choix de vie communautaire, marqué par la générosité et leur très grande ouverture d'esprit à l'égard de tous ceux et celles qui trouvaient accueil, mais aussi réconfort dans leur maison. Moi qui connaissais Daniel de Paris, mais que la distance géographique avait éloigné de lui, je me souviens encore du sentiment de sympathie que m'inspirait la vue de leur demeure, située à flanc de colline, au sortir de Jérusalem, chaque fois que j'entrais ou sortais de la ville, à l'occasion de mes voyages réguliers.

Les années ont passé, la communauté chaleureuse qui s'était développée autour de Daniel et Ilana s'était enrichie de la présence d'autres amis, hommes et femmes, en couple ou seuls, tandis que les enfants se multipliaient. Artiste né, s'étant éloigné de la grande carrière classique, promise à la reconnaissance et à la gloire publique, Daniel avait gardé de sa jeunesse le goût du spectacle, puis, en mêlant à sa première éducation celle qu'il s'était peu à peu donnée, au contact des maîtres de la tradition juive, il avait infléchi son projet de vie, en élevant ses propres enfants selon les principes de la générosité, de la tradition d'accueil et d'hospitalité, largement ouverte sur la société. En marchant dans les rues de Jérusalem, les passants reconnaissaient la famille de Daniel, à ses démonstrations de danse et de chant, pleines

[16] Le lecteur se reportera au site consacré à Daniel Ambash : www.danielambash.info

d'enthousiasme et de dévotion. Au fil du temps, le couple initial que formaient Daniel et Ilana a connu d'importants remaniements, engagés d'un commun accord, tant et si bien que cinq nouvelles compagnes se sont agrégées. Du même élan, ce modèle de polygamie respectueuse, fondée sur l'amour et le consentement entre adultes, s'est doublé d'un mode de vie collectif orienté vers leurs idéaux spirituels et la diffusion des livres de Rabbi Nachman de Braslav et de son disciple Rav Israel Ber Odesser, maître d'une branche marginale du hassidisme Braslav, qui vécut plus que centenaire (il est décédé à Jérusalem en 1994). La famille élargie se dévoua entièrement au rayonnement des leçons de vie de ce grand mystique.

Il est certain que cette organisation peu en phase avec les normes contemporaines valut à ce groupe autant de sympathie de la part des leurs, que de suspicion et d'inimitiés de la part de milieux, religieux ou séculiers, peu enclins à tolérer une dérogation franche aux conventions du jour : une famille organisée sur la polygamie (sans que toutefois il y eut de mariage officiellement célébrés, en vertu des interdits légaux), des enfants élevés à l'écart du système éducatif courant, des activités d'artistes de rue fondées sur des prestations parfois tapageuses, et des conduites naïvement prosélytes liées à la traditionnelle quête d'oboles, à la vente de livres et de disques ou à la distribution gratuite de prospectus à l'effigie de leur Rabbi.

Tout cela connut un essor et une fin que raconte le livre écrit à quatre mains que l'on va lire.

*

Daniel Ambash partage depuis quatre ans le lot des détenus de droit commun, dont le régime de vie ordinaire, tel que nous le percevons du dehors, ou bien à l'occasion des visites, au regard de ce que le citoyen en liberté peut en connaître, en dit long sur la violence pénitentiaire. Nous savons, depuis Deleuze et Foucault, qu'en dépit des garde-fous juridiques de la justice, au-delà de leurs enceintes, les prisons constituent bien souvent des zones de non-droit, où règne un ordre spécifique, fondé sur le rapport de force, les solidarités tacites ou clandestines, et le règne renforcé de l'arbitraire, de la ruse et de la brutalité légitimée. Le traitement pratique du détenu de droit commun est une contrainte de corps de tous les instants. Mais au-dehors, rien de ce qui nous en parvient ne trouble l'indifférence générale. Alors que ce qui advient au moindre des prisonniers, devrait être le souci de chaque citoyen. Ce qui le détourne de porter son regard dans ces recoins dissimulés de l'ordre social, vient de ce que le citoyen libre fait d'ordinaire confiance à ceux qui le dirigent, ou, dans le pire des cas, qu'il est entretenu dans son indifférence cruelle par l'état d'esprit vengeur selon lequel la séquestration légale que représente la prison est une peine méritée, parfois encore trop douce pour ce que les prévenus ont commis. En bref, ils doivent ''payer pour ce qu'ils ont fait''.

Arrêtons-nous un instant sur ce qu'il en coûte de vivre en prison, dans le moderne Etat d'Israël.

Lorsqu'un détenu doit se rendre aux convocations du tribunal, les convois de l'administration pénitentiaire font, selon chaque secteur, le tour des prisons de la région, ramassant les détenus un à un. On leur passe de longues chaînes aux chevilles et aux poignets, on les enferme dans des box métalliques, étroits, hermétiquement clos, sans fenêtre, avec juste l'espace nécessaire pour s'y tenir assis, encastrés entre trois fines parois qui ne communiquent pas entre elles. La paroi qui tient lieu de porte, et qui en s'ouvrant seulement de l'extérieur, donne sur le corridor étranglé du véhicule cellulaire, est aussi en métal, nuancé d'une vitre opaque et grillagée. Les détenus y sont poussés un par un, parfois dès après minuit, et ainsi jusqu'à l'aube, car il faut plusieurs heures à partir du petit matin pour arriver jusqu'à la cour du district. Confinés dans ces cercueils pour condamnés, ils roulent toujours enchaînés, dans le silence et l'oppression calculés du fourgon. L'été, on ne leur donne pas à boire. Souvent, chauffeurs et gardiens, au cours des arrêts, laissent en plein soleil cette oubliette à moteur. L'hiver, la buée et le givre assombrissent plus encore l'intérieur de chaque casemate. Ils y sont enfermés pendant des heures, n'ayant rien mangé avant d'embarquer, maintenus ainsi presque immobiles, sans pouvoir bouger, sans aliment et sans eau. Il n'y a ni bouche d'aération, ni chauffage, juste un trou sous leurs pieds pour uriner.

A leur descente, pour peu que des familiers les attendent, c'est une pitié de voir ces hommes et ces femmes, épiant un regard de bonté, cherchant un visage ami, se haussant au-dessus du rempart que forment autour d'eux leurs gardiens pour apercevoir le mouvement de la vie quotidienne. Une atmosphère morbide règne sur le passage de la troupe qui les encercle. Cette mise en scène de la puissance publique est dans ces moments un détail marquant de la violence d'Etat.

Pendant l'audience, qui dans l'affaire Ambash s'est tenu à huis-clos, les prisonniers vivent comme un repos cet instant de grâce où ils ne sont plus aussi contraints, mais ils sont si épuisés par le chemin, la fatigue et l'angoisse, qu'ils manquent de la force nécessaire pour affirmer une présence qu'on leur dénie, pour articuler librement une parole qui soit audible. Le plus souvent, on leur coupe la parole, on leur ordonne de se taire. Après la comparution qui s'est déroulée devant eux comme s'il ne s'agissait pas d'eux, on les embarque de nouveau, pour la même longue route de privation : d'eau, de pain, d'air, de lumière, de parole.

Retour à la prison vingt-deux heures plus tard : de nouveau enchaînés et convoyés dans leur cage mobile, dans les mêmes conditions qu'au cours de la nuit précédente, les détenus traversent les couloirs anonymes pour retrouver leurs murs. La cellule est un habitacle d'environ huit mètres carrés, où cohabitent six hommes. Une fois la porte refermée, ils survivent pendant des heures dans la promiscuité. La pièce où est enfermé Daniel Ambash ne comporte pas d'autre ouverture, il n'y a pas de fenêtre, pas même un hublot. En été, l'atmosphère est bouillante, empêchant le sommeil, en hiver les nuits sont glaciales. Tout est prévu pour distiller la souffrance.

Le hall collectif de la prison est le seul horizon de chaque jour : bruyant, surveillé, sans un espace de solitude. Il n'y a pas de promenade. On ne voit jamais le ciel, pas même d'une cour close qui ouvrirait sur un préau.

Mieux vaut se garder en bonne santé, mieux vaut éviter de tomber malade. L'absence de soin est complète. A l'infirmerie, on ne transporte que les détenus blessés dans une rixe, ou ceux qui sont déjà morts d'un malaise sans avoir été secourus. Les mesures de sécurité : appel, ouverture des sas, temps d'attente, procédure de vérification – sont si lentes, si minutieuses, que vous avez le temps de mourir avant d'avoir vu un médecin, bien peu soucieux de votre sort.

Le rythme, aussi bien que la durée des visites, en dépit du règlement, demeure à la discrétion du directeur de l'établissement. Il n'est pas rare qu'après un suicide ou une tentative de suicide, une bagarre entre détenus, ou un mouvement de protestation, le directeur décrète de boucler *sine die* tout l'effectif du pavillon. La dernière fois que j'ai rendu visite à Daniel, au bout de trente minutes c'était fini. Le nouveau directeur affirmait son style en diminuant de moitié la durée des rencontres au parloir, et en ramenant à une visite toutes les deux semaines la possibilité de venir. Jusque-là les visites avaient lieu chaque semaine, elles duraient une heure.

Contre toutes les dispositions légales, et réglementaires, Daniel Ambash n'a été autorisé à rencontrer aucune de ses compagnes, depuis le début de son incarcération en juillet 2011. Il est soumis à un régime d'exception, qui constitue une atteinte aux droits les plus élémentaires. Mais comme tous les autres, le téléphone demeure son seul lien avec elles. « Si elles et vous n'étiez pas là », me confie-t-il, « je me serai tué ».

En comparaison le sort des détenus politiques emprisonnés en Israël pour des attentats et des assassinats est plus enviable que celui des prisonniers de droit commun. Les premiers sont mieux traités : Ils ont la possibilité de faire du sport, reçoivent des visites conjugales et jusqu'à une époque récente, ils avaient même le droit de percevoir des organisations politiques dont ils sont des membres militants, le salaire de leur enrôlement ! Les assassins, les égorgeurs de femmes et d'enfants, animés de la haine fanatique d'Israël, ont plus de chance d'en sortir, parce que l'Etat d'Israël en outre peut avoir quelque intérêt à les libérer un jour en échange de la dépouille d'un soldat mort, ou contre le retour d'un captif. C'est ce qui s'est passé en 2011, lorsque Gilat Shalit, après cinq années passés aux mains du Hamas, dans les caves de Gaza, est « rentré à la maison », en échange de la libération de 3000 terroristes, dont certains ont repris du service.

Les détenus tels que Daniel Ambash n'ont pas le même horizon, ils ne peuvent pas espérer faire partie d'un quelconque échange. Les compagnes de Daniel : Ilana (dont il a dix enfants), Azamra (dont il a un enfant), Adéret et Shiran sont interdites de visite, sous le prétexte qu'elles ont-elles-mêmes fait de la prison. Selon l'acte d'accusation, elles ont enfreint l'obligation qui leur était faite de ne pas se rencontrer, ni se parler. Ayant dérogé à cette injonction, elles ont été jetées en prison, maltraitées, menacées, et ont passé une année dans des situations limites de dénuement et de violence psychologique et physique.

Dans l'optique bien singulière de la cour du district de Jérusalem, les compagnes de Daniel sont ses premières victimes : il les aurait violées, réduites en esclavage, et constamment soumises à des traitements humiliants, elles et leurs enfants. Ni la défense, ni les juges, personne n'a considéré que la parole de ces quatre compagnes – qui s'aiment comme des sœurs – était recevable, sous le prétexte que des esclaves mentalement subjuguées n'ont pas de jugement sain ni de témoignage valide.

Pourtant n'importe quel expert – psychiatre, psycholoque, médecin ou psychothérapeute expérimenté – établirait sans la moindre difficulté que rien dans la conduite d'Ilana, Azamra, Aderet et Shiran n'atteste d'un état de choc post-traumatique. Curieusement aucune expertise n'a été commanditée. Contrairement à des victimes, elles ne considèrent pas que Daniel soit un agresseur, ni d'adulte, ni d'enfant. Il n'a rien à faire en prison.

Une question se pose cependant : puisque le tribunal les tient pour des victimes, pourquoi n'a-t-il pas ordonné qu'elles soient protégées ? Pourquoi les a-t-il incarcérées une année durant ? Pourquoi la société ne les indemnise-t-elles pas de tous les préjudices que Daniel leur aurait infligés ? L'Etat d'Israël a détruit leur famille.

*

De son côté, la Diaspora se berce du doux rêve de la Terre Promise, et entretient souvent un lien idyllique avec l'Etat d'Israël, son enfant chéri, né au forceps dans les affres de l'Histoire, après un exil deux fois millénaire. La Diaspora ne veut pas voir, ni savoir ce qu'il s'y passe dès qu'il s'agit d'ouvrir les yeux sur les imperfections criantes de l'institution judicaire. Si la Diaspora savait ! Les geôles israéliennes sont pleines de pauvres gens, seuls, isolés, sans fortune, précipités à tort dans l'abîme, à l'issue d'instructions bâclées ; faute de moyens, ils n'ont pas la possibilité de s'offrir une défense digne de ce nom. Les honoraires des avocats sont rédhibitoires, la majorité des ténors du barreau se comportent comme des chefs d'entreprise cyniques, avant tout soucieux de la marge de profit de leurs affaires. Israël enregistre le score d'erreurs judiciaires parmi les plus élevés du monde libre.

A quoi donc ressemble cette justice pénale, en quoi consiste l'ordinaire de son fonctionnement ? Comme le rappellent les auteures du récit qu'on va lire, la bonne marche de la justice repose sur la ''bonne coopération'' de la police, des assistants sociaux, des enquêteurs, du ministère public et des juges. Rien que de très normal, voire souhaitable, du moins en apparence. Tout comme est normale, dans une société moderne et complexe, la fragmentation des responsabilités et la transmission de l'information, par paliers successifs.

Mais dans un pays en guerre, comme c'est le cas de l'Etat d'Israël, depuis sa fondation, l'idéologie sécuritaire, partiellement justifiée par la lutte légitime contre le terrorisme des irrédentistes ou des fondamentalistes, constitue, avec le temps, un facteur de corruption de la vie démocratique. Sans doute, de manière plus forte que partout ailleurs dans la sphère occidentale, les instances en charge de la présomption d'innocence, et la déontologie attachée aux droits de la défense, font peu de cas de ces prérequis. Une certaine corruption morale – peut-être naïve – règne sans partage. L'esprit de corps, au sein de la police, dans le milieu des enquêteurs, des assistants sociaux, bref chez tous les acteurs pénétrés du sens du devoir, a incidemment pour résultat de fonder la procédure sur des pratiques légalement aussi bien que moralement injustifiables, et finalement d'introduire de graves motifs de dysfonctionnement dans le système judiciaire.

Ce dysfonctionnement systémique – il n'est pas rare qu'il culmine en dysfonctionnement systématique – engage d'abord le degré d'intime conviction qui motive le comportement et la manière de juger des différentes instances impliquées à tous les niveaux de la hiérarchie judiciaire.

Chaque instance se met au travail selon les procédures qui caractérisent ses fonctions. La police enquête à partir d'un faisceau d'indices, et de preuves matérielles qui étayent ses soupçons (plaintes, enregistrements, déposition de témoins) mais peut aider la vérité à éclater en dissimulant les informations ou les preuves qui risqueraient d'introduire le doute, en corrompant ou violentant les témoins pour les aider à boucler un dangereux coupable[17]. Les enquêteurs ont exercé des pressions sur les enfants, leur suggérant des faux souvenirs en exigeant que ceux-ci les confirment en le reconnaissant par écrit[18] ! Les services sociaux, « la Révaha », ont toute autorité pour soustraire à un milieu qu'ils estiment dangereux des mineurs en péril et les services touchent 17 000 nis par mois pour chaque enfant placé en institution ou dans une famille d'accueil. Les journalistes qui ont vent d'une affaire à scandale exploitent les éléments dont ils disposent et font grand bruit ; le ministère publique suit la voie normale qui est de développer un discours à charge ; les juges, en majorité d'anciens procureurs, interviennent en dernière instance, avec les éléments de synthèse que leur ont fourni les instances précédentes, font leur travail, interrogent, évaluent, se font une opinion, tranchent et disent la loi.

Ce livre raconte comment sur une fausse accusation, la police de Jérusalem s'est lancée sans grande précaution dans la fabrication d'un dossier à charge, et comment pour gagner en crédibilité, elle n'a pas hésité à faire usage de violence, de chantage, de menaces, pour extorquer par ces moyens des témoignages ou aveux signés, que les intéressés (adultes ou enfants à l'époque des faits) ont par la suite récusés en expliquant dans quelles circonstances ils avaient 'témoigné' ou 'avoué'.

Ce livre raconte aussi comment les services sociaux du pays, forts de leur conviction « de démanteler une secte sadique », ont séparé les enfants de leurs mères, imposant aux mères des mesures d'interdiction, ou de restriction de leur prérogative, et quelles

[17] Le Prof Boaz Sangero, prof réputé de droit pénal israélien, le dit explicitement. Il compare les policiers israéliens à des chevaux portant des œillères.

[18] Les suggestions obscènes ne sont pas rares, avec des enfants âgés de 8 et 10 ans, à l'époque des faits. Une fois que l'enfant, a ''confirmé'', et ''avoué'', sous la menace de complicité s'il ne le reconnaît pas, il s'entend dire : « Ton père est un monstre qui a fait de toi un marginal, ce n'est pas ta faute, maintenant on va te protéger''. Cette conclusion est sensée lever la culpabilité de l'enfant. Sauf qu'aujourd'hui, ces enfants ont sombré dans l'addiction, et parfois, l'état suicidaire.

pressions les enfants ont dû subir dans les différentes institutions où ils ont été placés. Dans le cas qui nous occupe, les enfants religieux, talentueux et heureux de vivre ont été métamorphosés en adolescents ou jeunes adultes cyniques, désorientés, gravement perturbés, drogués ou suicidaires, avides de revanche, marqués comme leur père du sceau de l'infamie, peut-être irrécupérables. C'est sans doute là l'idée, que dans l'Etat moderne d'Israël, les services sociaux se font d'une « normalisation » réussie.

Ce livre raconte également par quelles ruses des journalistes de reportage, plus soucieux d'audimat et de scandale que d'exactitude, ont mené une campagne de diffamation contre Daniel Ambash et sa famille, avant même qu'il soit arrêté, commettant un lynchage médiatique dont on souhaiterait qu'il fût le seul exemple en Israël.

Ce livre raconte encore comment le ministère civil s'est acharné sur des témoins subornés, pour aggraver le poids des fausses accusations portées contre Daniel Ambash, sans le moindre souci de la vérification des faits.

Ce livre raconte enfin de quelle manière routinière, et finalement peu conforme aux critères d'une justice éclairée, certains juges du district de Jérusalem, ont pu énoncer, sous la pression des medias, mais aussi en faisant confiance à leurs différents collaborateurs, une sentence qui confirmait celle qu'avait décidée la vindicte organisée.

Ce livre surtout, montre comment l'action nuisible d'une association mafieuse – qui se pare du principe prétendu de la défense du bien commun et se pose en garante de la pureté des mœurs familiales – ayant gagné en pouvoir et en influence dans le pays d'Israël, peut orienter le cours de la justice ordinaire, et induire la subversion du système tout entier.

A tout cela s'ajoute à chaque étape, le motif du zèle professionnel et de l'intéressement personnel, dans chaque cas récompensé d'une promotion ou d'un surcroît de prestige. Ce procès est d'abord celui de la marginalité.

*

La tradition hébraïque n'a pourtant pas attendu le grand Cesare Beccaria pour codifier le domaine de la justice pénale, statuer sur la nécessité d'une enquête rationnelle, pour accorder à plusieurs témoignages concordants, obtenus sans contrainte, la valeur de la preuve, ni pour se prémunir contre les faux témoins, ou pour exiger des juges le sens de la mesure, la clarté du raisonnement et la plus parfaite équité. Toutes ces dispositions sont énoncées dans le *Deutéronome*, et développées par le menu dans différents traités du Talmud[19]. Pourtant, dans l'Etat d'Israël, moderne certes mais héritier du droit ottoman, du droit britannique et de certains traits du droit rabbinique, il est encore loin le temps où le citoyen ordinaire pourra se prévaloir de vivre dans un pays où la justice est juste.

Tout cela nous amène à nous interroger sur la manière dont l'instruction est conduite, mais aussi sur le sens de la peine. Du point de vue historique, trois conceptions prévalent : la peine doit être punitive et répressive, éducative ou réparatrice. La plupart des nations occidentales tendent, du moins en théorie, à adopter le principe de la peine réparatrice, au mieux de la peine éducative. L'une et l'autre doivent ouvrir sur le cercle vertueux de la réhabilitation et de la réinsertion. La peine répressive et punitive est de plus en plus considérée comme le trait majeur des législations archaïques. Il en va préalablement de même pour la conduite de l'instruction, puisqu'en principe, comme en droit également, la pratique de la torture et des mauvais traitements tend à céder le pas à l'investigation scientifique. Au regard de la manière dont la mise en accusation, le procès et le verdict de l'Affaire Ambash ont été organisés, il apparaît que – du fait peut-être de la mentalité de guerre – l'Etat d'Israël stagne laborieusement dans l'archaïsme d'un droit commun fondé sur l'infliction de peines grossièrement punitives : à la privation de liberté que constitue par principe la prison, s'ajoute la pratique amorale et vicieuse de la manipulation violente des prévenus comme des témoins, et l'humiliation constante du prévenu, et la très grande insuffisance du recours légal. A ces lacunes entretenues, s'ajoute l'administration d'une souffrance inutile et d'une cruauté mentale indignes des normes éthiques contemporaines. Ce paramètre, déplorable dans l'absolu, est à nos yeux aggravant dans le cas d'Israël, qui peut en revanche, en comparaison de l'histoire des autres nations, se prévaloir d'une

---

[19] Notamment, les traités *Sanhédrin* et *Makot*.

tradition éthique très élaborée, fondée sur l'étude et l'exemple plus que sur l'habitude.

A partir de l'incarcération de la sentence prononcée contre Daniel, cette affaire a eu de très graves conséquences. Arié Ambash n'a pas survécu à l'arrestation de son fils, il est décédé en novembre 2011, quatre mois après son emprisonnement. Fin 2014, la sœur de Daniel et mère de trois enfants, a développé un cancer de l'œsophage. Après huit mois de lutte contre la maladie, elle est morte à l'hôpital Hadassa En Kerem de Jérusalem, le 18/05/2015. Accablée par le sort fait à son fils, épuisée de chagrin après la disparition de son mari et de sa fille, Nina Ambash, la mère de Daniel, est morte à Jérusalem, deux mois après sa fille, le 29/07/2015.

L'administration pénitentiaire n'a pas permis à Daniel Ambash d'être présent à l'inhumation de son père, ni de sa sœur, ni de sa mère. Juste une semaine après l'enterrement de son père, il a pu venir au cimetière, sous bonne garde, menotté, enchaîné, tenu en respect par huit gardiens armés, sans autorisation de participer aux prières.

Les véritables coupables des faits qui ont pu être établis lors du procès de Daniel, sont toujours en liberté, et jouissent de la protection des autorités. La famille dispersée, condamnée, est en butte à d'incessantes tracasseries.

*

Qu'est-ce qu'un Etat moderne, présumé démocratique, en principe garant du droit des gens, dans lequel ce sont des policiers, des assistants sociaux, des journalistes, des témoins subornés, des responsables associatifs, des procureurs et des juges indignes qui devraient se trouver derrière les barreaux, à la place de ceux qu'ils ont injustement discriminés et arbitrairement condamnés ? Ni plus ni moins qu'une République de façade, usurpatrice des symboles de la tradition historique du peuple qu'elle prétend représenter, et se parant des atours illusoires des grands principes.

Ce n'est pas à sa Constitution idéale, ni à ses Lois fondamentales enchanteresses – comme celles qui en Israël régissent la vie entre ses citoyens – que se juge le degré de développement d'un Etat : Au contraire, c'est au sort que cet Etat fait à ses exclus, à ses marginalités, et d'abord à ceux qu'elle a condamné en justice.

Réveillez-vous, citoyens du monde, et citoyens d'Israël : au 21è siècle, certaines zones du monde libre, celles qui échappent à votre regard, certaines zones n'en ont pas fini avec les aberrations ni avec les cruautés du Moyen Age !

A cela s'ajoute que la société israélienne se distingue, entre toutes les sociétés du monde libre, comme une société des plus normatives. Difficile de se définir, sans être gentiment mis en demeure de se rattacher à un groupe, à une mouvance. L'état de guerre endémique n'est pas favorable à l'individuation, ni à la liberté de pensée. La critique y est paradoxale : toute licence est accordée à l'antisionisme, la langue de bois contre les minorités va bon train, la xénophobie n'y est pas absente, avec les avancées du néo-libéralisme, les écarts de condition se creusent inconsidérément. Si le tissu social y est encore résistant, et relativement stable, c'est que les valeurs de solidarité et d'humanité, issues de la tradition juive, y sont encore vivaces chez la majorité de ses habitants.

La critique est libre, mais elle se musèle d'elle-même, par crainte d'ajouter aux accusations des pires ennemis. Il n'est pas bon de s'attaquer aux institutions de l'Etat. Le peuple juif a trop souffert pour avoir enfin le droit de reconstituer une nation souveraine, sur la terre ancestrale, pour s'offrir le luxe de contester ses autorités. Tant de précautions, aux racines affectives profondes, finit par dévitaliser la fonction critique. S'il est commun de se déchaîner contre l'Etat d'Israël, y compris dans la presse israélienne la plus lue en dehors d'Israël – nous voulons parler du journal *Ha'aretz*, très complaisant à l'égard des thèmes de la modernité post-sioniste-, en revanche le fait d'exprimer son désaccord avec ceux qui sont en charge de la sécurité de l'Etat, est mal vu. La plupart adoptent une posture marquée par la confiance aveugle – confiance toute sentimentale pour ceux qui « gardent nos portes » –, parce que critiquer les institutions de l'Etat d'Israël au nom des valeurs du judaïsme ou du sionisme est ressenti comme une forme de faute, ou de trahison morale. C'est parce que les gens se taisent, ou se voilent la face, que le pire peut arriver, et que de fait le pire se produit. Israël est une société aveuglément conformiste, ce qui ne laisse de surprendre quand on se tourne vers l'acuité de la mentalité talmudique.

Pour expliquer certains évènement de grande ampleur – comme par exemple la Shoa – les historiens tendent à se partager entre deux tendances : ceux qui pensent que le génocide est le résultat d'un processus absolument intentionnel, et ceux qui pensent qu'il est la conséquence d'un concours d'initiatives, ayant abouti à ce fonctionnement global. Les premiers sont appelés intentionnalistes, les seconds fonctionnalistes.

Le procès de Daniel Ambash, au regard de la manière indigente dont l'instruction a été menée, et la grossièreté des conclusions qui fondent le verdict, il y a lieu de s'interroger de manière analogue : cette énorme erreur judiciaire est-elle le fruit d'un processus entièrement intentionnel, commandité de main de maître à chaque étape de son développement, ou bien est-elle le résultat d'un ensemble de petits fonctionnements aléatoires, procédant selon leur logique propre, et convergeant finalement dans cet immense fiasco national ?

Je dis ''fiasco national'', parce que la manière même dont cette affaire a été ficelée, médiatisée, et réglée accuse en son essence toutes les parties qui y ont joué un rôle, de près ou de loin. Fiasco national enfin parce que la mise en condition de l'opinion y a atteint des effets non moins considérables que ceux qu'obtient la propagande des pires dictatures. La justice d'un pays est une affaire trop sérieuse pour être abandonnée aux seuls experts.

Ce livre, écrit par quatre compagnes de Daniel Ambash, témoigne de l'intérieur de l'histoire de leur famille, et de la manière dont – dans un contexte policier, médiatique et judiciaire des plus troubles – l'Etat a mis un coup d'arrêt brutal et destructeur au mode de vie qu'ensemble ils s'étaient choisis. Il s'agit d'un document essentiel, qui tente de porter à la connaissance du public une vérité qui a été étouffée. Ce serait l'honneur des artisans de l'iniquité qui les frappe de reconnaître qu'ils se sont fourvoyés, en envoyant un innocent en prison. Par-delà leur propre situation, leur témoignage nous prévient contre le coup arbitraire qui peut, un jour ou l'autre frapper à notre porte.

Les témoins qui ont été bâillonnés, comme les citoyens du pays ou du monde qui ont le souci de ce que sont les véritables valeurs d'une démocratie sont les seuls enquêteurs et les seuls juges qui vaillent face à tant de bêtise, de manipulation et de violence arbitraire, de moralisme, de conformisme criminel et de volonté aveugle de bien faire. Ils ont le droit d'être en colère comme je le suis, et de demander des comptes comme je le fais. Ils ont le droit, et même le devoir d'exiger la vérité.

A qui s'en approche avec le souci de l'examen attentif, la justice pénale israélienne – et toutes les sphères qui en principe sont à son service – montre d'emblée que ses normes ont bien peu à voir avec les normes bibliques. C'est le premier point de désillusion pour la Diaspora. La pensée juive n'a pourtant pas attendu Beccaria pour statuer sur les conditions du témoignage, l'obligation de probité des témoins, l'équité des enquêteurs, la gravité d'une fausse accusation, la corruption ou l'intégrité des juges. Pétrie de nostalgie, à l'heure de l'occupation de la Terre d'Israël par les empires païens, la prière quotidienne du judaïsme – le *Chemonah essreh*[20] – demande à Dieu : « Rends-nous nos juges comme autrefois ».

Georges-Elia Sarfati
*Professeur des universités*
*Ancien professeur associé à l'université de Tel-Aviv*
*Membre de l'Institut Elie Wiesel (Paris)*
*Chargé d'enseignement (psycho-traumatologie) à la Faculté de médecine de Paris,*
*Et à la Sigmund Freud university (Vienne).*
*Directeur de l'Ecole française d'analyse*
*et de thérapie existentielles (logothérapie) V. Frankl*

[20] Littéralement les « Dix-huit » (bénédictions).

# THE STORY

On our conference call this morning with Daniel who spoke from jail, he told us that the social worker from the Israeli Prison Service threatened once again that she would prevent him from calling us.

The four of us sat at the park on our way to a meeting with the director of the documentary film about us. We squeezed ourselves onto one bench: Ilana, Azamra, and me, Aderet. Daniel is on the line with us. Missing him, worried, and unsure what to do, constantly scared that our one line of communication will be cut off.

We have been living like this for the past four years.

The park was desolate. We haven't heard children's laughter for a long time. They took them too.

They shut us up with a gag order, they prevented us from expressing ourselves and protesting, but the lies against us flooded the public via the press.

For many long months, the police forcefully closed us off separately, in different battered women's shelters all over the country. We were not allowed to leave, have a phone, or contact each other. Two armed policemen would come to take each of us in a police car to exhausting and violent interrogations.

They deprived us of our freedom to live and destroyed everything we had built over fifteen years.

Preceding this unbelievable arrest, we had the best lives imaginable; we couldn't understand how to live differently. We lived interesting, exciting, adventurous lives. A religious Breslev family with ties to Rabbi Israel Ba'ar Odeser, known as "ha Saba" (the grandfather), possessor of the famous Rabbi Na Nah Nahma Nahman from Uman note in Jerusalem. Our family was a special, nonconventional family – six friends who loved one man sounds odd, but there are many odd things in this world. And some people may find it hard to understand, but we got along pretty well and the problems that we had were 'normal' problems like in every household. That is why we were so shocked by our arrest. We couldn't imagine there is someone who wants to hurt us so much. Who were we bothering? What law did we break? Why would anyone care how we chose to live our lives? It was not clear to us who stood behind this and why. As time passed, the truth was revealed…

The plot against us was planned by "The Israel Centre for Victims of Cults" (ICVC) who tagged us a "dangerous cult" in the press in order to justify its existence and to enable the continued laundering of donation funds.

An exposé published by the newspaper "Yediot Ahronot" in March, 2011 revealed that the questionable "Centre" is actually a fake NPO working against religious streams which are unacceptable to them, and attacks any group of people who act in a way they don't like. The organization comprises two women and one doctor: Rachel Lichtenstein, Sharona Ben Moshe, and Dr. David Green.

*The European Interreligious Forum (EIFRF) published that the ICVC is actually a branch of FECRIS (European Federation of Centres of Research and Information on Cults and Sects), an 'anti-cult' organization existing in over thirty countries comprised of small NGOs often comprised of only two to three people in each country. (www.eifrf-articles.org)*

*FECRIS vice-president Alexander Dvorkin, a Russian citizen who is actively involved with the Russian Orthodox Church, explains the organization's anti-cult principles: "The Christian Orthodox faith is the original (...) a sect is a fake, something forged, something tawdry." Dvorkin also attacked the Muslim faith on several occasions and announced: "Either Mohammed suffered from a disease and it was a delirium vision; or it was demonic obsession."*

*Human rights experts worldwide strongly criticize FECRIS for their use of hate speech and their spread of intolerance in society against minority religions. A representative of the United Nations for Freedom of Religion said "there seems to be a negative and derogative connotation to the term "cult". This approach is evidence of a tendency towards generalizations, discrimination, and rejection, an approach which damages freedom of religion and harms basic defense of human rights".*

As opposed to other cases in which the police have a thread of evidence to make arrests and base indictments, in our case they had nothing. They could not even arrest us for "polygamy", because we were not formally married.

The slanderous articles in the newspaper and television came from Aliza's family, the fifth p ,;,ener. In the early years, we had excellent relations with her family, who visited often since they lived close by. Their relationship with Aliza and our family went south when Aliza decided to stop helping them financially because she felt that it was already too much after having giving them no less that eighty thousand shekels. They became violent when she refused to give in to their pressure, and ambushed us outside of our house with sticks and stones, cursed us and broke windows in the house until the children nearly got hurt – it could have ended in disaster. Her older brother, a criminal known to the police, threatened to kill Daniel and the children and burn our house down. Aliza did not give in and told them they went too far. She went to the police, filed a complaint, and demanded a restraining order. They apologized for their behavior, but simultaneously turned to the Israel Center for Victims of Cults, the press, and the police. So it happened that in 2008 the investigation began: surveillance, bugging, investigators, undercover activity. All of their efforts were in vain.

Three years later…

Sammy, Daniel's fourteen year old stepson, called the police because "Dad isn't home and a friend of my brother's older brother is hitting me". Even this was not cause for arrest. When the police called back and understood everything was okay, they did not even bother to come. A month and a half later, one of the boys saw a strange wooden box behind the closet and ripped it out. He couldn't know that it was a police wire. When he opened the box to see what it was, five undercover cops swarmed the house yelling that everyone is under arrest. Chief prosecutor Lilach Ranan admitted in county court that the arrest was not planned, but they had to arrest us since the listening devices which were supposed to help gather evidence were exposed. (Just to remind you, three years of close and intense surveillance yielded nothing).

The Jerusalem Police understood that their only way to get the court to extend our arrest was to mark us as a "sadistic cult", in which all of the family members are brainwashed slaves and sex slaves, and that the father of the family is no less than "the biggest criminal in the country" "the Satan from Jerusalem" "Head of a sadistic cult" as he was called in the media. In order to further their investigation, the police appointed the Israel Centre for Victims of Cults as "expert consultants" in the case against us. The ICVC provided the police with points of emphasis for the investigation and a list of questions for the interrogations. The police, in turn, sent them witnesses for bribing and "treatments" (i.e. to convince the people that they are indeed cult victims). Naturally, the police did not bother to check the credibility of the center or its active members, did not investigate the identity and quality of the "experts", their past, their personal issues and the millions in donations that they pocket under false pretenses and fraud.

Sharona ben Moshe, who presents herself as "legal consultant for the ICVC", is involved in the famous extortion case of Rabbi Nir Ben-Artzi and was the girlfriend of one of the partners in crime, Simon Katorza. For three years, they imprisoned Rabbi Ben-Artzi in different apartments in Tiberias under difficult conditions, took control of his assets and gave phony messages to the donors of his NPO. In this manner they fraudulently received funds. They fed him bread and margarine, and after forcing him to drink a liter of vodka, they made him sign a document in which he admits having sexual relations with sheep and other animals. In order to shift public attention and to cover her ties to the kidnapping and extortion, Sharona ben-Moshe became the "spokesperson" for the ICVC and fed false information to the press against "cults", and Nir Ben-Artzi was one of the first ones attacked. In the end, during their trial, the deceit was revealed; they were sentenced to jail, public service, and a fine.

It is interesting to note that in our case, the police succeeded in turning Aliza into a witness for the state after making great efforts over five long months and after “treatment” at the ICVC, Aliza began inventing hallucinatory stories, and slowly improved on them, until a year later she began to say that in the “cult” she was forced to have sexual relations with horses, snakes, spiders, mice, and cockroaches…

Rachel Lichtenstein, director of the ICVC, is a zealous, extremist Haredi woman and she felt she won the lottery when she brought forward her first witness, Timna.

Timna was a 19 year old girl from a religious family. According to her, her mother suffered from schizophrenia and was hospitalized in mental hospitals, her father of Yemenite descent, was a head of Yeshiva, and was involved in a famous case where he was accused of being married to several women simultaneously; at some point he left the house and divorced her mother. She also said that her uncle sexually abused her when she was a child. She was thrown to the streets, grew up in boarding schools, and dreamed of becoming a model. At a young age, she tried different drugs, and dealt. One day, Kary, Daniel’s second partener about whom you will read later, met Timna in downtown Jerusalem, and Timna asked to accompany her to Chanukah candle lighting. Timna enjoyed her visit with Kary, and continued their relationship via phone calls and the occasional meals at our house. We couldn’t imagine that she would develop an “obsessive love” for Daniel. Timna insisted unequivocally that she “marry” Daniel as his seventh partener, an idea that scared him very much, and therefore he requested Kary cease inviting her to the house. Nonetheless, Timna showed up, and with no shame, took Daniel for a discussion in which she told him that she could only be happy with him, and demanded that he “marry” her immediately. Daniel did not want to hurt her, and rejected her by claiming that he did not have any intentions to be with any more women. Timna left the house in a rage, and while obsessively kissing the Mezuzah she repeatedly said through her teeth: “You will regret this…”

Nevertheless, she continued coming to our performances and enthusiastically interviewed for a television show “360” that Channel Two edited, produced, and aired about us. She heaped praise on our family and our way of life: “… I’ve been in a lot of groups, and here I felt that this was a place of people of the truth and that I don't want to go..."

Four months later, while watching the show and hearing the presenter say: "More women are on the way to Ambash..." her pathological jealousy exploded and she called the ICVC who instigated the program and participated in it. She wrote to Rachel Lichtenstein, the director, and said she needed help. Lichtenstein invited Timna to a meeting. Timna was homeless and had an open criminal file for theft. Lichtenstein jumped at the opportunity that befell her, took advantage of Timna's weaknesses, and promised her financial and emotional support. She set up a meeting with police investigators from Jerusalem, and they took her to a hotel on the Tel Aviv coastline. The police investigators did not document the meeting, and used her burning desire for revenge to fabricate a story that the ICVC can fit to a "cult profile": 1. Sexual exploitation 2. Financial exploitation 3. Child rape 4. Sex with animals 5. Contempt by eating feces, and more. The police investigators broke every law possible, and even promised Timna an apartment, and also gave her bribe money. A year later, Timna was the prime witness in court and she said: "I was in shock that Rachel Lichtenstein passed this on to the police, I didn't think this would get to the police, they were just words I said and I didn't want this to have consequences but she said that I had no choice." It was important to Timna to emphasize her total love for Daniel in court, and she said: "I loved Daniel like I have never and will never love a man in my life." With Daniel in front of her, hands and feet chained, in prison garb and with guards around him, she stupidly revealed her motive when she told the judges that she is still hurt because she heard that Daniel once said her teeth were not pretty.

The FECRIS ideology is that a "cult" is a dangerous place for children, and that cult members are not legally competent and should have their children taken from them. Therefore, Dr. Green coached the police investigators that they need to prove that the children were sexually abused, and they should use any means necessary to prove it, as hard as they may be. From lack of evidence, they found a rabbit to pull out of the hat – the same phone call Sammy made to the police, the one we mentioned earlier and will now expand upon:

Sammy was a mischievous boy and he liked to sneak into the girls` dorms and peak in the showers. Once he touched six-year old Batya (Daniel and Aliza's daughter) on her lower parts above her clothes. Aliza got very upset and made a dramatic claim that Sammy raped Batya. When Daniel wasn't home, a friend of Sammy's older brothers, a 24 year old, American bully type came and heard Aliza's hysteria. He began to threaten Sammy that he would shove a broom pole in his rear end "to teach him a lesson". Sammy didn't want to come out a sucker, so he called the police. Three hours later, the police called to see what was going on, and when they understood that everything was alright they ignored the call. A month and a half later, under the guidance of the ICVC and under the theory that the "leader of the cult" is exclusively responsible for everything that happened, even if he wasn't there and didn't know about it – we were shocked to discover that on the basis of this story, they built an indictment that sits well with one of the characteristic of a profile of a cult leader: child abuse. Daniel was convicted of "sodomy", for a crime that may not have occurred, and if it did, all of the evidence indicates that he was not present while it was committed. Moreover, Sammy testified that had his father been home, he would have protected him and not let something like this happen. We sent the tape of Sammy's conversation with the police to a sound expert who investigates evidence admissibility, we were surprised to discover that the police committed a criminal act: They edited the tape and cut out the words: "Daddy's not home". In the interrogation room they threatened Sammy that he was suspected of raping his six year old sister and that if he didn't cooperate, he would sit in jail fourteen years. In this manner, they were able to plant different versions, detail after detail on the basis of this story and got to a long story with twenty charges against Daniel.

The police still needed more witnesses from within the house to create "credibility" and corroborate the story. Anastasia, Sammy's eighteen and a half year old sister, Daniel's step daughter, was disappointed that none of Daniel's sons wanted to marry her because she was known to be a liar and someone who "changes boyfriends like socks", and therefore she quickly decided that it would be more beneficial to her to accept the police bribe and help them and influence the others to testify against Daniel. She told the police that there was a rumor in the house about a week before the arrest that thirteen year old Akiva (Daniel and Ilana's son) played immodest games with his two little brothers. The police jumped at the story. Similar to Sammy's case, they threatened Akiva that if he did not testify against his father, he would be charged with raping his younger brothers. After a lot of pressure, Akiva became a witness for the prosecution against his father, and was considered the most reliable witness by the courts. A few months later, he sent a detailed letter to the Supreme Court in which he recanted his testimony, and provided details about how attorneys Sagi Ofir and Lizo Wolfos, together with the children's investigator Micah Haran, threatened him that if he didn't testify against his father, he would sit in jail in his stead, and taught him what to say in his testimony. He also explained that they were the reason he tried to commit suicide.

The Department of Welfare declared publicly that in the "Ambash" case, there was successful cooperation between the police, the ICVC, the prosecution, and the social workers. This was a golden opportunity for the Department of Welfare to kidnap children from their parents, to send them to boarding schools, and to get huge allocations for each child they hold.

The police identified the weak spots, failings, and sensitivities of each of the interviewees in the interrogations, and tortured each accordingly. With Aliza they had an advantage: her mother worked for them and put all possible pressures on her to convince her to divorce Daniel, whom she loved so much; furthermore, one of Aliza's relatives is a police investigator in the Jerusalem Region and she also pressured Aliza's mother to convince her to give in to the investigators. Actually, Aliza was very strong in her war to prove Daniel's innocence, so much so that they ended up using the weight of the whole of "Jerusalem Yamar" (Central Police Unit in Jerusalem – in charge of interrogations and intelligence in major crimes). They used different techniques: threats, screaming, degradation, flattery, and bribery. They scared her by saying she wouldn't see Batya, hers and Daniel's daughter, and explained her what she needed to say in order to save herself, otherwise she would sit in jail for years, because Anastasia, Kari's daughter, was prepared to testify that she raped her "under Daniel's orders". They also let her have a taste of a few days in solitary confinement in Ma'asiyahu Prison.

Aliza held out for a long while, yelled at the investigators, posted clips on YouTube in which she talked about the police corruption and the lies they were forcing her to tell. Unfortunately, she weakened five months later because they told her that Daniel would never get out of prison, and it would be a shame if she lost both her daughter and her life. Her older siblings, with her mother's cooperation, knew she couldn't live without a man and tempted her using a childhood friend who was several years younger than her and who had lived the past few years in the United States. They convinced him to come back to Israel to complete the mission. He began courting her and got her pregnant. The distance from here to becoming a witness for the prosecution was short. At this point, the police had victory at their hands.

In her testimony in court, when the defense asked her if she had any connection to theft of the Daniel's checkbook and forging of his signature, she played dumb and acted as if she didn't know what he was talking about. When the defense attorney showed the court a tape made by private investigators that proved that she and her childhood friend and big brother, forged checks in an amount of a quarter of a million shekels, Aliza did not know what to say. Despite this, the judges chose to ignore the fact that an ineligible witness sits before them. That must be the way it works when you decide to prosecute someone no matter what, even if there is no evidence against him and truthful testimony is not important…

The crumbling of Aliza's testimony as a witness for the prosecution is a turning point in the story because she was the only woman among us who became a witness for the prosecution and got benefits as a witness for the State.

Despite this whole house of cards, built on perjury after perjury (each witness recanted his or her testimony at some point after this and admitted to having lied) there is not any evidence to prove the charges against Daniel. Actually, evidence proving his innocence, like the police tapes and the beatings we got in the interrogations, was destroyed, made to disappear, or not recorded at all.

To my detriment, the police found twelve-year-old notebooks where I jotted down dreams, fantasies, imaginary things, and prayers. They gave their own interpretations to what I wrote, which were actually diametrically opposed to the truth, and despite the fact that the judges said the weight of the journal would be decided according the writer's explanation, they completely ignored my testimony, and thus manipulated me into "helping" them.

Six months after Daniel's arrest the police saw that despite the "treatment" at the battered women's shelter, despite the beatings, pressures, threats, and curses in the interrogation rooms, Ilana, Kary, Azamra, Shiran and myself, did not give into their lies. They decided to put all us, except for Kary, in the Neve Tirza Prison. Despite being a witness for the defense, she was the only one not imprisoned because her daughter Anastatsia threatened the head of the investigation team Asher Lizmi, that if her mother goes to jail, she will not testify against Daniel.

We sat in prison on a very heavy charge, about which we were not even questioned: child rape. Conviction could lead to a sentence of at least fourteen years. The state's attorneys tried to tempt us by saying: "If you sign that you were Daniel's victims, you will immediately be released from prison!" We sat for a whole year because we were not prepared to give in to the lie, and we insisted on waiting for trial so they could bring the evidence against us. Since they couldn't find any, they subpoenaed Timna, Sammy, and Aliza – their witnesses against Daniel, to bear witness against us. They contradicted each other and themselves, and were unable to answer even basic questions. It was so obvious that the witnesses were lying, that we were released the very same day. The judges reprimanded the prosecutor, Sagi Ofir, who was, not coincidentally, the same prosecutor in Daniel's case, that he had better sort the whole thing out immediately and that these women should not sit one moment in prison. The court cancelled the charges against us and only left that our meetings with Aliza were against a legal order, and forbid us to see each other. Today, we understand that this deal too was an exercise by the prosecutor, because his goal was to convict Daniel of the same charge.

In Daniel's trial, which was held simultaneously, with a different set of judges, in the same Jerusalem County court, with the same prosecutor, Sagi Ofir, with the same witnesses, with the same charge, which was proven to be a false story and was erased from the records, and against all criminal laws – the judges Jacob Saban, Refael Carmel, and Rebecca Friedman convicted Daniel.

In October 2013, in their ruling against Daniel, the judges wrote: "**A civilized society** cannot tolerate a way of life like that created by the defendant, with multiple wives".

And since we are more than one woman, they decided we were female slaves, and since female slaves have no free will, then sexual relations with us are considered non-consensual, and that is how they succeeded in convicting Daniel as a serial rapist.

In order to prove the theory of "possession under conditions of slavery" that Dr. Green invented, we were subject to violent police interrogations and intrusive and insulting questions about our sexual relations, because they wanted to prove forcefully sexual exploitation and humiliation. Their strategy was clear. It is not possible that a woman would share her man with five other women, unless he bewitched her and uses hypnotic suggestion on her brain, and since they had nothing real or tangible, they made up an accusation and called it "modern slavery", fruits of collaboration between the ICVC, the police, the welfare department, and the prosecutor's office. Daniel is the only one in Israel, maybe in the world, ever convicted on the charge that he has supernatural powers and charismatic powers that he can enslave other people's minds. Not a physical enslavement, but a "mental enslavement". It is unbelievable that in the 21$^{st}$ century a man is accused of using mystical powers, like in the times of the Inquisition.

Even in the Goel Ratzon case, the man who had more than 32 women and was arrested in January 2-1 – on charges of enslavement, polygamy, and rape of his daughters, which was the only case in Israel in which they wanted to convict a man for enslaving his family, he was not convicted on the enslavement charge. His case was completely different from ours: They believed in him, that he was a healer, they worshipped him and they called their children in his name, each of the women tattooed his image on wide areas of her body, and they had a rule book which defined proper behavior and what the punishments would be for not acting according to his will. They all lived with him in the same house. When he was arrested, most of them left him and testified against him, and he also admitted some of the charges. Despite all of this, the "enslavement" charge collapsed completely. As can be learned from the verdict in his case, the judges at the county court in Tel Aviv determined that the theory of "mental enslavement" created by the experts at the ICVC was not credible, not scientific, not accepted in the world or in professional circles, and determined: "There is no place to accept the theory regarding the existence of mental control over another person…". The Supreme Court also rejected the petition by the ICVC, who tried desperately to return the charge of enslavement in Goel Ratzon's case.

Despite this precedent, the judges in the Jerusalem County Court convicted Daniel on the charge of enslavement and mental captivity, since they had a problem: if they don't convict him on the charge of 'enslavement', then the whole indictment falls apart since it was all based on this charge. It is important to understand that once the whole family is defined as slaves and mind washed without an individual opinion, everyone is considered a victim, and automatically the head of the family is considered a "cult leader", and

Usually, when a woman complains about a man to the police, her first version is spontaneous and therefore the most credible. The first version is the deciding one, if the woman recants, says she lied, her second testimony is unacceptable. In our case, no woman complained. Moreover, the judges had to even admit in the verdict: "It has been proven that all members of the family appeared at the initial investigations as one with a unified version denying all of the allegations against Daniel."

When the prosecutors drew their card "mental slavery", they succeeded in misleading the judges. The system of the " victim witness" or "mental witness" enabled the prosecutors and the judges who decided to convict in any case, to achieve convictions, even if the prosecutor's testimonies are full of contradictions and different versions, they could always say the witnesses are "brainwashed victims", or if they went over to the prosecutor's side they were "brainwashed victims that sobered up", or if they switched sides and then went back to the defense and said they lied then they are "victims in the process of rehabilitation". In any case, the witness is a victim and the credibility of his testimony is decided upon by the prosecutor. No defense lawyer can deal with this system. Thus for example, when Aliza explained for five months that she determines how things work in her relationship with Daniel, they claimed that she was under "mental influence", and "her head was turned around", and she is, without a doubt, "brainwashed". They threatened her during the interrogations that until she "sobered up" and understand what they are telling her, she will not see her daughter, and will not get her back. Later, under the pressure of the investigation and emotional manipulation put on her by her mother and daughter, she skipped between different versions and couldn't remember key details in any one of them… Nonetheless, the judges determined that it did not matter that her versions were contradictory, because she is "in rehabilitation", and she should be allowed consideration and her testimony should be accepted as is. On the other hand, when they found my twelve-year-old journals they asked me to interpret things, rejected my answers all out, and decided on interpreting things exactly the opposite from my intentions. For example, when I wrote a prayer to G-d "Save me, Save me" which I copied from the books of Rabbi Nahman from Breslev, they used that as a type of evidence that I was in distress in my life with Daniel. They did not allow me to explain myself since I was "brainwashed", even though several times during the trial the judges and the attorney said I am an intelligent and well spoken woman…; … so clever, the most outstanding student, with multiple and rare abilities, who could easily be the Chief Rabbi's wife.

With unbearable ease and without any professional opinion or psychological testing, the judges decided that despite the fact that we are all independent, clever and intelligent; we are naught other than "a peloton of brainwashed people". The judges chose to convict only on the basis of the five witnesses for the prosecution, who recanted their testimony, and ignored completely all 16 witnesses for the defense. The judges even wrote about the defense witnesses in a general manner that: "... they were all cut from the same cloth of family members and often were partners themselves in the punishment he practiced."

When they said "Cut from the same cloth", did they mean that anyone who visits in our home is also a victim? Or maybe an accessory in crime? If so, why weren't they called in for questioning and indicted?

For example, when Dvora, a witness for the defense testified in court that she lived with us with her four children for six months, and that she liked the family and Daniel is a good father and nice and righteous man who never acted violently, the judges wrote in their verdict that "she is apparently an accomplice and is herself involved in the punishments that Daniel used, and was cut out of the same cloth as the family members, and that her positive impression of Daniel only strengthened his status among the household members..."

Daniel was sentenced to a harsh punishment, 26 years in jail. The prosecution appealed and asked for 65 years, and all this without one shred of evidence, no injured party.

Does a woman in a **"civilized society"** have to think "like the system", or she will be tagged a prostitute or sex slave?

Who decided that women supply sexual services and don't demand sexual services?

Who uses the term "feminism" and causes the oppression of women by preventing them to live as they choose?

Is it okay to decide in the name of "paternalism" what is love?

How is it possible that the same judges that call us "clever and smart" decide we are "sex slaves" just because we chose to love the same man together?

Is it possible that the courts will prosecute a man for raping his wife when she testifies sexual relations based on love?

The judges in Jerusalem determined that the State of Israel does not need proof to convict a man of rape, and doesn't even need a woman to claim she was raped. They decided to reinvent us as women who were raped, and supplied sexual services under duress. That is how they frame people in Israel: narrow minded zealous, money-grabbing, headline seekers play with people's lives, separate siblings, isolating each sibling in a different institution, sending children to destructive lives in boarding schools, incite them against their parents, teach them to be embarrassed of their origins, and to hate not only their father but also their mother who continues to love their father, who make them frustrated, desperate, and hopeless. It is interesting to note that when the State does that, it is not considered brainwashing and mental enslavement, but sobering… and the most important thing is the policeman who got the medal, the social worker who was promoted, the judge who got a certificate of excellence from feminist organizations, the ICVC who got the Speaker of the Knesset's Award, the press who gets scoops, and everyone makes a living.

We appealed to the Supreme Court, who allowed us visits and conjugal visits with Daniel. We sat in court. I very much wanted to respond to the lies of the prosecution, but the judge shut me up. He got a secret document from the Incest Committee, a committee of social workers, a document that said we could not meet with him since we were "his victims". Even our lawyer was not allowed to see what this was about, because it is a secret document. The judge added without hesitation that he could discontinue our phone calls with Daniel…

And now, sitting on the bench, we ask each other what to do, what will be? How will the world know our real story, four woman from different cultures, with rich life experiences, determined, who decided to live together with one man, how will our children get the real story of how we lived together?

Only we, who built the home, can tell how it really was there. Our cry is deep and painful, nested deeply in our hearts and will not give us rest – until the truth is told.

We created a website (www.danielambash.info), put on a show, and a movie about us is about to come out, but we have so much more to tell. We decided that the best thing to do is to write a book, which will be comprised of four parts. Each of us will write her personal story, and together we will get our true story out, with each of us presenting her point of view. That is how this book was born. An authentic story of four women and one man who despite everything, did not give up on love.

# L'HISTOIRE

Lors de notre conversation téléphonique avec Daniel, ce matin, qui nous appelait de la prison, il nous a informées que l'assistante sociale du service pénitentiaire d'Israël le menaçait à nouveau de lui interdire de nous téléphoner.

Nous nous sommes assises toutes les quatre dans l'aire de jeux publique, avant de nous rendre à une réunion prévue avec la réalisatrice du documentaire sur notre histoire. Nous étions tassées sur un même banc, Ilana, Azamra, Shiran et moi, Aderet, Daniel en ligne. Abattues, inquiètes, ne sachant que faire, avec la peur permanente d'être coupées de cette ligne téléphonique qui constitue notre seul lien restant avec Daniel.

Nous vivons ainsi depuis quatre ans.

Durant toutes ces années, on ne nous a jamais laissé voir Daniel. Pas de visites conjugales auxquelles, normalement, chaque prisonnier a droit. Aucune visite au parloir.

L'aire de jeux était abandonnée… nous non plus n'entendons plus depuis longtemps le rire de nos enfants. Eux aussi nous ont été enlevés.

On nous a bâillonnées : en nous interdisant de publier, en nous privant de la possibilité de nous exprimer ou de protester. En revanche les médias ont été inondés de mensonges à notre égard.

Pendant des mois, la police a enfermé chacune de nous séparément, elle nous a dispersées dans différents refuges pour femmes battues, aux quatre coins du pays. Interdiction de quitter les lieux, d'avoir un téléphone portable sur nous, d'entrer en contact l'une avec l'autre. Deux policiers armés venaient nous chercher dans un véhicule de la police pour nous mener à des interrogatoires épuisants et violents.

On nous a privées de notre liberté de vivre et on a détruit tout ce que nous avions construit pendant quinze ans.

Jusqu'à cette détention cauchemardesque, nous menions la meilleure vie du monde, nous ne comprenions pas comment il serait possible de vivre autrement. Notre existence était intéressante, animée, pleine d'aventures et d'enthousiasme. Nous étions une famille religieuse, des Hassidim Breslav attachés au Rabbi Israël Ber Odesser, le dépositaire du Petek qui est aussi surnommé « le grand-père » ou « Rabbi Na Na'h Na'hma Na'hman de Ouman à Jérusalem ». Une famille particulière, inhabituelle : six amies qui aimaient le même homme. Cela peut paraître étrange, mais beaucoup de choses le sont dans ce monde. Certains auront sans doute de la peine à le croire, mais nous nous entendions bien et nos problèmes n'étaient pas différents de ceux d'autres ménages. Voilà pourquoi le choc de l'arrestation fût si brutal, nous ne pouvions pas imaginer que quelqu'un veuille nous nuire de cette façon. Qui avions-nous dérangé ? Quelle loi avions-nous enfreinte ? Pourquoi quelqu'un se soucierait-il de la façon dont nous avons choisi de mener nos vies intimes ? Nous ne comprenions pas qui avait pu orchestrer tout cela ni pourquoi. Avec le temps la vérité s'est révélée...

Ce complot diabolique contre nous a été concocté par le *Centre Israélien pour les Victimes de Sectes* qui, pour justifier son existence et blanchir de l'argent recueilli par des dons, nous a étiquetés de « secte dangereuse » dans les médias.

Des recherches menées en mars 2011 par le journal *Yediot A'haronot* ont révélé que ce « Centre » douteux est en fait une organisation d'imposteurs qui agit contre tous courants ou tous groupes inacceptables à leurs yeux. Le « centre » s'attaque à toutes sortes d'associations ou d'individus dont les critères religieux ne correspondent pas aux leurs. L'organisation est composée de deux femmes et d'un médecin : Rachel Lichtenstein, Sharona Ben Moshe et le Dr David Green.

Le Forum européen pour la liberté religieuse[21] a publié que le *Centre Israélien pour les Victimes de Sectes* est essentiellement une

---

[21] EIFRF – European interreligious forum for religious freedom, site www.eifrf-articles.org

extension du *FECRIS* en Israël. Le *FECRIS* étant un organisme « antisecte » qui a essaimé dans plus de trente pays, chaque succursale étant constituée de deux ou trois membres.

Le vice-président du FECRIS, Alexander Dvorkin, est un citoyen russe, activiste de l'église russe orthodoxe, qui explique les principes de l'organisme antisecte comme suit : « La foi chrétienne orthodoxe est la foi originelle (...) d'autres cultes sont des falsifications, des inventions bon marché. » Dvorkin a également attaqué la foi musulmane à plusieurs reprises en déclarant : « soit Mohamed souffrait d'une maladie grave qui lui donnait des hallucinations soit un démon s'est emparé de lui ».

Des experts internationaux des Droits de l'Homme critiquent le FECRIS pour son incitation à l'intolérance à l'encontre de religions minoritaires et sa prédication à la haine. Le représentant des Nations Unies dans le domaine de la liberté de conscience a déclaré : « Il semble qu'une connotation négative et irrespectueuse soit attachée au terme de « secte ». Ce type d'approche encourage l'amalgame, la discrimination, le rejet et incite à violer un des droits humains fondamentaux : la liberté de culte. »

Contrairement aux cas où la police possède un indice pour établir un acte d'accusation et procéder à des arrestations aucun indice, dans notre cas, ne justifiait notre mise en accusation. Même la « polygamie », proscrite par la loi civile israélienne, ne justifiait pas nos arrestations : civilement, nous n'étions pas mariés.

La diffamation à notre égard faite d'articles de presse et de reportages télévisés provenait, en grande partie, de la famille d'Aliza, la cinquième compagne. Les premières années nous avions d'excellentes relations avec eux, ils nous rendaient souvent visites, ils habitaient près de chez nous. Nos relations se sont dégradées à partir du moment ou Aliza a décidé de cesser de les soutenir financièrement. Elle trouvait qu'ils exagéraient : nous leur avions déjà donné un montant de pas moins quatre-vingt mille shekel. Ils ont réagi violemment lorsqu'elle a refusé de céder à leurs pressions : ils avaient pris l'habitude de nous attendre devant notre maison avec des bâtons et des pierres, ils nous maudissaient, ils ont brisé les vitres de nos fenêtres en jetant des pierres et ont même blessé des enfants. Cette agression aurait pu tourner au drame. Le frère aîné d'Aliza, un délinquant connu des services de police, a menacé de tuer Daniel, de nuire à ses enfants et de brûler notre maison. Aliza n'a pas cédé. Elle leur a déclaré qu'ils avaient franchi les limites du tolérable. Elle a porté plainte contre sa famille et a obtenu une « interdiction de périmètre ». Ils se sont excusés mais parallèlement ils ont contacté le *Centre Israélien pour le Victimes de Sectes*, des journalistes et des policiers. Et à partir de 2008, a commencé leur poursuite. Ils ont obtenu que nous soyons placés sur table d'écoute. Des enquêteurs nous ont envoyés des « espions » qui ont échoué à trouver des éléments autorisant nos arrestations.

Trois ans plus tard.. .

Appel téléphonique au commissariat de Samy, beau-fils de Daniel, âgé de 14 ans, demandant une intervention policière parce qu'un ami des fils aînés de la famille l'aurait battu en l'absence de « son père » (son beau-père). Lorsque le policier a rappelé trois heures plus tard et a compris que tout allait bien, il n'a même pas pris la peine de venir vérifier. Cet appel n'a donc pas fourni de prétexte à des arrestations. Un mois et demi plus tard, un des garçons de la famille a découvert une boîte en bois étrange derrière un placard et l'a prise. Il ne pouvait pas imaginer qu'il s'agissait d'un appareil d'écoute camouflé là par la police. Quand il l'a ouvert, cinq policiers en civil sont entrés, hurlant que toute la famille était en état d'arrestation. L'enquêtrice principale, Lilah Renan, a admis devant la Cour du district que les incarcérations n'étaient pas prévues mais qu'elle avait dû y procéder parce que le système de surveillance qui était censé donner une orientation à leur enquête, donc les motifs des arrestations, avait été démasqué. (Je rappelle, qu'après trois ans de surveillance étroite et intensive de tous nos faits et gestes, la police ne disposait pas du moindre commencement de preuve d'une activité ou d'un comportement illicites).

La police de Jérusalem savait que pour obtenir la prolongation des incarcérations, la seule solution était de nous présenter comme « une secte sadique » dont tous les membres étaient endoctrinés, réduits à l'esclavage par « un monstre », le père de famille, « le plus grand criminel du pays », « le prêtre d'un culte néfaste et pervers ». Et les médias ont répercuté telles quelles les informations. La police a nommé le *Centre Israélien pour les Victimes de Sectes* comme « expert » pour encadrer l'enquête diligentée contre nous. Le *Centre* a briffé les enquêteurs, les guidant sur les points où il convenait de mettre l'accent durant les interrogatoires, et le même *Centre* a envoyé une liste de questions-types. Bien entendu, la police n'a pas pris la peine d'examiner les activités du *Centre* ni la fiabilité des intervenants. Elle n'a vérifié ni l'identité, ni les qualités, ni le passif, ni les intérêts personnels des soit disant « experts ». La police n'a pas été intriguée par les millions de shekel de dons qu'empoche cet organisme.

Sharona Ben Moshe, qui se présente comme conseillère juridique du *Centre Israélien pour les Victimes de Sectes*, a été impliquée dans l'affaire d'enlèvement du célèbre rabbin Nir Ben Artzi. Elle était à l'époque la compagne et la complice du kidnappeur. Durant trois ans, ils ont détenu le Rabbin Ben-Artzi dans différents appartements de Tibériade, le traitant de façon inhumaine. Ils ont pris le contrôle de ses biens et ont transmis, en son nom, de faux messages aux donateurs de l'organisation qu'il avait fondée. Ainsi, ils se sont frauduleusement emparés de fortes sommes d'argent. Ils l'ont nourri de pain et de margarine, puis après l'avoir obligé à boire un litre de vodka, ils lui ont fait signer un document dans lequel il admettait avoir eu des relations sexuelles avec des moutons et d'autres animaux. Afin de détourner l'attention du public et de brouiller toutes les pistes relatives à son enlèvement et aux extorsions de fonds dont elle s'était rendue coupable, Sharona Ben Moshe est devenue la représentante du *Centre israélien pour les Victimes de Sectes* en diffusant de fausses informations contre les « sectes ». Nir Ben Artzi était au nombre de leurs premières victimes. Finalement, au terme d'un procès, la fraude a été prouvée, les responsables condamnés à de l'emprisonnement ou à du travail d'intérêt général et à une amande[22].

Il est intéressant de savoir que, dans notre affaire, la police a réussi à convaincre Aliza de devenir témoin à charge après cinq mois d'efforts acharnés et suite à un « traitement » au *Centre pour les Victimes de Sectes*. Aliza a commencé à inventer et développer des

[22] Cf. http://mishpatsheker.com/tag

histoires invraisemblables, expliquant que la « secte » l'avait forcée à avoir des rapports sexuels avec des chevaux, à introduire des serpents, des araignées, des souris et des cafards dans son vagin !

Rachel Lichtenstein, la directrice du *Centre pour les Victimes de sectes*, qui attaque fanatiquement tout ce qui dévie de l'idée qu'elle se fait de ce que devrait être un judaïsme orthodoxe, a du avoir l'impression de gagner à la loterie lorsqu'elle a reçu Timna, le premier et principal témoin.

Timna, âgé alors de 19 ans, avait grandi dans une maison religieuse. Elle nous a raconté que sa mère souffrait de schizophrénie et était internée dans un hôpital psychiatrique. Son père, d'origine Yéménite, était Roch Yechiva (responsable d'une école talmudique) et a été impliqué dans une affaire très médiatisée dans laquelle on l'accusait d'avoir été simultanément marié à plusieurs femmes. Il a fini par quitter le domicile conjugal et divorcer de la mère de Timna. Cette dernière disait aussi qu'enfant, son oncle l'avait agressée sexuellement. Jetée à la rue, elle grandit dans des internats, rêvant de devenir mannequin. Très jeune, elle a touché à diverses drogues et a même été impliquée dans un trafic. Kari, la seconde compagne de Daniel dont il sera question plus tard, a fait sa rencontre dans le centre-ville de Jérusalem. Timna a demandé à l'accompagner pour l'allumage des bougies de la fête de Hanoucca. Ravie de sa rencontre avec Kari, les deux femmes sont restées en contact téléphonique. Parfois elle venait aussi partager nos repas. Nous ne pouvions pas imaginer qu'elle tomberait éperdument amoureuse de Daniel, de façon maladive et obsessionnelle. Timna voulait absolument devenir une des compagnes de Daniel, sa septième femme. L'idée effrayait terriblement Daniel, il a donc demandé à Kari de cesser de l'amener chez nous. Timna revenait malgré tout nous voir. Sans la moindre gêne, elle a pris Daniel à part pour lui déclarer son amour, lui dire qu'elle ne souhaitait aucun autre homme que lui, qu'elle ne pourrait être heureuse qu'avec lui. Elle a exigé qu'il l'accepte immédiatement comme l'une de ses compagnes. Daniel ne voulait pas la blesser, il a rejeté ses avances, lui expliquant qu'il n'avait pas l'intention d'avoir de nouvelles compagnes. Timna est sortie de notre maison, répétant furieusement, en embrassant la *mezouza* de façon compulsive : « Tu vas le regretter... »

Pourtant, elle a continué à assister à nos concerts et s'est répandue en éloges sur notre famille et notre mode de vie lorsque l'émission de télévision '360' de la chaîne 2 l'a interviewée. Elle a notamment dit : « ... J'ai vécu dans divers groupes, mais ici j'ai rencontré des individus authentiques que je ne voulais plus les quitter ».

Quatre mois plus tard, en regardant l'émission '360' diffusée, elle a entendu le présentateur annoncer que « d'autres femmes s'uniraient à Daniel Ambash ... ». Elle a dû en concevoir une jalousie maladive : elle s'est rendue sur le site du *Centre Israélien pour les Victimes de Sectes* – qui a initié cette émission et qui y a participé – et a écrit à la directrice, Rachel Lichtenstein, pour lui demander de l'aide. R. Liechtenstein lui a donné rendez-vous. Timna se trouvait sans domicile et aussi sous le coup d'une procédure pénale pour vol. R. Liechtenstein profité de l'occasion qui s'offrait à elle pour exploiter la faiblesse de Timna et lui a promis un soutien psychologique et financier. Elle a organisé une rencontre avec les enquêteurs de la police de Jérusalem, qui l'ont emmenée dans un hôtel, situé sur la plage de Tel-Aviv. La police n'a pas enregistré la rencontre mais a utilisé le désir brûlant de vengeance de Timna pour l'encourager à fabriquer un tissu de mensonges correspondants au document « profil d'une secte » fourni par le *Centre Israélien pour les Victimes de Sectes :*

1. exploitation sexuelle
2. exploitation économique
3. viols sur mineurs
4. zoophilie
5. traitements dégradants (forcer les gens à manger des excréments, etc.).

Les enquêteurs ont retenu tous les points d'accusation précédemment mentionnés et ont promis à Timna qu'ils la logeraient. Ils l'ont ainsi soumise à un chantage.

Un an plus tard elle comparaissait devant le tribunal en qualité de témoin à charge. Timna a déclaré à la barre : « J'étais choquée d'apprendre que Rachel Lichtenstein avait informé les services de police de mon appel. Mon intention n'était pas de me plaindre et je ne souhaitais pas de telles conséquences mais Rachel Lichtenstein m'a affirmé que je n'avais pas le choix. »

Il était également important pour Timna de rappeler, lors de sa déposition devant la Cour, à quel point elle avait été amoureuse de Daniel. Elle a déclaré : « J'ai aimé Daniel comme jamais je n'avais aimé un homme et comme je n'en aimerai jamais de toute ma vie. » Face à Daniel vêtu de l'uniforme des prisonniers, enchaîné pieds et mains, elle a très naïvement révélé aux juges son véritable motif : son dépit et l'offense d'avoir une fois entendu Daniel dire qu'elle n'avait pas de belles dents !

L'idéologie du FECRIS prétend que de grandir dans une secte est dangereux pour les enfants car les membres y sont irresponsables. Par conséquent le FECRIS préconise de retirer aux parents la garde de leurs enfants. Ainsi le Dr Green a conseillé aux enquêteurs de la police de Jérusalem de prouver que les enfants avaient subi des agressions sexuelles. Faute de preuves, ils ont tiré, comme un lapin du chapeau, la conversation téléphonique de Samy évoquée précédemment et que nous détaillerons maintenant.

Samy était un garçon un peu voyou qui avait l'habitude de se faufiler dans le dortoir des filles et de les épier dans les douches. Une fois, il a touché Batia, âgée de six ans (la fille d'Aliza et de Daniel), « à l'endroit de la culotte, par-dessus ses vêtements ». Aliza a été choquée, en a fait un drame, prétendant que Samy avait violé sa fille. Daniel était sorti lorsqu'un des amis du frère aîné de Samy, un Américain, costaud, âgé de 24 ans, est venu à la maison et a entendu d'Aliza sa version des faits. Il a menacé aussitôt Samy de lui « donner une leçon » en introduisant un manche à balai dans son anus. Effrayé, Samy a téléphoné à la police. Trois heures plus tard un agent a appelé pour vérifier si la situation était rentrée dans l'ordre. Lorsqu'il a compris que tout était calme, il n'a pas donné suite.

Selon les instructions du *Centre pour les Victimes de Sectes* et en conformité avec leur théorie selon laquelle le chef d'une secte est le seul responsable de tout ce qui s'y produit (malgré son absence, malgré son ignorance des faits) nous étions tous en état d'arrestation et en état de choc, un mois et demi plus tard ; mais Daniel était « le coupable ». Nous comprenions que l'appel téléphonique interprété comme preuve d'une « maltraitance d'enfant » associé au descriptif du « profil de chef de secte » suffisaient à l'accuser. Daniel a été condamné pour acte de sodomie sur mineur, sur la seule allégation d'un fait dont nous doutons qu'il se soit réellement produit et où l'alibi de Daniel prouvait son absence de la maison, lieu d'où Samy a téléphoné au commissariat. Plus encore, Samy a précisé durant les interrogatoires que si « son père » (son beau-père) avait été présent, il l'aurait protégé et n'aurait pas laissé une telle chose se produire. Lorsque nous avons envoyé l'enregistrement de la conversation entre Samy et le policier du commissariat à un analyste expert du montage son et de ses manipulations, nous avons été surprises de découvrir que la police s'était permise un acte criminel, celui de supprimer les mots « Papa n'est pas à la maison » puis d'utiliser la conversation tronquée comme preuve à charge.

Durant son interrogatoire les policiers ont déclaré à Samy qu'il serait suspecté d'avoir violé sa sœur de six ans s'il ne coopérait pas et que le viol était puni de quatorze ans d'incarcération. Les enquêteurs ont ainsi réussi à lui faire « avouer » des faits précis et détaillés dont ils se sont ensuite servis pour les vingt chefs d'accusations.

La police avait besoin de témoins supplémentaires venant de l'intérieur de la famille, afin de renforcer la « fiabilité » des accusations. Anastasia, dix-huit ans et demie, la demi-sœur de Samy, une belle-fille de Daniel, était déçue qu'aucun des fils de Daniel n'ait voulu l'épouser. Elle était connue pour son problème de mythomanie et ses fréquentations peu honorables. Cette fille a vite compris que le plus avantageux pour elle serait de collaborer avec la police et de tenter d'influencer d'autres détenus de a famille à témoigner contre Daniel. Elle a révélé à la police qu'une rumeur avait commencé à circuler une semaine avant les arrestations selon laquelle Israël, âgé de 13 ans à l'époque, fils de Daniel et d'Ilana, aurait joué avec ses deux plus jeunes demi-frères des jeux inappropriés. La police en a profité pour également menacer Israël, comme elle avait menacé Samy : s'il ne témoignait pas contre son père il serait emprisonné pour le viol de ses frères. Israël a fini par céder aux menaces de la police, en devenant un témoin de l'accusation contre son père ; il a été considéré comme le témoin le plus fiable par les juges. Quelques mois plus tard, il a envoyé une lettre détaillée à la Cour suprême – lettre que nous avons intégré au livre – dans laquelle il révèle ses faux témoignages contre son père. Il y raconte comment les procureurs Sagi Ofir et Lisa Wolfus, assistés d'une enquêteur spécialisé en interrogatoire pour enfants, Micha Haran, l'ont menacé de l'emprisonner à la place de son père s'il ne témoignait à charge. Ils l'on préparé au témoignage devant la Cour. Dans la même lettre, il déclare qu'il a tenté de se suicider à cause d'eux et des pressions qu'ils ont exercées sur lui.

Le Ministère des Affaires Sociales a ouvertement déclaré que dans le dossier « Ambash » il y avait une coopération réussie entre la police, le *Centre Israélien pour les Victimes de Sectes*, le parquet et les services sociaux. Pour le Ministère des Affaires Sociales ce fût l'occasion de remplir les institutions spécialisées en retirant plusieurs enfants du domicile de leurs parents et donc de toucher les fortes sommes d'argent que verse par l'État pour chaque enfant placé (17 000 shekel par mois et par enfant).

Les enquêteurs de la police ont identifié les sensibilités et les faiblesses et de chacun et s'en sont servis pour nous manipuler ou torturer en conséquence. Avec Aliza ils étaient avantagés : sa mère collaborait avec eux et faisait pression pour que sa fille se sépare de Daniel. Une des enquêtrices de la police de Jérusalem était un membre de leur famille. Elle a encouragé la mère d'Aliza à convaincre sa fille de céder aux exigences des enquêteurs. En fait, Aliza était tellement déterminée à prouver que Daniel était innocent que la police de Jérusalem a usé de tous les moyens possibles pour parvenir à ses fins : menaces, cris, humiliations, mais aussi flatterie et chantage. Les policiers l'ont menacée de ne plus jamais revoir sa fille Batia, et le chantage consistait aussi à lui faire comprendre ce qu'elle devrait dire pour faire avancer l'enquête si elle voulait sauver sa propre peau. Autrement elle risquait également de passer de nombreuses années en prison, vu qu'Anastasia était disposée à témoigner contre elle pour l'avoir violée « sur les instructions » de Daniel. Les inspecteurs l'ont aussi enfermée quelques jours « en isolation » dans un cachot pour lui donner un avant-goût de ce qui l'attendait.

Aliza a tenu le coup un certain temps, elle s'énervait contre les enquêteurs, elle a posté des vidéos sur YouTube où elle décrivait la corruption des policiers et comment ils l'ont contrainte à mentir. Mais au bout de cinq mois de ce régime, elle n'avait plus de forces et a cessé de protester. Les enquêteurs lui ont garanti qu'ils veilleront à ce que Daniel ne sorte jamais de prison, qu'il serait dommage qu'elle gâche sa vie, qu'elle soit privée de la garde de sa fille et qu'elle finisse enfermée en prison comme lui. Ses frères plus âgés, en collaboration avec sa mère savaient qu'elle ne pourrait pas vivre seule ; ils ont recontacté un de ses amis d'enfance afin de la séduire. Un peu moins âgé qu'elle, ce dernier avait vécu au Etats-Unis au cours des dernières années. Ils l'ont convaincu de rentrer en Israël dans cet objectif. Il a commencé à lui faire la cour, elle est tombée enceinte. Le cheminement nécessaire pour devenir témoin à charge fut court. À ce stade, il est possible de dire que la police a gagné.

Lors de son témoignage au procès, l'avocat de la défense a interrogé Aliza sur son implication dans le vol du chéquier de Daniel et ses fausses signatures. Elle a fait semblant de ne pas savoir de quoi il s'agissait. Lorsque l'avocat de la défense a présenté sur un écran une vidéo de caméra cachée tournée par des détectives privés qui prouvait qu'elle et son ami d'enfance, avec la complicité de son frère aîné, avaient falsifié les signatures sur des dizaines de chèques pour un montant qui atteignait un quart de millions de shekel, Aliza s'est tue. Néanmoins, les juges ont préféré ignorer ces vols. C'est probablement ainsi que fonctionne le système lorsqu'il a décidé de condamner quelqu'un à n'importe quel prix, même s'il ne possède aucune preuve contre lui, même si le serment de dire toute la vérité au tribunal n'est pas respecté par les témoins…

L'effondrement d'Aliza fût un tournant net dans le cours des événements parce qu'elle fût la seule des six compagnes à devenir témoin à charge, témoin d'État au service de la procuration. Elle a reçu, en échange de son « repentir » et de ses délations une immunité pénale et des avantages matériels.

Ce château de cartes a été construit avec le concours de faux témoins (certains se sont rétractés au cours de l'instruction, tous ont déclaré avoir menti sous pression). Aucune preuve ne soutient les accusations portées contre Daniel.

Malheureusement, la police a trouvé mon journal intime qui datait d'une douzaine d'années et dans lequel je notais mes rêves, mes fantasmes, mes fantaisies et mes prières. Ils ont donné à mes mots l'interprétation qu'ils voulaient bien leur donner, interprétation fausse. Si les juges ont statué que la valeur testimoniale de mon journal dépendrait des explications fournies par son auteure, ils n'ont, en fin de compte, pas tenu compte de mon témoignage dans le jugement et se sont servis de mon journal intime de façon abusive et mensongère.

Six mois après l'arrestation de Daniel, les enquêteurs de polices ont réalisé qu'en dépit des « soins psychologiques » reçus dans les foyers pour femmes battues, malgré la violence physique, les chantages, les menaces et les insultes dans les salles d'interrogatoires, Ilana, Kari, Azamra, Shiran et moi-même refusions de mentir comme on nous demandait de le faire, nous avons été incarcérées dans la prison de Nevé Tirtza. Bien que demeurée témoin de la défense Kari fût la seule d'entre nous à ne pas avoir été incarcérée. Parce que sa fille, Anastasia, a prévenu l'enquêteur chef – Asher Lizmi – qu'elle ne témoignerait contre Daniel qu'à condition qu'il préserve sa mère de la prison.

Nous avons été emprisonnées conséquemment à une accusation très lourde, au sujet de laquelle personne ne nous a interrogé : viol sur mineur. Crime puni d'une peine d'au moins 14 ans de prison. Les procureurs ont essayé de nous convaincre de nous présenter comme des victimes : « Si vous signez que vous êtes des victimes de Daniel, nous vous libèrerons immédiatement de prison ». Nous avons donc passé un an en prison uniquement parce que nous refusions de céder et de mentir. Nous avons persévéré jusqu'au procès où devaient être produites les preuves de notre culpabilité. Les enquêteurs n'ayant rien trouvé, ils ont fait comparaître Timna, Samy et Aliza, les témoins à charge contre Daniel, pour témoigner également contre nous. Les témoins se sont contredits les uns les autres devant la Cour, ils ne savaient pas répondre aux questions les plus élémentaires. Il était évident qu'il s'agissait de faux témoignages par conséquent nous avons été libérées le jour même. Les juges ont réprimandé le procureur Sagi Ofir, celui-là même qui menait le procès contre Daniel : il était préférable d'annuler les plaintes et que les femmes soient relaxées instamment. Le tribunal a effacé toutes les charges contre nous sauf celle qui nous condamnait pour réunions illégales avec Aliza ; en tant que témoins nous avions l'interdiction de la rencontrer.

Aujourd'hui, nous comprenons que cette affaire était un coup monté par Sagi Ofir. Le procès contre Daniel était mené parallèlement au nôtre, avec le même procureur, Sagi Ofir, avec les mêmes trois témoins à charge mais avec trois juges différents du même tribunal – Jacob Tzaban, Raphaël Carmel et Rebecca Feldman-Friedman. Or Daniel a été condamné sous le même chef d'accusation pour lequel nous avons été relaxées.

En octobre 2013, le verdict stipulait : « Une société civilisée comme l'est la société israélienne ne peut pas tolérer la vie que l'accusé a mené, la polygamie. »

Comme il était inconcevable que nous étions plusieurs compagnes consentantes, les juges ont décidé que nous étions des esclaves. Et parce que les esclaves ne disposent pas de libre arbitre, ni de volonté propre, nos relations intimes avec Daniel ont été considérées comme des relations obtenues sans consentement mutuel. Ainsi ont-ils pu condamner Daniel de divers viols sur nous….

Pour confirmer la théorie de l'« esclavage » inventée par le Dr Green, nous avons subi des brutalités policières lors de nos interrogatoires, nous avons du faire face à des questions indiscrètes et insultantes au sujet de notre intimité, les enquêteurs voulant à tous prix montrer que nous avions subies des agressions et des humiliations sexuelles. Ils postulaient qu'aucune femme ne serait prête à partager son mari avec cinq autres femmes, à moins qu'il ne les ensorcèle et fasse usage de méthodes hypnotiques ! Mais comme ils ne disposaient d'aucune preuve tangible, ils ont inventé un chef d'accusation désigné par le terme d' « esclavage moderne ». Cette trouvaille fut le résultat de la collaboration entre le *Centre Israélien pour les Victimes de Sectes*, la police, le Ministère des Affaires Sociales et le parquet. Daniel est le seul dans ce pays, peut-être le seul dans le monde, a être condamné pour usage de « pouvoirs surnaturels » et d'une force charismatique telle qu'elle subjugue les esprits. Il ne s'agit pas d'« esclavage physique » mais d'« esclavage mental ». Il est proprement incroyable qu'au XXIe siècle un homme soit accusé de posséder des pouvoirs surnaturels comme du temps de l'Inquisition.

Même dans le cas de « Goel Ratzon », l'homme qui avait plus de 32 femmes, arrêté à Tel Aviv en Janvier 2010 et accusé d'esclavagisme, de polygamie et de viols sur ses propres filles (seul cas en Israël, où il a été question de condamner un homme pour mise en esclavage de toute sa famille), le chef d'inculpation d'esclavagisme n'a finalement pas été retenu. Son histoire était totalement différente de la nôtre. Ses femmes croyaient en lui, c'était un guérisseur, elles l'admiraient, l'adoraient et ont nommé tous leurs enfants « Goel Ratson », comme lui. Leurs corps étaient tatouées de son portrait et il possédait un livre de lois qui règlementaient leurs façons de se comporter avec lui. Ce règlement prévoyait même un certain nombre de sanctions si elles ne lui obéissaient pas. Elles vivaient toutes avec lui sous le même toit, et lorsqu'il a été incarcéré la plupart d'entre elles ont témoigné contre lui. Il a également reconnu un certain nombre d'actes illicites. Dans son verdict, les juges de la Cour du district de Tel-Aviv ont statué sur le fait que la théorie « d'esclavage mental », inventé par les soit disant experts du *Centre Israélien pour les Victimes de sectes*, est dénué de fondement légal ; il ne repose sur aucune base scientifique et n'est pas avéré par la communauté professionnelle qui a ainsi déclaré : « Il n'y a pas lieu d'accepter la théorie de l'existence d'un contrôle mental qui s'exercerait sur un autre individu. » Même la Cour Suprême a rejeté la requête du *Centre Israélien pour les Victimes de Sectes*, qui a déployé tous ses efforts pour rétablir le chef d'accusation d'esclavagisme dans le dossier de « Goel Ratzon ».

En revanche les juges de la Cour du district de Jérusalem ont retenu dans leur condamnation de Daniel la thèse de l'asservissement mental. Pourquoi ? parce qu'ils se sont heurtés à un problème ; s'ils ne le condamnaient pas d'abord pour « esclavagisme », sa culpabilité s'effondrait étant donné qu'elle repose entièrement sur ce postulat. Dès qu'on désigne tous les membres de la famille comme « esclaves ayant subis des lavages de cerveau », sans libre arbitre, ni opinion indépendante, tout le monde est automatiquement considéré comme « victime ». Il en résulte alors que le chef de la famille peut être défini comme « chef de secte » et qu'il devient possible de le condamner pour une infinité de crimes.

La question qui se pose est la suivante : Comment l'Etat peut-il établir des faits contradictoires ? D'un côté on nous étiquète de « victimes » de l'autre côté on nous emprisonne ! Est-ce ainsi qu'on traite les « victimes » en Israël ? Et si nous sommes définies comme des victimes, pourquoi nous priver du support financier que l'État accorde normalement aux victimes ?

Habituellement, le droit israélien considère que lorsqu'une femme porte plainte contre un homme, la première version est la plus spontanée donc la plus fiable.Sur le plan juridique, la première version prévaudra. Si la femme se ravise, en déclarant qu'elle a menti, son second témoignage n'est pas retenu. Dans notre affaire, aucune compagne n'avait porté plainte. Même les juges ont admis dans le verdict « qu'il a été démontré qu'au cours du premier interrogatoire toute la famille est arrivée unie comme une seule personne avec une version homogène des faits, niant les accusations portées contre Daniel ». Le parquet a donc tiré la carte de l' « esclavage mental » et a réussi ainsi à convaincre les juges.

La tactique du « témoin victime » ou de la « victime mentale » a permis au parquet et aux juges, de condamner Daniel malgré tout, de le reconnaître coupable en dépit des nombreuses contradictions et divergences contenues dans les divers témoignages. Il est toujours possible de prétendre que si le témoin est un témoin de la défense c'est qu'il est, par ailleurs, « encore sous l'emprise des lavages de cerveau ». À contrario, si un témoin de la défense se ravise et devient témoin de l'accusation, on prétend alors que « cette victime qui a subi un lavage de cerveau a enfin retrouvé ses esprits ». Ou encore, si on réussi à faire qu'un témoin de la défense devienne témoin de l'accusation puis se rétracte et admet qu'il a menti sous la pression de la police et du parquet, on prétend alors que le processus est en cours, qu'il est une « une victime en voie de réhabilitation ». Quoiqu'il en soit, le témoin est toujours considéré comme « victime » et son « degré de fiabilité » dépend des ordres du parquet. Les avocats de la défense sont impuissants face à de telles méthodes.

Ainsi lorsqu'Aliza durant cinq mois s'est efforcée d'expliquer aux enquêteurs que sa relation avec Daniel était ainsi menée avec son entier consentement, ils ont affirmé qu'elle était encore sous « influence mentale », que les « lavages de cerveau » lui paralysait l'esprit. En salles d'interrogatoires, les policiers l'ont aussi menacée, lui disant que si elle n'« ouvrait pas les yeux », si elle se refusait d'entendre ce qu'ils lui expliquaient, elle ne reverrait jamais plus sa fille qu'ils donneraient à l'adoption. Plus tard, sous les pressions et les manipulations émotionnelles exercées par l'intermédiaire de sa mère et de sa propre fille, Alisa a commencé à être confuse, à mélanger diverses versions de ses témoignages, incapable de se souvenir des informations données préalablement... Pourtant, les juges ont statué que cette confusion ne prêtait pas à conséquence, elle ne faisait qu'exprimer le processus : « en cours de réhabilitation ». Par conséquent, il ne fallait tenir compte que de son témoignage à charge et l'accepter tel qu'il était. En revanche, lorsque les enquêteurs se sont servis de mes journaux intimes, vieux de douze ans, et m'ont posée des questions sur le sens de certaines phrases, ils ont refusé mes explications, et ont donné à mes mots une signification opposée à celle que je leur avais donné. Par exemple, lorsque ils ont trouvé une prière recopiée des livres de Rabbi Na'hman de Breslav avec les termes « au secours, au secours », ils l'ont utilisé comme preuve que je demandais à être sauvée de l'existence menée avec Daniel. Ils n'ont pas voulu entendre ce que j'expliquais, car ils ont affirmé d'emblée que j'avais subit un « lavage de cerveau », bien qu'à d'autres occasions les juges et le procureur ont indiqué que j'étais une femme « intelligente et structurée », « la meilleure élève », « dotée de nombreuses et rares qualités, si sage que je pourrais facilement être la femme d'un grand rabbin ».

Avec une facilité intolérable et sans l'aval d'aucun point de vue d'experts ou de tests psychologiques, les juges ont décidé que, même si nous étions toutes autonomes, intelligentes et avisées, nous ne formions qu'un groupe d'individus endoctrinés. Les juges ont choisi de condamner Daniel sur la foi de cinq témoins à charge qui se sont ensuite, d'une façon ou d'une autre, rétractés. Par contre ils ont totalement ignoré les seize témoins de la défense. Les juges ont même écrit à propos des témoins de la défense que, de manière générale, ils étaient tous : «... faits du même matériau que la famille et qu'ils participaient au système de punitions ordonnées. »

Lorsque les juges ont écrit, « faits du même matériau », insinuaient-ils que tous ceux qui nous rendaient visite étaient des victimes ? Ou peut-être des complices ? Si tel était vraiment le cas, pourquoi n'ont-ils pas convoqué tous ces gens pour les interroger ? Et pourquoi ne les ont-ils pas associés à cette histoire de « secte », inventée de toute pièce ?

Par exemple, lorsque Devora, témoin de la défense, a témoigné devant la Cour, rappelant qu'elle avait vécu chez nous pendant six mois avec ses quatre enfants, qu'elle aimait notre famille et que Daniel était un merveilleux père, un homme agréable, plein d'attentions, de gentillesses, qui n'avait jamais fait preuve de violence, les juges ont écrit dans le verdict qu'elle était « probablement une complice impliquée dans le système de punitions instituées par Daniel » et qu'elle était « faite du même matériel que la famille ce qui justifie son impression positive... ».

Daniel a été condamné à une peine extrêmement sévère : une peine d'emprisonnement de 26 ans. Le procureur a lancé un appel dans lequel il réclame 65 ans de prison, sans étayer son exigence de la moindre preuve, sans que Daniel n'ait commis le moindre délit ni le moindre crime.

Dans une « société civilisée » une femme doit-elle penser d'une façon normative au risque d'être identifiée comme une « femme menant un mode de vie dissolue » ou encore comme « une femme-esclave » ?

Qui a décidé que les femmes sont des prestataires de services conjugaux et qu'elles ne sont pas elles-mêmes détentrices des mêmes droits ?

Qui se sert du terme de « féminisme » dans le seul but d'interdire aux femmes de vivre comme elles le souhaitent ?

Au nom du féminisme, est-il permis de déterminer ce qu'est l'amour, et comment il doit être vécu entre adultes consentants ?

Comment les mêmes juges qui nous nous ont décrites comme « intelligentes et structurées » ont-ils pu décider que nous sommes des

« esclaves sexuelles », uniquement parce que nous avons choisi ensemble d'aimer le même homme ?

Comment est-il possible que le tribunal définisse notre conjoint comme agresseur, alors que nous ne cessons de déclarer qu'il ne nous a jamais contraintes à quoi que ce soit et que nos relations intimes avaient notre plein consentement ?

Les juges de Jérusalem ont jugé que dans l'État d'Israël il n'est pas nécessaire de disposer de preuves pour condamner pour viol un homme, même si ses supposées victimes clament son innocence. Contre notre gré, les juges nous ont étiquetées de « victimes de viols », « forcées à fournir des services sexuels ». En Israël, c'est ainsi qu'on fabrique des dossiers à charge contre des innocents. Une bande de criminels professionnels jouent avec la vie des gens, séparant les familles, jetant les enfants dans des institutions, leur préparant des avenirs brisés, les montant contre leurs parents, leur enseignant à avoir honte de leurs origines, leur inculquant la haine de leur père mais aussi la haine de leur mère tant que celle-ci ne s'est pas désolidarisée du père, les privant de leur cadre, les jetant dans le désespoir. Pourquoi, lorsque l'État agit de cette façon, ne parle-t-on pas aussi de « lavages de cerveaux », d' « emprisonnement mental », pourquoi parle-t-on, au contraire de « processus de réhabilitation » ?

L'officier de police en charge a reçu une médaille, l'assistante sociale a été promue, le juge a reçu un certificat d'excellence des organisations féministes, *le Centre Israélien pour les Victimes de Sectes* a été récompensé par le président du parlement, les médias récoltent des scoops, tout le monde prospère et s'engraisse au prix de notre malheur.

Nous avons soumis une demande à la Haute Cour de justice pour nous permettre de rendre visite à Daniel, et être rétablies dans nos droits, notamment nos droits conjugaux. Chaque prisonnier y a droit. Nous non. Nous nous sommes donc assises dans la salle d'audience. Je voulais réagir à tous les mensonges du parquet, mais le juge m'a interrompue. Il a reçu devant nos yeux un document secret, « une lettre de cachet ». De la procuration ? Des services sociaux ? Une missive affirmant sans doute qu'en tant que « victimes » il fallait nous protéger et nous interdire de rencontrer Daniel. Même notre avocat ignorait de quoi il s'agissait, étant donné le caractère confidentiel du document. Le juge n'a donc pas autorisé les visites au parloir, ni les visites conjugales et il ajouté, sans hésitation, qu'il pouvait aussi nous interdire nos conversations téléphoniques avec Daniel ...

Et maintenant, assises sur un banc, pleines de doutes, nous nous demandons que faire et quel sera notre avenir ? Comment le monde connaîtra-t-il notre véritable histoire, l'aventure de quatre femmes de cultures différentes, riches de leurs expériences de vies, fermes dans leurs convictions, qui ont décidé de vivre ensemble et d'aimer le même homme. Comment les événements de nos vies communes pourront-ils être transmis à nos enfants ?

Seules nous, qui avons construit ce foyer, pouvons raconter ce qui s'y est vraiment passé. Ce cri de détresse, issu du plus profond de notre cœur, ne nous donnera pas de répit tant que la vérité n'aura pas éclaté au grand jour.

Nous avons construit un site internet ; nous avons écris une pièce de théâtre, nous collaborons à un film documentaire, mais nous avons encore tellement de choses à raconter. Nous avons décidé que le mieux était d'écrire un livre, notre livre, composé de quatre parties.

Chacune y relate sa vision de notre histoire commune, nous le publions ensemble. C'est ainsi qu'est né le projet de ce livre. L'histoire authentique de quatre femmes et d'un homme, qui malgré tout, n'ont pas renoncé à l'amour.

# AMBASH FAMILY משפחת אמבש

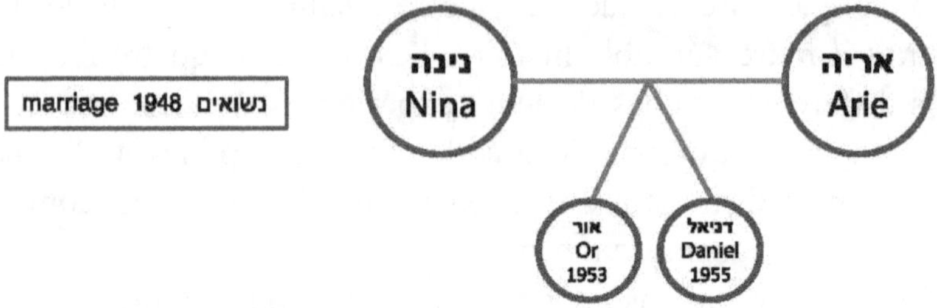


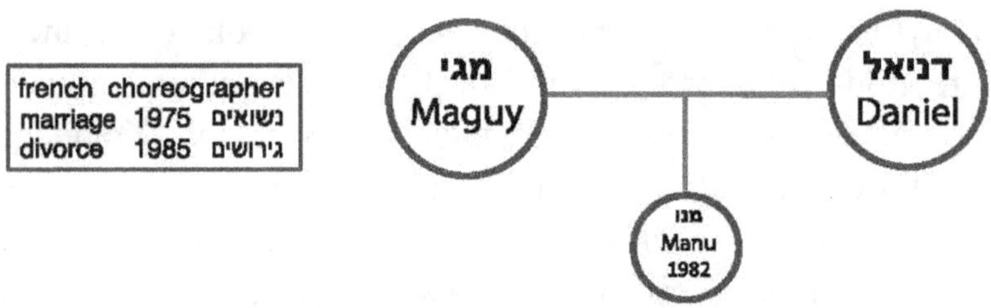


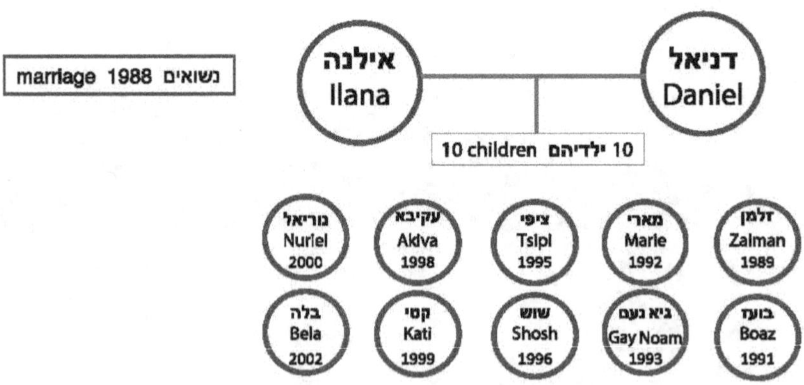

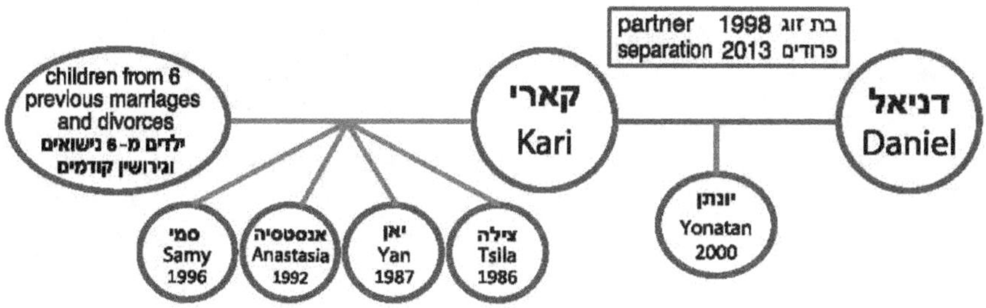
partner 1998 בת זוג
separation 2013 פרודים
children from 6 previous marriages and divorces
ילדים מ-6 נישואים וגירושין קודמים
קארי
Kari
דניאל
Daniel
יונתן
Yonatan
2000
סמי
Samy
1996
אנסטסיה
Anastasia
1992
יאן
Yan
1987
צילה
Tsila
1986

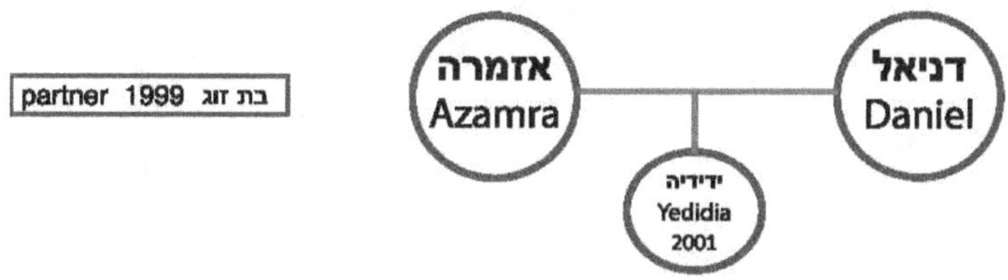
partner 1999 בת זוג
אזמרה
Azamra
דניאל
Daniel
ידידיה
Yedidia
2001

partner 2000 בת זוג
אדרת
Aderet
דניאל
Daniel

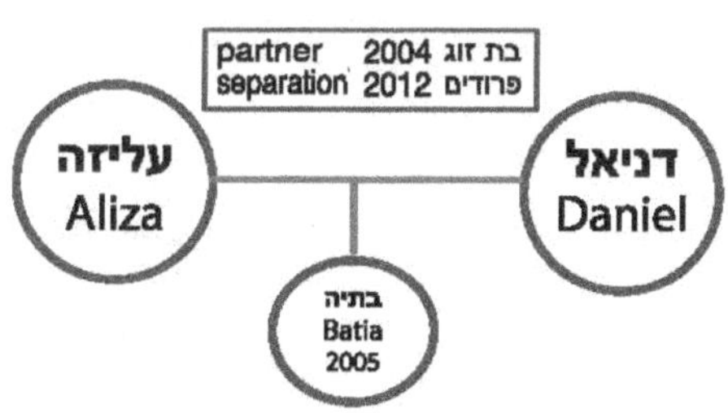
partner 2004 בת זוג
separation 2012 פרודים
עליזה
Aliza
דניאל
Daniel
בתיה
Batia
2005

partner 2009 בת זוג
שירן
Shiran
דניאל
Daniel

בשיחת הוועידה הטלפונית שלנו הבוקר עם דניאל מהכלא, הוא סיפר לנו שהעובדת הסוציאלית של "שירות בתי הסוהר" שוב איימה שלא תאפשר לו להתקשר אלינו יותר.

התיישבנו ארבעתנו בגן השעשועים הציבורי, בדרכנו לפגישה עם במאית הסרט הדוקומנטרי עלינו. נדחקנו על ספסל אחד, אילנה, אֲזַמְּרָה, שירן ואני אדרת. הוא אתנו על הקו. מתגעגעות, מודאגות ולא יודעות מה לעשות, בחשש מתמיד מניתוק קו הקשר היחיד שנותר.

כבר ארבע שנים שאנחנו ככה.

במשך כל השנים האלה לא נותנים לנו לראות אותו. לא ביקורים. לא התייחדויות.

גן השעשועים היה שומם. גם אצלנו כבר מזמן לא נשמע צחוק של ילדים. הם לקחו לנו גם אותם.

על ידי צו איסור פרסום, סתמו לנו את הפה, סתמו לנו את האפשרות להביע את עצמנו ולמחות, אבל את השקרים נגדנו בתקשורת הם שפכו.

במשך חודשים ארוכים, סגרה המשטרה בכפייה כל אחת מאתנו בנפרד, במקלט אחר ברחבי הארץ המיועד לנשים מוכות. אסרו עלינו לצאת משם או להחזיק טלפון או ליצור קשר בינינו. שני בלשים מזוינים היו מגיעים לקחת כל אחת מאתנו ברכב משטרה לחקירות מתישות ואלימות.

שללו מאתנו את החופש לחיות והרסו את כל מה שבנינו במשך 15 שנה.

עד המעצר ההזוי הזה, היו לנו חיים – הכי טובים שיש, לא הבנו איך אפשר לחיות אחרת, זכינו לחיות חיים מעניינים, תוססים, מלאי הרפתקאות וריגושים. משפחה דתית ברסלבית המקושרת לרבי ישראל בער אודסר בעל הפתק הקדוש המכונה 'הסבא', רבי נ נח נחמ נחמן מאומן בירושלים. משפחה מיוחדת ולא שגרתית, שש חברות שחיו באהבה אחת עם אותו איש. אולי זה נראה מוזר, אבל יש עוד כמה דברים מוזרים בעולם, ואולי לכמה אנשים זה נשמע תמוה, אבל הסתדרנו לא רע בכלל והבעיות בינינו היו רגילות כמו בכל בית. זו הסיבה שהיינו כל כך המומות מהמעצר, לא יכולנו לדמיין שיהיה מי שירצה להזיק לנו בצורה שכזו. למי הפרענו? על איזה חוק עברנו? למה בכלל היה אכפת למישהו איך בחרנו לחיות? לא היה מובן לנו מי עומד מאחורי כל זה ולמה. עם הזמן האמת נחשפה ...

העלילה השטנית נגדנו נרקחה על ידי "המרכז הישראלי לנפגעי כתות" שכדי להצדיק את קיומו, וכדי להלבין את כספי התרומות שגייס, תייג אותנו בתקשורת כ"כת פוגענית".

בתחקיר שנערך במרץ 2011 על ידי עיתון "ידיעות אחרונות" התגלה, כי אותו "מרכז" מפוקפק הוא בעצם עמותה מתחזה הפועלת נגד זרמים שלא מקובלים בעיניה, ומתנפלת על כל התאגדות אנשים שלא לרוחה. העמותה מורכבת משתי נשים וד"ר אחד: רחל ליכטנשטיין, שרונה בן משה וד"ר דוד גרין.

*האיחוד האירופי לחופש דת European interreligious forum for religious freedom) EIFRF באתר: (www.eifrf-articles.org פרסם ש'המרכז הישראלי לנפגעי כתות' הוא בעצם שלוחה של 'פקריס' (FECRIS) בישראל. 'פקריס' הוא ארגון 'נגד כתות' שהקים ביותר מ-30 מדינות עמותות קטנות המורכבות משניים עד שלושה אנשים בלבד.*

*סגן הנשיא של FECRIS אלכסנדר דבורקין, אזרח רוסיה, פעיל בכנסיה האורתודוכסית הרוסית, מסביר את עקרונות הארגון נגד כתות: "האמונה הנוצרית האורתודוכסית היא האמונה המקורית ... כת היא זיוף, דבר מומצא, משהו זול". דבורקין תקף גם את האמונה המוסלמית בכמה הזדמנויות והכריז: "או שמוחמד סבל ממחלה קשה ומה שראה היה הזיה או שהשתלט עליו שד".*

*ברחבי העולם מומחים בתחום זכויות האדם מותחים ביקורת חריפה נגד 'פקריס' על ההטפה לשנאה ועל ליבוי אי סובלנות בחברה נגד דתות מיעוט. נציג האומות המאוחדות בנושא חופש הדת אמר: "נראה שקיימת קונוטציה שלילית ומזלזלת למונח "כת". גישה מסוג זה מעידה על נטייה להכללות, לאפליה ולדחייה, נטייה אשר מזיקה לחופש הדת ופוגעת בהגנה הבסיסית של זכויות אדם".*

להבדיל מתיקים אחרים שבהם למשטרה יש קצה חוט לבצע מעצרים ולבנות כתבי אישום, במקרה שלנו, לא היה להם כלום. אפילו על "פוליגמיה" לא יכלו לעצור אותנו, כי לא היינו נשואים רשמית.

כתבות הדיבה בעיתונות ובטלוויזיה הגיעו מכיוון המשפחה של עליזה, האישה החמישית. בשנים הראשונות היינו בקשרים מצוינים אתם, הם היו באים לבקר אצלנו הרבה כי גרו קרוב. קלקול היחסים שלהם עם עליזה ואתנו התחיל כשעליזה החליטה להפסיק לעזור להם כלכלית כי הרגישה שזה כבר מוגזם שהעברנו להם סכום של לא פחות משמונים אלף ₪. הם הפכו לאלימים כשהיא לא הסכימה להיכנע ללחצים שלהם, וארבו מחוץ לביתנו עם מקלות ואבנים, קיללו וניפצו את החלונות בבית עד שכמעט נפגעו

ילדים וזה יכול היה להיגמר באסון. האח הגדול שלה, עבריין ידוע למשטרה, איים לפגוע בדניאל ובילדים ולשרוף לנו את הבית. עליזה לא ויתרה להם ואמרה שהם הרחיקו לכת. היא הלכה למשטרה, הגישה תלונה נגדם ודרשה צו הרחקה. הם התנצלו על התנהגותם אך במקביל פנו למרכז הישראלי לנפגעי כתות, לעיתונאים ולמשטרה. כך משנת 2008 החלו מעקבים עלינו, תצפיות, האזנות סתר, נשלחו אלינו תחקירנים ומתחזים רבים, וכולם העלו חרס בידם.

כעבור שלוש שנים ...

אפילו שיחת הטלפון של סמי בן ה-14 הבן החורג של דניאל למוקד המשטרה שבה הוא מזעיק את המשטרה לבוא כי "אבא לא בבית וחבר של אחיו הגדולים מרביץ לו", לא סיפקה עילה מספקת למעצר. כשהמשטרה התקשרה שוב לבית והבינה שהכול בסדר, היא לא טרחה אפילו להגיע. חודש וחצי לאחר מכן, כשאחד הבנים ראה קופסת עץ מוזרה מאחורי ארון ותלש אותה, הוא לא יכול היה לדעת שזוהי הסוואה ל"האזנות הסתר" של המשטרה. כשפתח אותה לנסות להבין מה זה, פרצו לבית חמישה סמויים שצעקו שכולם עצורים. החוקרת הראשית לילך רנן הודתה בפני בית המשפט המחוזי שהמעצר לא היה מתוכנן, אך נאלצו לעצור אותנו כיוון שנחשפו האזנות הסתר שהיו אמורות לתת להם כיוון לחקירה. (להזכירכם, אחרי שלוש שנים של מעקב צמוד ואינטנסיבי עלינו, מתברר שעדיין אין להם אפילו כיוון לחקירה!).

משטרת ירושלים הבינה שהפתרון היחיד שלה לקבל הארכת מעצר מבית המשפט הוא לסמן אותנו כ"כת סדיסטית", שבה כל בני המשפחה שטופי מוח, שפחות ועבדים, ואבי המשפחה הוא לא אחר מאשר "הפושע הגדול ביותר במדינה", "השטן מירושלים", "ראש הכת הסדיסטית" כפי שהכריזו עליו בתקשורת. לשם כך, מינתה המשטרה את המרכז הישראלי לנפגעי כתות כ"מומחה מלווה" לחקירה נגדנו. המרכז לכתות סיפק למשטרה דגשים לחקירה, ושלח לה רשימת שאלות לנחקרים. המשטרה שלחה אליהם נחקרים לקבלת שוחד ו"טיפולים" (כלומר, לשכנע את האנשים שהם אכן נפגעי כתות). כמובן שהמשטרה לא טרחה אפילו לבדוק את מהימנות המרכז או את מהימנות הנפשות הפועלות בו, לא חקרה את זהות ואיכות "המומחים", את עברם, את עניינם האישי ואת מיליוני התרומות שהם משלשלים לכיסם תחת מצג שווא ובמרמה.

שרונה בן משה, המציגה עצמה כ"יועצת משפטית במרכז הישראלי לנפגעי כתות", מעורבת בפרשת הסחיטה המפורסמת של הרב ניר בן ארצי והייתה בת זוגו של אחד מהשותפים לפשע, שמעון קטורזה. במשך שלוש שנים, הם כלאו את הרב בן ארצי בדירות שונות בטבריה בתנאים קשים, השתלטו על נכסים שבבעלותו ומסרו בשמו מסרים פיקטיביים לתורמים לעמותה שהקים. כך גרמו לקבלת כספים במרמה. הם האכילו אותו בלחם ובמרגרינה, ואחרי שדחפו לו ליטר שלם של וודקה החתימו אותו על מסמך שבו הוא מודה בקיום יחסי מין עם כבשים ועם חיות אחרות. כדי להסית את תשומת הלב הציבורית ולטשטש את הקשר שלה למעשה החטיפה ולסחיטת הכספים, הפכה שרונה בן משה להיות ה"דוברת" של המרכז הישראלי לנפגעי כתות והפיצה בתקשורת הודעות כוזבות נגד "כתות", וניר בן ארצי היה מראשוני המותקפים. בסופו של דבר, לאחר שנערך משפט נגדם, התגלתה התרמית, נגזר עליהם מאסר, עבודות שרות וקנס כספי.

מעניין לשים לב שבתיק שלנו, כשהמשטרה הצליחה להפוך את עליזה לעדת תביעה לאחר מאמצים כבירים משך חמישה חודשים ארוכים ובאמצעות "טיפול" במרכז הישראלי לנפגעי כתות, עליזה לפתע החלה להמציא סיפורים הזויים, ולאט לאט שדרגה אותם, עד שלאחר שנה החלה לספר שהכריחו אותה ב"כת" לקיים יחסי מין עם סוסים, נחשים, עכבישים, עכברים וג׳וקים ...

רחל ליכטנשטיין, מנהלת המרכז לכתות, חרדית קנאית-קיצונית הרגישה שזכתה בפיס כשהשיגה עבור המשטרה את העדה הראשית והראשונה, תמנע.

תמנע, בחורה בת 19 מבית דתי. לדבריה אמה סבלה מסכיזופרניה ואושפזה בבתי חולים לבריאות הנפש, אביה ממוצא תימני, היה ראש ישיבה, והיה מעורב בפרשה מתוקשרת שבה האשימו אותו שהיה נשוי בו-זמנית לכמה נשים; בשלב כלשהו עזב את הבית והתגרש מאמה. היא סיפרה גם שדוד שלה ניצל אותה מינית כשהייתה ילדה. היא נזרקה לרחובות, גדלה בפנימיות, וחלמה להיות דוגמנית. בגיל צעיר התנסתה בסמים שונים, וסחרה בהם. יום אחד קארי, האישה השנייה של דניאל, שעליה תשמעו בהמשך, פגשה לראשונה בתמנע במרכז העיר בירושלים, ותמנע ביקשה להתלוות אליה להדלקת נרות חנוכה. תמנע התלהבה מהביקור עם קארי, ומאז שמרה עמה על קשר טלפוני והגיעה מדי פעם לסעודות. לא יכולנו לדמיין שהיא תפתח מחלה של "אהבה כפייתית" כלפי דניאל. תמנע בכל תוקף רצתה להתחתן אתו כאישה שביעית, רעיון שהבהיל אותו מאוד, ולכן ביקש מקארי לא להביא אותה יותר אלינו לבית. תמנע בכל זאת שוב הגיעה אלינו, ובלי בושה תפסה את דניאל לשיחה שבה אמרה לו שרק אתו היא תהיה מאושרת, ודרשה שיתחתן אתה מיד. דניאל לא רצה לפגוע בה, ודחה את חיזוריה באמרו שאין בכוונתו להתחתן עם עוד נשים. תמנע יצאה מביתנו בזעם, וסיננה בעודה מנשקת בצורה אובססיבית את המזוזה שוב ושוב: "אתה עוד תצטער על זה..."

בכל זאת המשיכה לבוא להופעות שלנו והתראיינה בהתלהבות לתוכנית הטלוויזיה "360" שערוץ 2 ערכו, הפיקו ושידרו עלינו. היא הרעיפה שבחים על משפחתנו ועל אורח חיינו ואמרה: "...הייתי בהרבה קבוצות, ופה הרגשתי שזה מקום של אנשי אמת ושאני לא רוצה ללכת...".

כעבור ארבעה חודשים, כשצפתה באותה תכנית ושמעה שהמגיש אומר: "נשים נוספות בדרך לאמבש...". התפוצצה מקנאתה החולנית, נכנסה לאתר המרכז הישראלי לנפגעי כתות שהיו אלה שיזמו את התכנית והשתתפו בה, וכתבה לרחל ליכטנשטיין מנהלת המרכז שהיא צריכה עזרה. ליכטנשטיין הזמינה את תמנע לפגישה. תמנע הייתה ללא קורת גג ועם תיק פלילי פתוח על גנבה. ליכטנשטיין עטה על ההזדמנות שנפלה לידיה, ניצלה את חולשתה של תמנע, והבטיחה לה תמיכה נפשית וכלכלית. ארגנה לה פגישה עם חוקרי המשטרה מירושלים, והם לקחו אותה למלון על חוף הים בתל אביב. חוקרי המשטרה לא תיעדו את המפגש, והשתמשו ביצר הנקמה הבוער בתמנע לתפירת סיפורי בדים, כדי שהמרכז לכתות יעבד את החומר באופן שיתאים ל"פרופיל כת": 1. ניצול מיני; 2. ניצול כלכלי; 3. אינוס קטינים; 4. מין עם חיות; 5. ביזוי דרך אכילת צואה, ועוד. חוקרי המשטרה עברו על כל החוקים האפשריים, ואף הבטיחו לתמנע שיתנו לה דירה, וגם העבירו לידיה כספי שוחד. שנה לאחר מכן תמנע העידה בבית המשפט כעדת תביעה ראשית, וכך אמרה: "הייתי בשוק שרחל ליכטנשטיין העבירה את זה למשטרה, לא תיארתי לעצמי שזה יגיע למשטרה, זה רק מילים שאמרתי ולא רציתי שיהיה לזה השלכות אבל היא אמרה לי שאין לי ברירה". לתמנע היה חשוב להדגיש לבית המשפט את האהבה הטוטאלית שלה לדניאל, וכך אמרה: "אהבתי את דניאל כמו שלא אהבתי ולא אוהב יותר אף גבר בחיים". כשדניאל מולה, אזוק ידיים ורגליים, במדי בית סוהר ושומרים סביבו, בטיפשותה הסגירה את המניע שלה כשאמרה לשופטים שהיא עדיין פגועה ששמעה שדניאל אמר עליה פעם שהשיניים שלה לא יפות.

האידיאולוגיה של "פקריס" קובעת ש"כת" הוא מקום מסוכן לילדים, ושחברי כת אינם כשירים משפטית, ויש לקחת מהם את ילדיהם. לכן ד"ר גרין הדריך את חוקרי משטרת ירושלים שעליהם להוכיח שילדים נפגעו מינית, ולשם כך עליהם לפעול בכל דרך אפשרית, תהיה קשה ככל שתהיה. מחוסר ראיות שלפו כמו שפן ממגבעת את אותה שיחת הטלפון של סמי למוקד המשטרה, כפי שהזכרנו לעיל וכעת נפרט:

סמי היה נער שובב שהיה נוהג להתגנב למגורי הבנות ולהציץ להן במקלחת. פעם אחת הוא נגע לבתיה בת השש (הבת של דניאל ועליזה) באזור התחתון מעל הבגדים. עליזה נרעשה ועשתה דרמה שסמי אנס את בתיה. כשדניאל לא היה בבית, חבר של אחיו הגדולים של סמי, בריון אמריקאי בן 24 הגיע ושמע את ההיסטריה של עליזה, החל לאיים על סמי שהוא יכניס לו מקל בתחת, "ללמד אותו לקח". סמי שלא רצה לצאת מפסידן, התקשר למשטרה. כעבור שלוש שעות התקשרו מהמשטרה לבדוק מה המצב, וכשהבינו שהכול בסדר, התעלמו מהקריאה. חודש וחצי לאחר מכן, בהדרכת המרכז לכתות ובהתאם לתיאוריה שלהם ש"ראש כת" הוא האחראי הבלעדי על כל מה שקורה, גם אם לא היה שם ולא ידע מזה – נדהמנו לגלות שעל בסיס הסיפור הזה, בנו כתב אישום שתואם לאחד ממאפייני הפרופיל של ראש כת: התעללות בילדים. דניאל הורשע ב"מעשה סדום", על אירוע שספק אם קרה, שכל הראיות הוכיחו שדניאל לא היה שם, ויתרה מכך, סמי העיד שאם אבא היה בבית, הוא היה מגן עליו, ולא היה נותן שדבר כזה יקרה. כששלחנו את הקלטת השיחה של סמי עם המשטרה לבדיקה אצל מומחה סאונד החוקר קבילות ראיות, נדהמנו לגלות שהמשטרה עשתה מעשה פלילי: היא ערכה את ההקלטה, וחתכה מהשיחה את המילים: "אבא לא בבית". בחדרי החקירות איימו על סמי שהוא חשוד באונס אחותו בת השש, ושאם לא ישתף אתם פעולה, הוא ישב 14 שנה בכלא. כך הצליחו לשתול בפיו גרסאות, פרט אחר פרט, ולבנות על סמך סיפור זה עלילה שלמה של עשרים אישומים נגד דניאל.

במשטרה עדיין היו זקוקים לעדים נוספים מתוך הבית כדי לייצר "אמינות". אנסטסיה, בת ה-18 וחצי, אחותו של סמי, בת חורגת של דניאל, הייתה מאוכזבת כשאף אחד מהבנים של דניאל לא רצה להתחתן אתה כי היא הייתה ידועה כשקרנית וכמי ש"מחליפה חברים כמו גרביים", לכן מהר מאוד החליטה שיותר משתלם לה לקבל שוחד מהמשטרה ולעזור להם להשפיע על נחקרים להעיד נגד דניאל. היא סיפרה למשטרה שהייתה שמועה בבית מהשבוע האחרון לפני המעצר שעקיבא בן ה-13, הבן של דניאל ואילנה שיחק עם שני אחיו הקטנים במשחקים לא צנועים. המשטרה קפצה על הסיפור הזה כמוצאת שלל רב ואיימה גם על עקיבא, בדומה לסמי, שאם לא ידבר נגד אביו, ישב בכלא על אונס שני אחיו הקטנים. עקיבא, לאחר לחצים רבים, הפך להיות עד תביעה נגד אביו, ונחשב העד האמין מכולם בעיני השופטים. מספר חודשים לאחר מכן הוא שלח מכתב מפורט לבית המשפט העליון, כפי שתקראו בהמשך, שבו הוא חוזר בו מעדותו נגד אביו, ומפרט איך הפרקליטים שגיא אופיר וליזו וולפוס יחד עם חוקר הילדים מיכה הרן, איימו עליו שאם לא יעיד נגד אביו, ישב בכלא במקומו, ולימדו אותו מה להגיד בעדות, הוא גם מסביר באותו מכתב שבגללם הוא ניסה להתאבד.

משרד הרווחה הכריז ברֵיש גלי שבתיק "אמבש" התקיים שיתוף פעולה מוצלח בין המשטרה, למרכז הישראלי לנפגעי כתות, לפרקליטות ולעובדים הסוציאליים. עבור משרד הרווחה הייתה זו הזדמנות פז לחטוף ילדים מהוריהם, להעבירם לפנימיות ולקבל תקציבי עתק מהמדינה על כל ילד שברשותם.

חוקרי המשטרה זיהו את נקודות התורפה, את החולשות ואת הרגישויות של כל אחד מהנחקרים, ועינו אותנו בהתאם. אצל עליזה היה להם יתרון: אימא שלה עבדה בשבילם והפעילה עליה את כל הלחצים האפשריים על מנת לשדל אותה להתגרש מדניאל שאותו כל כך אהבה; וכן, קרובת משפחה של עליזה היא חוקרת משטרה במרחב ירושלים, וגם היא פעלה עם אמה של עליזה על מנת לשכנע אותה להיכנע לחוקרים. למעשה, עליזה הייתה כל כך חזקה במלחמה שלה להוכיח שדניאל חף מפשע, עד כדי כך שנאלצו להפעיל נגדה את כל ימ"ר ירושלים (יחידה מרכזית במשטרת ירושלים, האחראית על חקירות ומודיעין בפשעים חמורים) בשיטות שונות: איומים, צעקות, השפלות, חנופה ושוחד. הפחידו אותה שלא תראה יותר את בתיה, הבת שלה ושל דניאל, והסבירו לה מה היא צריכה להגיד כדי לעזור לחקירה וכדי להציל את

עצמה, אחרת תשב שנים רבות בכלא, כי אנסטסיה, בתה של קארי, תהיה מוכנה להעיד נגדה שאנסה אותה ב״הוראת״ דניאל. גם נתנו לה לטעום למספר ימים צינוק בכלא מהו.

תקופה ארוכה החזיקה עליזה מעמד, צעקה על החוקרים, העלתה סרטונים ליו-טיוב שבהם סיפרה על השחיתות של המשטרה ועל השקרים שאילצו אותה להגיד. אך לאחר חמישה חודשים נחלשה כי החוקרים הבטיחו לה שהם ידאגו לזה שדניאל לא יצא לעולם מבית הסוהר, ושחבל שתפסיד גם את הבת שלה וגם את החיים שלה. אחיה הגדולים, בשיתוף אמה ידעו שהיא לא יכולה לחיות בלי גבר, ופיתו אותה באמצעות חבר ילדות שלה שצעיר ממנה בכמה שנים וגר בשנים האחרונות בארצות הברית. הם שכנעו אותו לחזור לארץ לשם המשימה. הוא התחיל לחזר אחריה והכניס אותה להיריון. מכאן הדרך להפוך לעדת תביעה הייתה קצרה. בשלב זה אפשר להגיד שהניצחון כבר היה בידיים של המשטרה.

בעדותה בבית המשפט, כששאל אותה הסנגור אם יש לה קשר לגנבת פנקס הצ׳קים של דניאל ולזיוף חתימתו, היא היתממה כלא מבינה על מה מדובר. כשהסנגור הציג על גבי מסך סרטון ממצלמה נסתרת של חוקרים פרטיים שמוכיח שעם אותו חבר ילדות ואחיה הגדול, זייפה חתימות בעשרות שקים בסכום שהגיע לרבע מיליון ₪! עליזה לא ידעה מה להגיד. אף על פי כן השופטים העדיפו להתעלם מהעובדה שמולם עדה פסולה. כנראה ככה זה עובד כשמחליטים להרשיע מישהו בכל תוקף, גם אם אין שום ראיות נגדו, אפילו השבועה להגיד אמת בבית משפט לא חשובה...

הקריסה של עליזה כעדת הגנה מהווה תפנית חדה בכל מהלך העניינים כיוון שהיא האישה היחידה מבינינו שהפכה להיות עדת תביעה וקיבלה הטבות של עדת מדינה.

אך עם כל בניין הקלפים הזה, הבנוי מעדי שקר (שכל אחד מהם חזר בו מעדותו בשלב מסוים והודיע ששיקר) אין ראיות להוכחת ההאשמות נגד דניאל אלא להפך, ראיות חשובות המוכיחות את חפותו, כמו הקלטות של חקירות חשובות ומכות שקיבלנו בחדרי החקירות, הושמדו או הועלמו או לא תועדו כלל.

לרוע מזלי, השוטרים מצאו מחברות שלי מלפני 12 שנה שבהם הייתי משרבטת חלומות, פנטזיות, דמיונות ותפילות. הם נתנו לדברים הכתובים בהם פרשנות משלהם, הפוכה מהאמת, ועל אף שהשופטים קבעו בהכרעת הדין שמשקל היומן ייקבע לפי ההסבר שייתן הכותב, התעלמו לגמרי מעדותי, וכך בדרכים מניפולטיביות השתמשו גם בי.

חצי שנה אחרי המעצר של דניאל, כשהשוטרים ראו שלמרות כל השיחות ה״טיפוליות״ במקלטים לנשים מוכות, ולמרות כל המכות, הלחצים, האיומים והקללות בחדרי החקירות, אילנה, קארי, אזמרה, שירן ואני, לא נכנענו לשקר שלהם. הם החליטו לסגור את אילנה, אזמרה, שירן ואותי בכלא נווה תרצה. קארי היחידה מבינינו הנשים, שעל אף שהייתה עדת הגנה, לא ישבה בכלא אפילו יום אחד, והסיבה לכך הייתה שאנסטסיה בתה איימה על ראש צוות החקירה אשר לזמי, שאם יכניס את אמה לכלא, היא לא תעיד נגד דניאל.

ישבנו בכלא על אישום כבד ביותר, שעליו אפילו לא חקרו אותנו: אינוס קטין. הרשעה שאפשר לקבל עליה מאסר של לפחות 14 שנה. הפרקליטים ניסו לפתות אותנו ואמרו: ״אם תחתמו שאתן קרבנות של דניאל, תשוחררו מידית מהכלא!״ ישבנו שנה במאסר כי לא היינו מוכנות להיכנע לשקר, והתעקשנו לחכות למשפט שבו יובאו הוכחות נגדנו. מאחר שלא מצאו, זימנו את תמנע, סמי ועליזה העדים נגד דניאל, שישמשו כעדים נגדנו. הם סתרו זה את זה ואת דברי עצמם, ולא ידעו לענות על שאלות בסיסיות. זה היה כל כך בולט שהעדים משקרים, כך ששוחררנו כבר באותו היום. השופטים גערו בפרקליט שגיא אופיר, שהיה, ולא במקרה, אותו הפרקליט התובע במשפט נגד דניאל, שכדאי לו להסדיר את העניין הזה מיד, ושהנשים האלו לא היו צריכות לשבת רגע אחד בבית הסוהר. בית המשפט ביטל את כל כתב האישום נגדנו, והשאיר רק סעיף שאומר שהמפגשים שקיימנו בינינו ועם עליזה היו נגד ההוראה החוקית, שאסרה עלינו להתראות. כיום אנו מבינות שגם העסקה הזו הייתה תרגיל של הפרקליט, כיוון שהמטרה שלו הייתה להרשיע את דניאל באותו אישום.

במשפט נגד דניאל, שהתנהל במקביל, עם הרכב אחר של שופטים, באותו בית משפט מחוזי בירושלים, ועם אותו פרקליט, שגיא אופיר, עם אותם עדים, ועל אותו אישום, שכבר הוכח במשפט שלנו כעלילה ונמחק כליל, נגד כל חוקי המשפט הפלילי – הרשיעו השופטים יעקב צבן, רפאל כרמל ורבקה פרידמן פלדמן את דניאל.

באוקטובר 2013, בהכרעת הדין נגד דניאל כתבו השופטים: ״**חברה מתוקנת** לא יכולה לסבול אורח חיים כפי שיצר לעצמו הנאשם, ריבוי נשים״.

כיוון שאנו יותר מאישה אחת, קבעו שאנחנו שפחות. והיות שלשפחות אין רצון חופשי משלהן, לכן כל יחסי המין בינינו נחשבים ליחסי מין ללא הסכמה, וכך הם הצליחו להרשיע את דניאל באונס סדרתי.

כדי להוכיח את התיאוריה על ״החזקה בתנאי עבדות״ שהמציא ד״ר גרין, נאלצנו לספוג בחקירות האלימות של המשטרה שאלות פולשניות ומעליבות על יחסי המין שלנו, כי רצו בכוח להוכיח ניצול וביזוי מיני. האסטרטגיה שעליה החליטו הייתה שקופה: לא ייתכן שאישה תחלוק את הגבר שלה עם עוד חמש נשים, אלא אם כן הוא מכשף אותה ומפעיל עליה תהליכים היפנוטיים על המוח, והיות שלא היה להם שום

דבר אמתי ומוחשי, המציאו הרשעה וקראו לה "עבדות מודרנית", תוצאה של העבודה המשותפת בין המרכז לכתות, המשטרה, הרווחה והפרקליטות. דניאל הוא היחיד בארץ, וכנראה בעולם, שהצליחו להרשיע אותו באשמה שהוא בעל כוחות על-טבעיים וכוח כריזמטי שמצליח לשעבד מוחות של אחרים. לא מדובר בשעבוד פיזי אלא ב"שבי מנטלי". לא יאומן שבמאה ה-21 מאשימים אדם בכוחות מיסטיים, כמו בתקופת האינקוויזיציה.

אפילו תיק גואל רצון, האיש שהיו לו מעל ל-32 נשים ונעצר בינואר 2010 באשמת שעבוד, פוליגמיה ואונס בנותיו, שהיה התיק היחיד במדינת ישראל עד התיק שלנו, שבו רצו להרשיע גבר בשעבוד בני משפחתו, בסופו של דבר הוא לא הורשע בגין עבדות. המקרה שלו היה שונה בתכלית משלנו: הן האמינו בו, הוא היה מרפא, הילר, הן סגדו לו והעריצו אותו וקראו לכל ילדיהן על שמו, כל אחת מהנשים קעקעה את דמותו על גבי אזורים נרחבים מגופה, היה להם ספר חוקים הקובע איך צריך להתנהג אתו ומה כללי העונשים אם לא מקיימים את רצונו, הן חיו כולן יחד אתו באותו הבית. עם מעצרו רובן עזבו אותו והעידו נגדו, והוא גם הודה בחלק מהמיוחס לו. עם כל זה, סעיף ה"עבדות" נגדו קרס לחלוטין. כפי שניתן לראות בהכרעת הדין בעניינו, קבעו שופטי בית המשפט המחוזי בתל אביב כי התיאוריה של "שבי מנטלי" שיצרו מומחי המרכז לכתות איננה אמינה, איננה מדעית ואיננה מקובלת בעולם או בקהילות המקצועיות, וקבעו: "אין מקום לקבל את התיאוריה בדבר קיומה של שליטה מנטלית באדם אחר...". גם בבית המשפט העליון דחו את העתירה של המרכז הישראלי לנפגעי כתות, שניסו בכל תוקף להחזיר את סעיף העבדות בתיק של גואל רצון.

לעומת זאת, הרשיעו שופטי בית המשפט המחוזי בירושלים את דניאל בסעיף עבדות ושבי מנטלי, כיוון שנתקלו בבעיה: אם לא ירשיעו אותו בסעיף הראשון 'עבדות', יתבטל כל כתב האישום, שהרי כולו בנוי על סעיף זה. צריך להבין שברגע שמכריזים על כל בני המשפחה כעל עבדים ושפחות שטופי מוח ללא דעה עצמאית, כולם נחשבים קרבנות, ואוטומטית ניתן להגדיר את ראש המשפחה כ"ראש כת", וכך להרשיע אותו על כל מה שרק רוצים.

השאלה המתבקשת היא: איך יכולה המדינה להחזיק את החבל משני הקצוות, בקצה אחד הכריזו עלינו כקרבנות, ובקצה שני סגרו אותנו בבית הסוהר... האם כך מטפלים ב"קרבנות" במדינת ישראל? ואם קבעו שאנחנו קרבנות, למה לא מעניקים לנו סיוע כלכלי מטעם המדינה כפי שמגיע לקרבנות?

בדרך כלל כשאישה מתלוננת על גבר, הגרסה הראשונה שהיא מוסרת במשטרה היא הספונטנית, ולכן האמינה ביותר. הגרסה הראשונה היא הקובעת, ואם האישה חוזרת בה, ואומרת ששיקרה, לא מקבלים את עדותה השנייה. במקרה שלנו, אף אישה לא התלוננה, ויתרה מכך, השופטים היו חייבים להודות בהכרעת הדין: "הוכח כי כל בני המשפחה התייצבו לחקירות הראשונות כאיש אחד בגרסה אחידה ומכחישה את ההאשמות נגד דניאל".

כשנציגי הפרקליטות שלפו את הקלף "עבדות מנטלית", הצליחו להטעות את השופטים. שיטת "העד הקרבן" או "קרבן מנטלי" אפשרה לפרקליטות ולשופטים שהחליטו בכל מקרה להרשיע, לייצר הרשעות, גם אם בעדויות של התביעה קיימות אין-ספור סתירות וגרסאות משתנות, תמיד אפשר להגיד שאם העד הוא עד הגנה אז הוא "קרבן שטוף מוח", או לחלופין אם הופכים אותו לעד תביעה אז הוא "קרבן שהיה שטוף מוח והתפכח", או לחלופין אם הצליחו להפוך עד הגנה לעד תביעה ושוב הוא חוזר בו ואומר ששיקר מתוך לחץ אומרים שהוא "קרבן בתהליך שיקומי"... בכל מקרה הוא תמיד בגדר "קרבן", ואמינותו נקבעת לפי הכוונות הפרקליטות. אין שום עו"ד מצד ההגנה שיכול להתמודד מול שיטה זו. כך למשל, כשעליזה, במשך חמישה חודשים, הסבירה לחוקרים שהיא זו שמובילה את הדברים כרצונה במערכת היחסים שלה עם דניאל, טענו נגדה שהיא עדיין תחת "השפעה מנטלית", ש"סיבבו לה את המוח" והיא מבחינתם ללא ספק "שטופת מוח". עוד איימו עליה בחדרי החקירות שעד שהיא לא "תתפכח", ותבין את מה שהם מסבירים לה, לא תראה את ילדתה, ולא תקבל אותה חזרה. בהמשך, תחת לחץ החוקרים ומניפולציה רגשית שהפעילו עליה באמצעות אמה וילדתה, דילגה בין גרסאות ולא זכרה פרטים עיקריים באף אחת מהן... בכל זאת קבעו השופטים שלא משנה שהגרסאות שלה סותרות זו את זו, כיוון שהיא ב"שלב שיקומי", יש להתחשב בה ולקבל את עדותה כמות שהיא. לעומת זאת, כשנמצאו יומנים שלי מלפני 12 שנה ושאלו אותי על פרשנות הדברים, שללו את דבריי באחת, וקבעו ההפך מהמשמעות שאליה התכוונתי, כמו למשל כשכתבתי תפילה להשם "הצילו הצילו" שהעתקתי מספרי רבי נחמן מברסלב, השתמשו בזה כמין הוכחה שאני במצוקה בחיים עם דניאל. לא אפשרו לי להסביר את עצמי כי עוד קודם קבעו שאני "שטופת מוח", על אף שמספר פעמים במהלך המשפט אמרו השופטים והפרקליט שאני אישה אינטליגנטית ורהוטה...; ...נבונה כל כך, התלמידה המצטיינת ביותר, עם יכולות מרובות ונדירות, שיכולה להיות בקלות רבה הרבנית הראשית.

בקלות בלתי נסבלת וללא שום חוות דעת מקצועית או בדיקה פסיכולוגית, החליטו השופטים שעל אף שכולנו עצמאיות, נבונות וחכמות, איננו אלא "דבוקה אחת של שטופות מוח". השופטים בחרו להרשיע רק על סמך חמשת עדי התביעה שחזרו בהם מעדותם, והתעלמו כליל מכל 16 עדי ההגנה. השופטים אף כתבו על עדי ההגנה באופן גורף כי: "...קורצו מאותו חומר של בני המשפחה ופעמים רבות הם היו שותפים בעצמם בענישה שהנהיג".

כשכתבו "קורצו מאותו חומר", האם התכוונו שכל מי שביקר בביתנו גם הוא קרבן? או אולי שותף לפשע? אם כן, מדוע לא זימנו אותם לחקירה, ולא הוציאו נגדם כתב אישום?

לדוגמה: כשדבורה, עדת ההגנה העידה בבית המשפט שגרה אצלנו עם ארבעת ילדיה, משך חצי שנה, שאהבה את המשפחה ושדניאל הוא אבא טוב ואיש נחמד ובעל חסד שמעולם לא התנהג באלימות, כתבו השופטים בהכרעת הדין כי "כנראה היא שותפה ומעורבת בעצמה בענישה שהנהיג דניאל, וקורצה מאותו חומר של בני המשפחה, וכי התרשמותה החיובית מדניאל רק חיזקה את מעמדו בעיני בני הבית...".

גזרו על דניאל עונש חמור ביותר, מאסר של 26 שנים. פרקליטות המדינה מערערת ל-65 שנים, וזאת כשאין ברשותה שום ראיה, ובלי שום נפגע.

האם ב"**חברה מתוקנת**" אישה חייבת לחשוב בצורה "סיסטמתית", אחרת תתויג כזונה או לחלופין שפחה?

מי החליט שנשים הן ספקיות שירותי מין ולא אלו הדורשות שירותי מין?

מי הוא שמשתמש בשם "פמיניזם", וגורם לדיכוי נשי בכך שמונע מנשים לחיות כרצונן?

האם מותר בשם ה"פטרנליזם" לקבוע מה זו אהבה?

כיצד ייתכן שאותם שופטים שמגדירים אותנו "נבונות חכמות", קובעים שאנו "שפחות מין" רק כי בחרנו לאהוב איש אחד ביחד?

הייתכן שבית משפט מרשיע בעל באונס אשתו כאשר היא מעידה על יחסי מין מאהבה?

השופטים הירושלמים קבעו שבמדינת ישראל לא צריך הוכחות כדי להרשיע גבר באונס, וגם לא צריך שהאישה תגיד שהיא נאנסה. החליטו להמציא שאנחנו נשים שעברו אונס, ושסיפקנו שירותי מין בכפייה. כך תופרים תיקים במדינת ישראל: צרי המוח הקנאים, רודפי הבצע והכותרות הם שמשחקים בחיי אדם, שמפרידים בין אחים, שמבודדים כל אח ואחות במסגרת אחרת, שמשליכים ילדים לחיים הרסניים בפנימיות, שמסיתים אותם נגד הוריהם, שמלמדים אותם להתבייש במוצא שלהם ולשנוא לא רק את אבא אלא גם את אימא כל זמן שהיא ממשיכה לאהוב את אבא, שגורמים להם לתסכול, לייאוש ולאיבוד התקווה. מעניין שכשהמדינה מתנהגת כך זה לא נקרא שטיפת מוח ושבי מנטלי, אלא התפכחות... והעיקר שהשוטר קיבל מדליה, העובדת הסוציאלית קיבלה קידום, השופט מקבל תעודת הצטיינות מארגוני הפמיניסטיות, המרכז הישראלי לנפגעי כתות מקבל פרס יו"ר הכנסת, התקשורת מקבלת סקופים, ולכולם יש פרנסה.

הגשנו עתירה לבג"צ, שיאפשרו לנו לבוא לביקורים ולהתייחדות עם דניאל. ישבנו באולם בית המשפט. רציתי מאוד להגיב על כל השקרים של הפרקליטות, השופט השתיק אותי. הוא קיבל מסמך סודי מ"וג"ע", ועדת גילוי עריות, ועדה של עובדות סוציאליות, מסמך הטוען שאסור לנו להיפגש עם דניאל כי אנו לדבריהם "קרבנותיו". גם עוה"ד שלנו לא יכול היה לדעת במה מדובר, כי המסמך סודי. השופט ללא היסוס הוסיף שבקלות הוא יכול גם להשבית לנו את שיחות הטלפון עם דניאל...

ועכשיו, יושבות על הספסל, מתלבטות, שואלות אחת את השנייה מה לעשות, מה יהיה? איך העולם ידע את הסיפור האמתי שלנו, ארבע נשים מתרבויות שונות, בעלות ניסיון חיים עשיר, נחושות בדעתן, שהחליטו לחיות יחד עם איש אחד, איך יישארו לילדינו הסיפורים האמתיים על איך חיינו יחד?

רק אנחנו, שהקמנו את הבית יכולות לספר מה באמת היה. הזעקה עמוקה וכואבת, מקננת עמוק בתוך הלבבות שלנו, ולא תיתן מנוחה – עד שהאמת תצא לאור.

הקמנו אתר אינטרנט, העלנו מופע, ועומד לצאת עלינו סרט, אך יש לנו עוד כל כך הרבה מה להגיד. החלטנו שהדבר הנכון ביותר יהיה לכתוב ספר, שיהיה מורכב מארבעה חלקים, כל אחת מאתנו תכתוב את הסיפור האישי שלה, ויחד נוציא לאור את הסיפור האמתי שלנו, כשכל אחת מציגה את הזווית שלה. כך נולד הספר הזה. סיפור אותנטי של ארבע נשים ואיש אחד שלמרות הכול, לא ויתרו על האהבה.

חלק מהשמות בספר שונו.

**הסיפור האישי שלי – אדרת**

**שנת 2012**, 16 בדצמבר לפנות בוקר. אני, אדרת דורית אמבש, הובאתי על ידי פרקליטות ירושלים, עם אזיקים בידיים וברגליים, מכלא נווה תרצה, לבית המשפט המחוזי, להעיד מטעם התביעה נ ג ד בעלי דניאל אמבש ונגד הגרוש שלי אסא מיראש.

קדמה לכך מסכת חקירות קשה במשטרה במחלקת תשאול ימ״ר ירושלים בשנת 2011 שניסתה להפוך אותי לעדת תביעה.

עד היום, ארבע שנים אחרי, אני כועסת על עצמי ולא מצליחה להבין איך חוקרי המשטרה הצליחו בסופו של דבר להביא אותי למצב שאני מאשרת להם חלק מהשקרים שסיפרו לי? למה לא התעקשתי אתם עד הסוף על האמת? ממה פחדתי? מהצעקות האלימות והקללות המבזות שלהם? או מכך שאשב בכלא? אולי בגלל האיום שיפרסמו בתקשורת את השם שלי אם לא אהיה בצד שלהם? או בגלל שדאגתי שייפגע הכבוד של ההורים שלי? האם זה בגלל שעוד הייתי בטראומה מהאופן שבו עצרו את כל המשפחה לחקירה? למה ויתרתי על האמת הפנימית שלי, ועל בסיסי המוסר והצדק שאני מאמינה בהם ונכנעתי לשוחד ולחנופה? האם זה השימוש הציני שעשו ביומנים האישיים שלי שגרם לי להיכנס למבוכה ולנסות ״לכסות צואה בצואה״?

שאלות קשות מעיקות עליי ולא נותנות לי מנוחה. כשאני נזכרת בתחושה, באווירה ובריח שבחדרי החקירות עוברת בי צמרמורת בכל הגוף. אני חיה מחדש את הסבל ואת הפחד שעברתי בחדרי הימ״ר במשך שעות על גבי שעות, לפעמים גם בצום, ללא אכילה ושתייה, כשהראש מתפוצץ מכאב, והלב – כבר לא יכול להכיל את הצער. אני שומעת מחדש את הצעקות והאיומים של לילך רנן, איציק לוי, רויטל צרף, גדי לובין, אשר לזמי, עודד שמע, עודד יניב... החוקרים, שבאו עם כל הכוח כדי להשפיל, לבזות, לצעוק, לקלל ולאיים בצורה שיטתית; היו פעמים שהתקיפו אותי חמישה חוקרים יחד, היו פעמים שרק חוקר אחד, הכול לפי ״תרגילי החקירה״ שתכננו. מבחינתם ״המטרה מקדשת את האמצעים״, והכול ״כשר״ כדי להוציא ממני דיבור מפליל נגד בעלי. הם היו אחוזי טירוף ודבקים במטרתם להרשיע, אחוזים בעצמות של שנאה שלא ידעתי שקיימות. עברה לי בראש המחשבה: ״הם מסוגלים לגרום לאדם חף מפשע לחשוב ולהאמין שהוא רצח, ולהודות על רצח שהוא לא ביצע...״.

בחקירות הראשונות הייתי נחושה בדעתי לא להיכנע ללחץ שלהם, ולדעת להישמר מהתחבולות המניפולטיביות שלהם. אני מנסה להסתכל דרך המרחק של הזמן על מה שקרה שם בחדרי החקירות, כדי להבין מה גרם לי מאוחר יותר ליפול בבור שהם חפרו לי ולחשוף בפניהם את ״האגדות האורבניות״ של ״סיפורי הצואה״ שהיו ביני לבין עליזה; איך לא הבנתי שהם ישתמשו בסיפורים האלה כדי להפליל את דניאל? למה לא הבנתי שהם יכולים לתפור לתוך כל סיפור את דניאל, אפילו אם הוא לא ידע ולא שמע ממנו, ולייצר באופן זה הרשעות שווא? איך הייתי כל כך טיפשה להאמין בהם שהם מחפשים לדעת את האמת ורוצים לעשות משפט צדק? מה באמת קרה לי בחדרי החקירות? למה חשבתי שאני חייבת לרצות את החוקרים? האם זה בגלל שפחדתי שיתפרו גם לי תיק פלילי כמו שהבטיחו? האם זה היה סוג של הלם קרב?

**שנת 2011** הצצה לחדר חקירות ימ״ר ירושלים:

״את חשודה בהתעללות בחסרי ישע ותקיפה, בכך שאת יחד עם אחרות תקפת נשים שחיו אתך בבית משפחת אמבש, וגרמת להתעללות בילדים, וכל זאת בניגוד לחוק. אני מודיעה לך שיש לך את הזכות להיוועץ עם עו״ד. כל שתאמרי עלול לשמש ראיה נגדך. יש לך כמובן גם את זכות השתיקה, אך עליי לידע אותך שזה עשוי לחזק את הראיות נגדך, כלומר את נחקרת במצב של חשודה, שזה אומר שהמצב שלך הוא לא מצב טוב... את מבינה, אדרת, על מה אנחנו מדברים?״

החוקרת לילך רנן, הישירה לעברי מבט מאיים, מרוכז, מצמצמת את שתי עיניה השחורות כשהיא מתריסה לעברי: ״את לא הולכת לראות את דניאל לפחות לשלושים שנה, גם לא את הילדים, זהו, נגמר אדרת, היא צעקה בזעם, אין לך יותר משפחה, תשכחי מדניאל, הוא כבר לא קיים, תקבלי את זה כעובדה״. ואז לפתע היא שינתה את הטון והוסיפה בלחש, כמו מנסה לשתף אותי בסוד: ״עכשיו מה שנשאר לך זה רק להציל את עצמך...״. היא קיוותה שלאחר שעות ארוכות, ימים ולילות של חקירות מתישות, היא תצליח לסחוט ממני את ההודאה שהיא מצפה לה בקוצר רוח, שאני הקרבן של דניאל. היא המשיכה במסע ההתעללות

שלה בנפש שלי והזהירה: "ואני מציעה לך לא להמשיך ללכת ראש בראש נגדי, כי אז אני אאלץ לכתוב לך כתבי אישום על ימין ועל שמאל, ואת לא תדעי איך לצאת מהם, אני מבטיחה לך!". הבטתי בה בהלם. למה מותר לה לאיים עליי בצורה כזו? מה אני עושה פה? כשהיא ראתה שהאיומים לא פועלים, היא ניסתה לשוות לקולה טון רך יותר: "תקשיבי אדרת, כישרון הכתיבה שלך הוא בלתי רגיל, אני ישבתי כל השבת וקראתי את הכתבים שלך, היומנים שלך, והם מאוד נגעו ללבי, את כתבת בדם לבך, כל מילה ומילה שלך ממש מרגשת. לא חבל עלייך? לא חבל על כישרון כתיבה כל כך מבוזבז? הרי בין השורות רואים שאת סובלת, למה את לא מוכנה להודות על אמת כל כך פשוטה?".

הרגשתי שאני רוצה לצרוח עד לב השמים. היא מנסה להשתמש בי ובכתבים שלי, נגד בעלי! מה לעזאזל היא מבינה מהם? איך יש לה רשות לחטט במחברות אינטימיות שלי שכתבתי בהם פנטזיות והרהורים שהצניעות יפה להם, ושלעולם לא הייתי מראה אותם למישהו זר, בוודאי לא לגבר, ובטח שלא לה! הייתכן שאין במדינה שום חוק שמגן על צנעת הפרט? על כבוד האדם? האם באמת הכול מותר לה וכל האמצעים כשרים כדי לסגור את בעלי בכלא? היא הרימה את רגליה על שולחן המחשב, נשענה לאחור ופרצה בצחוק מאולץ: "את כל כך תמימה, את חושבת שכל הנשים מגנות עליו כמוך? את נשארת לבד אדרת, כולן הבינו שאין להן ברירה, שאם הן רוצות לראות את הילדים שלהן, הן חייבות לעזור לחקירה. אז נכון, לך אין ילדים, אבל החיים לפנייך, לא חבל עלייך? תשתחררי. קחי את החופש שלך. שיהיה לך ברור, את דניאל את לא תיראי לא בקרוב ולא עוד הרבה זמן... אני מוכנה להפגיש אותך עם אחת מהנשים כדי שתאמיני לי שכולן הבינו שהן חייבות לשתף פעולה אתנו, ורק את נשארת טיפשה ולא לוקחת אחריות על החיים שלך. את מי מהן את רוצה לראות? את עליזה? גם היא דיברה כמוך בהתחלה ואמרה שדניאל לא עשה שום דבר רע, אבל עם הזמן היא התפכחה ועשתה אחד ועוד אחד והבינה שזה לא שווה לה להתעקש, אני גם בטוחה שדניאל היה אומר לה שזה השיקול היותר נכון, איפה ההיגיון שלך?"

"אני לא מאמינה לך שעליזה דיברה נגד דניאל, את פשוט משקרת", אמרתי בכעס.

"אני משקרת"?! היא צעקה עליי, "עכשיו אני אביא את עליזה ותראי אם אני משקרת לך". היא קמה בבת-אחת מהכיסא, ובצעדים גדולים עזבה את החדר, משאירה אותי רגע לבד, מתחבטת בשאלות: האם היא משקרת לי או לא? האם ייתכן שעליזה מדברת נגד דניאל? יכול להיות שהיא משתפת פעולה אתם? לא, לא יכול להיות, חשבתי לעצמי, זה לא ייתכן. לא ייתכן שהיא תסכים לשתף פעולה עם העלילה הזדונית שלהם. החוקרת בטח משקרת בקשר לעליזה, כמו ששיקרה לי בקשר לשאר הנשים והילדים. נזכרתי בציפי, הבת של אילנה ודניאל, בת ה-16. אתמול כשהחוקר אמר לי שציפי לא רוצה לראות אותי יותר הדלת הייתה פתוחה וראיתי את ציפי בקצה השני של המסדרון. כשהיא הבחינה בי היא שמה את שתי ידיה מסביב לפה כדי ליצור אפקט של רמקול וצעקה לי: "אדרת, אל תתייחסי למילה ממה שהם אומרים לך, הם **שקרנים**!" בלי שיכלה לדעת שבאותו רגע החוקר אמר לי שציפי אמרה שהיא כועסת עליי שעשיתי דברים רעים לאבא שלה. הצטערתי שכמעט נתתי לחוקרת לסכסך ביני ובין עליזה.

החוקרת יצאה מהחדר ולפתע נכנסה עליזה. קפצנו אחת על השנייה בהתרגשות, התחבקנו ארוכות. עברו כבר כמה שבועות מיום המעצר, שתינו היינו נעולות במקלטים לנשים מוכות בתנאי מעצר, ואסרו עלינו לדבר בינינו או להיפגש.

לחשתי לה באוזן: "זה נכון מה שהם מספרים עלייך?"

עליזה הרחיקה אותי ממנה באחת ואמרה בקול: "את מאמינה להם???"

"מה פתאום", אמרתי, "אני לא מאמינה להם, בשביל זה אני שואלת אותך...".

האמת שהיה קשה לי להאמין לסיפורי החוקרים בקשר לעליזה כי האמנתי בה ובאהבה שהייתה בינה לדניאל, אבל אני מוכרחה להודות, שאף על פי כן, באותו הרגע חשדתי בה, וכנראה שהיא הרגישה את זה, כי אני לא שחקנית מוצלחת במיוחד ותמיד היא הייתה אומרת שאני שקופה... היא לקחה צעד אחורה ממני, הביטה בי משתאה...

"הצילו, את עם מלא מסכים וחומות ממני, מה יש לך ? את יודעת מה אני עברתי? 48 שעות אני בתוך חדר כזה קטן שאין בו אפילו שירותים רק חור, חור... ואני כל יום בחקירה, כל יום בחקירה, הם אומרים לך שאני דיברתי נגד דניאל ואת מאמינה להם? את אוכלת את החרא הזה?"

"נראה לך שאני אוכלת את זה? מיהרתי להתגונן.

"אני רואה את ההתנהגות שלך, אני רואה איך את באת אליי, אני בהלם ממך. אני, רק אמרו לי שמפגישים אותי עם אדרת נשבר לי הלב, כל כך התרגשתי, אני מתפלאה עלייך אדרת, כמה שנים אנחנו חברות ואת מאמינה להם? מה קרה לך?"

"אני... אני אמרתי לך שאני לא מקבלת שום דבר ממה שהם אומרים".

"כולך ב..ב.. את כן מקבלת", גמגמה.

"אני לא מקבלת".

"בלב שלך את כן".

"לא אני לא".

"את כן בחששות".

"אני לא מאמינה להם".

"את מתנהגת כאילו אנחנו זרות, למה את כל כך קרה אתי? אני כל כך חיכיתי לפגוש אותך וזה מה שיש לך להגיד לי, שאת מאמינה להם? כאילו למי את מאמינה, לאחות שחיית אתה שמונה שנים או למה?"

בעצם לא יכולתי להפסיק לחשוב שהיא עושה הצגה. היא נעמדה ליד הדלת והתחילה לצעוק: "איפה החוקרת, אני רוצה שתבואו לכאן, אני רוצה שמישהו יעזור לי".

"למה עליזה עושה את זה?" חשבתי בלבי, "היא לא משאירה לנו רגע אחד להיות לבד. ממה היא מפחדת? האם היא משקרת או לא?"

נכנסו לחדר החוקרת לילך יחד עם החוקר עודד שמעא.

"תגידי את האמת", פנתה עליזה לחוקרת: "אתם אומרים שאני מדברת נגד דניאל? אני אמרתי משהו נגד דניאל? אני לא מבינה מה קרה לאדרת, אני כל כך התרגשתי לראות אותה והיא ממש קרה אתי. אני מחבקת אותה בחום, והיא מחבקת אותי בקרירות ואומרת לי שהיא חושדת בי ששיקרתי בקשר לדניאל, מי אמר לה כזה דבר?"

"מה פתאום", אמרה לילך החוקרת לעליזה והמשיכה: "אני אמרתי משהו כזה? לא אמרתי שאת מדברת נגדו, למה צריך לדבר נגדו? אמרתי שאת התחלת להבין מה את צריכה להגיד".

עליזה היססה לרגע ואז אמרה בקול רם:

"תביני אדרת, אני הבנתי שאין לי ברירה, הם יודעים עליי כל מיני דברים, אם אני הולכת להיות בכלא, זה אומר שבתיה הולכת לאימוץ או למשפחה בחו"ל, הבנת? זה לא משחק. אדרת, כשיש ילד זה כבר לא משחק, זה משהו שאת לא יכולה להבין".

"בשביל מה את מגבירה את הקול?" שאלתי.

"אני מנסה להסביר לך שזו נקודה שכואבת לי, זו נקודה שכואבת לי. אני חולמת על הילדה הזאת כל לילה, אני קמה בסיוטים שהילדה לבד בלי אבא, בלי אימא. אני עוברת דברים שאת לא יכולה להבין, מה אני עוברת כל לילה, כל לילה, אני לא יודעת איך את חיה. אני לא חיה...".

"את חושבת שמישהו חי טוב עכשיו?" שאלתי בתמיהה.

"אבל יש לי סיוטים, סיוטים, את קולטת? סיוטים על הילדה הזאת", הוסיפה לקולה נימה היסטרית.

"אז הם הבטיחו לך שאם תדברי נגדו תקבלי אותה?" ניסיתי לברר...

"אדרת, עוד לא נפל לך האסימון? אני מדברת אתך על החיים של הילדה, אנחנו לא באיזשהו משחק, איך את מחזירה את בתיה?"

"כשהם יבינו שכל זה, זה לא קיים – אז היא תחזור, מה זה הסיפורים שאת מספרת להם?" שאלתי.

"אני לא מרבה לדבר" הצטדקה, "מה שאני מדברת זה דברים שהם אומרים לי, ואם אני רואה לנכון לאמת אותם, אני מאמתת אותם".

"עליזה, את מוכנה לאשר דברים שקריים רק כדי שאת לא תשבי בכלא? את שומעת מה שאת אומרת לי?!" הזדעזעתי. הרגשתי שאני בתוך איזה חלום בלהות, לא רציתי להאמין למשמע אוזניי.

"היא מנסה להציל את הילדה שלה", התערבה החוקרת להגנתה של עליזה.

"הילדה צריכה לגדול עם אבא שלה", כעסתי.

"את יודעת מה?" עליזה ניסתה להסביר: "את לא מבינה איך אני מנהלת את הדברים, ואת לא מבינה מה המחשבות שלי, ואת לא מבינה איך אני פועלת, את חושדת בי, אני יודעת שאת חושדת בי, זה כנראה עוד תהליך שאני אצטרך לעבור, אבל עברנו הרבה חוויות ביחד, הקשר שיש לנו הם לא יוכלו לגעת בזה, גם אם יעשו חקירה אלף שנים הם לא יוכלו לגעת בזה, תאמיני לי שאני בוכה בלילות. אבל המלחמה שלי עכשיו זה להחזיר את בתיה, את צריכה להבין, את לא מבינה את זה, ולהחזיר אותה זה בכל מחיר".

החוקרת לעגה לי שאין לי ילדים, ושזו הסיבה שאני לא יכולה להבין מה זה להיות אימא. היא ביקשה מעליזה לצאת מהחדר ואז פנתה אליי בטון קשה ואמרה: "שיהיה לך ברור, בגישה שלך את לא תצאי החוצה, אני אומרת לך, את תועמדי לדין. ולדעתי את צריכה להיות עם בושה שאת יושבת מול האישה הזו ושופטת אותה בגלל שהיא מנסה להציל את הילדה שלה. את צריכה לקחת את האחריות ואני לא מבקשת ממך לספר לי שום דבר, אני אספר לך, ואת רק תאשרי ותנסי להסביר ולנמק מה היה בסיטואציה".

"את רוצה שאני אשקר?"

לא רציתי להאמין שזה קורה. אני, שחונכתי שהמשטרה היא גוף שמגן על האזרח, מציל ועוזר בשעת צרה, זקוקה להצלה מהמשטרה בעצמה. עומדת מולי חוקרת משטרה בימ"ר ירושלים שמבזבזת את כל המשאבים והכוחות של משטרת ישראל על איומים עליי ועל החברות שלי, או כמו שהם אומרים: "איומים על חסרי ישע", שאם לא נשקר ונסייע לה להושיב את מי שהיא סימנה כ"פושע" בכלא, היא, יש לה את הכוח להושיב אותנו בכלא ולקחת לנו את הילדים!

והחוקרת המשיכה: "אני רוצה לראות אותך מעזה לעמוד מול עליזה בבית משפט, מתה לראות אותך, את חושבת שאת גיבורה? בואי נראה, רק תנסי לקרא לה שקרנית, רק תנסי אדרת. אם תשחירי אותה, את לא יודעת כמה שחורה את תצאי, אין לך מושג. אלף כמוך לא יצליחו נגדי. את חושבת שאת חזקה, אדרת? את חושבת שאת מסוגלת לזה? משפט זה דבר קשה. לא היית רוצה להיות מהצד השני. אני אשאל אותך שאלות, ואת תיתני את הפירוש שלך לזה, ואת תתנצלי על זה ותבקשי סליחה, ואת תסבירי בצורה מאוד לא הגיונית, אני יודעת, מאוד לא הגיונית, כולם פה הסבירו בצורה מאוד לא הגיונית, אבל גם בחוסר ההיגיון הזה יש איזה שהוא היגיון מסוים. את רוצה? זה הזמן. את לא רוצה? בואי נתהפך, אין לנו שום בעיה. אני נותנת לך פייר פייט, הבחירה היא אצלך. את מבינה מה אני אומרת, אדרת? אם אנחנו נפרדות היום, אנחנו כבר יותר לא ניפגש, אבל את לא תעזבי פה לפני שאני כותבת את כל הדברים, מעלה אותם יפה יפה, מסדרת תיק יפה יפה, אני אעבוד היום, עוד יום, עוד יום, אעשה לך תיק. אני אכתוב לך שלושים אירועים שהשתתפת בהם, אני אאמת אותם, וככה אני אציג את הדברים. פעם הבאה שאני אראה אותך זה כשתנסי להשחיר אנשים על דוכן העדים, אז אני אעלה, את לא יודעת איך תצאי משם, את לא מבינה, אז תראי משטרה אחרת. עדיף לך להיות אתי, עדיף לך להיות אתי, עדיף לך שאני אגיע אתך ולא נגדך. עדיף לך שהמשטרה תבוא אתך ולא נגדך, עדיף לך שהמדינה תבוא אתך ולא נגדך, עדיף לך שבית המשפט יהיה אתך ולא נגדך, עדיף לך. את לא חזקה כמו שאת חושבת, את יומיים בכלא נווה תרצה לא שורדת, לא שורדת, ההחלטה בידייך. זאת תכנית א', זאת תכנית ב', ההחלטה היא שלך... לי כואב רק על ההורים שלך...".

היום אני מסיימת את החקירה הזו ככה או אחרת, מחר זו ההזדמנות האחרונה שלך.

אחרי כל השעות האלו לקחו אותי באזיקים והעלו אותי על רכב המשטרה חזרה למקלט לנשים מוכות. נכנסתי למכונית, מלווה בשני חוקרים חמושים שמנסים לתת לי את ההרגשה שאני פושעת מבוקשת והם אחראים שלא אברח. אחד מהם התיישב ליד ההגה והשני ישב על הספסל האחורי לידי. התיישבתי צמוד לחלון, השעה הייתה סמוך לשקיעה, והשמש צבעה את השמים באדום לוהט כמו לאות הזדהות עם השרפות שחשתי בתוך לבי. הגעגועים לדניאל, והחרדה לשלומו הציפו אותי בסערת רגשות שאיימה להתפרץ בדמעות. הייתי עדיין בהשפעת הטראומה של החקירה, ובהלם מהמפגש עם עליזה. לא ידעתי מה לחשוב עליה, מה שבטוח זה שהיא הצליחה לבלבל אותי, ולא הבנתי באיזה צד היא. האם היא עשתה

משחק מול החוקרת כי היא רוצה לרכוש את האמון שלה ולהבטיח לעצמה את בתה חזרה, או שהיא משחקת אתי ומשקרת לי?

האמת היא שאף פעם לא הצלחתי להבין אותה ולדעת אם היא מאמינה במה שהיא אומרת או שהיא מנסה להציג מה שמתאים לאינטרסים זמניים בלבד. חשבתי על הניסיון שהיא עוברת בתור אימא. מה אני הייתי עושה אם היו שמים על מאזניים את בעלי מצד אחד ואת בתי מצד שני ואומרים לי את מי את בוחרת לקבור?... אולי באמת אין לה ברירה... זו הפעם הראשונה שחשבתי שמזל שאין לי ילדים, ושאני לא צריכה לעמוד בניסיון הזה.

התחלתי לחשוב שאולי אני אטומה לצער של עליזה, ואולי אני צריכה לשנות גישה בחקירות, ולספק תשובות שירצו את החוקרים, כדי שבתיה תקבל את אימא שלה בחזרה ואולי נצליח לסדר את הדברים והם יניחו לנו...

רכב המשטרה חנה סמוך למקלט לנשים מוכות בתל אביב. שני החוקרים ליוו אותי עד הכניסה, צלצלו בפעמון לוודא שפותחים לי את הדלת, ואז עזבו. נכנסתי לחדר שאותו חלקתי יחד עם פיליפינית והבן שלה בן החמש, רציתי רק להיכנס למיטה ולהיעלם מתחת לשמיכה, בלי שאף אחד יבחין שנכנסתי לחדר. הראש שלי התפוצץ בכאב חד, והלב פעם בחזקה. אני מתגעגעת למיטה שלי, לחיבוק של דניאל; צריכה אותו צמוד אליי, מה קורה אתו עכשיו? מה הוא עובר? מה הם מעוללים לו? בחדרי החקירות, נתקלתי באיבה כזו מצד החוקרים כלפי דניאל שזה מאוד הדאיג אותי. לא ידעתי למה לצפות. למצוא את עצמי כבר כחודש במקלט לנשים מוכות, הרחק מבעלי וממשפחתי היה בשבילי זעזוע קשה. עוד טכניקה מלוכלכת של המשטרה, בשיטת "הפרד ומשול". לנסות לשכנע אותי ואת כל הנשים, שאנחנו שייכות לקטגוריה של "נשים מוכות", שעברנו סוג של התעללות. מתי ייגמר הסיוט הזה?

למחרת, בחדר החקירות, החוקרת לילך, בתגבור החוקר עודד שמעא ורויטל צרף, גדי לובין ואיציק לוי הטיחו בי סיטואציות הזויות, נאלמתי ללא זיע. לא ידעתי מה לעשות. הם התקיפו מכל כיוון. הרגשתי מול כיתת יורים, הפחד שיתק אותי. לדבריה, כל דבר שאומר ישמש לרעתי. האופציה היחידה שהיא נתנה לי הייתה לחזור אחריה מילה במילה.

"תודי שאתן אכלתן צואה!" היא צעקה. "את ועליזה אכלתן צואה כדי לרצות את דניאל", קבעה. "את חושבת שאני לא יודעת הכול? עליזה אכלה צואה גבישית ואת אכלת צואה נוזלית!" ניסתה להשחיל לדבריה את האינפורמציה על הסיפור שדרשה שאאשר לה. הזדעזעתי. מה קורה פה, ריבונו של עולם, היא באמת חושבת שאכלתי צואה? מאיפה היא הביאה את ה"יציאה" הזו?

"אני לא מבקשת ממך שתספרי על אחרים, כל מה שאני אומרת זה שאם לא תיקחי אחריות על מעשים שאת עשית, ותודי בהם, ותנסי לתת הסבר הגיוני לכל סיטואציה שאספר לך, את לא תצאי מפה עוד הרבה זמן, אני מבטיחה לך, מילה שלי!"

היא גם הטילה עליי את האחריות לכך שעליזה הולכת לאבד את בתיה בגללי. "תיזהרי אדרת, את הולכת בכיוון לא טוב. את רוצה ככה? אין בעיה, רק תזכרי שבדרך הזו בתיה לא תראה את עליזה יותר. אני יוצאת מהחדר ואני נותנת לך זמן לחשוב עוד פעם מה את מעדיפה לענות לי... הגורל של הילדה הזאת בידיים שלך".

היא עזבה את החדר והשאירה אותי לבד. הייתי מותשת משעות רבות של חקירות. ניסיתי להתנער מהפחד מהאיומים שלה. חיפשתי מה העצה שיכולה לעזור לי לסיים כמה שיותר מהר את הסיוט הזה של החקירות. חשבתי שאולי אם אספר לה את האמת על החברות המיוחדת שהייתה ביני לבין עליזה, על ההרפתקאות שחווינו יחד, על הרצונות של שתינו להתחזק בתשובה וביראת שמים ביחד, על התחרותיות והקנאה שהיו בינינו ועל ה"עקיצות" שהיינו מטיחות זו בזו – היא תבין ללא שום ספק שבחיים לא אכלנו צואה אלא רק דיברנו שיחות נשים על "פֶטישים" מיניים.

עליזה ואני באנו מרקע שונה לחלוטין. זו גם אחת הסיבות לתחרות שהייתה בינינו. היא צעירה ממני בשמונה שנים, מבית מסורתי; היא סיפרה לי שלהוריה היו הרבה בעיות שלום בית, וחובות "בשוק האפור", אחיה הסתבכו עם המשטרה, היא התנסתה בסמים ועברה הרבה הרפתקאות ותנודות בחיים. היא סיפרה שמגיל 16 פיתחה מערכות יחסים שונות ומגוונות עם גברים, ומכיוון שגדלה בתוך הבלגן הזה של החיים ניסתה לבנות את עצמה על בסיס היופי החיצוני שלה. תמיד אמרו שהיא יפה, וזה נתן לה הרבה ביטחון עצמי. היא הציעה תמיד שכדאי ללמוד ממנה, כי עם ניסיון החיים שיש לה, היא יודעת מה גבר

צריך. ושהדבר הכי חשוב במערכות יחסים זה הכנות. היא ידעה איך לשחק ולהציג את עצמה כאישה הכי אמתית ופתוחה.

אני לעומתה באתי מבית מבוסס מאוד מבחינה כלכלית, וגדלתי ביציבות עם הורים שתמיד חיו בזוגיות יפה. הבית היה דתי-לאומי, ועם השנים התחזקנו לכיוון חרדי-ליטאי, כל האחיות שלי גרות בבני ברק, מורות, נשואות לאברכים; אבי – לאחר שנים של עבודה כסמנכ״ל של חברה למוצרי בניין, נכנס גם הוא לישיבה ליטאית, ואמי החלה להעביר שיעורי תורה לנשים. גדלתי בחינוך שמרני, ללא מגע עם בנים. כשהתחתנתי עם אסא הייתי בת 21 והוא היה הבחור הראשון שהכרתי. עם דניאל התחתנתי כשהייתי בת 26, ושלוש שנים לאחר מכן עליזה הגיעה לבית.

עליזה הייתה אומרת שהיא מקנאה בקשר שלי עם דניאל. שכשאני אתו לבד ואנחנו סוגרים את הדלת של החדר זה ״מפוצץ אותה מבפנים״, והיא הייתה כועסת עליי שאני טיפוס סגור ומופנם, ושאיני פותחת את לבי ומשתפת אותה במה שקורה ביני לבינו, כי אולי אם אספר לה זה ירגיע אותה. אני חשבתי שיש דברים שהצניעות יפה להם, ושמרתי על הפרטיות שלי מכל משמר. עצבן אותי שהיא מנסה להתערב בכל מה שקשור אליי, אבל גם קינאתי בה כי ידעתי שדניאל אוהב את ה״דוגריות״ שלה. היא ״לקחה את ההגה לידיים״, תרתי-משמע: הייתה כריזמטית ואסרטיבית, ידעה איך לשלוט במצבים ולארגן את כולם; וגם אהבה לנהוג על המכוניות הגדולות של ההפצה. היו מתחים לא מעטים בינינו. אך עם כל העליות והירידות, עם השנים בנינו חברות חזקה.

כשלילך החוקרת חזרה לחדר החקירות, סיפרתי לה בדיוק מה היה עניין הצואה ביני לבין עליזה: ״יום אחד עליזה כעסה עליי שאני לא מנסה לשבור את הבסדרניקיות שלי, ואמרה לי שזה לא העיקר בחיים להיות ׳בסדר׳... כלומר, לדעתה בן אדם צריך להיות כן עם עצמו, ואם הוא מרגיש שקוע באיזו תאווה, זה לא עוזר שישים מסֵכה על הפנים, או שיתקע את הראש בחול ויגיד: אני בסדר, אני לא כזה מלוכלך..., אלא שיתמודד עם עצמו ויעבוד על המידות, וישבור את עצמו אם צריך״. ״מתי זה היה?״ שאלה לילך. ״עליזה תמיד הייתה צוחקת אתי על איך שאני אוהבת להיות ׳בסדר׳, אבל השיחה שאני מספרת לך עליה הייתה בשנה האחרונה״, הסברתי. לילך החלה להקליד על המחשב את דבריי, והמשכתי לספר: ״שנאתי שעליזה מטיפה לי מוסר, גם לא אהבתי את הטון המתנשא שלה, ואמרתי לה: ״את יודעת לדבר יפה על אחרים, אבל מתי את ניסית לשבור את עצמך?״ עליזה בתגובה, כדי להוכיח לי שהיא לא רק מדברת, אלא גם עושה אמרה לי שיום אחד שהרגישה שהתאווה לגברים תפסה אותה חזק, היא לקחה גוש של חרא ובלעה אותו כדי להרגיש מלוכלכת״. ״מה את אומרת״ צחקה לילך, ״ואת האמנת לה?״ שאלה. ״אמרתי לה שהיא שקרנית, ושאני לא מאמינה לה. עליזה נפגעה וזה התפתח לריב בינינו. עצבן אותי מאוד שהיא מרגישה שהיא יכולה לספר סיפורים הזויים, ושאני חייבת ״לאכול״ אותם. החלטתי לעשות לה תרגיל. יצאתי מהבית והלכתי לכיוון ״סנטר 1״ שליד התחנה המרכזית בירושלים. התעכבתי עד שעליזה התקשרה לשאול מה קורה אתי ואיפה אני, ואז עניתי לה בציניות: ״אני בסנטר 1 ובדיוק עכשיו אני אוכלת צואה כדי לשבור את הבסדירניקיות שלי...״ את עליזה זה בכלל לא הצחיק. היא אמרה לי: ״שקרנית. מה את מנסה לחקות אותי? את צוחקת עליי? את חושבת שמישהו מאמין לך?״ ״זה הסיפור״, אמרתי ללילך.

מאוחר יותר, כשראיתי שבכתב האישום נכתב שבשל האימה שדניאל הטיל עלינו, עליזה ואני אכלנו צואה כחלק ממערך הענישה, מתוך כוונה להוכיח את כפיפותנו המוחלטת אליו ובמטרה למצוא חן בעיניו... הבנתי שאני נמצאת בתוך סיוט קפקאי מול מערכת אטומה ומושחתת, שלא בוחלת בשום שקר כדי להרשיע את מי שסימנה עליו איקס.

חמישה חודשים לאחר מכן אני ועליזה ישבנו בתחנת הרכבת בירושלים. היא הביטה בי בעיניים דומעות. שאלתי אותה מה קרה והיא השפילה מבטה ואמרה בקול נמוך ומהסס: ״תשמעי אדרת, יצר אתי קשר בפייסבוק חבר ילדות שלי, הוא אמר שהוא מתגעגע אליי ודואג לי וחוזר לארץ במיוחד בשבילי... חשבתי על הכול, החוקרים אמרו לי שדניאל לא יצא בשלושים השנים הקרובות... את צריכה להבין אותי, אני לא יכולה להיות בלי גבר״.

עליזה קיבלה את בתיה בחזרה בתמורה לכך שהפכה לעדת מדינה. מסתבר שהיה לה מניע נוסף מלבד בתיה, כי כשדיברה איתי היא כבר הייתה בהיריון מאותו הגבר.

עליזה הפכה את כל החברות בינינו לכתב אישום, ועל כל מחווה שביקשה ממני ונעתרתי לה, נכתב לי סעיף נוסף. ישבתי בכלא שנה שלמה על עבֵרות שלא ביצעתי. עליזה הגיעה להעיד נגדי. גרסתה הייתה בלתי אפשרית וסתרה את עצמה, היה ברור לשלושת השופטים במחוזי שהיא לא אמינה, שיחררו אותי באותו יום.

גדלתי בבת ים, בת שלישית מתוך ארבע בנות. כשההורים והאחיות שלי התחברו לזרם החרדי, אני לא הייתי בטוחה שהכיוון הליטאי שהם בחרו בו זה מה שמתאים לי, אבל בכל מקרה, לא הסכמתי שאף אחד ישפיע על החיפוש האישי שלי אחר הדרך בעבודת השם.

ביום האחרון של הלימודים, אחרי 12 שנות לימוד, כשכל שנה קיבלתי תעודת הצטיינות, הצלחתי אמנם להגשים את השאיפות הפרפקציוניסטיות שלי, אבל חשתי ריקנות איומה. הסתובבתי בבית הלוך ושוב חסרת מנוחה, הרגשתי שבזבזתי את החיים שלי בתחרות, שהעניקה לי אמנם כבוד, אך לא נתנה לי תשובה לצעקה הפנימית של הנשמה שלי. להפך, ההישגים הגשמיים אפילו איימו להטביע אותי במאבקים על תארים מכובדים וכך לחנוק את הכיסופים האמתיים שבלב שלי. התעורר בתוכי רצון חזק, מתוך הכרת הטוב לבורא עולם, לעשות לו נחת רוח, אבל איך?

את שנת השירות לאומי שלי עשיתי בירושלים. במדרשה לבנות, שמשלבת את שנת השירות עם לימודי יהדות. המשך ישיר של שנת השירות הזו היו הלימודים במכללה להשכלה גבוהה באופקים לתואר "מורה בכירה לחינוך רגיל ולחינוך מיוחד". במשך שלוש שנים השתתפתי כל בוקר בשיעורים עם מיטב המרצים בזרם החרדי-ליטאי, ובשעות הצהריים והערב היו הלימודים האקדמיים לתואר מורה בכירה לכיתות ג׳-ח׳ עם התמחות בחינוך מיוחד על גווניו השונים. השקעתי בלימודים, אהבתי את הדיונים בסוגיות החיים. החלטתי בשלב ההוא שגם אני, בדומה לאחיותיי, אקדיש את חיי כדי להקים בית של תורה, כלומר, אתחתן עם בחור ישיבה שיהיה "עילוי", כלומר "השפיץ של הישיבה"... ואביא ילדים לעולם ש"תורתם תהיה אומנותם".

בתור סטודנטית שנה ב׳ במכללה, אני זוכרת איך ישבתי על הדשא, מביטה בבנות שהיו משוחחות זו עם זו, וחושבת לעצמי בהתפארות, הנה כל היום אני עסוקה בצדקה וחסד, עוזרת לנשים בקהילה, עוזרת לבנות במכללה, אף פעם לא היה לי קשר אסור עם בנים, הרגשתי שהגעתי לשיא של רוחניות, הגשמה עצמית, ובעצם לשלמות, מה עוד אפשר לבקש?...

בדיוק אז באו שתי בנות וקראו לי לשיחה עם הרבנית-המנהלת. נכנסתי לחדרה במעט חשש, למה הרבנית קוראת לי? זו הייתה הפעם הראשונה שהוזעקתי כך לחדרה. היא פנתה אליי בחיוך מרגיע, ולאחר שהתעניינה בשלומי אמרה: "תשמעי אדרת, המדיניות של המכללה קובעת שבשנה הראשונה של הלימודים אנחנו לא מאשרים לבנות לצאת לשידוכים, כיוון שאנחנו מעדיפים שהבנות תכרנה את הקהילה ואת אורח החיים החרדי לפני שהן מקימות בית משלהן. אך הגיעו אליי במקביל שלוש הצעות שידוכים שונות בשבילך, ורציתי שתבררי עליהם פרטים, ותחליטי עם מי את רוצה להיפגש".

אמנם נכון, הבנתי שלהקים בית של תורה זה העיקר בחיים, אבל לא הייתה לי כוונה להתחתן לפני שאסיים את הלימודים. הייתי כבר בת עשרים, ולפי לוח הזמנים של החברה החרדית בגיל הזה כבר הייתי אמורה להיות אם לילד, אבל לי היו תכניות אחרות. תכננתי לעשות קריירה. חתונה נראתה לי מסגרת סוגרת ומחייבת שאולי עדיף לדחות ולהרוויח עוד קצת זמן. הרבנית עברה אתי במהירות על הרשימה של הצעות השידוך, והתעכבה על הצעה שבאופן מפתיע גם אבא שלי הציע לי יום לפני כן. בחור שהיה קרוב משפחה של מי שעבדה אצלו במשרד. "הוא לומד היום בישיבת 'תפארת צבי' בירושלים", היא עדכנה אותי בפרטים: "גם הוא נולד בבת ים, בן יחיד להורים חילונים. בגיל עשר התייתם מאביו ומאז החל את דרך התשובה. למד בישיבה תיכונית והיה פעיל ב'בני עקיבא'; בצה"ל שירת בישיבת ההסדר 'הר עציון' באלון שבות. עבר חצי שנה בקורס מ"כים, היה מ"כ והדריך טירונים. שירת בזמן האינתיפאדה ברמאללה ובבית אל, וסיים את שירותו ב'בור' בקריה. אחרי הצבא החל ללמוד תורה בישיבה החרדית בקריית מלאכי ולאחר מכן בישיבת 'מיר'. הוא לומד בחברותא עם הרב אליהו הורוביץ שהוא היה החברותא של הרב שך. קוראים לו אסא מיראש".

הרבנית הביטה בי ושאלה: "מה את חושבת?". "אני אברר לגביו ואחזיר לך תשובה", ניסיתי להתחמק ולהרוויח זמן. "כשאדע יותר פרטים אודיע לך". יצאתי מחדרה בסערת רגשות. מצד אחד רציתי להגיד לה שאולי נחכה עוד קצת זמן, אני רוצה להחליט אם בכלל להיכנס לעניין של שידוכים עכשיו, מצד שני הצעת השידוך עם אסא, שהגיעה באותו הזמן בשתי דרכים שונות, עם סיפור חיים שהתנהל די במקביל לחיי, נראתה לי כ"השגחה משמים", ולהשגחה – הרגשתי שאסור לסרב. אולי זה רצון השם שאכיר אותו?! כששם פותח פתח, זה לא נכון לטרוק את הדלת ולהפנות גב להשגחה, חשבתי. זו הסיבה שהסכמתי להצעת השידוך הזאת. אחרי ארבע פגישות קצרות החלטנו שאנחנו רוצים להתחתן.

בזרם החרדי אין נגיעות בין בני זוג עד לליל החתונה. החתן מקבל שיעורים פרטיים אצל רב שמדריך אותו איך להתנהג עם הכלה לפי כללי הבית היהודי, והכלה הולכת לרבנית מדריכת כלות. אני חייבת להודות שהשיעור האחרון אצל הרבנית שמלמדת מה עושים "בלילה הראשון" השאיר אותי במבוכה. אני זוכרת איך ישבתי באוטובוס אחרי השיעור די בהלם, מתאפקת לא לבכות מהגילוי החדש, ותוהה בלבי: "מה הולך להיות?". עד אותו שיעור לא ידעתי איך בדיוק מקיימים את מה שנקרא "המצווה" – מצוות עונה, בחברה הדתית זה לא נושא שמדברים עליו, ובאמת לא דיברתי על זה אף פעם, לא עם אימא שלי, לא עם אחיות שלי, ואפילו לא עם החברות שלי שכולן היו דתיות, ואני מאמינה שגם היו בורות בתחום זה כמוני. המקור היחיד עד אז שסיפק לי איזשהו כיוון של חשיבה לגבי איך מתקיימים היחסים בין בעל ואישה היו הרומנים שאהבתי לקרוא, אך גם הם לא הסבירו את המעשה עצמו, והשאירו מין ערפל מסביב. השיעור עם הרבנית השאיר אותי במתח מהבאות, הרגשתי שכללי הצניעות שהקפדתי עליהם עד אז צריכים להעביר הילוך, ובבת-אחת אני צריכה לשנות את כל עולם המושגים שלי. אך הייתה בי גם סקרנות וציפייה דרוכה לבאות, וחיכיתי בהתרגשות לחוויה של הלילה הראשון. לאחר כמה חודשים התחתנו. בתור אברך אסא למד ב"כולל באר שבע" וב"ישיבת אופקים", ואני שילבתי את הלימודים במכללה עם עבודה כמחנכת כיתה ד' בנות באופקים, במקביל לאתגר החדש של הקמת הבית.

החתונה חשפה אותי להרגשות ולתחושות שלא הכרתי, ולהתמודדויות שהיו חדשות לי. בליל החתונה, כשהייתי כולי נרגשת, אסא הפתיע אותי כשלפתע הציע ש"אולי עדיף לדחות את קיום המצווה לזמן שנהיה פחות עייפים"?! הלב שלי החסיר פעימה, זה לא מה שראיתי ברומנים שאהבתי לקרוא. למה אין לו חשק להיות אתי? האם משהו בי לא בסדר? העזתי והתעקשתי שזה לא צריך להיות ככה, והצלחתי לגרום לו למספיק רגשי אשמה עד שהוא נאלץ לקיים את "המצווה", אך לרוע המזל, עם כל ההשתדלות לא הצלחנו לעשות מה שצריך. לא הבנתי למה זה לא הולך. לכזה דבר הרבנית לא הכינה אותי. מה אני עושה לא נכון? לא ידעתי איך לפרש את הכישלון הזה. אסא החליט שהוא עייף ושננסה שוב בפעם הבאה. הוא נרדם. נשארתי ערה במיטה הרבה זמן, מנסה לעכל את מה שחוויתי זה עתה, ולהתגבר על ההצפה הרגשית שאיימה להטביע אותי באכזבה כואבת. במשך כל אותה שנה נאלצנו להתייעץ עם כל מיני רבנים ולקבל הדרכה כדי להצליח להתגבר על הבעיות שעלו בקשר הזוגי, אפילו נסענו לטיפול רפואי אצל ד"ר מנדלסון, שניסה דרך היפנוזה לגרום לי להסכים להיפתח לבעלי ולרצות אותו ורק אותו. הטיפולים לא עזרו. סחבנו את הבעיה במשך כשנה ללא פתרון, מתוסכלים ומבולבלים. עם הזמן נקשרתי אליו, אך הרגשתי יותר ויותר חסרת אונים כי לא הבנתי למה אנחנו לא מצליחים ושום דבר לא עוזר. התחלתי להאשים את עצמי. אולי משהו אצלי לא בסדר, מה קורה כאן? מה לא נכון? כל לילה הייתי בוכה בשקט במיטה, מרגישה אבודה בתוך סערת רגשות, ולא מצליחה לדבר אתו על זה. הפריע לי שאני זקוקה לאהבה שלו ועוד יותר הפריע לי שלא הבנתי מה עובר עליו.

הוא ניסה לתרץ את חוסר החשק שלו אליי בכך שהוא עושה עבודה של "פרישות", כאילו שזה חלק מעבודת השם שלו. הוא טען שתלמיד חכם צריך להיות עם אשתו רק משבת לשבת, כלומר פעם בשבוע, ונתן לי להרגיש שאם היה חיוב מהתורה להיות עם אשתו רק פעם בחודש או פעם בשנה או בכלל לא, זה היה עוד יותר טוב. הרגשתי שהוא מתחמק ממני ומחפש לכך תירוצים וחיזוקים מהתורה, כעסתי עליו, אך משום מה גם ריחמתי עליו. היה נראה לי שהוא סובל. הרבה פעמים קרה שהוא לא רצה לקום בבוקר ולצאת מהמיטה, כמה שניסיתי לדובב אותו ולהבין מה קרה, הוא נשאר סגור ומופנם ורק היה אומר שהוא במשבר.

כשהתארחנו בשבת אצל ההורים שלי והוא היה במרה שחורה ובדיכאון במיטה, הרגשתי שאני לא יכולה לסבול את זה יותר. בשלב מסוים הבטן שלי כאבה כל כך שהרגשתי כאילו משהו בפנים התפוצץ. לא יכולתי לשאת עוד את הכאב. ההורים שלי הזמינו אמבולנס, הרופא בדק אותי וקבע שכאבי הבטן הם מעצבים. ידעתי שזו תגובה ישירה להצטברות של המתח מחיי הנישואין שלנו.

מה שהחזיק עדיין את הקשר בינינו היה החיפוש המשותף אחר "רצון השם". יום אחד אסא הגיע הביתה בשמחה גדולה, ובידיו ערמה של כל ספרי רבי נחמן. אני זוכרת לצערי, את השרפה שבערה בתוכי כמו אש מהגיהינום, אש של מחלוקת ששרפה אותי מבפנים, ולא נתנה לי בשום פנים ואופן להסכים שהוא יתחיל ללמוד את הספרים של רבי נחמן. לא ידעתי להסביר לעצמי את ההתנגדות הפנימית הזו, אך היה לי ברור שאני אעשה הכול כדי להניא אותו מהרעיון החדש. כל ארבע שנות הלימוד בעולם הליטאי, החרדי-השחור, המתנגד לחסידות צפו ועלו בבת-אחת עם סערה פנימית שלא נתנה לי מנוחה. אמרתי לו ש"הרבנים הליטאים" מתנגדים לרבי נחמן, ורציתי להבין מה גורם לו לעשות משהו נגד כולם. הוא ניסה להסביר לי ששנים הוא מחפש עצות ל"פגם הברית" ולחטאי נעורים, ובעולם הליטאי הוא לא מצא להם פתרון, כי שם לא מדברים על זה, ושרק לרבי נחמן יש פתרונות לבעיות האלה, והספרים שלו מלאים בעצות איך להתמודד עם הכול. הוא אמר שרבי נחמן גם גילה את "התיקון הכללי" שהוא תיקון גדול ל"פגם הברית", וביקש שלא אדבר שטויות לפני שאני אקרא את הספרים ואבין קצת יותר. כך בעצם התחלתי לקרוא את

הספרים של רבי נחמן, מתוך רצון להוכיח לאסא שהוא טועה, אבל ככל שקראתי יותר, התחלתי להבין שהטעות היא אצלי. עברתי מלחמה פנימית סוערת בין הלימוד הליטאי שהערצתי לבין החשיפה לחסידות, אך אהבתי את ההתמודדות. זה היה מרתק. השאלות האמתיות בעניין ההתקרבות לצדיק מאוד העסיקו אותי, והייתי מחפשת להן תשובות. נהניתי שלמדנו יחד מהספרים. הוא גם הזמין איזה אברך ברסלבר שהגיע אלינו באופן קבוע להעביר לנו שיעור משותף ב״ליקוטי מוהר״ן״. במובן מסוים הפכתי להיות ״החברותא״ שלו, הוא אפילו אמר שחבל שהוא לא יכול להלביש אותי בבגדים של בחור ישיבה ולהביא אותי אתו ל״כולל״. הרגשתי שהלימוד ביחד מחזק את הקשר בינינו, ונותן לי מעין פיצוי על המרירות שהצטברה אצלי מהתסכולים הרבים שנגרמו בגלל הבעיות בחיי האישות.

עם כל ההשתדלות שלי למצוא חן בעיניו, לא הצלחתי להבעיר בו את החשק אליי, והוא נשאר אדיש מול הניסיונות שלי. אני זוכרת ימים ולילות שאני יושבת לבד ומחכה לו, בוכה על כך שהוא לא זוכר אותי, או משתדל כמה שיותר להיות עסוק בדברים אחרים ואינו זקוק לי בעצם... וכשהוא סוף סוף חוזר הביתה אז היו אין-ספור מריבות על: ״למה שכחת אותי?!״ הרגשתי שאני מפתחת סוג של תלות בתשומת הלב שלו, וסבלתי מזה. הוא לעומת זאת, בכל הזדמנות היה אוהב להגיד לי שאישה היא עול בשבילו כמו רחיים על הצוואר, אז איך הוא יכול לעבוד את השם? והיה משתדל שאני לא אהיה המכשול שלו בדרך. לאורך כל השנים לא הצלחנו לפתח קשר בריא של בעל ואישה, ואני הרגשתי שהנה הקללה והעונש של חוה התקיימו בי במלואם: ״ואל אישך תשוקתך, והוא ימשול בך״. וכשאין לו תשוקה – אז את בבעיה...

בשנה השלישית לנישואין אסא שמע ברדיו שיש ערוץ חרדי-ספרדי שנקרא ״קול הנשמה״, שמבצע התרמות, והחליט שהוא רוצה לתרום להם את הבית שלנו. בהתחלה זה היה נשמע לי הזוי. למה צריך לתת כל מה שיש לך לצדקה? אתה לא יכול להפריש מעשר או אפילו חומש? אמרתי לו שישכח מזה ושבשום אופן אני לא מסכימה להישאר בלי בית. הוא אמר שאם הייתי חיה את מה שהוא חי לא הייתי אפילו לרגע מהססת אם לתת צדקה או לא, שאני לא חיה אותו ולא מבינה מה הוא מרגיש ומה עובר עליו, ובשבילו – לתרום את הדירה זו הצדקה שיכולה להציל אותו. לא יכולתי להבין על איזה הצלה מדובר, כי עדיין הסתיר ממני את הבעיה שלו. הרגשתי שהוא זועק מתוך נקודה פנימית שכואבת לו, שהוא מתמודד לבד עם איזושהי בעיה. הוא אמר שהוא לא מרגיש שהעבודה שלנו על התחזקות בביטחון בהשם היא אמתית, הרי איך אפשר לקרוא לזה ״ביטחון בהשם״ כשיש לנו בית משלנו ויש לנו ״ביטחון כלכלי״? הוא למד שהצדקה שקולה כנגד כל המצוות, ורצה לקיים אותה בהידור. אני הייתי נסערת מאוד: מצד אחד ההיגיון אמר לי שבשום פנים ואופן לא להסכים לכזה צעד, איפה נגור אם נתרום את הבית שלנו, ואיך נחיה? אך מצד שני, משהו בחיפוש האמת של אסא משך אותי להיזרק אתו למים, ולצפות שייפתח לנו הים. סך הכול כבר תקופה ארוכה ששנינו לא עבדנו כי רצינו לסמוך על ״אמונה וביטחון״, ובאמת הצלחנו להסתדר. התפללתי להשם שיכוון וידריך אותנו מה רצונו. בסופו של דבר הסכמתי לשתף עם אסא פעולה. אסא התקשר לערוץ הרדיו ״קול הנשמה״ להציע להם כתרומה את הבית שלנו. תוך שעה הגיעו אלינו לבית שלושה רבנים של הערוץ והסבירו לנו בדרך של גימטריות כמה אנחנו צודקים ברצוננו לתרום להם את הבית שלנו. הם אמרו גם שלא נדאג כי אסא הוא בן יחיד ובוודאי בעתיד יקבל ירושה. לחיזוק דבריהם טענו ששם המשפחה של אסא הוא מיראש, ואם נשנה את סדר האותיות יצאו המילים: ״אם ירש״, ומכאן שאנחנו יכולים לשמוח שבחרנו בעצה הנכונה. לא יכולתי לסבול את השיחה אתם. אנשים ששומרים היטב על הבית שלהם, ומעודדים אחרים לתרום להם את ביתם, לא הבנתי איך הם יכולים להיקרא רבנים. כשהם עזבו את הבית החלטנו שנשאיר את הרעיון לתרום פתוח עד שנמצא את המקום שאליו ראוי לתרום.

אסא רצה שנתארח אצל משפחות מברסלב, ולפעמים לתקופות ארוכות, כי רצה ללמוד על אורח החיים שלהם. אני הרגשתי שהוא חיפש דרך איך להתחמק ממצב שנהיה לבד כדי שלא יצטרך להתמודד אתי ועם הדרישות שלי, וזה פגע בי מאוד. רציתי שתהיה לנו פרטיות כי קיוויתי שנוכל להשקיע בקשר בינינו, ולא הבנתי למה לו זה לא חשוב. שנאתי להיות אורחת ולוותר על הפינה השקטה שלי, אבל גם היה לי קשה להרגיש שהוא עושה לי טובה להישאר אתי בבית כשהלב שלו בכלל לא שם. העדפתי לנסוע אתו, וחשבתי שאולי זה ירענן ויחדש את האווירה בינינו. התארחנו כמה שבתות ביישוב ברסלבי בצפון הארץ. לא הרגשתי שייכת.

יום אחד אסא חזר הביתה בהתלהבות גדולה, הוא דיבר ברחוב עם איזה ברסלבר מרכב של הפצה שסיפר לו על רבי ישראל ועל ״הפתק הקדוש״ שבו התגלה השיר נ נח נחמ נחמן מאומן. הוא היה כולו נלהב ונרגש, והסביר לי שהפתק הזה הוא עניין גדול מאוד, ושרבי ישראל אמר שזה הנס והפלא הגדול ביותר שהיה מיום בריאת העולם. באותה שבת התארחנו אצל ההורים שלי. אימא שלי, שידעה שאנחנו מתקרבים לרבי נחמן קנתה לנו ממפיצים שעברו ברחוב חוברת שנקראת ״אני נ נח נחמ נחמן מאומן״. על הכריכה יש תמונה של רבי ישראל מרים ידיים כלפי מעלה על רקע ים המלח. מהרגע שהתחלתי לקרוא את החוברת, גמעתי כל מילה שלה בצמא, ולא יכולתי לעזוב אותה עד שסיימתי לקרוא את כולה. החוברת ענתה על כל הקושיות שהיו לי, ונתנה הסבר לכל מה שהציק לי. (לימים התברר לי שמי שליקט את המקורות מדברי

חז״ל, והוציא לאור את החוברת הזו היה דניאל, אבל אז עוד לא הכרנו אותו). בחוברת היו ציטוטים מהתנ״ך ומהזוהר על השיר העשירי שכתוב שעתיד להתגלות (תשעת השירים הקודמים מופיעים בתנ״ך, כגון ״שירת הים״, ״שירת חנה״, ״שירת האזינו״), רבי ישראל בער אודסר אמר שה״שיר חדש״ התגלה והוא נ נח נחמ נחמן מאומן, שהוא שיר הגאולה, שיר לכל העולם, גם הגויים עוד ישירו נ נח. הוא גם אמר שעכשיו ההפצה עולה על הכול, וזה מה שיקרב את הגאולה.

הסכמתי שאסא יצא להפצות עם החברים של ההפצה כי הבנתי שזה דיבור של רבי ישראל שאמר שצריך לארגן רכבים של הפצה, להתחיל מודה חדשה של מכירת ספרים של רבי נחמן, לעצור ברמזורים, לשיר ולרקוד, ולהודיע שיש רבי נחמן בעולם.

באותה תקופה היינו נשואים כשלוש שנים. שכרנו דירה בצפת כדי להיות חלק מהקהילה של ״הנ-נחים״ שם. הם היו יוצאים כל השבוע להפיץ יחד, ונשותיהם היו ביחסי חברות טובים . אסא הצטרף אליהם להפצה באזור המרכז, ואני הייתי בבית לבד משבת לשבת, מחכה לו שיחזור. שמחתי שסוף סוף אני בפינה משלי ולא מתארחת בבית זר, אך הרגשתי מאוד בודדה. אני זוכרת שנכנסתי למיטה, כיסיתי את עצמי בשמיכה עד מעל הראש ובכיתי וצעקתי להשם שקשה לי, שאני לבד. בסמוך אליי, על המיטה היה טייפ. לא ידעתי אם יש בפנים קלטת אך הרגשתי צורך להפעיל אותו. לחצתי על כפתור ה-PLAY. לפתע שמעתי את קולו של הסבא אומר בטון מרגיע: ״רבנו הקדוש נמצא עם כל אחד ואחד״. התמלאתי בשמחה, הבנתי שאני לא לבד. הרגשתי שרבי ישראל, הסבא, הוא אתי, יודע מה אני מרגישה, מבין את הצער שלי ויורד עד אליי לחזק אותי, הרגשתי שהוא עוטף אותי באהבה, וזה נתן לי הרבה כוח להתגבר ולהתחזק.

כששמענו שרבי ישראל בער אודסר לא השאיר ירושה לילדיו, אלא אסף את כל הכספים שקיבל מ״ביטוח לאומי״, מצדקות ומפדיונות והקים קרן על סך מיליון וארבע מאות אלף שקלים להפצת הספרים של רבי נחמן במחיר הדפוס, התפעלנו מאוד. ב״אבי״ הנחל״ הסבא כתב: ״אני מוכן למסור את חיי נפשי ממוני וכל אשר לי בשביל נפש אחת של יהודי אפילו בשביל רגע אחד לגרום לו להרהור של תשובה״, ראינו שהצדיק מקיים את כל הדיבורים שלו, ושאפנו ללמוד ממנו להפקיר, בפרט ששמענו שכששאלו את רבי ישראל מה הוא חושב על השיחה שרבנו אמר (בשיחות הר״ן נאי) ״שלא צריך להפקיר את הכול כדי להתקרב לצדיק״ ורבי ישראל ענה: ״נכון שרבנו אמר כך, אבל היום, בדור שלנו, בשביל להתקרב לצדיק צריך להפקיר הכול״. זה חיזק בנו את החשק להפקיר את הבית לצדקה. הרגשנו שסוף סוף התפילות שלנו התקבלו ומכוונים אותנו משמים, כי עכשיו כששמענו שיש ״קרן של רבי ישראל להדפסת והפצת ספרי רבי נחמן״ זה אומר שיש מקום שאפשר לתרום לשם בלי שאנשים ינצלו את זה לרווח שלהם. התפללנו שנזכה למכור מהר ובקלות את הבית שלנו, כדי לתרום את הכסף ל״קרן של רבי ישראל להפצת הספרים״.

כשחיפשנו קונים, התחילו אצלי חששות וספקות, האם אנחנו עושים דבר נכון? באחד הימים החלטתי לפתוח את ספר אבי״ הנחל, ולבקש מהסבא שיראה לי מה העצה. הספר נפתח לי על המילים: ״והעיקר אין שום קביעות בעולם כלל״. סגרתי את הספר במהירות, לא רציתי להאמין שבאמת קיבלתי תשובה לשאלה שלי. החלטתי לפתוח שוב, אולי הפעם ייפתח לי ההפך? הלב שלי התחיל לדפוק חזק כשנפתח לי מכתב אחר לגמרי שבסופו היה כתוב: ״אין שום קביעות בעולם כלל וכלל״. סגרתי את הספר, הבנתי שהסבא עונה לי בדיוק על השאלה. כמו תזכורת, שהעולם הזה הוא עראי ואין בו שום קביעות. החלטתי לפתוח שוב, וכשבפעם השלישית ראיתי שכתוב ״רבנו הקדוש אמר שאין שום קביעות בעולם כלל״, הרגשתי שקיבלתי את החיזוק שחיפשתי. החלטתי לעזור לאסא לחפש קונה לבית ולמכור.

קיבלנו אור גדול מההתקרבות לרבי נחמן, אך יחד עם זאת הבעיות שהיו בינינו לא פסקו. הייתי בוכה וכואבת מכך שהוא לא זקוק לי, והוא היה נותן לי להרגיש ולהבין היטב שהמחויבות שלו כלפיי כבעל, מציקה לו ומפריעה לו להתקדם בעבודת השם כרצונו.

באחד מערבי החורף, היינו בדירה בצפת, שנינו לבד. אסא היה מאוד לא רגוע. הוא התיישב על המיטה בחדר שינה, החזיק את ראשו בשתי ידיו ולא זז במשך שעה ארוכה. כששאלתי מה מציק לו, הוא הרים את הראש, הסתכל עליי במבט שנתן לי להבין שיש לו משהו מאוד חשוב להגיד לי. לא ידעתי למה לצפות. ואז הוא אמר שכבר הרבה זמן שהוא מתלבט אם אנחנו צריכים להמשיך את הקשר בינינו, והיום הוא הגיע למסקנה סופית שאנחנו צריכים להתגרש. לא הספקתי לעכל את מה שאמר לי ומיד הוסיף שכיוון שהגיע להחלטה כזו, אז מבחינה הלכתית אסור לנו לישון באותו הבית, ולכן הוא יחפש לעצמו מקום לישון ללילה. די הופתעתי מהנחרצות שבה הוא אמר את הדברים. מה גרם לו להחליט פתאום החלטה סופית שכזו? היינו נשואים כבר שלוש וחצי שנים. לבסוף אמר שיש לו וידוי שהוא רוצה להגיד לי. הוא היה נבוך ואמר שהוא מצטער שלא אמר לי את זה קודם כי הוא לא היה בטוח שזו באמת המציאות והוא באמת חשב שחתונה תעזור לו להתמודד עם הבעיה שהוא סוחב אתו מאז שהוא ילד, אבל הוא רוצה להיות כן אתי כי הוא מרגיש שהגיע למבוי סתום, וכמה שניסה להכחיש הוא בעצם חייב להודות שיש לו מלחמה עם היצרים

של משיכה לגברים...! הוא הסביר שברור לו שזה איסור תורה ותמיד נלחם לא להיכשל בזה, אך הוא חי בתוך מלחמה יומיומית עם עצמו כדי להתגבר על הדחף הפנימי של התאווה למשכב זכר, ולבסוף אמר שהוא חושב שהנישואין שלנו לא יובילו לשום מקום, ולכן הוא רוצה להתגרש.

לא רציתי להאמין למה ששמעתי. לא הייתי מוכנה לקבל בשום אופן שזו האמת. רציתי להאמין שדברים יכולים להשתנות, שאולי זה רק מצב הרוח שלו. התקפתי אותו בצרור של שאלות, כדי שיסביר לי למה הוא מתכוון. הייתי מבולבלת מאוד, לא ידעתי מה לחשוב. עברנו כל כך הרבה ביחד בשנים האחרונות, נקשרתי אליו כל כך, איך הוא עושה לי את זה? במקום לכעוס עליו ולשמור לו טינה. למה סיבך אותי כל כך עם עצמי ואתו, ולמה הוא לא סיפר לי את זה לפני החתונה ולא נתן לי את האפשרות לבחור איך אני רוצה לחיות, ולמה ניצל את האמון המלא שלי בו? הרי אם זה נכון מה שהוא מנסה להגיד לי, אז כל הקשר שלנו הוא מקח טעות, במקום זה הרגשתי שוב שאני מרחמת עליו ולא מסוגלת לכעוס עליו. הרגשתי שאולי אם אני אעזור לו יותר הוא יצליח לצאת מהבעיות שלו, אבל הוא המשיך להתעקש שאני לא מבינה כלום, ואני לא יכולה להבין מה הוא חי ומה הוא עובר, ושהעצה הכי נכונה היא שאני אניח לו. כשהבחין שאני נסערת הוסיף שהוא מאוד אוהב אותי, אבל דווקא בגלל זה הוא חושב שיהיה לשנינו טוב יותר אם נתגרש, ונלך כל אחד לדרכו. באותו הזמן לא קלטתי שהוא סוף סוף, אחרי שלוש וחצי שנים, פתח את הלב וסיפר לי את האמת. אני חשבתי בכנות שהוא בתוך איזה פלונטר עם עצמו, ושאסור לי לשחרר אותו בצורה כזו, כי מה שהוא עושה זה כמו סוג של התאבדות, או ענישה עצמית על משהו שהוא הסתבך עם עצמו. התעקשתי אתו שהוא מדבר שטויות ושהוא לא יצליח להשתחרר ממני. בהתחלה לא רציתי להתמודד עם הגילוי החדש. העדפתי להדחיק את הדברים, להכחיש את המציאות, לקוות שאולי נתעורר למציאות אחרת. הערצתי את המלחמה שהוא עשה כדי להתגבר על הבעיה שהוא חי בתוכה, הערכתי את העובדה שהוא לא נכנע ליצרים ואת העקשנות שלו לחפש פתרונות בצורה אמתית, לכן כל פעם שהוא חיפש דרך להשתחרר ממני, ולשכנע אותי שצריך להתגרש, אני הייתי מחזיקה בו חזק ולא עוזבת, אך יחד עם זאת הייתי זועקת להשם מעומק הלב שיעשה איזה נס שהמצב ישתנה, שמשהו טוב יקרה, שנמצא איזה פתרון, כי קשה לי, כי קשה לו, כי אנחנו לא יכולים יותר, שאנחנו בתוך מבוי סתום, ואי-אפשר יותר להמשיך את חיי הנישואין!

כך סחבנו בכל זאת עוד תקופה ביחד, מנסים לדלג ולהבליג על הבעיות, ולשים אותם איכשהו בצד עד שנגיע להחלטה שקולה וברורה.

באחד הפעמים שאסא יצא להפיץ עם החברים, הם סיפרו לו שיש בירושלים חבר, מפיץ של הנ-נח, ששנתיים קודם לכן, מיד לאחר ההסתלקות של רבי ישראל, מכר את הבית שלו ותרם את הכסף כדי להפיץ את הספרים של רבי נחמן, וגם את הרכב שלו הקדיש להפצה. הוא הראשון בארץ שכיסה את הרכב שלו בסטיקרים של נ נח נחמ נחמן מאומן ושמו דניאל אמבש. היינו סקרנים להכיר את דניאל ואשתו, ולשמוע מהם איך התמודדו עם הקשיים אחרי שתרמו את הבית שלהם לצדקה, בפרט ששמענו שיש להם גם שבעה ילדים ולפני שבוע נולד להם בן נוסף. אסא חיפש להכיר את דניאל, וכששמע על הברית של התינוק, ראה בזה הזדמנות ונסע לירושלים. הוא שמח מאוד להכיר חבר שמשתדל בכל יכולתו לחזק את ההפצה. באותו זמן רצינו לעזוב את הדירה השכורה בצפת, ולמצוא מקום בירושלים. אסא הודיע לי שהוא ביקש מדניאל ואילנה שנגור אצלם לתקופה קצרה כדי שיהיה לנו קל יותר לחפש דירה. הוא ביקש שאבוא אתו לירושלים. הם פינו לנו חדר, והתארחנו אצלם בבית מספר חודשים. לא היה קשה לראות עליי שאני בצער מהבעיות עם אסא, והם השתדלו לעזור לנו לשלום בית. אילנה ודניאל מצאו את עצמם מזכירים לאסא להתקשר אליי כשהוא בהפצה, נעלם לי לשעות ארוכות ולפעמים לימים, החברים בהפצה היו מפצירים בו לחזור הביתה לאשתו. עם הזמן, הבנתי שזה לא הולך להשתנות, ושום דבר לא יכול לעזור, עם כל הרצון הטוב, אין פתרון עבורנו. דניאל חשב שאולי עדיף שנשכור דירה רק לשנינו. מצאנו דירה בגבעת שאול. גרנו שם כמה חודשים עד שלא יכולנו להחזיק מעמד יותר. אסא אמר שהוא רוצה להיות חופשי, ושלקשר בינינו אין עתיד. כאב לי, אבל הסכמתי אתו שאין טעם להמשיך לגרור את החיים ביחד, והגיע הזמן לסיים את הקשר בינינו, החלטנו סופית להתגרש. מיד למחרת התגרשנו בבית הדין של הרב קרליץ בבני ברק. את הדירה שהייתה לנו בבני ברק מכרנו, ואת הכסף, כמו שהחלטנו כבר מזמן, תרמנו ל"קרן של רבי ישראל דוב אודסר להפצת הספרים של רבי נחמן". הרגשתי שסוף סוף עשיתי את הצעד הנכון.

הגירושין מאסא השאירו אותי עם מועקה ותחושה של כישלון. גם שנים אחר כך, עדיין היה לי קשה להשלים עם העובדה שאסא לא נמשך לנשים, ושהוא לא רצה אותי. כבודי נפגע. לא הבנתי למה השם עשה לי את זה. איך ייתכן שאני, שחשבתי שאני כל כך מושלמת ובעלת רצונות טובים, קיבלתי שידוך משמים עם בחור עם נטיות הומוסקסואליות, ושאני לא מעניינת אותו בכלל!!

ניסיתי להתגבר, לשכוח ממנו, ולהתחיל חיים חדשים. שכרתי דירת קרקע קטנה בת שתי חדרים בשכונת קריית משה, ליד אילנה, ויחד אתה החלטתי שזו ההזדמנות להשקיע בהקמת בית ספר לילדים ממשפחות

ברסלביות שמאמינות בנ-נח, היות שבתקופה ההיא לא הייתה שום מסגרת מתאימה לילדים של משפחות המאמינות בנ-נח, והרגשתי שיש לי אחריות חינוכית כמורה.

קארי הייתה בת 38 כשהכרתי אותה. היא עלתה לארץ מאמריקה כדי להתגייס לצה"ל, ומשחזרה בתשובה, התחתנה והתגרשה שש פעמים. היו לה ארבעה ילדים מבעלים שונים, והיא הייתה חולה במחלות קשות, אחת מהן סופנית, הרופאים נתנו לה שנתיים לחיות. היא הגיעה לדניאל ואילנה הרבה פעמים לשבתות, וביקשה מהם עזרה. היה חשוב לה שילדיה יקבלו חינוך טוב, ושיהיה לה כוחות להחזיק מעמד כמה שאפשר. היא אמרה להם שרק אתם "עדיין יש לה תקווה". דניאל ואילנה ניסו לדבר עם אנשים כדי לעזור לה, אך כולם מסביב משכו ידיהם מהמקרה הקשה שלה. בפרק של "הסיפור האישי של אילנה" אתם תקראו איך התגלגלו הדברים עד שקארי הפכה להיות האישה השנייה. אך ללא ספק זו הייתה החלטה לא פשוטה, ובעיקר אמיצה. ילדיה של קארי: צילה בת 13, יאן בן 11, אנסטסיה בת שש, וסמי בן שנה, היו ילדים לא קלים. צילה ויאן נפלטו מהמסגרות הקיימות של בתי הספר כיוון שהיו עם קשיי למידה, בעיות קשב וריכוז ובעיות התנהגות. בית הספר היחיד שקיבל אותם היה בית ספר לחינוך מיוחד "תדהר", וזה פגע בדימוי העצמי שלהם. קארי ביקשה שנמצא פתרון עבורם, כיוון שעברו חיים קשים. כמעט בכל שנה עברו דירה, עם אבא מתחלף, ובחוסר יציבות מתמיד. יחד עם אילנה החלטנו לראות את זה כפרויקט של חסד, ועם עוד משפחה של חברים, ניסינו להקים בית ספר לבנות של הנ-נח. אהבתי מאוד להשקיע את כל כולי בעבודה. בהתחלה הפכנו את הדירה שלי לבית ספר, ומאוחר יותר שכרנו מקום ברחוב "נגיארה", במיוחד עבור בית הספר. העבודה כמורה וכמחנכת, מילאה אותי בסיפוק. אני ואילנה הפכנו להיות חברות יותר ויותר קרובות. הערצתי את המסירות של דניאל ואילנה כלפי ילדיה של קארי. יאן למשל, היה בן 11, אך לא ידע לדבר. הוא היה מגמגם כל מיני הברות והתקשה לבטא את עצמו, אולי זו הסיבה שהיה נוהג באלימות, והיה מאוד קשה להרגיע אותו. גם צילה הייתה ילדה פרועה ותזזיתית, הם היו מציקים לילדים של אילנה תוך כדי דהירה בבית וברחוב על רולרס, היה קשה מאוד לעצור אותם. דניאל ואילנה טיפלו בהם מכל הלב, והשקיעו בהם אהבה עד בלי די. לראשונה בחייהם, הילדים של קארי הרגישו מוגנים ובטוחים. אני זוכרת את היום שיאן וצילה החליטו לקרא לדניאל אבא, זה היה מרגש מאוד. יאן חיבק את דניאל בחזקה, והיה ניכר עליו שהנפש שלו מצאה מרגוע. לקארי הם היו קוראים "מאמי", ולאילנה "מאמו" (אימא בצרפתית) זו הייתה חוויה נפלאה לראות איך נבנה תא משפחתי חדש ומיוחד כל כך. אני זוכרת את עצמי מביטה בדניאל, וחושבת שהייתי רוצה בעל אחראי ומסור שיהיה אבא לילדים שלי בדיוק כמו דניאל שאוהב את הילדים שלו ואת הילדים של קארי...

אזמרה הייתה אז בת 18, מפיצה שהגיעה ממושב בדרום לחזק את ההפצה בירושלים, ואהבה מאוד את המשפחה. הפכנו להיות חבורה שכזו: אילנה, קארי, אני ואזמרה. היינו לומדות יחד, מכינות שבתות יחד ומארגנות הפצות לנשים יחד. והפכנו להיות כמו משפחה אחת. הערצתי את אילנה שפתחה את הבית ואפשרה להשגחה לגלגל את הדברים כמו שהתגלגלו. קארי, לתדהמת הרופאים, הבריאה מהמחלה, והתמלאה אמביציה ומרץ לחיים. היו לה רעיונות גרנדיוזיים להפצה, והיא הכניסה בכולנו הרבה התלהבות. אפילו שהרופאים אמרו לה שמסוכן בשבילה להיכנס להיריון, היא התעקשה שהיא רוצה עוד ילד.

היה לי כיף עם כולם. עברה כבר שנה מהגירושין מאסא, והרגשתי שאני סוף סוף חוזרת לעצמי, שוכחת מהעבר ומכל הצרות, ומתחילה לחשוב ולחפש מי הוא הזיווג האמתי שלי.

היינו יושבים כולנו יחד, מתכננים הופעות מוזיקה, הפצות מקוריות, לומדים יחד מהספרים ומדברים שעות על הסבא. דניאל סיפר לנו על ההפצות הראשונות, ועל הזמן שהסבא חי אתו ועם אילנה בבית. מצאתי את עצמי חולמת בהקיץ "הלוואי והייתי חלק מסיפור החיים שלו", בתוכי ידעתי שאתו אני רוצה להביא ילדים לעולם. מיום ליום הרצון שלי להיות אתו התחזק. חשבתי לעצמי שאם יש לו כבר שתי נשים, אילנה וקארי, אז למה שלא נהיה שלוש? יום אחד החלטתי שאני אעשה צעד אמיץ, ואציע לו נישואין. ביקשתי לשוחח אתו. וסיפרתי לו על מה שאני מרגישה. היה ניכר על דניאל שהוא היה מופתע. הוא לא ציפה ממני לכזו הצעה. הוא חשב שמין הראוי כמחווה חברית, לשאול תחילה את אסא מה הוא חושב, ואיך הוא מרגיש עם זה, מכיוון שהם חברים טובים. אסא שמח מאוד, ואיחל לנו הרבה מזל טוב. הוא אמר שכבר מזמן הייתה לו הרגשה שדניאל ואני זה זיווג אמת, ובסתר לבו חיכה שזה יקרה, כי זה ישחרר אותו מהעול של האחריות שהרגיש כלפיי.

החיים עם דניאל החזירו לי את שלוות הנפש שלי. הנשיות חזרה אליי, ואתה גם כבודי האבוד. לאט לאט החוסרים שהטרידו את ימיי, התחילו להתמלא. שמחתי להגשים את עצמי בתור אישה. היחסים עם דניאל, מכל הבחינות, היו בדיוק מה שחיפשתי. הפתיחות, תשומת הלב, השיחות, ההבנה, העבודה המשותפת, נסכו בי רגיעה ותחושה של שלמות. התחרות הסמויה עם שאר הנשים הגבירה עוד יותר את האתגר...

אילנה, קארי ואזמרה (שתקראו בפרק שלה איך גם היא בחרה להצטרף למשפחה) היו מלאות חיוניות, בעלות שמחת חיים, חיוביות, אינטליגנטיות ונעימות. החיים אתן, החברות המיוחדת, הקנאה, המריבות, האילוצים, הצורך להתגבר ולהסתדר בינינו, הכניס ממד של הבנת החיים מזווית אחרת. פתאום, מאותה סטודנטית שלומדת ספרי מוסר כתיאוריה על עבודת המידות, העבודה הפכה להיות מציאות יומיומית. אני בטוחה שהניסיונות שעברו על אימהותנו הקדושות, עוברים על כל אישה גם בדור הזה. חז״ל הכינו לנו מראש חיזוק לדורות, בגמרא מסכת יומא לח׳ ב כתוב: ״אין אדם נוגע במוכן לחברו ואין מלכות נוגעת בחברתה אפילו כמלא נימה״, כלומר: אף אחת לא יכולה לגעת במוכן לי, במלכות שלי, במה ששייך לי, על החלק שלי אני לא צריכה לוותר, כל אחד מקבל במדויק את מה שמגיע לו לפי חשבונות שמים. לרצות שגם לשנייה יהיה טוב, לשמוח מההצלחה של השנייה, זה עוד עניין שבוודאי מצריך עבודה אינטנסיבית, אך זה מה שנקרא להיות ברסלב: ״לב הבוסר בחלק חברו״, שרוצה את טובת חברו. נהגנו לצחוק בינינו הנשים כשכל אחת היא מלכה, המלחמות בינינו הן סוג של מלחמת עולם, וכל חיבור של שלום בינינו הביא אותנו לחשוב שאנחנו בתהליך של גאולה.

אסא שכר את הבית ששימש כבית מדרש למפיצים בשכונת גבעת שאול וגר שם. היה בבעלותו רכב גדול, הוא ארגן את ההפצה של הבנים, והיה הגבאי של בית הכנסת. בשלב מסוים הוא ניסה שוב להתחתן, אך זה לא החזיק מעמד יותר משבוע והם התגרשו.

קארי נכנסה להיריון, היינו בהתרגשות. זה היה נס אמתי, וגם הרופאים היו המומים. בחודשי ההיריון המתקדמים שכרנו בית בליפתא, על מנת שתוכל להיות במנוחה לקראת הלידה. ניכר היה עליה שהיא מאושרת ורגועה. משלד עצמות היא הבריאה, והשמינה בצורה יפה. לאורך כל ההיריון היא התפללה להשם שלתינוק יהיה לב טוב כמו של אבא שלו. כיוון שבילדים טיפלנו אילנה אזמרה ואני, לקארי הייתה הפריבילגיה לטפל בעצמה בשקט, בנוף הקסום של הבית החדש בליפתא. היא קראה הרבה מספרי רבי נחמן, וכך גם שיפרה את העברית שלה (כזכור שפת האם שלה היא אנגלית). ליוויתי אותה לבדיקות אולטרא סאונד אצל רופאת הנשים הפרטית שלה, והיא ביקשה שאהיה אתה בזמן הלידה.

באותה תקופה עבדתי עם דניאל בהוצאת ספר חדש על ההפצה והמפיצים. שעות על גבי שעות ישבנו יחד מול המחשב, עד השעות הקטנות של הלילה, בריכוז מקסימלי, עברנו על ההגהות. לא היינו שמים לב לזמן שעובר. אילנה או אזמרה היו דואגות לנו לשתייה. אני זוכרת את הטלפון של קארי ב02:00 לפנות בוקר מהבית בליפתא, כשהודיעה לנו שהלידה מתחילה וביקשה שדניאל יגיע אליה מהר לקחת אותה לבית החולים. דניאל זינק מהכיסא ורצנו לרכב. נסענו כולנו יחד לבית החולים. דניאל, קארי, אילנה, אזמרה ואני. בדרך ליוו אותנו ארבע יונים לבנות. הרגשנו שזה סימן לברכה. הלידה של יהונתן, בניגוד ללידות הקודמות של קארי, הייתה לידה מהירה וקלה, וקארי הייתה מאוד נרגשת.

אהבתי להפיץ בעיר, בכפר, בקניון וברחוב. בכל מקום, לחלק לנשים צילום של הפתק מרבי נחמן, להסביר להן מה זה נ- נח, ולמכור ספרים של רבי נחמן ושל שיחות מתומללות של רבי ישראל.

בשלוש השנים הראשונות אמנם נבנה קשר מאוד מיוחד בין ארבעתנו: אילנה, קארי, אזמרה ואני, אך היו לא מעט מריבות וויכוחים בינינו. לפעמים המריבות האלה הכבידו עליי כל כך, שמצאתי את עצמי מתגעגעת לתקופה שהייתי לבד עם אסא, בלי שאישה נוספת מעבירה עליי ביקורת או מנסה להשתלט, אבל יחד עם זאת, לא הייתי מוכנה בשום אופן לוותר על החיים עם דניאל, וכשהסתדרתי טוב עם הנשים, הרגשתי שקיבלתי את החיים הכי יפים שיכולתי לבקש. דניאל חשש מהמריבות בינינו, לפעמים זה היה מכניס אותו לספקות אם המבנה של כמה נשים נכון או לא נכון. הוא אפילו אמר פעם שאולי המבנה הזה מקשה עלינו, אולי אנחנו רוצות לחיות אחרת, ואולי יהיה לכל אחת טוב יותר אם כולנו נתגרש ונפרק את החבילה.

לא רציתי שהוא ייכנס לספקות, וכאב לי שזה מה שהוא חושב. לא רציתי שנתגרש, וגם הנשים האחרות לא. החזקנו בעמדה ברורה שלא נוותר, לא עליו ולא זו על זו. ניסינו להסביר לו שגם אם לפעמים קשה לנו, אין שום סיבה לדאגה, טוב לנו ביחד אפילו אם אנחנו רבות, ככה זה נשים וכמו שאחיות רבות, ואנחנו קרובות יותר מאחיות, וזה אך טבעי.

הרגשתי שלפרק את מה שבנינו יחד זו כפיות טובה כלפי ההשגחה שחיברה בינינו. אני מאמינה שכל הסיפור שלנו לא היה מתקיים אם זו לא הייתה השגחה פרטית מדוקדקת ומדויקת. רציתי מאוד שיהיה איזשהו סימן משמים שישים סוף לספק, ושנפסיק לחשוש אם זה נכון או לא נכון שאנחנו חיים ככה, אם זה רצון השם או לא רצון השם ויוכיח לדניאל שאנחנו בדרך הנכונה. עד היום אני נדהמת מעצמת הביטחון שהייתה לי כשאמרתי לדניאל שאני בטוחה שעד כ״ג באדר, תאריך יום ההולדת שלי ויום הנישואין שלנו, יגיע סימן משמים שיחזק את כולנו.

כל הנשים רצו שיגיע סימן. אמנם לא קבענו מה צריך להיות "הסימן משמיים", אבל הסכמנו שכל דבר טוב יכול להיות סימן. אם יצטרף מפיץ חדש, או שתתגלה קלטת חדשה של הסבא שלא ידענו עליה, כל חיזוק שיגיע ויראה שאנחנו בדרך הנכונה, ייחשב לסימן טוב עבורנו. חשבתי לעצמי שצורת החיים שלנו מאפשרת לי מעין הזדמנות להגשים את החלום שלי להביא ילד לעולם. כיוון שכבר תשע שנים איני מצליחה להרות בעצמי, אם אתפלל שתגיע אישה אחרת לבעלי, ייחשב לי לזכות הילד שתביא. חשבתי שמצאתי רעיון גאוני. כשסיפרתי לדניאל, זה לא כל כך מצא חן בעיניו, הוא אמר שלהכניס עוד אישה למשפחה זו אחריות גדולה, שיכולה גם חס ושלום להרוס את הכול. הוא ניסה לנחם אותי שגם אני עוד יכולה להביא ילדים, וזו לא סיבה להכניס עוד צרות; ושאם אני רוצה להתפלל, אז שאתפלל על עצמי שיהיו לי ילדים; ושרבי נחמן אמר שגם "מעשים טובים" נחשב לילדים. חשבתי בלבי: "אני עוד אפתיע אותו..."

אילנה, קארי, אזמרה ואני ידענו שהצדקה והחסד בינינו הנשים, פותחים את הברכה. היינו נחושות להצליח במשימה ששמתי לנו כמטרה. קארי כינסה אותנו לאספת חירום בעניין התכנית עד כ"ג באדר. היא הציעה שנחזק את ה"יחד" שלנו, שנעשה יותר דברים שיחזקו את הקשר בינינו, ואולי זה יביא לנו ברכה, למשל היא אמרה שהיא רוצה שיהיו לי ילדים, והיא מאמינה שזה יכול לקרות דרך ההשגחה, שאישה תצטרף אלינו. מימוש התכנית הפך להיות חוויה משותפת מדהימה. החלטנו שכדי שנהיה מרוכזות במטרה, נקום כל בוקר ביחד בעלות השחר, ונתחיל את היום בריצה למעיין של ליפתא, שהיה בעמק הסמוך, נתרכז יחד כעשר דקות וכך נכין עצמנו לתפילת שחרית ביחד, אחר כך נאכל ארוחת בוקר ביחד, נלמד ביחד, ונקבע את המשך התכנית של אותו היום. בסך הכול הצלחנו לבצע את התכנית. האתגר יצר אווירה מאוד דינמית בינינו. זה היה חודש עמוס פעילויות; התפללנו הרבה אצל הסבא ובכותל, חילקנו תהלים וכיפות לחיילים, הלכנו ביחד לחזק חולים בבתי חולים, הקדשנו אלבום תמונות של הסבא לעשרות קברי צדיקים ברחבי הארץ. ככל שהזמן התקרב לתאריך היעד, המתח גבר וחיפשנו מה לעשות. קראנו את הספרים של רבי נחמן שדיבור אמת מעלה את התפילות, החלטנו להתחזק בדיבורי אמת בינינו. פתחנו את לבנו אחת בפני השנייה וסיפרנו את כל הסודות הכמוסים שלנו, ניסינו להיות כנות ככל שאפשר, וחיכינו במתח ובציפייה...

באחד הימים, כשחשבנו מה לעשות, קיבלתי הודעה כתובה לנייד: "קבר רחל נפתח לציבור הרחב". קפצנו משמחה. הרגשנו שרחל אמנו מזמינה אותנו להתפלל אצלה. נסענו מיד. בכינו בתפילה לרחל אמנו שתעזור לנו ללכת בדרכה ובדרך אימהותנו הקדושות, ותתפלל עלינו שיהיה לנו סימן טוב.

הגיעו ימי הפורים, עשרה ימים לפני התאריך שקבענו. הגיעו אורחים רבים לסעודת פורים. קארי מצאה פנקס טלפונים ישן שלה, והתקשרה למספרי הטלפון שמצאה בו כדי להזמין את כולם לסעודה. בין המוזמנים הייתה עליזה. עליזה הגיעה מחופשת לכיפה אדומה עם חברה שהייתה מחופשת לזאב, כשסלסלת ממתקים בחיקה, היא נכנסה לבית בריצה תיאטרלית וצעקה: "הצילו! הצילו! מי יכול להציל אותי?" היא חילקה ממתקים לילדים. קארי הציעה לה ללכת להתפלל ב"ציון" (מקום קבורה) של רבי ישראל, והיא הלכה לשם. אחרי החג המשכנו בתכנית, והתפללנו לישועת השם.

כ"ג אדר הגיע. הכינו לי מסיבת יום הולדת, ערכו שולחן בשפע ומכל טוב, קישטו את הבית, דניאל ניגן באורגן, וכולנו רקדנו. אף שהגענו לתאריך ועוד לא היה שום סימן מיוחד עבורנו, בתוך לבנו קיווינו כולנו שבכל זאת יקרה משהו ברגע האחרון של כ"ג באדר.

באותה תקופה לא סיפרנו עדיין לאף אדם מחוץ למשפחה שאנחנו נשואים ביחד. חמש שנים שמרנו על זה בסוד.

עליזה הפתיעה אותנו, והגיעה למסיבת יום ההולדת עם מגן דוד מבמבוק שהכינה לי במתנה. ישבנו יחד הנשים, והיא סיפרה לנו שחלמה חלום, והיא מתביישת לספר לנו. לפתע היא קמה וביקשה מדניאל שיפסיק לנגן כי היא חייבת לדבר אתו, ותוך דקות מספר סיפרה לו שבחלום ראתה שהוא מנגן באורגן, ואילנה, קארי, אדרת ואזמרה רוקדות סביבו; והיא רוצה לדעת אם זה נכון שכולנו נשואות לו. דניאל ענה לה בפשטות: "כן". בהתרגשות גדולה הכריזה עליזה, בלי להתבלבל, שהיא היא האישה החמישית!

אז היה סימן.

כשעליזה התחתנה עם דניאל הרגשתי גאוות ניצחון. היא הייתה בשבילי סימן של הצלחה. כשהיא ילדה את בתיה, אחרי עשר שנים שלא נכנסתי להיריון, היה זה סגירת מעגל. עם התלתלים הזהובים והחיוך המתוק שלה היא שבתה את הלב של כל מי שראה אותה. ילדה מלאת שמחה, שרה במשך שעות, רוקדת ומוחאת כפיים.

עליזה ואני הסתדרנו לא רע, אבל היה קל בהרבה אם היא לא הייתה מתערבת בענייני כל אחד בבית וגורמת לסכסוכים. תמיד הייתי אומרת לה שמה שקורה עם אחרים "זה לא עניינה" והיא הייתה אומרת: "אנחנו משפחה אחת, וכולם צריכים לדעת הכול על כולם". את עצמה היא לא הייתה באמת חושפת, אבל היה לה כישרון – להיראות כנה.

היו שבתות שאכלנו בבית המדרש, כל המשפחה והמפיצים. באחת הפעמים, עליזה סיפרה לי שהיא נמשכת לאסא, ולכן שמה לב למבטים שלי אליו, ואמרה שמעניין אותה לדעת מה באמת אני מרגישה כלפיו. היא שאלה אותי אם זה לא מפריע לי שלפעמים הוא אוכל אתנו בשבתות בבית המדרש. אני מצדי לא אהבתי את השאלות שלה, ולא רציתי לדבר אתה על זה. כשחזרנו לבית, היא הפתיעה אותי כשאמרה לדניאל: "אדרת משקרת לך, אני ראיתי איך היא הסתכלה על אסא בסעודה, והיא לא באמת אוהבת אותך". נפגעתי וכעסתי מאוד.

האמת שהיא נגעה לי בנקודה רגישה. בגלל שאסא הוא זה שיזם את הגירושין בינינו ולא אני, באיזשהו מקום גם אחרי ארבע שנים נשארתי קשורה אליו רגשית, ולא הצלחתי להתנתק. בהתחלה היה לי קשה להודות שיש בי עדיין אהבה אליו. בגלל שבאתי מרקע חרדי ורציתי להיות "אישה כשרה" חשבתי שהרגשות שלי כלפיו הם בגדר משהו "לא כשר", שהרי אני התגרשתי ממנו והתחתנתי עם מישהו אחר, ולפי התורה אסא אסור עליי לנצח נצחים. כשהרהרתי על אסא או שהתגעגעתי אליו, השתדלתי בכל הכוח לדחוק ולהכחיש את המחשבות, כדי להרגיש שלא פגמתי, שאני "בסדר", שלא הייתה לי, חס ושלום, איזו מחשבת "תועבה" עליו. מצד אחד היה לי נוח עם הדימוי השקרי הזה של "הצדקת" שיצרתי לעצמי, זה חיבר אותי לעולם החרדי שממנו באתי, ועזר לי להרגיש טוב עם עצמי; אך מצד שני, הניסיון לטשטש את הרגשות כלפיו, גרם לי עם הזמן להפוך את המציאות, ולרחם עליו כאילו אני זאת שעזבתי אותו והשארתי אותו לבד. זה היה מעוות לחלוטין לחשוב בצורה כזו, הרי הוא זה שעזב אותי, ואפילו התעקש על כך. וידעתי שטוב לו להיות חופשי מעול של אישה, סוף סוף הוא קיבל את השקט שחיפש. נוצר אצלי קונפליקט בין השכל שמבין ורואה את האמת, לבין הרגש שלא מוכן להשלים עם העובדה שאסא אף פעם לא היה מעוניין בי. רציתי להצליח לנתק את התלות שחשתי כלפיו ולהרגיש משוחררת, וכיוון שלא הצלחתי, התאכזבתי מעצמי. למה אני לא מצליחה לשלוט ברגשות שלי? למה אחרי שעברו שנים מאז שהתגרשנו, אני עדיין מחפשת את תשומת הלב שלו? מצאתי את עצמי מתייסרת, זה לא לפי כבודי לרדוף אחרי מי שלא צריך אותי, במיוחד שאני נשואה למישהו אחר. לא הבנתי למה אני עדיין מחפשת את אסא, בזמן שקיבלתי מדניאל את כל האהבה שיכולתי לחלום עליה. התחלתי להוציא את התסכול שלי בכעס על הבעל החדש שלי. כנראה בתת-מודע, האשמתי אותו בכך שאני לא יכולה יותר לחזור לאסא, כי לפי התורה גרושה שנישאה לאחר, אסורה לבעלה הראשון. הרגשתי מאוד רע עם המחשבות האלה שעלו בי. מצד אחד, הרתיח אותי שאחרי שאסא התגרש ממני בגלל שהוא לא נמשך לנשים, הוא עמד להתחתן עם אישה אחרת; אבל מצד שני, הצטערתי בשבילו שאחרי שבוע הוא ברח ממנה. הפריע לי שעדיין דאגתי לו וריחמתי עליו. הציק לי גם שדאגתי לו יותר משדאגתי לדניאל. ייסורי המצפון שלי מהמחשבות עליו לא הניחו לי, ושיתפתי את דניאל בכעסים ובתסכול שהצטברו בי. עם כל זאת, מצאתי נחמה: לפחות אני לא לבד עם כל זה.

לכן כעסתי כל כך כשעליזה נגעה בנקודה הזו, הרגשתי שכדי להכשיר כל מיני פנטזיות שלה על אסא היא משתמשת בי. היא הייתה אומרת לדניאל שמתוך כנות ואמת, חשוב לה שידע, שהיא נמשכת לאסא ויש לה ביטחון שהיא היחידה שיכולה להוציא אותו מהמשיכה שלו לגברים. לא הצלחתי להבין אם בכל הצגת הכנות שלה, היא מספרת את האמת על עצמה, או שהיא עושה את כל זה רק בשביל למשוך תשומת לב, לי היא הייתה אומרת שהסודיות המסתורית שלי בקשר לאסא, מבלבלת אותה. לבסוף היא הצליחה לגרור את דניאל, את אסא ואותי לשיחות, שבהן רצתה לברר מה כל אחד מרגיש. אני חייבת להגיד לזכותה של עליזה שהשיחות האלה עזרו לי להיפתח, ולהשתחרר מהמועקה.

דניאל לא היה כל כך שלם עם הביקורים של אסא בבית, בגלל המורכבות של העניין מבחינה הלכתית, אבל אחרי שראיתי את התועלת בשיחות המשותפות, אמרתי לדניאל שפתרון חיצוני, למשל להגיד לו לא לבוא לא יהיה פתרון לבעיה שלי, כי גם כשהוא נמצא בגבעת שאול אני חושבת עליו ודואגת לו, ואני מעדיפה שנמצא פתרון אמיתי לקשר שלי אתו. כשהתייעצתי עם "יועצת חרדית לענייני זוגיות" איך לפתור את הקונפליקט שאני חיה בו, היא אמרה שהמקרה שלי הוא מקרה מיוחד, ובגלל שלאסא אין משיכה לנשים, ואין חשש שיפגום כתוצאה משיחה אתי, חשוב שאשתף אותו ואת דניאל ברגשות שלי, ואשתדל כמה שיותר לפרוק את המטענים שלי. עד היום אנחנו לא בטוחים שפעלנו נכון כששמענו לעצה הזו אבל היינו בתוך מצב מורכב. דניאל גדל בעולם התיאטרון ולכן ראה את הדברים אחרת ממני. הוא חשב שאני מייסרת את עצמי לחינם, ושזה טבעי שאני לא אשכח את אסא שהיה "האהבה הראשונה" שלי, ושאני צריכה ללמוד להשלים עם עצמי, ולא להתכחש לרגשות ולרצונות שלי. בשיחות עם הנשים עליזה לקחה מקום של מנחה ושכנעה את דניאל להדגים לנו מה שלמד בעולם הריקוד והבמה. דרך משחק ואלתורים שחררנו רגשות והצלחנו להביע את עצמנו. זה היה בשבילי הפתרון המושלם. לפעמים הייתי מרגישה

תקועה ועצורה, אבל רציתי להשתחרר, כי הפנימיות רצתה לפרוץ החוצה, רציתי לחיות איך שבא לי באמת, בלי לעשות חשבון של "בסדר" ו"לא בסדר". הרגשתי חופשיה אפילו עם אסא, עד כדי כך שפתחנו את כל הקלפים ודיברנו על הכול. צחקנו על עצמנו, והפכנו את הדברים למשחק. אהבתי את משחקי האלתור, ראיתי שזה עושה טוב גם לאסא, הרגשתי שסוף סוף, בזכות הפתיחות של הקבוצה, אני אמתית עם עצמי. לפעמים השיחות היו יותר אינטימיות וגרמו להתפרצות רגשית ולמתחים בינינו, לפעמים נסחפנו עם היצרים וגלשנו, אך כיוון שרצינו לנתב את האנרגיות נכון, דווקא מהעליות ומהירידות התחזקנו כל אחד בעצמו, והתחזקו הקשרים בינינו. עליזה ידעה לשחק ולהכניס את כולם לאווירה שרצתה, יותר מכולם היא ידעה לתת פורקן לרגשות, ולפעמים הייתי מקנאה בספונטניות שלה ובכישרון הדרמה שהיה לה. היו פעמים שעשינו את השיחות האלה בחדר הצמוד לבית, שכונה בפינו "המחסן". ביום, המחסן שימש כחדר התפירה של אנסטסיה והיה בו שקט ופרטיות. משחקי האלתור עזרו לכולנו להבין טוב יותר אחד את השני וכל אחד את עצמו, ואת מה שעובר על כל אחד ואחת, בצורה הרבה יותר טובה. עליזה אהבה להגיד ש"חברים אמתיים כאלה אף פעם לא היו לה, וגם אי-אפשר למצוא בשום מקום בעולם".

בשנת 2009 הגיעה שירן, האישה השישית.

יחד עם שירן היינו שש נשים, וגרנו בכמה דירות באזורים שונים – בירושלים, במרכז ובצפון הארץ, לפי הצרכים של ההפצה. בטבריה שכרנו קרוון יפהפה, בהרים מאחורי הציון של רבי מאיר בעל הנס. מסביב לקרוון היה שטח גדול של דשא, מקום חניה נוח לכל הרכבים של ההפצה, הייתה שם אורוות סוסים, והקמנו ברכה לילדים. הכינרת הייתה בסמוך, והנוף היה חלומי. אהבנו מאוד להיות בטבריה, לטייל באזור ביחד, לרדת לכינרת, ולארגן משם את ההופעות של הלהקה ואת ההפצות באזור הצפון.

ב-4.7.11 לפתע עצרו לנו את החיים. הטראומה וההלם עדיין טריים. הזיכרונות של אותו הלילה רודפים אותי מאז, והגעגועים שורפים לי את הלב. עד היום אני חיה בזיכרוני את הרגעים האחרונים כאילו שזה קרה עכשיו. היינו שירן ואני עם הבנות בבית בטבריה, מחכות על הנדנדה במרפסת העץ שמשקיפה לאגם הכינרת, לאבא ולבנים שיחזרו מהתפילה. כבר היה מאוחר, ולא הבנתי מדוע הם מתעכבים. לפתע עצרו בחזית הבית שלושה רכבים לבנים, ומתוכם יצאו כעשרה גברים חמושים, ובריצה הקיפו את הבית. חשבתי שזו פעולת טרור. קראתי לבנות להיכנס מיד לבית, הבנות בכו והיו מבוהלות. ניסיתי לסגור את דלת הכניסה, אך אחד מהם דחף את הדלת בחזקה ואתו התפרצו פנימה עוד שניים. הם נעלו אותנו בבית, ואחד מהם אמר: "אני שוטר ואני יכול לעשות מה שאני רוצה". הם צעקו, קיללו והפכו את הבית. איימו על כולנו שנזדרז להיכנס לרכבים שלהם לנסוע לחקירה בירושלים. כשניסיתי להתקשר לדניאל ולבנים, לא הייתה תשובה. לא ידעתי מה לחשוב.

מאז אותו הלילה החיים הם לא חיים. ב 02:00 לפנות בוקר אילצו אותי להיפרד מהבנות, ולהשאיר אותן ב"מרכז חירום" בפרדס חנה. ניתקו לי מהידיים את בלה, הבת הקטנה של אילנה. אני זוכרת איך היא חיבקה אותי חזק כדי שלא אעזוב אותה ולא אשאיר אותה לבד, אני עדיין מרגישה את הלב שלה פועם בחזקה על הלב שלי, ואני שומעת אותה בוכה שהיא רוצה הביתה ושלא אעזוב אותה. אני זוכרת איך הבנות החזיקו ידיים חזק במעגל, ובבכי הבטיחו אחת לשנייה שהן לא ייפרדו זו מזו. עד היום אני לא מבינה איך העולם יכול להמשיך להתנהל כאילו כלום לא קרה כשהילדים שלנו, מאותו היום, חיים כיתומים להורים חיים.

---

בכתב האישום כתבו על דניאל שבשליטה מנטלית גרם לגירושין שלי מאסא כדי להתחתן אתי, ושבמסגרת הנישואין, כעונש עבורי, היה שולח מדי פעם את אסא למחסן לאנוס אותי.

לא טרחו אפילו לשאול אותי בחקירות ובבית המשפט אם כל זה נכון ואם בכלל נאנסתי והתעלמו מהעובדה שאסא לא נמשך לנשים. כשהציגו אותי בתור עדת תביעה בחלק מתרגיל של הפרקליטות, הסברתי שההאשמות שקריות וחסרות היגיון. אותם שופטים ציינו לשבח את רמת האינטליגנציה הגבוהה שלי, את השכלתי, ואף הוסיפו שיכולתי להיות הרבנית הראשית. לא יכולתי לדמיין שבהכרעת הדין יחרצו שאני שפחה, ושעברתי מספר מעשי אינוס על ידי אסא בהוראת דניאל.

---

הלינץ' התקשורתי שעשו לדניאל היה מזעזע. לא האמנתי ששחיתות כזו יכולה לקרות בשנת 2011 בפרהסיה. בדיוק 27 יום מהמעצר, כשהיינו רק בתחילת החקירות, עוד לא נערך משפט, ובעצם זה היה הרבה לפני שהצליחו להשפיע על עדי התביעה העיקריים להתהפך נגד דניאל, הם כבר תפרו לו את התיק ללא פתח יציאה, חרצו את דינו. מסביב לשולחן ענק קיימו מסיבת עיתונאים צמאי דם, וראיינו אנשים

מדרגות בכירות במשטרה וברווחה ששכחו שכל עוד לא נעשה משפט, יש לכל אזרח את זכות החפות, והתחרו ביניהם מי יצליח לתאר טוב יותר את דניאל כמקרה החמור ביותר בארץ. זה היה מחריד. הם ביצעו רצח אופי לאור יום. לא הבנתי איך ייתכן שמי שנקראים "אנשי החוק" או "אנשי הרווחה" במשרות בכירות, ירשו לעצמם להוציא דיבה, לצאת בהצהרות כוזבות, ולהכריז על אדם שהוא פושע, בלי שנעשה לו עדיין משפט! מי שם אותם לשופטים? איפה הצדק? לאט לאט התחוור לי שזוהי תחבולה שטנית של "אנשי מקצוע", שמכינים מלכודת של דעת קהל לשופטים, שלא יוכלו לזכות חשודים, שהרי אז יצטרכו להתמודד עם כל המדינה!

ניגשתי לחדר הישיבות של המקלט לנשים מוכות כדי לצפות בחדשות. עוד לא עבר חודש מהמעצר, עוד לא הסתיימו החקירות של המשטרה, וכבר הלכלוך בתקשורת היה בשיאו. הזדעזעתי כששמעתי: "הותרה לפרסום אחת הפרשות המזעזעות שהתרחשו בישראל בשנים האחרונות. המשטרה חושדת בתושב ירושלים שהקים כת אכזרית, על פי החשד הוא התעלל בנשותיו..."

על גבי מסך הטלוויזיה, ראש ימ"ר ירושלים שלמה דאי, הכריז במסיבת העיתונאים: "החוויות שהנשים האלה עברו הן חוויות קשות, ואני כאיש משטרה ותיק גם קשה לי לתאר מה שהן עברו...". איזה שקרן! חשבתי בזעם עמוק, הרי אני בעצמי הייתי אצלו בחדר בזמן החקירות, ואמרתי לו בפירוש שטוב לנו ביחד, ושדניאל אף פעם לא פגע בנו! המשנה למנהל משרד הרווחה ניסה להישמע יותר סנסציוני, והצהיר: "עשיתי לא מעט תפקידים במשרד הרווחה בחיים שלי, כולם היו בתחומים הקרובים לעניין הזה, אני חושב שהוא אחד המקרים החמורים ביותר, או אני אפילו יכול לומר שהחמור ביותר מבחינת העצמות שלו", עוד יותר התרעמתי כששמעתי את רות מטות, מנהלת "היחידה לילדים בסיכון" של עיריית ירושלים: "כשאני ראיתי את הדברים ושמעתי, כשראיתי את הילדים ואת האימהות, היה לי קשה מאוד לראות ולשמוע את הדברים..." אבל היא מעולם לא פגשה אף אחת מאתנו! צעקתי בלבי, למה היא משקרת ככה? והיא המשיכה להכפיש: "זה אחד המקרים הכי מזעזעים שאני ראיתי ושמעתי, ואני 30 שנה במקצוע", וראש מפלג התשאול בימ"ר ירושלים, במין ניסיון להתחרות בסופרלטיבים בקודמיו, הצהיר: "זה המקרה הכי חמור שאני נתקלתי בו, ונתקלנו בתיקים קשים!" ראיינו כל מיני פרשנים שמסרו את הגרסה שלהם ל"מה שקרה בבית". תמיד ידעתי שהתקשורת משקרת, אבל עד שחוויתי את זה על בשרי, לא ידעתי עד לאן זה יגיע!

הייתי נחושה בדעתי להגיב במהירות, ולפרסם בכל כלי התקשורת, ברדיו, בטלוויזיה ובעיתונים את הסיפור האמתי. הרי אנחנו במדינה דמוקרטית, אמורה להיות לי זכות לחופש הביטוי...

חיכיתי לבוקר. במקלט אסרו עליי להחזיק טלפון. ב-08:00 בבוקר נכנסתי בחשאי למשרד של המקלט. היה שם טלפון. התקשרתי במהירות לרדיו אמרתי שמדברת אשתו של דניאל אמבש וברצוני להגיב על כל מה שנאמר נגדנו בתקשורת. אמרו לי להתקשר בדיוק ב-10:00 ויעלו אותי לדבר בשידור חי. חיכיתי בקוצר רוח לשעה 10:00. ב-09:30 הודיעה לי מנהלת המקלט שעוה"ד של המקלט מחכה לי עכשיו. ניסיתי לדחות את השיחה הזו כדי שלא תהיה לי מניעה להתקשר לרדיו, אך ללא הועיל. הייתי חייבת להיכנס לפגישה, עם זאת החלטתי, אני אתקשר לרדיו ויהי מה. ב-09:55 התנצלתי בפני עוה"ד, ויצאתי לרגע. חמקתי לחדר הסמוך, היכן שנמצא מכשיר הטלפון וסגרתי אחריי את הדלת. חייגתי לרדיו. הודיעו לי שמעלים אותי לשידור. התחלתי לספר על ההלם שלי מהשקרים שמספרים על דניאל ושמפרסמים בתקשורת, על הדרך שלקחו מאתנו את הילדים, ושניתקו לנו את הקשר איתם, מגיש התכנית שאל אותי שאלות והתחלתי לענות לו, כשלפתע מישהו ניסה לפתוח את הדלת. נלחמתי תוך כדי שיחה להשאיר את הדלת סגורה. זו הייתה עוה"ד שיצאה לחפש אותי. היא הורתה בקול רם שאפתח לה את הדלת, ניסיתי להתעלם ממנה ולענות על השאלות ברדיו, אך היא המשיכה ודפקה על הדלת, החזקתי את הדלת סגורה אך היא הצליחה לפתוח, נכנסה וביקשה ממני לנתק מיד את הטלפון. ניסיתי למרות ההפרעה שלה להתרכז בשיחת הטלפון ואמרתי בשידור שחלק מהעוול שנעשה לנו הוא שלא מרשים לנו לדבר ולהשמיע את קולנו בעוד מספרים לציבור שקרים בקשר אלינו. היא הפצירה בי להניח את השפופרת. ניתקתי ונשארתי עם טעם מר שלא הצלחתי להגיד כל מה שיש לי בלב. היא דיווחה למנהלת של המקלט שהתקשרתי לרדיו, וזו נזפה בי והזהירה אותי שאסור לי ליצור קשר עם התקשורת. לא הסכמתי בשום פנים ואופן שיסתמו לי את הפה או שיגידו לי מה לעשות, בוודאי שלא אכנע, בפרט בזמן שהתקשורת מלאה שקרים עלינו. קבעתי פגישות עם עיתונאים של העיתונים המובילים במדינה, "ידיעות אחרונות", "מעריב", "הארץ", "מקומון ירושלים"... חיפשתי דרכים לצאת מהמקלט בלי שידעו לאן אני הולכת, כי הייתי צריכה לבקש רשות על כל יציאה, ולדווח בדיוק היכן אהיה ועם מי אפגש. בדרך לא דרך התקיימו המפגשים עם העיתונאים. הם הקשיבו במשך שעות למה שיש לי להגיד, אך לאחר שנפרדנו התקשרו להודיע לי שהעורך של העיתון אסר לפרסם את הכתבה כי יש צו איסור פרסום. ניסיתי להתעקש, הרי זה לא ייתכן שהמשטרה והפרקליטות יכולות לפרסם מה שהן רוצות ולהוציא דיבה בלי הגבלות. הרי מדובר בי. משתמשים בי כדי להפליל את דניאל עד כדי קביעה שביצע בי מעשים, בעוד אני מעידה לטובתו ואומרת בפירוש שהם משקרים, והם אוסרים עליי

להגיב בתירוץ שיש צו איסור פרסום?! מי הוא זה שקובע מה יצא לתקשורת ואיך יתפרסמו הדברים וחוסם את הקול שלנו? האם צו איסור פרסום הוא צו שבא להגן על האזרח או שהוא מין תחפושת שמאפשרת לשחיתות נוראית להתבצע תחת כיסוי של איסור פרסום?!

חיפשתי חיזוק. באחד הימים ב״מעון לנשים מוכות״ פתחתי את הספר אב״י הנחל של הסבא, והתעודדתי מהכתוב:

״...עטרת חן וכבוד וגדולה וניצחון ייתן השם להולכים בתמים בכל לב באש ובמים **ומוסרים את נפשם ואת ביתם** על עם ישראל וארץ ישראל, אשר השם יתברך מתפאר בהם ועושה בשבילם ניסים. הראם השם חסדך וישעך תיתן להם להצילם מידי אויביהם, אוהב אותם בכל איבר ואיבר שלהם ומצילם!...״ (רלו׳ בחלק שני).

המתיקות של האהבה של הסבא עטפה אותי בביטחון שעוד תהיה ישועה והצלה, הרגשתי שהוא כתב את המכתב הזה במיוחד בשבילנו, הרי למי עוד הסבא יכול להגיד ״שמוסרים את ביתם״?!

בהזדמנות הראשונה שהייתי ליד טלפון ניסיתי לחייג לצילה, הבת של קארי. כל כך התרגשתי לשמוע אותה, אך מיד היא חסמה את השמחה שלי כשבישרה לי שאבא של דניאל מאושפז בבית חולים במצב אנוש עקב אירוע מוחי. נבהלתי מאוד. מיד, אף שהמשטרה אסרה עלינו להגיע לירושלים, נסעתי לבית החולים לראותו. שם פגשתי את כל הנשים והילדים הגדולים, את אימא של דניאל ואת אחותו. הפגישה הייתה מרגשת וכואבת. הוא שכב על המיטה, מחובר למכונות, חסר אונים, כואב. עליזה גם הגיעה לבית החולים. היא נעמדה ליד המיטה שלו הסתכלה עליו כמה דקות, ואז התקרבה לאוזן שלו ולחשה בקול: ״אני מבקשת סליחה. אני יודעת שאני אשמה במצב שלך, אני יודעת שגרמתי לך צער גדול במה שעשיתי לבן שלך, אבל אני מבקשת שתסלח לי״. אימא של דניאל, ניצולת שואה, שמאז המעצר של הבן שלה עוברת שואה נוספת. סימנה לעליזה לגשת אליה וסיפרה לה שבתאי הגזים היה אפשר לראות שני סוגי יהודים, היו כאלה שמסרו נפשם כדי להציל את האחר וחילקו את פרוסת הלחם שלהם עם השני כדי שגם הוא יוכל לחיות והיו כאלה שהיו מוכנים לדחוף את השני לתאי הגזים כדי להציל את עצמם. עליזה השתתקה, ולא הצליחה לזוז כמה שניות, לאחר שהתעשתה התחמקה ויצאה מהחדר.

אבא של דניאל נפטר. שירות בתי הסוהר אסר על דניאל להגיע להלוויה. קשה לתאר במילים את גודל הצער. אחרי שהקדיש את חייו למען המדינה, לחם ב״הגנה״, נפצע קשה במלחמת יום העצמאות, דאג לעלייה של יהודים לארץ ישראל, המדינה לא אפשרה לבנו היחיד, דניאל, לבוא לומר עליו קדיש בהלוויה שלו. ההלוויה נערכה ב״הר המנוחות״, ירושלים. מנהג עתיק בירושלים אוסר על נשים להיכנס לבית הקברות בהלוויה, לכן נשארו כל הנשים בחניה, והגברים התקדמו וליוו את הרכב שמסיע את הנפטר. עליזה לא התביישה להיות האישה היחידה שהתלוותה לגברים, להיות נוכחת בכל שלבי הקבורה ולהסתכל מקרוב דרך משקפי שמש שחורות גדולות שמסתירות את פניה, איך מכסים את אבא באדמה. רק לאחר מכן היא הלכה.

יום ההולדת של עליזה הגיע. ערכנו לה מסיבת הפתעה היא הייתה נרגשת מאוד ורצתה להצטלם עם כולנו. היא סיפרה לנו שחלמה על דניאל, ולכבוד יום ההולדת שלה היא מבקשת מתנה מבורא עולם, שדניאל ישתחרר מהר. זו הייתה הפעם האחרונה שראיתי אותה.

חודשיים לאחר מכן, הייתי בתל אביב. לילך החוקרת התקשרה שאגיע לשיחה קצרה אצלה במשרד. נסעתי מיד לירושלים.

המסדרונות האפלים של ימ״ר ירושלים העלו בי זיכרונות טראומטיים מהחקירות האלימות שבוצעו נגד כל המשפחה חצי שנה קודם לכן. הטעם המר של הניתוק מדניאל, הדאגה והפחד מהלא נודע חזרו לכרסם בתוכי. נכנסתי לחדר החקירות בלי לדעת שבעצם נכנסתי למלכודת, ששנה שלמה לא אצליח לצאת ממנה.

״זימנתי אותך, כיוון שעברה תקופה ארוכה שלא שמעתי ממך ואני רוצה לדעת היום מה המצב שלך?״

״מה זאת אומרת מה המצב שלי?״

״האם את עדיין תומכת בדניאל או לא?״

״בוודאי שאני אתו, הוא בעלי ואני אוהבת אותו והוא לא עשה שום רע״.

״את בטוחה?״

"בוודאי".

"אני חשבתי שאת יותר אינטליגנטית, אדרת, ומבינה עניין, אבל אם את הולכת עם כוח והתנצחות, אני כבר הסברתי לך שזה לא יהיה משתלם לך. לפחות לא תוכלי להגיד שלא הזהרתי אותך!"

"דניאל לא עשה שום דבר רע".

"לא מוצא חן בעיניי איך שאת מדברת, אבל אם את בטוחה בעמדה שלך, אז פתחת חזית אתי ומעכשיו את נחקרת בתור חשודה".

"על מה את מדברת?" לא הבנתי.

היא הישירה מבט לעברי, ודקלמה את הטקסט שהיה שגור בפיה: "אני מודיעה לך כי הנך חשודה בקשירת קשר לביצוע פשע, הדחת עד, שיבוש מהלכי חקירה ומשפט וכן בחטיפה והתעללות בילדים. יש לך את הזכות להיוועץ בעו"ד, אין את חייבת לומר דבר, כל שתאמרי עשוי לשמש ראיה נגדך, הימנעות מלהשיב לשאלות עשויה לחזק את הראיות נגדך".

"זו בדיחה?!" שאלתי, לא מאמינה למשמע אוזניי.

"ספרי לי מה את עושה בשבועות האחרונים, והיכן את מתגוררת", היא פתחה בחקירה. שתקתי. הבנתי שהיא מקיימת את מה שהבטיחה לי חצי שנה קודם לכן, כי אם לא אשתף פעולה נגד דניאל ואאמת את כל מה שהיא אומרת, היא תכתוב נגדי כתבי אישום. הפעם, החלטתי, אני לא עונה לה.

"יש כלפייך האשמות קשות, האם את לא רוצה לתת לגביהם איזו פרשנות?" בוודאי שלא, חשבתי בלבי, כל מילה שלי היא מפרשת לפי רצונה, לפחות הפעם אלמד מהניסיון הקודם בחדרי החקירות...

"האם נפגשת עם מי מנשותיו של דניאל מיום מעצרו?" היא שאלה.

שתקתי.

"מחומר החקירה עולה כי נהגתן להיפגש כולכן באופן קבוע, כל פעם במקומות שונים, מה תגובתך?"

שמרתי על זכות השתיקה.

"מחומר החקירה עולה כי נהגתן להיפגש כולכן והלכתן לעליזה כדי להניאה מלהעיד במשפטו של דניאל אמבש, מה תגובתך?"

מאיפה היא המציאה את הרעיון הזה? חשבתי. הרי עליזה היא זו שיזמה את הפגישות בינינו, ביקשה מאתנו לבא לבית הוריה, לא יכול להיות שעליזה התלוננה על כך.

"מדוע את שותקת? אלו טענות קשות של הדחת עד, שזו עברה מסוג פשע. מדוע את לא מספרת את גרסתך? אני מזכירה לך שזה הזמן. מחומר החקירה עולה כי נפגשת עם עליזה ונתת לה 2000 ₪, מה תגובתך? עליזה מסרה למשטרה על כך. מה תגובתך לזה?"

המשכתי לשתוק, ולא רציתי להאמין שאחרי שבכתה לי שנבלע לה כרטיס האשראי והיא בחובות וזקוקה לכסף דחוף כי אין לבתיה בגדים לחורף וכבר קר, עליזה משתמשת בעזרה שנתתי לה נגדי? הרי עשיתי הכול כדי להשיג לה 2500 ₪, לקחתי הלוואה שעד היום לא מצאתי דרך כיצד להחזיר אותה!

"אני מציגה בפנייך מכתב בן שמונה עמודים שעליזה מסרה למשטרה, שאת כתבת לה ומסרת לה, ובכך עברת על הטרדת עד".

"מה?!" הייתי בהלם. ראיתי בידיה של החוקרת את המכתב שכתבתי לעליזה בשעות הלילה בדמעות כשלא הצלחתי להירדם בגלל מחשבות ודאגה לה ולבתיה. לא יכול להיות שעליזה מסרה אותו למשטרה. רק אז "נפל לי האסימון", עליזה היא לא העליזה שחשבתי. היה לי קשה מאוד לקבל את האמת הזו. לא רציתי לקבל את זה. הרגשתי שהיא נעצה חרב עמוק עמוק בלב שלי, ולאט לאט מסובבת אותה כדי להכאיב לי, כדי להרוג אותי ואת כל המשפחה, במוות אטי ואכזרי. אבל למה? איך זה ייתכן?! נוכלת!... זה לא אנושי, איך ייתכן שהיא עושה לי את זה?!

"עליזה מסרה כי את, ביחד עם שאר הנשים, נפגשתן עם הכתבת דינה אברמסון, ואת שכנעת אותה להצטלם, מה תגובתך?"

מה קורה פה? כמה ביזיונות ספגתי ממנה כשכעסה עליי כי אני לא עושה מספיק, כמוה, למען דניאל, הרי היא זו שהזמינה את העיתונאית ועודדה את כולנו להצטלם ולספר על השחיתות של המשטרה, של הרווחה ושל הפרקליטות. הייתי מזועזעת, אך המשכתי לשתוק, היא לא תצליח להוציא אותי מהכלים.

"מחומר החקירה עולה כי את נפגשת עם הנשים בניגוד למותר בבית החולים ,שערי צדק", מה תגובתך? האם את מבינה שאת חשודה בעברות חמורות מאוד, וכי זה הזמן שלך לדבר ולספר תגובתך?"

האמת על עליזה הכתה אותי בתדהמה. בסיוט הכי נורא שלי לא יכולתי לדמיין שהיא תתנהג כך. בחלום בלהות לא יכולתי לחשוב שהיא תפעל לסגור אותנו החברות שלה ואת דניאל בכלא.

"זה ברור לך שאת עצורה?!"

לא האמנתי למשמע אוזניי. על מה ולמה? איך ייתכן שעל סמך שקרים כל כך גסים היא סוגרת אותי בכלא?! מה המזימה הנבזית הזו, ומי עומד מאחורי כל זה? אבל מעל הכול הייתי נסערת לגלות את דו-הפרצופיות של עליזה, איך כל זה קרה? מתי עליזה החליטה להתהפך? איך היא הצליחה לשחק מולנו עד עכשיו?

החוקרת שלחה אותי לצילומים ולבדיקות משפילות כדי להמחיש לי היטב את העובדה שאני עצורה. צילמו אותי מהחזית ומהפרופיל, לקחו ממני טביעת אצבעות, הסוהרת מישׁשה אותי בצורה מבזה כדי לבדוק שלא הכנסתי לתוך גופי איזשהו חומר, מעולם לא הרגשתי מושפלת כמו בבדיקות לפני המעצר. עצורה אחרת שעברה את הבדיקות האלה אחריי, נשברה והתייפחה בבכי שזה לא אנושי שהם מרשים לעצמם להתנהג אלינו כאילו אנחנו בהמות. הרגשתי כמוה, אך ניסיתי לחזק אותה. החוקרת קראה לאחת הסוהרות ללוות אותי לתא המעצר ב"מגרש הרוסים", ובטון מאיים אמרה: "את עוד תצטערי שעשית את הבחירה הלא נכונה, אדרת!"

המעצר קרה לי באופן בלתי צפוי, כשהייתי לגמרי לא מוכנה. הסוהרת הכניסה אותי לתא, ונעלה אחריי. הטריקה של דלת הברזל, ורעש המפתחות הנועלות אותי בפנים גרמה לי לזעוק זעקה עמוקה בתוך הלב. התא היה קטן וצר, בלי חלונות ובלי סירקולציה של אוויר. על הקירות היו מרוחות כתובות נאצה בחום גבישי שהשאירו למזכרת אסירות שהיו לפניי בתא הזה. שתי מיטות קומתיים משני הצדדים ועליהם מזרנים דקים ומוכתמים בכתמי שתן, ו"שמיכת סקביאס" על כל מיטה. בין המיטות היה שביל צר שהוביל לחדר שירותים מצחין שבו מקלחון ישן וכיור מחליד – המקור היחיד למי שתיה. לא ידעתי איך אני הולכת לשרוד במחנק הזה. לפתע, כמשב של חמצן טרי, הכניסו לתא את אילנה. כל כך שמחתי לראות אותה, זה השכיח ממני את עליזה ואת כל שעברתי בשעות האחרונות. התחבקנו. היא נעצרה יום לפניי, ולא ידעתי מה אתה. כיוון שלא נתנו לנו אפשרות להתקשר בטלפון, אילנה הייתה בחרדות שלא תוכל להיות בקשר עם הילדים. דיברנו על העוול הנוראי של המערכת כלפינו, אבל יותר מהכול כאבה לנו ההתהפכות האכזרית של האנשים שהיו קרובים לנו.

בכלא "ספירה" מתבצעת חמש פעמים ביום על ידי הסוהרים, החל מ-5:00 לפנות בוקר. הם מתפרצים לתאים בצעקות: "לעמוד על הרגליים", כשבידיהם מקל שאתו הם דופקים על הקירות. משך חצי שעה ביום הסוהרת מוציאה אותנו ל"חצר", ריבוע תחום בקירות בטון אפורים וכבדים; בשביל לראות את השמים מבעד לגדרות התיל צריך להתאמץ. כשבוע לאחר מכן עצרו את אזמרה, והכניסו אותה אתנו לתא. לא בגלל שרצו שנהיה ביחד, אלא רק בגלל שלא היה תא נוסף לנשים. לפני חצי שנה הפרידו בינינו, ועכשיו הרגשנו שצריך להעריך כל רגע שאפשר להיות ביחד, אפילו במקום כזה. חיזקנו את עצמנו בשירה ובריקודים. הסוהרות הביטו אחת בשנייה מבולבלות, וצרחו עלינו "סתמו תיפה!"

לאחר כמה ימים קיבלנו את כתב האישום. נחרדתי לגלות שבנוסף לכל הדברים שהחוקרת האשימה אותי בהם, הוסיפו אישום חדש שבכלל לא נחקרתי עליו: "אינוס קטין". וכך מתועד בו: בזמן לא ידוע, במקום לא ידוע, בגיל לא ידוע, החזקנו את סמי הבן של קארי, אני בידו האחת, ועליזה בשנייה, כשאזמרה בתחתונים ובחזייה מבצעת בו מין אוראלי, בפקודה של דניאל. אישום זה היה יכול לסגור אותי לפחות לעשר שנים בכלא. תהיתי, אם עלה חשד שדבר זה אכן התרחש, איך ייתכן: 1. שלא נחקרנו על כך לפני שסגרו אותנו בכלא 2. למה חיכו חצי שנה עד שעצרו אותנו? 3. מדוע הייתה צריכה החוקרת לילך רנן לברר מה עמדתי כלפי דניאל לפני שהחליטה אם לחקור אותי או לא? 4. לשם מה התאמצו במשך חצי שנה, מאז המעצר של דניאל ועד למעצר שלנו הנשים, לשכנע אותנו ב"מעון" על ידי עובדות סוציאליות, שיחות קבוצתיות, שוחד ואיומים שאנחנו "נשים מוכות?"

המסקנה המתבקשת היא שיצרו את כל המעצר הזה כתרגיל כדי למנוע מאתנו לפעול לשחרורו, וגם כדי להפעיל עלינו לחץ שנעיד נגדו כדי להציל את עצמנו, כמו שהודיעו לנו הפרקליטים: "אם תחתמו שאתן קרבנות שלו תשוחררו מיד מהכלא".

במשך שנה שלמה הובאנו במשאיות פח לוהטות, אזוקות ידיים ורגליים, לדיונים להארכת מעצר. הכאב מהאזיקים המהודקים לרגליים עדיין חד בזיכרון.

ט"ו בשבט 2012, אני ואזמרה בבית המעצר בירושלים. דניאל בכלא "רימונים" בצפון, ואין לנו אפשרות ליצור אתו קשר, ואילנה בכלא "נווה תרצה". הסוהרת הוציאה אותי לפגישה עם עוה"ד שצילה שלחה אליי, היא פתחה את דלת הברזל הענקית של האגף, והלכתי אחריה במסדרון צר שהוביל לחדר הפגישות. שמעתי רעש של אזיקים שמגיע מקצה המסדרון. הרמתי את עיניי, הלב שלי ניתר ממקומו מרוב שמחה... נתקלתי פנים מול פנים בדניאל (!). מה הוא עושה כאן בבית מעצר בירושלים? כשהסוהר שליווה אותו נעצר בדיוק ליד הסוהרת שליוותה אותי, זה היה פלא כזה ששניהם החליטו לשחרר לשנינו את האזיקים באותו מקום, באותו הזמן... דניאל לא ידע שנעצרנו, ונדהם לראות אותי שם. התרגשנו כל כך. הרגשתי שחזרה אליי נשמתי. הספקנו להעביר בינינו כמה מילים עד שהסוהר הוביל אותו לחדר צדדי. הסוהרת הורתה לי ללכת בעקבותיה והתקדמה לפניי, אבל אני רציתי לראות את דניאל. חצי שנה לא ראיתי אותו. לא יכולתי להמשיך ללכת אחריה. הרגליים שלי לקחו אותי בדיוק לכיוון ההפוך... הגעתי לתא שבו היה דניאל. הוא ישב בין המון גברים וטמן את ראשו בין שתי ידיו. הבחנתי בו לפי הכיפה הלבנה שלראשו. נצמדתי לסורגים וצעקתי לעברו: "דניאל!" הוא הרים את הראש והתקרב במהירות לעברי. לחשתי לו "אני כל כך מתגעגעת אליך, תהיה חזק אל תישבר!" הוא הספיק להגיד לי שהוא אוהב אותי לפני שהסוהרת הגיעה אליי בצעדים מהירים, בצעקות ובנזיפות, וניתקה אותי מהסורגים. שלחנו נשיקות באוויר זה לזה והיא הובילה אותי לחדר עוה"ד. כשנכנסתי, עדיין נרגשת, ראיתי שאזמרה כבר משוחחת עם עוה"ד. "דניאל כאן" עדכנתי אותה בהתלהבות.

"באמת?!" היא כמעט בכתה, "איך זה יכול להיות? מה הוא עושה פה? מה אמרת לו? איפה הוא?" היא לא רצתה לפספס שום פרט. "אני חייבת לראות אותו".

"אל תדאגי" אמרתי לה. "בדרך חזור לתא ננסה לעשות משהו..."

כמעט ששכחנו מנוכחותו של עוה"ד. השתדלנו לסיים מהר את השיחה אתו. הסוהרת הגיעה והורתה לנו ללכת אחריה. קיווינו שנוכל לראות את דניאל. לפתע, כשהסוהרת התקדמה במסדרון, הגיעה קבוצה גדולה של אסירים מלווים בסוהרים, שמילאה בבת-אחת את המסדרון והסתירה אותנו לרגע מעיניה של הסוהרת. לא היססנו, ובמהירות לקחתי את אזמרה לתא שבו ראיתי את דניאל. אזמרה צעקה: "דניאל איזה נס לראות אותך" דניאל התקרב אלינו. אזמרה החזיקה חזק בסורגים, נלחמת בסוהרת שהגיעה אלינו בריצה וניסתה לשחרר את אחיזתה של אזמרה מהסורגים. אזמרה לא שמעה לאף אחד, היא הסתכלה רק על דניאל, וניסתה להעביר לו כמה שיותר מסרים של חיזוק ואהבה. הגיעה עוד סוהרת, והן החזירו אותנו בעל כורחנו לתא המעצר. לא הייתה שום סבירות שבדיוק באותו היום, באותו המקום ובאותו הרגע, למרות כל המאמצים הכבירים של ה"מערכת" לנתק כל קשר בינינו, נפגשנו למספר רגעים שאת המתיקות שלהם לא נוכל לשכוח לנצח.

מאוחר יותר, התברר לנו שדניאל היה בהמתנה בבית המעצר בירושלים, כי זומן לדיון בבית דין רבני כדי שייתן גט לעליזה.

כמה ימים לאחר מכן הודיעו לי שאני עוברת מבית המעצר "מגרש הרוסים" לכלא לנשים "נווה תרצה". ארזתי את הטרנינג האפור שקיבלתי שם עם המגבת ועם עוד כמה פריטים בתוך שקית פח שחורה וגדולה, וחיכיתי שיקראו לי לנסיעה. לקחו אותי במשאית שב"ס ("פוסטה") גדולה בתוך תא נפרד, מבודד, כשעל ידיי ועל רגליי אזיקים. שוב הייתי צריכה לעבור בדיקות קבלה משפילות. אחרי המתנה ארוכה, לקחה אותי סוהרת לאגף של "המתחם", האגף שבו משאירים את הבנות עד שוועדת קבלה תחליט היכן לשבץ אותי. הלכתי אחריה, אוחזת את שקית הפח השחורה בידי. היא העבירה אותי במסדרון ארוך שמשני צדיו רכבת של תאים חשוכים שמכמה מהם הציצו לעברי אסירות. אחת צעקה: "הנה עוד דתייה מסריחה הגיעה", אחרת צעקה: "בואינה, יש לך סיגריה?" מישהי קראה לסוהרת להתלונן על אחת מהחדר שלה, ואחרת התחננה שהסוהרת תביא לה מים, הסוהרת צרחה עליה "שקט!!" עברנו את כל המסדרון עד החדר האחרון. חשבתי בלבי: "לא על חינם רבי נחמן אמר שהוא מאמין שיש עולם הבא, אבל שאת העולם הזה הוא לא רואה איפה יש, כי פה זה נראה הגיהינום. הרגשתי בתוך סיוט. לא רציתי להאמין שזה אמתי. הסוהרת אחזה צרור מפתחות ענק, ופתחה לי את התא. החדר היה חשוך. מתוך החשכה הבחנתי בחמש זוגות עיניים שבוחנות אותי ואת השקית שהחזקתי. עוד לא הספקתי להתפכח מההלם של המעמד,

כשלפתע, כמו מתוך עולם אחר אני שומעת את קולה של אילנה מקבל אותי בהתלהבות: "הנה אדרת הנהדרת, סוף סוף הגעת"! היא אחזה בשתי ידיי, וסחבה אותי לריקוד. הנשים בחדר חייכו, וחלקן הצטרפו אלינו למעגל של ריקודים. הרגשתי שהאהבה שיש בינינו יכולה להאיר גם את החושך של שאול תחתיות.

על פניו, כל אחת מאתנו יוצגה על ידי עו"ד מטעם הסנגוריה הציבורית. בדיון שבו היה צריך להגיב לכתב האישום, ממש לפני שהשופטים נכנסו לאולם, עורכות הדין של אזמרה ושלי ניגשו אלינו להודיע לנו שאנו לא נאהב לשמוע את מה שהן הולכות להגיד בדיון בתגובה לכתב האישום, אך זו החלטה שהן החליטו עליה ערב לפני, וכדאי שאנחנו נשב בשקט ולא נתערב בדיון, וניתן להן לעשות את העבודה שלהן כדי לשחרר אותנו. לא ידענו למה לצפות. אך בדיון, כששמענו את עורכות הדין מנסות להסביר לשופטים שבעצם אנחנו קרבנות של דניאל ולכן צריך לשחרר אותנו, הזדעזענו. הן פעלו בניגוד מוחלט לכל מה שסוכם בינינו. הן לא ייצגו כלל וכלל את האמת שעליה נלחמנו, ושבשבילה היינו מוכנות אפילו לשבת בכלא. הן ידעו בדיוק כמונו שהמטרה של המשטרה במאסר שלנו הייתה רק כדי להפעיל עלינו לחץ לדבר נגד הבעל שלנו, ולספר סיפורים שלא היו ולא נבראו. העובדה שעורכות הדין בחרו בדרך הקלה והשקרית, ולכאורה, בצורה קרה ומשפטית טענו שאנחנו לא מכחישות את הטענות נגד הבעל שלנו, אלא שאנחנו במצב של הכחשה בגלל שטיפת מוח, ולכן ראוי לרחם עלינו, ולשחרר אותנו מהכלא – הכעיסה אותנו מאוד, והתפרצנו לתוך דבריהן בצעקות שאנחנו לא מסכימות בשום פנים ואופן עם מה שהן אומרות, אמרנו לשופט שאנו מוכנות לשבת בכלא אפילו שנים אם צריך, אבל על האמת אנחנו לא נוותר! ולהפוך את דניאל למתעלל אכזר שביצע מעשים מגונים ושלט בנו – זה שקר שאין כדוגמתו, אנחנו לא קרבנות של דניאל, ואנחנו רוצות שהצדק והאמת ינצחו! השופט ניסה להרגיע אותנו, והסביר לנו שמדובר רק במושגים משפטיים ושאין בדבריהן להוכיח איזושהי אמת. אנו התנגדנו בכל תוקף שהן ימשיכו לייצג אותנו, וביקשנו מהשופט להחליף עורכי דין, או שנייצג את עצמנו, ושהאמת תהיה עדה לעצמה. בדיונים אחרי כן עורכי דין אחרים ייצגו אותנו. הם התייחסו עניינית לכל סעיף של אישום בכתב האישום במטרה להראות את השקר שבו.

לאחר שנה שישבנו בכלא, הגיעו שלושת העדים שהעידו נגד דניאל להעיד גם נגדנו: סמי, עליזה ותמנע. שוב לקחו אותנו מ"נווה תרצה" ברמלה לבית המשפט המחוזי בירושלים בנסיעות קשות ב"פוסטה". אני לא האמנתי שעליזה תעז להגיע לבית המשפט ותסתכל לנו בעיניים, תראה אותנו באזיקים בידיים וברגליים, ותוציא עדות שקר מפיה כדי לסגור אותנו ולקבל במרמה את הבת שלה. לא האמנתי שהלב שלה ייתן לה לראות אותנו, החברות שלה, במצב הזה, ולרצות שנהיה סגורות בכלא, בפרט בידיעה שהילדים של אילנה ושל אזמרה גם סובלים מכך שהאימהות שלהם כלואות. אך התברר שטעיתי. עליזה הגיעה להעיד, ונעמדה על דוכן העדים כמו שחקנית קרת מזג שמחכה שיתרגשו מהמשחק שלה וימחאו לה כפיים. היא הסתבכה בשקרים גסים. היא לא ידעה את מקום האירוע שסמי היה מעורב בו, לא את זמן האירוע, ואפילו לא זכרה מי נכח באירוע, היא גם לא ידעה להגיד מה בדיוק קרה באירוע, היא סתרה את עצמה וסתרה, את עדותו של סמי ויחד עם תמנע הם יצאו כולם שקרנים. השופטים החליטו שזה יהיה מיותר לבזבז את הזמן של בית המשפט לשמוע עוד כארבעה דיונים של ההגנה, והציעו לפרקליטות "לסגור אתנו עסקה". הוחלט לבטל את כל כתב האישום נגדנו, כולל הרקע הכללי לכתב האישום. השופטים כתבו בגזר הדין ש"לאור הראיות שלפניהם החליטו לשחרר אותנו מיד", וכדי להצדיק את השנה שישבנו במעצר, הרשיעו אותנו בהפרת הוראה חוקית ובהדחה בחקירה על כך שהודינו שנפגשנו בינינו הנשים כשהיה אסור לנו להיפגש.

באופן לא מובן ומאוד מכעיס, אצל דניאל בהכרעת הדין אותם הסעיפים לא בוטלו, והוא הורשע בגינם.

בתאריך 17.12.12 ביום השמיני של חנוכה, שוחררנו מהכלא. ברגע שיצאנו מהדלת הראשית של בית המשפט המחוזי בירושלים, אחרי שנה של מעצר, אילנה התחילה לרוץ ברחוב מרוב שמחה, ואזמרה ואני אחריה. הרגשנו כמו ציפורי דרור שהחזירו להן את החופש שלהן, הודינו להשם יתברך על נס חנוכה, אך עננה של עצבות הייתה מרחפת בינינו עדיין – הבעל שלנו עוד לא שוחרר!

תשעה חודשים לאחר מכן, באוקטובר 2013, היה יום הכרעת הדין של דניאל. עוה"ד מהמשרד של הסנגור אביגדור פלדמן הסבירה לנו שאין סיכוי שהשופטים ירשיעו את דניאל על עבודות. היא אפילו צחקה והוסיפה: "נשים חזקות ועצמאיות כמותכן זה יותר נכון שהוא הקרבן והעבד בסיפור". היא אמרה בניצחון שהם הצליחו להוכיח לבית המשפט שכל עדי התביעה שקרנים, ושהדבר היחיד שקצת מדאיג זה שבית המשפט חושב שתמנע אמינה. מהר מאוד היא גם הוסיפה שלא צריך לפחד מזה, כי הם הצליחו להוכיח לבית המשפט שתמנע היא רק עדת שמיעה של הסיפורים ששמעה ותו-לא. הזכרתי לה שכשהגיעה תמנע לעדות בבית המשפט, עוה"ד פלדמן הבריז ולא הגיע לדיון. עו"ד אחר מהמשרד התנצל שאינו מוכן לחקירה, והשופטים נתנו אפשרות לזמן את תמנע שוב לחקירה נגדית. שאלתי אותה: "למה החלטתם לוותר על האפשרות הזאת?" היא ענתה לי: "לא צריך לזמן שוב את תמנע, זה מיותר".

הגענו להכרעת הדין בתקווה ובציפייה שדניאל יחזור אתנו הביתה. חיכינו באולם בדריכות לשמוע את ההחלטה של השופטים. השופטים נכנסו לאולם בצעדים מהירים. קמנו לכבודם. אב בית הדין ביקש מכולם לשבת ואמר: "הכרעת הדין כוללת 152 עמודים. אני אסכם הכול במשפט אחד: מתוך עשרים אישומים לנאשם 1 (דניאל), אנו מרשיעים אותו בשמונה עשר אישומים, ואת נאשם 2 (אסא) אנו מרשיעים בארבעה אישומים". התפרצתי בצעקות על השופטים: "זה לא משפט אמת! דניאל חף מפשע! איך אתם עושים דבר כזה?!" הרגשתי שהעולם התמוטט. אזמרה בכתה וצעקה: "זה לא ייתכן שאתם מקשיבים לעליזה, אישה זונה אחת ולא לחמש נשים שהעידו לטובתו!" השומרים הוציאו אותנו מהאולם בכוח. אילנה ושירן נשארו המומות.

העיתונאים חיכו מחוץ לאולם, ורציתי לפנות אליהם ולספר על העוול הנורא שנעשה כאן, אך השומרים של בית המשפט הורידו אותי לקומה התחתונה, ואסרו עליי לדבר עם העיתונאים. ישבתי על ספסל סמוך לכניסה הראשית. בכיתי מעומק הנשמה. אחת השומרות נעמדה לידי להשגיח שלא אעלה למעלה. כשראיתי את עו"ד פלדמן יוצא באדישות מבית המשפט, מסתכל עליי במבט אטום, וממשיך ללכת, נשברתי וצרחתי לעברו עם כל כוחות הנפש שעוד היו בי: "מה עשית?!... איך זה יכול להיות?!... איך עשית עבודה כל כך גרועה?!" הייתי היסטרית, ואיבדתי שליטה על עצמי. אף פעם לא צרחתי ככה על מישהו. בכיתי בקול. הרגשתי שאני מתפרקת. עד היום אני לא מעכלת ולא רוצה לעכל את הבשורה המרה. על דניאל גזרו 26 שנים של מאסר בפועל, ועל אסא – 6 שנים. אני בתוך סיוט שעוד לא נגמר, מנסה להתעורר, ולא מצליחה. זועקת לעזרה, אף אחד לא שומע.

אילנה שירן אזמרה ואני נסענו לבית המעצר בירושלים. ידענו שיובילו את דניאל לשם להמתנה ב"פוסטה" עד שיסעו לכלא. קיווינו לראות אותו מעבר לחריצים הקטנים בחלונות המשאית המשטרתית. כשהגענו לחניה של בית המעצר, היו כמה "פוסטות" זהות, ולא יכולנו לדעת אם דניאל באחת מהן או שעוד לא הגיע. לפתע ראינו אצבע שיוצאת מאחד החורים שבחלון המשאית. ידענו שזה הוא מסמן לנו שהוא רואה אותנו. הוא היה מרוסק נפשית וכואב, ניסינו לסמן לו שיהיה חזק, היה לנו חשוב שידע שאנחנו אתו, אוהבות אותו, ונילחם ביחד להחזיר אותו הביתה. אחד הסוהרים של בית המעצר התעצבן כשראה אותנו, ואמר: "אני אראה לכם מה זה!", הביא מקל ארוך, וסגר את החלון של דניאל. חשבתי: איזה רוע, איזו אכזריות יש בעולם, למה אנשים מנצלים את התפקידים שלהם כדי לעשות רע לאחרים! הכול היה יותר מדי. שום דבר לא יוכל יותר להפתיע אותי. אך מאוחר יותר, כשהקשבתי לחדשות, ספגתי את הזעזוע הגדול ביותר של חיי. הפרקליטות הודיעה שהיא מערערת על "קלות העונש", והם דורשים 65 שנות מאסר לדניאל, ולאסא – 20.

**ניצול ציני של יומנים אישיים:**

כפי שסיפרתי, השתמשו בי, בכתבים הפרטיים שלי כראיה להרשיע את דניאל. ההתעקשות הזאת להשתמש בכתבים האלה נובעת מכך שלא היו ראיות להרשעה, לא היה להם עמוד שדרה משמעותי שיכול להצדיק את העלילה ההזויה והאכזרית הזאת... לכן היו צריכים לנקוט בווירטואוזיות משפטיות, ולבנות פאזל מפלצתי כמו בניין קלפים, שאם מוציאים חתיכה – כל הבניין נופל. עצם השימוש בכתבים אישיים שבן אדם כותב בינו לבין עצמו, זו בושה, זו חדירה ופגיעה עמוקה בפרטיות ובכבוד האדם ובחירותו, בפרט כשמשתמשים בזה כתמיכה מפוקפקת לראיות כושלות, ונותנים פירוש ציני וכוזב לציטוטים מהכתבים, שהוצאו לגמרי מהקשרם, רחוק מהכוונה שבה נכתבו הדברים. זה מזכיר לי סיפור ששמעתי על קיסר סיני שציווה על ההמון לכתוב יומנים אישיים. לאחר זמן-מה ציווה שיביאו אליו את כל היומנים, ועל פיהם החליט להעמיד לדין ולהרוג את כל מי שכתב מה שאינו לרוחו. ביהדות יש איסור הלכתי שנקרא "חרם דרבנו גרשום", שאותו אוהבים לצטט כשמדובר בחרם הזמני שעשה רבנו גרשום על עניין ריבוי נשים בארצות אשכנז, ומעניין שלא מצטטים אותו על האיסור שגזר שלא לפתוח מכתבים אישיים...

על אף שכתבו בהכרעת הדין: "שהמשקל הראייתי של היומן ייקבע על פי עמדת העד כלפי תוכן הרישום, מהותו, אימותו או הפרכתו...", התעלמו לגמרי מהעדויות המפורטות והמפורשות שנתתי. בהכרעת הדין ציטטו השופטים ממחברת אישית שלי, ונדהמתי לראות שכתוב שם בשמי: "אין לי רצון משלי אין לי מחשבה משלי מה נכון מה לא". (עמוד 57 בהכרעת הדין) זה לא ייתכן שכתבתי דבר כזה! ניגשתי למחברות שלי, ולאחר חיפושים רבים מצאתי את הכתוב. מקריאה שטחית מבינים מיד שמדובר בשאלה רטורית, "אין לי רצון משלי?! אין לי מחשבה משלי?!". שאלה שבאה בקונטקסט של שאלות פילוסופיות, המתלבטות במשמעות של הפסוק: "בטל רצונך בפני רצונו כדי שיבטל רצון אחרים בפני רצונך". פסוק

הלקוח מ"פרקי אבות", ומדבר על כך שביטול רצון האדם כלפי רצון השם גורם שהשם מבטל את הרצון של האנשים בפני רצונו. כתבתי כמו דיון ביני לבין עצמי על אודות משמעות הביטול בפני השם: האם המשמעות היא שאין לי רצון משלי או שיש לי רצון אך אני, מתוך עבודת השם, מבטלת את רצוני בפני רצון השם? רק התעלמות גסה ובוטה מתוכן הכתוב יכולה ליצור מציאות שיצטטו השופטים את המשפטים שכתבתי כשבסופם סימן קריאה(!) במקום סימן שאלה(?) וישייכו את תוכנם ל"כניעה" לדניאל. השופטים נאלצו להישען על המחברת שלי כדי לאשר את קביעתם השרירותית: "שהנשים שטופות מוח וללא דעה עצמאית" (כפי שכתבו בהכרעת הדין), ולא טרחו אפילו לדרוש בדיקה מקצועית של פסיכולוג או איש מקצוע שיאבחן אם אנחנו בעלות דעה עצמאית או לא. איך ייתכן שהשופטים שינו את תפקידם לצורך המשפט ל"פסיכולוגים לפי שעה", ונותנים לעצמם רשות לקבוע בהכרעת הדין (עמ' 38): "הנשים מבחינה שכלית ופסיכולוגית לא היו מסוגלות לעזוב את הנאשם ואת הבית...", ועל סמך אבחנה זו מרשיעים ב"החזקה בתנאי עבדות". האם השופטים במדינת ישראל שכחו והזניחו לחלוטין את הערכים הבסיסיים המנחים בערכה משפטית?

הפרקליט (התובע) שגיא אופיר, ניסה להוכיח שלדניאל הייתה שיטה לשלוח את הנשים "לגייס נפשות", כפי שכתוב בהכרעת הדין (עמ' 2): "במשך השנים פעלו נשותיו של נאשם 1 לאתר מועמדות נוספות להיות נשותיו ולהצטרף למשפחה, על מנת להפיץ את משנתו של הסבא", וראיה לכך הביא מהיומן שלי, וכך אמר: "אדרת מתמללת שיחה עם דניאל, ושם כותבת שהוא אומר: יש כאן עניין גדול להכניס אישה למשפחה". אם השופטים היו קוראים עוד שתי מילים קדימה באותו המשפט, היו מבינים שהתובע לקח חלק ממשפט, הוציא אותו מהקשרו, והפך את המשמעות שלו לשונה בתכלית. המשפט המקורי היה: "יש כאן עניין גדול להכניס אישה למשפחה <u>זו אחריות גדולה שיכולה גם חס ושלום להרוס את הכול!</u>" משפט שאמר דניאל דווקא במשמעות ההפוכה. זו הייתה שיחה שהתפתחה בעקבות התאריך שקבעתי כשרציתי שעד יום ההולדת שלי יהיה סימן טוב, ורציתי להתפלל שתגיע אישה. ודניאל ניסה לצמצם את ההתלהבות שלי ואומר שם בפירוש: "זה לא עניין האישה, גם את יכולה עוד להביא ילדים... להכניס אישה למשפחה זו אחריות גדולה שיכולה גם חס ושלום להרוס את הכול!". איך ייתכן שהשופטים לא עשו את המאמץ לקרוא עוד שתי מילים קדימה ביומן? האם זה מכיוון שרצו לקבל את דברי התובע כ"תורה מסיני", בלי לבדוק ולחקור את אמינותם, או מכיוון שזה פשוט התאים למה שהחליטו, לפני שניגשו למשפט?!

כאשר התובע האשים את דניאל ששלח אותי ל"עונש בגלות" על סמך היומנים שלי, חשבתי שאני יוצאת מדעתי. הייתכן? בדקתי שוב ביומנים, ומצאתי את הציטוט שהביא התובע כראיה, מתוך תפילה שכתבתי לבורא עולם, תפילה בחרוזים שמדברת על גלות הנפש וגעגועיה לאביה שבשמים. ציפיתי שהשופט יבין את האמת ויגער בפרקליט שמנסה בכוח לעוות את הדברים, נדהמתי לראות שבקלות יתר השופט אימץ את עמדת התובע.

יש אין-סוף דוגמאות מהיומנים המראות איך עיוותו את הנאמר ונתנו לכתוב פרשנות משלהם לפי התכנית להרשיע. על פי האמת היומנים מעידים על היותי עצמאית ובלתי תלויה, ולמעשה היו צריכים להוות ראיה של ההגנה אם רק היו השופטים מסתכלים בהם בצורה אובייקטיבית.

---

אני לעולם, אבל לעולם לא אסלח לכל מי שהשתתף בפשע הנורא הזה, לכל מי שנתן יד לעיוות הדין האיום הזה, ולכל מי שיש לו חלק בשואה שפקדה את משפחתי. בתוכי אני יודעת שהאדמה לא תשקוט. אני יודעת שהשמים לא ישקטו. אני רוצה להעתיק כאן תפילה מתוך ליקוטי תפילות של רבי נתן:

> "ותשפיע עלינו כח וגבורה מאתך בזכות הצדיקי אמת. ותעזרנו ותושיענו שנזכה להכניע ולהשפיל עדי ארץ כל המתנגדים החולקים על האמת ונזכה לעקור ולשבר ולבטל כל המקטרגים והמלשינים על הרחוקים הבאים להתקרב אליך באמת, החפצים ליראה את שמך, אף על פי שאין אנו כדאים להתקרב אליך לפי מעשינו, אף על פי כן 'רחמיך רבים השם' רחמיך רבים מאוד, עשה אתה עמנו מה שתרצה וכרצונך עשה עמנו. ומי יאמר לך מה תעשה, אבל מי שם אותם לדין ושופט, לדון אותנו חס ושלום, ולקטרג עלינו חלילה. מי ביקש זאת מידם לרמוס על הנרדפים חלילה. 'כי אתה אשר הכית רדפו, ואל מכאוב חלליך יספרו. אפלה נא ביד השם כי רבים רחמיו וביד אדם אל אפולה'. רבונו של עולם, שומע צעקה מעמקי השאול תחתיות ומתחתיו, שמע צעקתי ואנחתי המרה מאוד, הכבדה מאוד העמוקה מאוד!"

אילנה היא האישה הראשונה של דניאל, שיחד הביאו לעולם עשרה ילדים, ולאחר עשר שנות נישואין אתו פתחה את ביתה לנו, חברותיה. לדעת כולנו זוהי "אשת חיל" אמתית. וכעת נעבור לסיפור האישי שלה.

**הסיפור של אילנה האישה הראשונה, חלק ראשון**

אני אילנה אמבש. הייתי אלופת צרפת בקונג פו. נסעתי לרפובליקה של סין בטאיוואן יחד עם המשלחת מצרפת כדי להתמודד באליפות עולם בקונג פו ובוקס סיני, לא בגלל שרציתי מדליה, לא הלכתי לחפש כבוד, המאסטר הסיני הזקן לצ'י קונג שלמדתי אצלו אמר שזה יהיה לי לניסיון חיים.

במשך ימי התחרות היינו מגיעים לאצטדיון כדי להסתכל על הקרבות של החברים מהמשלחת. רק שעה לפני הקרב הודיעו לי שהיום זה הסיבוב שלי ואני צריכה להתמודד מול אלופת סין.

ההודעה על הקרב הייתה די מפתיעה ולא כל כך הוגנת. אפילו שלא הייתי מוכנה לאותו היום, וגם הייתי אפילו בצום קיבלתי את ההודעה בקור רוח. הלכתי להתאמן בחדר צדדי מבודד, סמוך לאולם האימונים. ישבתי ישיבה מזרחית על הרצפה והתרכזתי בצ'י קונג ובמדיטציה כדי להכין את עצמי לקרב. אחרי כמה תנועות הרגשתי מוכנה.

חודש לפני אליפות העולם הלכתי לחנות מכולת בצרפת ונשבר בקבוק זכוכית על הרגל שלי. הוא חתך לי חלק מהגיד ברגל. במיון של בית החולים הרופא אמר שבשום אופן אינני יכולה להתחרות באליפות עולם לפחות שלושה חודשים. החלטתי שאני אסע. התרכזתי כדי לרפא את הרגל בעזרת המחשבה, לפי מה שלמדתי ברפואה הסינית, ואפילו שהייתי קצת צולעת הלכתי להילחם.

האצטדיון היה מלא באלפי צופים מכל העולם. כשהגעתי לזירת הקרב נתנו לי קימונו כחול, ומולי ניצבה אלופת סין, לבושה קימונו צהוב. היא הייתה הרבה יותר גבוהה ממני. לא הסתכלתי עליה. השיטה שלי הייתה לא להסתכל על האויב, רק להרגיש אותו.

הקרב היה מאוד קצר. אלופת סין רצתה לגרום לי לצאת מהזירה, נתתי לה להרגיש שהיא עומדת לנצח ואז הפכתי את זה נגדה, ובסיבוב מהיר, במכת מחץ אחת, הפלתי אותה בנוקאאוט רציני. היא שברה את האף והוצאה באלונקה מהזירה. זכיתי במקום רביעי בעולם.

באימוני הלחימה של הקונג פו הייתי האישה היחידה בקבוצה של גברים. שניים היו מחזיקים שק אגרוף, ואני, בבעיטה אחת שלי תוך כדי קפיצה, הייתי מעיפה את שניהם.

לקונג פו הגעתי מתוך חיפוש רוחני. האימונים היו עבורי חיבור לאמונה. אהבתי את האצילות, את השליטה, את הריכוז הנדרש בחוקי הלחימה הסינית. אהבתי את האימונים ואת העבודה הקשה, גם את העליות, הירידות והמלחמות. לא מצאתי את התכלית בחכמות של המזרח הרחוק, והחלטתי לחזור לשורשים שלי – ליהדות.

הבנתי שהאתגר האמתי בשבילי, שעליו אני רוצה להילחם, זה לחיות בארץ ישראל, לעבוד על המידות של עצמי, להביא ילדים לעולם ולטפל בהם. כשהתחלתי לחזור בתשובה והייתי בשידוך עם דניאל רציתי להוליד ממנו 26 ילדים. היה לי סוג של חלום, ובו אני מגדלת הרבה ילדים, שעומדים על הר גבוה בטבע, מתפללים ושרים ומהללים את השם יתברך. החלום שלי התגשם, עליתי לארץ ישראל, נהייתי אימא לעשרה ילדים, וגידלתי עוד תשעה ילדים עם האימהות האחרות. הקדשתי להם את כל כולי, טיפלתי בהם עם כל הלב והנפש, הם היו שמחת החיים שלי. התרגשתי מאוד שכל הילדים רקדו ושרו להשם עם אבא שלהם בהופעות שמוקדשות להילולות של הצדיקים מול אלפי אנשים. הייתי מאוד גאה שזכיתי להיות המפיקה של ההופעות האלה. הבנים הגדולים נהיו חזנים בבית הכנסת של רבי נ נח נחמ נחמן מאומן.

כשסוף סוף הגעתי לתכלית הרוחנית שחיפשתי כל חיי, ולהגשמת השאיפות שלי, "חטפתי מכה מתחת לחגורה". השופטים במדינת ישראל תקעו לי סכין בגב נגד כל כללי ההגינות. בשנת **2011**, בלי לשאול אותי, בלי לחקור, בלי לבדוק, בלי לחפש אמת, הם קבעו שאני השפחה של בעלי, שהוא מנצל אותי מינית

וכלכלית, והכריזו עליי שאני אישה מוכה. לקחו לי את הילדים, הפרידו ביניהם, פיזרו אותם במוסדות סגורים של הרווחה, ושלחו את בעלי בעקבות עלילות שווא למאסר של 26 שנה!

נולדתי במרוקו, ובגיל שנתיים המשפחה שלי עברה לצרפת. גדלתי בעיקר בין לא-יהודים. המשפחה של אימא שלי הייתה ממשפחה מכובדת מאוד שייחוסה ניתן לה בזכות אחד מגדולי חכמי מרוקו מהמאה ה-19, שהיה אב בית דין בפס, וראש בית דין גבוה ברבאט. נכדו היה סבא שלי, הדיין האחרון בשושלת של 23 דיינים במשפחה. גם הוא היה ראש אב בית דין בפס וברבאט, אך בתור ילדה הייתי מופתעת לשמוע את סבתא מתלוננת ובוכה לי שהיא חושדת שהוא מתעסק עם השפחות הערביות שעבדו אצלם בבית. היא פחדה שאולי בגלל זה נפטר לה תינוק קטן, משה. אימא שלי לא נשארה דתייה וגידלה אותי באווירה חילונית. אבא שלי שהיה בעל תואר ראשון בכימיה, שנא את הדת ואת האנשים הדתיים. הוא האמין במדע וברציונליות. בבית היו מעט מאוד סממנים יהודים מסורתיים. לפעמים כשאימא התגעגעה לשמירת שבת והייתה עורכת שולחן לכבוד השבת, אבא היה הופך את השולחן תוך כדי צעקות וגידופים. הדודים שלי מצד אימא היו יהודים הדוקים, והדודות שלי מצד אבא היו נשואות לנוצרים וחגגו את החגים הנוצריים, ואני גדלתי בתוך הקונפליקט הזה. מאז שהייתי בת שמונה, אני זוכרת שהתארחתי אצל אחות של אימא שלי, שהייתה חרדית; והייתי הולכת אתה ביום כיפור לבית הכנסת, אך כיוון שלא כל כך הבנתי, ולא ידעתי מה צריך לעשות בתפילה, הייתי בוכה. נשבר לי הלב, רציתי לדבר עם השם ולא ידעתי איך. כשהייתי חוזרת לאורח החיים החומרי, בבית של ההורים שלי, זה היה מדכא אותי. כשגדלתי, חשבתי שדרך חכמת סין אצליח להתעלות מעל החומר ולהבין את תכלית החיים. בפרט התלהבתי מאומנויות הלחימה של המזרח הרחוק, והחלטתי ללמוד אותן. ההורים שלי לא הבינו אותי, ולכן הייתי מסתירה את כפפות הקרטה ואת המגנים מתחת לבגדים, והולכת לאימונים נגד רצונם. כשהייתי בת עשרים הם רצו לחתן אותי עם הבן של המנהלת של אבא שלי, כיוון שהיה עשיר, ולא הפריע להם שהוא שנא יהודים. כששאלתי אותם איך הם מציעים כזו הצעה הרי הוא אנטישמי, הם ענו לי: "תגיירי אותו, העיקר שיש לו כסף". היה לי קשה שהם לא רגישים לחיפוש שלי.

חשבתי שמתוך עבודה על היכולות הפנימיות, אפשר להגיע לחיבור להשם. למדתי שיש שני מושגים הודיים: "אוטו גדול", ו"אוטו קטן". כלומר, יש שתי גישות לחיים. או שאתה כמו באוטו קטן ומסיע רק את עצמך, או שאתה נוהג באוטו גדול ולוקח אתך גם אחרים. בחרתי באוטו הגדול. הקונג פו כולל את הרפואה הסינית. האמנתי שאפשר להתחבר לטבע ולהשם ודרך זה לרפא אחרים. לכן השקעתי בלימודים ובאימונים.

הייתי נוהגת להיכנס לעומק היערות הסמוכים לפריז עם מקל, עם חרב אימונים ועם תיק קטן על הגב ובתוכו לחם כפרי ומימייה שאותה הייתי ממלאה במי המעיין שתחת ההר. לפעמים הייתי נשארת שם בלילות כדי להמשיך להתאמן. בלילה הייתי מדליקה אש, והמקום שם הפך להיות כמו הבית השני שלי. אהבתי לאכול את פרות היער; הייתי עולה להר בריצה; הייתי מתאמנת גם בשלג בלי נעליים ובלי גרביים. שיפרתי את היכולות שלי גם בלימודי הצ'י קונג שמלמד שליטה באנרגיה ובנשימה על פי עקרונות הרפואה הסינית. בעזרת ריכוז ותנועות מפעילים את האנרגיה הפנימית (הצ'י). בעזרת שליטה באנרגיה אפשר להגיע להישגים מדהימים בלחימה, לשליטה עצמית, לאיזון רגשי, לפיתוח החושים ולפיתוח כוחות פיזיים, עבודה שדרשה ריכוז רב. פעם אחת, תוך כדי אימונים ביער, הרגשתי בלי לראות שמישהו במרחק של כמאתיים מטר מתקרב אליי כדי להתקיף אותי. הפחדתי אותו כשביצעתי תנועות לחימה במקל. הוא הבין שלא כדאי לו להתקרב אליי וברח במהירות.

את הפארקים בפריז היו נועלים בשעה 21:00. לפעמים הייתי מטפסת על הגדר כדי להיכנס לפארק הנעול בלילה ולהתאמן בשקט. באחד הלילות, כשהייתי מאוד מרוכזת בתנועות לחימה של קונג פו וצ'י קונג, ראיתי לפתע מולי ארבעה בריונים ערבים מלווים בכלב גרמני גדול. לא התייחסתי אליהם. אחד מהם צעק על הכלב: "תקוף!" הכלב רץ במהירות לכיוון שלי. באותו רגע התחברתי בלב ובנפש להשם והתעלמתי מהם. הכלב רץ עד למרחק של חצי מטר ממני, וחזר אליהם בהליכה אטית. אחד מהם התעצבן וצעק עליו שוב: "תקוף!" הוא רץ לעברי בשנית וחזר אליהם. אחרי הפעם השלישית שניסו לשווא, הם כנראה הבינו שלא כדאי להם להתעסק אתי ועזבו. הודיתי להשם.

כשהתחלתי את לימודי הקונג פו, ידעתי שבודהה ופסלים הם עבודה זרה, והיה לי ברור שאני לא אפול בזה, כי אמנם לא הייתי דתייה, אך האמנתי תמיד בהשם יתברך. אבל בסופו של דבר, התאווה ללמוד רפואה אלטרנטיבית; הספרים של טיבט ולימודי הרפואה הטיבטית – גרמו לי לחשוב שיש סודות, ואלה משכו אותי, לצערי, לאמונות זרות.

התפנית החדה שעוררה את הנשמה היהודית שלי הייתה כשהייתי בת 22, אחרי האליפות בטאיוואן. בדרך לעוד אימון ביער, פנתה אליי אישה יהודייה ואמרה לי: "את יודעת שכל הגוף שלך זה אותיות של שם

השם?" המילים שלה חדרו ללבי. היא נתנה לי להבין שביהדות יש אוצר רוחני מאוד גבוה, וכך התחלתי ללמוד מה יש ביהדות. באותה תקופה, בחודש אב, הגעתי לאזכרה של סבא שלי שאול, אבא של אבא. כשהשתטחתי על קברו, נפתח לי הלב והתחלתי לזעוק "איפה האמת". הרגשתי שאני מבולבלת מכל חכמות המזרח הרחוק. בכיתי מתוך צעקה להשם שיראה לי מה האמת (באותו זמן עוד לא ידעתי שבדיוק באותו חודש דניאל נסע לאומן שבאוקראינה לקברו של רבי נחמן להתפלל על זיווג). כשחזרתי מבית הקברות, הערוץ היהודי בטלוויזיה היה דלוק, הייתה תכנית על רבי נחמן, והראו חסידי ברסלב רוקדים. הרגשתי שזו התשובה לתפילתי על קברו של סבא שלי. מיד הלכתי לקנות את הספרים של רבי נחמן, כדי ללמוד איך לחזור בתשובה.

בחופשת הקיץ הייתי מתפללת הרבה בחדר בבית הוריי. כל ערב הייתי הולכת לשיעורי תורה. יום אחד, לכבוד ט"ו בשבט הלכתי עם אימא שלי להרצאה בבית הכנסת, ישבנו בעזרת נשים, ואימא שלי אמרה לי להסתכל על בחור חרדי שישב בשיעור. זה היה דניאל. הוא היה בעזרת גברים, ולא ראה אותי.

מהקהילה היהודית פנו אליי בבקשה ללמד ילדים קונג פו. התחלתי ללמד, עד שהרגשתי שאני לא יכולה בשום אופן להיות גורם למכשול. פחדתי שההתלהבות של הילדים מהקונג פו תרחיק אותם מהדת, והם יתפתו לעבודה זרה, לכן הפסקתי את השיעורים. התנצלתי בפני האימהות שאיני יכולה להמשיך. באותה תקופה המשכתי ללמוד סיפורי מעשיות וליקוטי תפילות של רבי נחמן, ולהתבודד שעות בתפילה.

סבא שלי, הדיין ממרוקו, רצה שאתחתן עם רופא שיניים עשיר שהיה ממשפחה של כוהנים. סירבתי, כי כבר החלטתי שאני רוצה להתחתן עם בחור שאוהב את רבי נחמן. לא רופא שיניים, ולא מהנדס.

עבדתי שלושה ימים בחנות ששמה "כי טוב", באזור היהודי בפריז. התיידדתי עם בחורה שעבדה בחנות ספרים סמוכה, סיפרתי לה שאני חוזרת בתשובה. הייתי שם ביום שישי כשדניאל הגיע לאותו אזור כדי לקנות חלות וספר לכבוד שבת. מסתבר שאותה בחורה הייתה חברה של אחות של דניאל, ושלחה אותו לראות אותי כשידוך. יצאתי מחוץ לחנות כדי לסדר את המגבות ופריטים אחרים, והבחנתי בדניאל מעבר לכביש. חייכתי אליו והוא הלך.

ביום האחרון לעבודה שלי בחנות, הגיעה אחותו של דניאל עם בעלה לחנות, להציע לי להיפגש עם אחיה ל"שידוך". היא לקחה ממני מספר טלפון, והעבירה לדניאל. כשהתקשר אליי, הזמין אותי למסיבת יום ההולדת של אחותו. מיד אחרי העבודה עליתי על הרכבת התחתית ונסעתי לשם. הייתה אווירה חמה ונעימה. בסוף המסיבה, מנו, בנו בן החמש מנישואים קודמים אמר: "אבא, אולי תתחתן אתה?" התרגשתי.

דניאל למד גמרא בישיבת "פאווה" בפריז. במוצאי יום כיפור, לאחר ברכת לבנה, החליט הרב של הישיבה לעשות לנו טקס אירוסין. מוצאי יום כיפור נקרא בספרים "יום הגדלת שם השם", ואחרי ברכת לבנה זו הייתה הרגשה מיוחדת של עת רצון. של התחלה חדשה. היו לי כיסופים חזקים לתשובה ולהגדלת שם השם בעולם. למדתי ב"ליקוטי מוהר"ן" של רבי נחמן כי: לכל צדיק יש חיידר, שהבל פה של הילדים נותן כוח לאותו צדיק לנצח את המלחמה נגד עמלק. רציתי שיהיו הרבה ילדים לחיידר של הצדיק רבי נחמן.

התחתנו בשמיני של חנוכה. אחרי החופה הייתה לי מין ידיעה פנימית שבשביל להגשים את השאיפות שלי ולהצליח לגדל 26 ילדים, אני אצטרך עזרה של עוד נשים. כמובן שלא סיפרתי לדניאל על הרעיון שלי. ידעתי שהוא רוצה שנחיה כמו כל האנשים בקהילה החרדית בפריז, אך בלבי קיוויתי שהרצון שלי יתגשם.

שנה לאחר החתונה נולד לנו בן. דניאל חזר מהקיבוץ של ראש השנה באומן, וסיפר לי שקיבלנו מהתלמיד היקר של רבי נחמן, רבי ישראל בער אודסר, המכונה "הסבא", ברכה שנזכה לעלות לארץ ישראל. התרגשתי מאוד. חודש לאחר מכן זה קרה, הודיעו לנו מהסוכנות היהודית" שיש עבורנו מקום במרכז קליטה במבשרת ציון. עלינו לארץ ישראל!

בארץ, זכינו לארח אצלנו בבית, לתקופה מיוחדת במינה, את רבי ישראל בער אודסר, שקיבל מכתב בכתב ידו של רבי נחמן חתום ב-נ נח נחמ נחמן מאומן גילוי הסוד של ה"שיר חדש". בעקבות הסבא, היו מגיעים אלינו כל מיני אנשים לדבר אתו. זה היה תענוג לשמוע את הסבא שר ניגונים נפלאים מאוד עם החברים. כששמעתי שאמר שההפצה עולה על הכול; שחשוב שבכל בית בישראל יהיו הספרים והפתק של רבי נחמן; ושאם כל בנות ישראל היו לובשות את הקמע של נ נח נחמ נחמן מאומן, היו כולן טהורות וקדושות, ויהיה נולד דור חדש ירא השם, חשבתי שחשוב מאוד שאתחיל להפיץ לנשים, ולהכין קמעות בכל מיני צורות. באותה תקופה לא היו עדיין הרבה נשים מפיצות. הייתי מפיצה לבד. כמעט כל שנה ילדתי. היו חודשים שלא יכולתי להפיץ, כי הייתי עסוקה עם הלידה ועם התינוק החדש. התפללתי שיגיעו נשים שירצו גם הן להפיץ יחד אתי, ויחזקו את ההפצה לנשים.

כשהבן השני שלנו היה בן חודשיים, הסבא היה אצלנו בבית, והוא אמר: "תגידו לי כשהוא יתחיל לשיר". באותו זמן לא הבנתי למה הוא התכוון. שנים אחר כך, כשהבן הזה גדל והפך לזמר הראשי של להקת "הבעטלירס", הבנו, שאת הכישרון היוצא מן הכלל שלו, הוא קיבל במתנה. שוב ראיתי במו עיניי איך מתקיימות הברכות של הצדיק. כשנולד עוד בן, הסבא היה הסנדק שלו בברית המילה, ונתן לו את שמו.

בי"ח בחשוון תשנ"ה (1995), מוצאי שבת, הייתי בבית עם הילדים. דניאל היה עם החברים בבית חולים "הדסה", ליד רבי ישראל שהיה מאושפז. אני והילדים התפללנו בשירים ובריקודים לרפואת הצדיק. לפתע, בבת-אחת נכבה ה"נר תמיד" שהדלקנו בבית לכבוד רבי נחמן, וכן כל האורות בסלון. כמה דקות לאחר מכן דניאל התקשר והודיע לי שרבי ישראל הסתלק. אמרתי לו שכשהאורות וה"נר תמיד" כבו, הרגשתי שמשהו קרה.

אחרי פטירת הצדיק, הרגשנו שצריך לעשות משהו. דניאל דיבר אתי על זה. הוא חשב למכור את הבית שקנינו מכספי עבודתו ככוריאוגרף באירופה, ולתרום את הכסף לצדקה ולהדפסת הספרים של רבי נחמן ושל הסבא. אמנם זה היה צעד נועז שדורש אומץ כדי לעשות אותו, בפרט שהיו לנו שישה ילדים לכלכל, אבל האמנו שזה צעד נכון, שיביא ברכה. חיזקתי את דניאל לקיים ולעשות זאת. מה שהגדיל את התלהבותנו זה שרבי ישראל, בימי חייו, אסף כל פרוטה וצדקה שקיבל, ואת כל כספי הביטוח הלאומי שלו כדי להקים קרן להדפסת הספרים של רבי נחמן והפצתם במחיר הדפוס (בלי רווח). דניאל הצטער מאוד שהוא לא תרם את הדירה שלנו לפני פטירת הצדיק, ועד היום הוא מצטער על זה. הייתה בנו אמונה חזקה שזה מה שצריך לעשות. אחרי שזכינו לחיות עם הסבא בבית, היה לנו מאוד חשוב להפקיר הכול למען ההפצה. דניאל אפילו הקים תחנת רדיו בשם "נ-נח" שפעלה 24 שעות ביממה. שמחתי וחיזקתי את בעלי להפיץ לכל עם ישראל. במבט לאחור, אני שמחה שבחרנו לעשות את הצעד הזה שבזכותו היו השגחות נפלאות, אם לא הייתי רוצה בזה, ודאי היה מתפתח סיפור אחר לגמרי. דניאל הדהים אותי במסירות הנפש שלו, באכפתיות שלו, בארגון ההפצות ובחיזוק החברים. הבית היה פתוח להכנסת אורחים לכל המפיצים בשבתות ובמשך כל השבוע, וראיתי בזה זכות גדולה. אחרי שמכרנו את הבית והקדשנו את כל הכסף לצדקה לרבי ישראל, נסענו לחפש דירה להשכרה בשכונת נווה יעקב. ראינו מודעה של דירה זולה בת ארבעה חדרים. הגענו לשם, ונשארנו שלוש שנים. בעל הבית היה נחמד ומתחשב, ואמר לנו שנוכל לשלם לו מתי שנוח לנו. הדירה הייתה מרווחת ובעלת נוף ליער, יכולנו לראות רועי צאן עם כבשים. דניאל ואני היינו לוקחים את כל הילדים לטיולים ביער, והילדים חוו הרפתקאות כמו ב"סיפורי מעשיות" של רבי נחמן.

בכוח הכסף הזה שהופקר ממכירת הבית, דניאל בכל שנה, ביום ההסתלקות של הסבא, י"ח בחשוון, ארגן והפיק עם החברים את ההילולה לכבודו. אירוע ענק לציבור הרחב בחינם. כל שנה הם מצאו מקום מתאים לאלפי אנשים, הזמינו להקות מוזיקה מפורסמות, הקרינו סרטים על רבי ישראל במסך ענק, העמידו שולחנות עם ספרים למכירה במחיר הדפוס, ודאגו לכיבוד משובח לבאים. בסיום ההילולה חיכו אוטובוסים להסיע את הקהל הרחב ל"הר המנוחות", לציון של רבי ישראל. שבוע לפני האירוע היינו תולים מודעות ענק להזמנת הקהל הרחב. את קארי הכרתי בהילולה השלישית. היא הגיעה עם בתה צילה בת ה-11. היא ניגשה אליי, וניסתה להיות נחמדה. היא סיפרה לי שאצלם בבית, היא והילדים כל היום מאזינים לתחנת נ-נח ברדיו. היא הייתה מתקשרת לרדיו, ומבקשת שידאגו לה ל"שידוך". ככה היא פגשה את הבעל השישי שלה. אמריקאי כמוה. נזכרתי שכבר קודם ראיתי אותה, באיזו חתונה, מפיצה אתו ספרים של רבי נחמן באנגלית. היא סיפרה לי שקנתה לו מחשב כדי לעודד אותו לתרגם ולהדפיס. היא התנדבה למכור את הספרים בשולחן ההפצה לנשים בהילולה, והייתה מלאת התפעלות מהאירוע. היא סיפרה לי שעלתה לארץ מאמריקה לפני 19 שנה כדי להתגייס לצה"ל. אחרי הצבא היא לקחה חלק בהקמת קיבוץ בצפון הארץ, ואפילו קיבלה שם בית. היה לה חבר במשך כמה שנים, הוא לא רצה להתחתן אתה והם נפרדו. איכשהו הגיע לידיה "סיפורי מעשיות" באנגלית, ואחרי שקראה אותו חיפשה שידוך ברסלב. הכישלונות של ששת נישואיה הקודמים, גרמו למשברים קשים ולבעיות התנהגות אצל ילדיה, והיא לא הצליחה להשתלט עליהם. היא אמרה שההפצה תמיד נתנה לה כוח לשרוד כי למעשה המצב הבריאותי שלה החמיר. הבעל האמריקאי עזב אותה ונעלם כשהרופאים הודיעו לה שחלתה בסרטן סופני. קארי הייתה בת 38 ונראתה מבוגרת הרבה יותר. רזה וצנומה עד כדי כך שהלחיים כמעט נדבקו אחת לשנייה, ועיגולים שחורים נראו מסביב לעיניה. גופה היה חלש ונאבק במחלות רבות, ניכר שעברה לא מעט תלאות. היא ביקשה רחמים שניקח את הילדים ונגדל אותם אצלנו עם הילדים שלנו. היה זה בחודשי הקיץ, ימי החופש הגדול. הילדים של קארי הרגישו טוב בבית שלנו, וקיבלו הרבה אהבה ותשומת לב ממני, מדניאל ומאדרת, שהייתה מורה מוסמכת והקימה כיתה לבנות בביתה. ביום ההילולה של האר"י הקדוש, כשדניאל והחברים נסעו לצפת להפצה, אני חשבתי לשמח את קארי, ולהזמין אותה לצאת להפיץ יחד אתי בבית חולים. שיתפתי את אדרת ברעיון שלי, והיא אמרה שטוב שאני חושבת על קארי, והציעה לי שהיא תישאר לעשות "קייטנה" לילדים. קארי שמחה מאוד, והייתה אווירה טובה בינינו. זמן קצר אחר כך, ביום חמישי אחד, רציתי להכין את הבית ואת הבישולים לשבת, אבל לא יכולתי, כי יאן דהר בתוך הבית על הרולרס, עדיין פרוע ולא

ממושמע, אפילו שבכל זאת הוא היה מתוק, הוא פתח את המקרר כל חמש דקות, וכל הילדים רצו אחריו בכל הבית והרגשתי שאני מאבדת שליטה עליהם. הייתי בהיריון השישי, לא ידעתי מה לעשות, פתאום יאן שם לב לדאגה שלי, ובלי שביקשתי ממנו, הוריד את הרולרס שהיו כקבע לרגליו, והתחיל לשפוך מים עם סבון על הרצפה ולקרצף את הרצפות במטבח עם מטאטא. הוא לא נרגע עד שהמטבח היה מצוחצח כמו מעבדה, אז מיד התחלתי ללוש בהתלהבות בצק לחלות לכבוד שבת. חזרה האווירה הנעימה מאוד בבית עם ההכנות של שבת. פתאום צלצל הטלפון, כשידיי מלאות בצק, קולעת חלת צמות. זו הייתה קארי. בשמחה ובספונטניות סיפרתי לה על הנס שקרה לי בבית, איך שהכול היה מבולגן, עד שיאן ריחם עליי, תפס את העניינים לידיו, וניקה לי את כל המטבח כך שיכולתי להתקדם בהכנות לשבת... קארי הגיבה בזעם יוצא דופן, ואמרה במבטא האמריקאי שלה: "הבן שלי מנקה אצלך ולא אצלי! תעלי את הילדים שלי עכשיו על מונית ותשלחי לי אותם חזרה! מיד!" אמרתי לה שאני לא יכולה לשלוח ילדים לבד במונית בדרך מסוכנת, שעוברת דרך כפר ערבי... הצעתי לה לחכות שדניאל יחזור בערב והוא יחזיר אותם אליה ברכב שלנו. היא אמרה: "מה? אני אשלח לך עו"ד עכשיו!" הרגשתי שחטפתי סטירה מצלצלת דרך הטלפון, ולא הבנתי מה יש לה. גם אדרת שנכחה בסיטואציה הייתה בהלם. כשדניאל חזר בערב הביתה הוא מיד נסע להחזיר לה את הילדים, ואמר לה שתעזוב אותנו בשקט ושלא תצער אותי עוד, הרי עזרתי לה עם הילדים. אחרי כמה ימים היא התקשרה בטון מתחנחן וביקשה סליחה על כפיות הטובה שלה. אני ודניאל החלטנו לסלוח לה ולרחם עליה בגלל כל הייסורים שהיא עוברת בגלל מחלתה. היא והילדים שוב הגיעו אלינו הרבה, ויאן עבר ללמוד עם הבנים שלנו באופן קבוע ב"חיידר" שנקרא "אבי הנחל" בבית המדרש בגבעת שאול היא ראתה שהילדים שלה מתקדמים בלימודים, יאן, שלא ידע קרוא וכתוב, הפתיע במוטיבציה שלו ללמוד, וגם בתוצאות. בשבת היא הייתה לוחשת לי באוזן: "איך ב ע ל ך מטפל טוב בילדים!" ומגלגלת את הלשון במבטא אמריקאי כבד, ומאריכה בהדגשה: "...ב ע ל ך...". לא ידעתי אם אני צריכה לפחד או לשמוח...

כעבור כמה חודשים, היא ביקשה לדבר אתי ועם דניאל בפרטיות, והושיבה אותנו לשיחה בסלון. בקול נמוך ורך אמרה שהמחלה מתפשטת בגופה, ולפי דברי הרופאים לא נותר לה הרבה זמן לחיות. היא אמרה שהיא קצת מתביישת, אפילו שהיא לא הייתה ביישנית בכלל, ובכל זאת, אמרה, שהיא מבקשת שנרחם עליה וניקח אותה כאישה שנייה. אני ודניאל השתתקנו, היא המשיכה והסבירה את עמדתה, שלפי דעתה, צורת החיים שלנו היא הכי קרובה למה שכתוב בספרים של רבי נחמן; והאהבה שלנו לצדיק מעניקה חינוך טוב ובריא לילדינו, וזה משהו שהיא לא ראתה בשום משפחה אחרת, גם לא אצל הבעלים הברסלבים הקודמים שהיו לה, בפרט לא את שמחת החיים הזו, עם המוזיקה והריקודים, שלדבריה "החיו אותה"; היא אמרה שראתה שאנחנו בית יציב, ושהילדים מסתדרים טוב ביניהם, והם משפיעים לטובה על ילדיה, וגורמים להם לרצות ללמוד ולהיות רגועים יותר; ושדניאל הוא בעל רגיש ומתחשב, שזה דבר נדיר שלא ניתן למצוא היום. היא ניסתה לשכנע אותנו שזו תהיה מצווה לקחת אותה בתור אישה שנייה, אחרי כל מה שהיא עברה מהבעלים הקודמים שלה. ונתנה פירושים דרך "סיפורי מעשיות" ומשלים שזה הרי משמים ושהיא במצב של פיקוח נפש, וילדיה אינם יכולים לגדול בלי אבא. היא ביקשה שנבין אותה, שהיא לא יכולה להישאר לבד, ולא רוצה להתחתן שוב, כי מניסיונה המר, היא לא רוצה לעשות עוד טעויות, והיא סומכת רק עלינו. היא אמרה שהיא יודעת שלפי ההלכה אין שום איסור ליהודי להתחתן עם כמה נשים, וגם בדקה את זה עם רבנים. היא סיפרה לנו גם שהכירה כמה משפחות שחיות ככה, ביישוב ראש העין, שם גרה עם בעלה הראשון, בשכונות לתימנים רבים, ואצלם זה מקובל ורגיל, ומה גם שהיא יודעת ש"חרם דרבנו גרשום", שאסר על אשכנזים ריבוי נשים, היה תקף רק לאלף שנה, וכבר מזמן הסתיים. היה ברור שהיא מאוד רוצה שזה יקרה ושהיא לא תקבל "לא" כתשובה. אני לא ידעתי מה להגיד. הייתי נשואה לדניאל כבר עשר שנים, היו לנו שבעה ילדים, והייתי בהיריון. אמנם תמיד רציתי שהמשפחה תגדל, אבל קארי לא הייתה טיפוס קל, וכבר הספקתי לחוות כמה שיגעונות שלה... זו הייתה נראית לי משימה קשה ביותר, אולי אפילו בלתי אפשרית. כשקארי ראתה שאני יודעת איך להגיב, היא הודתה בפניי שביום חתונתה עם האמריקאי שהכירה בשידוך מהרדיו, היא פזלה לעבר דניאל, שהיה אחד העדים תחת החופה, ולמעשה כבר אז הצטערה שלא הוא החתן שלה... הרגשתי שהיא מחזירה אותי לתקופה שהייתי במזרח הרחוק, לפני שחזרתי בתשובה, והייתי מאוהבת בגבר נשוי ואב לילדה, ומאוד רציתי שאשתו תקבל אותי כאישה שנייה, ונגדל יחד את הילדה שלהם. זה לא קרה, אבל זה גרם לי להבין את קארי. לא רציתי שהיא תסבול מה שסבלתי אני, בצעירותי, באהבה האפלטונית שהייתה לי. ידעתי שזה באמת מה שייתן לה, כמו שהיא אמרה, תקווה לחיים. דיברתי על זה עם דניאל והסברתי לו את המצב מנקודת מבט של אישה, ומהניסיון שלי. התייעצנו גם אנחנו עם רבנים אורתודוקסים, והבנו שההלכה מתירה לערוך חתונה כשרה על פי דת משה וישראל, ואין צורך לעבור על חוקי המדינה, כיוון שאפשר לחיות יחד, לפי התורה וההלכה, בלי להיות נשואים באופן רשמי ובלי לעבור על החוק. עשינו את זה. לא ציפיתי לזה ששבועיים אחרי שהתחתנה עם דניאל היא תגיד לו שיתגרש ממני. בכיתי הרבה בשנה הראשונה בגלל ההתנהגות שלה כלפיי. לא הבנתי איך היא יכולה לצעוק עליי מול כולם, כשאני זאת שפתחתי לה את הבית. כשדניאל העיר לה, היא הייתה עושה לו מהומות בצעקות היסטריות במשך שעות ארוכות ברחובות. טיפלנו בילדיה כמו היו ילדינו שלנו, במסירות ובאהבה. היא גרה בבית משלה, ואת ילדיה הייתה שולחת אליי כדי שתוכל לשכב לנוח

ולהתרפאות. היא לא הייתה מסוגלת לעשות כמעט כלום מעבר לכך. דניאל ואני היינו מכינים לה מאכלים בריאים, ולאט לאט היא התחזקה והתרפאה, ואמרה שהרגישה שקיבלה את החיים במתנה. העיגולים השחורים נעלמו, ובמקומם קיבלו פניה צורה נאה והתמלאו בצבע ובשמחה. הרופאים אמרו שזה נס, ולא ידעו איך להסביר את זה, הרי היא הייתה גוססת, על סף מוות, והבריאה להיות חזקה מאי-פעם. היא הייתה גאה שהצליחה לתת לילדיה בית חם ומשפחה לגדול בה. ילדיה הפכו להיות בעלי ביטחון עצמי, מלומדים, מחונכים ובעלי מקצוע. היה ניכר על קארי שהיא התאהבה בחיים.

במשך השנים, כפי שיסופר בהמשך, המשפחה התרחבה, והצטרפה גם אזמרה, עליזה ושירן, והיה לי הרבה יותר קל לא להתמודד לבד מול קארי. התוודענו אחת לחסרונות וליתרונות של השנייה, ולמדנו חברות אמת מהי. באש ובמים. וכמו שרבי נחמן אומר: "השלום הוא לחבר הפכים". שמחתי שההפצה של הנשים התחזקה, הכנו קמעות עם ה"שיר חדש": נ נח נחמ נחמן מאומן, והפצנו לנשים את הפתק ואת הספרים במדרשיות, בהילולות, בבתי חולים ובאקראי. הקשר שנוצר בינינו הנשים גרם לכל מי שהכיר אותנו להתפלא... אפילו שהיינו שש נשים, הכול היה טבעי ונוח לכולם, המשפחה נעה בין כמה בתים: אחד בטבריה, אחד בתל אביב, שניים בירושלים, ובחגים ובשבתות היינו תמיד יחד. בשבילנו היו אלה חיים נורמטיביים למדי במשך חמש עשרה שנה, ואפילו היינו צוחקות בינינו הנשים שאנחנו לא מבינות איך אפשר לחיות אחרת.

דניאל והבנים הקימו להקת מוזיקה ותיאטרון שהופיעה ברחבי הארץ באירועים חשובים כגון: כליזמר בצפת, בכותל, במועדי העלייה לרגל, ביום ירושלים ובהילולות בכל הארץ. הלהקה הוציאה לאור חמישה אלבומי מוזיקה בסגנונות שונים, ו-DVD מהמופע של ההילולה לכבוד רבי ישראל ב-2010. בית המדרש שבו למדו הבנים, היה צמוד לדירת קרקע בעלת חצר גדולה ונוף ירוק, הדירה שימשה כסטודיו לריקוד עם רצפת פרקט, אולפן הקלטות ומשרד הפצה, ובה הבנים הגדולים גרו ועבדו. את השבתות היינו עושים בדרך כלל שם, כיוון שהיה בה די מקום לשולחן שבת ארוך לכל המשפחה ולאורחים הרבים שהיו מגיעים, חלקם באופן קבוע. דניאל היה מתאמן עם הבנים במשך שעות אחר הצהריים רבות, ויחד הם היו מכינים את ההופעות של הלהקה. כל כך שמחתי והייתי גאה להפיק את ההופעות של בעלי ושל הילדים, ובגלל שהיינו כמה אימהות, היה נוח להתארגן עם כל פעילות שכל אישה חפצה בה, בתורנות בישולים, כביסות וטיפול בילדים. לאורך השנים המשכתי להקפיד על אימוני הספורט שבהם הייתי רגילה. כשהייתי בחוגי אירובי ואמנות לחימה, הילדים היו לומדים בחוג קרטה באותו מכון. בערבים, אחרי שהילדים הלכו לישון, היינו עורכים ארוחות ערב ביחד כל המבוגרים, מעבירים חוויות מהיום שעבר, ובונים תכנית ליום המחרת.

בשנת 2011, משטרת ישראל פרצה לבית שלנו בקללות ובצעקות. בלי שום סיבה פירקו לנו את הבית. השוטרים תלשו לי בברוטליות את הילדים מהידיים כשהם צורחים: "אימא, אימא"; דחפו והפילו אותי לרצפה לעיני הילדים, ולא נתנו לי להתקרב אליהם. לקחו את דניאל למעצר, הפרידו בינינו הנשים, ואחרי חקירה לאורך כל הלילה ועד הבוקר, אחרי שדרשתי לראות עו"ד והתעלמו ממני, עובדת סוציאלית ושני שוטרים כלאו אותי בכוח, ללא הסכמתי, ועל אף התנגדותי, במקלט לנשים מוכות תחת האיום שאם לא אשמע לכללים של המקלט לא יהיה סיכוי שאקבל את הילדים שלי בחזרה. אמרתי לפקידת הסעד שאני רוצה ללכת למקום שבו שמו את דניאל, ושאני מעדיפה להיות במעצר. היא לא שמעה לי, והמשיכה לשכנע אותי שאני חייבת להיות במקלט אם אני רוצה יום אחד לקבל את הילדים. לא החזירו לי אף אחד מהילדים, ורק נתנו לי לבשל ולנקות לארבעים, חמישים נשים ותינוקות כל יום, כל יום. בשביל לראות את הילדים שלי, שסגרו אותם בפנימיות ברחבי הארץ, הייתי צריכה לקום ב04:00 בבוקר, לנקות את המדרגות של המקלט, את חדר האוכל ואת הסלון, ולנסוע שעות, כל פעם לעיר אחרת, בקצוות הארץ (בנימינה, אשדוד, באר שבע, חברון, מושב אורה וכו') לפגוש את ילדיי במשך חצי שעה עד שעה, בפיקוח עובדת סוציאלית. וכשהייתי חוזרת למקלט, היו צועקים עליי שאיחרתי ושאתחיל לנקות ולבשל מיד! בכל תקופת המאסר במקלט העבירו אותי ואת כל בני המשפחה חקירות משטרתיות אלימות תחת האיום: "או שאתה מאשים או שאתה נאשם", כלומר; או שתאשימי את דניאל במה שנגיד לך, או שתהיי מואשמת בתיק שנתפור לך...

לגודל האבסורד, כתב האישום מבוסס על המצאות נבזיות שדניאל השתמש בי ובשאר הנשים כ"שפחות מין ועבודה" הכלואות בכפייה. אני ודניאל חיים יחד 27 שנה, ויחד הבאנו עשרה ילדים לעולם – פרות אהבתנו.

פגעו בי ובדניאל עד כדי כך שלקחו מאתנו אפילו את זכות האדם הבסיסית להתייחדות, למה? במטרה ליצור את הרושם השקרי שאני צריכה הגנה מפניו? אבסורד! כאן אני רוצה לספר לכם איך פעם אחת בפריז, שדניאל ואני היינו בשידוך, נסענו ב"מטרו" (הרכבת התחתית), דניאל היה בלבוש חסידי, עם זקן, פאות וכיפת ברסלב, כשלפתע התקרב אליו בריון שהיה נראה עבריין תוקפני. אני, באופן ספונטני, כנראה בהשראת אימוני הלחימה, נדחפתי בין שניהם, עם הגב לדניאל ועם הפנים לבריון, במבט מזהיר, שאם

יעשה תנועה אחת נגד האהוב שלי, הוא יצטער על זה... דניאל היה מופתע מהתגובה שלי, והבריון התוקפני הניח לנו.

במערכה הזו של החיים, אני עומדת בזירת הקרב, כשבלבי תפילה שהאהבה האמתית והאמונה התמימה ינצחו. אני יודעת שמולי עומדים לא רק לוחם אחד, אלא מערכת מפלצתית של מדינה, שמקריבה את בעלי על מזבח השחיתות והמשכורות השמנות של בעלי הדרגות והתפקידים שמרוויחים על גב ילדיי, שזועקים כבר ארבע שנים שהם רוצים לחזור הביתה! ונציגי משרד הרווחה משלשלים לכיסם 17,000 ₪ על כל קטין שלי בכל חודש, ומעזים לכנות את עצמם "חברה מוסרית". השופטים כתבו בגזר הדין: "עונשו של נאשם 1 צריך לשקף תפיסה מוסרית של החברה העומדת על משמר עקרונות בסיסיים, שהרי צריך להיות ברור לכל כי בלי ערכים יסודיים ועקרונות בסיסיים **לא תיכון חברה אנושית**...". ואני שואלת את עצמי: על איזה עקרונות בסיסיים, ובאיזה ערכי יסוד מוסריים יכולה להתגאות מערכת המדינה, שאפילו לא שומרת על "חוקי לחימה" הוגנים וכולאת חף מפשע ל-26 שנה, לוקחת אותו מילדיו, מאוהביו, מחריבה משפחה בישראל, בלי שום ראיות, בלי שום הוכחות, בלי שהייתה תלונה נגדו, בלי שפגע באף אחד, בלי שום עברה פלילית ובלי עבר פלילי!

**זו החברה האנושית שעליה מדברים השופטים?! מאו ותהיו אתם חבר המושבעים...**

בס"ד

**מכתב אישי לכל העולם מאזמרה:**

"...זה התחיל כשהפסקנו לחלום כשהפסקנו כבר לקוות... הייתי צועק לכולם תסתכלו זהו סוף העולם..." (אביב גפן).

בטיולים של בית הספר, כשישבנו כמה חיברה בספסל האחורי של האוטובוס, לא יכולתי שלא לשיר בקולי קולות את השירים של אביב גפן; "...ילד סינתטי כבוי מול מסך שדולק... מגפה אורבת לנו בכל פינה, מחכה שנחטא במגע, כבר שכחנו מה זאת אהבה... סוף העולם סוף העולם!..." רציתי לחיות את השירים, שחלקם היו שירי מחאה, המעוררים ומבטאים בעיות של הדור הצעיר במדינה שלנו. אבל הפתרונות שהציע בשיריו הם שבעצם אין פתרונות. היינו בהופעות, אלפי בני נוער, צועקים את המילים יחד: "לכבוד מיליארד מיליארד טועים, שאת דרכם עוד מחפשים, אם לא מצאתם זה אולי סימן שאין..." איזה מין סימן זה?! זה דיכא אותי, כי לא חיפשתי סימנים שאין. חיפשתי איפה נמצאות התשובות לטעויות, ואיך לשנות את סוף העולם.

נולדתי במושב זרחיה שבדרום הארץ, ולמדתי בבית ספר ממלכתי דתי. השיעורים היחידים שעניינו אותי באמת היו שיעורי התנ"ך, שנתנו לי חיזוק שיש דרכים נכונות להשיג שינוי. ההרגשה של הייסורים ושל הרדיפות שעברו על אבותינו חיה בתוכי כאילו זה קורה עכשיו. כשקראתי על דוד המלך, רציתי לבוא ולעזור לו. כששאול רדף את דוד, רציתי לעצור אותו ולהגיד לו שדוד אוהב אותו. הצער של דוד ויהונתן כשהיו צריכים להיפרד בעולם הזה מסיבה שנראתה לי לא מוצדקת, שבר אותי. כל שנה, כשלמדנו על מכירת יוסף, כעסתי על האחים שמתנהגים כך כלפיו. כל זה השפיע על דרך החשיבה שלי. חייבים לעשות משהו כדי לתקן את הפגמים והפגיעות שנעשו בעולם. פרדות היו בשבילי דבר עצוב שהשאיר אותי בהלם ובשאלות למה? לא הבנתי למה בבית ספר יסודי (כתות א'-ו') צריך לעזוב את כל החברות ולעבור לחטיבה (כיתות ז'-ט') ולמה שוב צריך להיפרד מהחברים החדשים ולעבור לתיכון (כתות י'-יב'). אף פעם לא קיבלתי את העובדה שמשהו צריך להפריד בין אנשים. תמיד רציתי לפגוש את אברהם אבינו, את אהרון הכהן ואת בועז. בתוכי הרגשתי קשר נצחי אליהם, וביטחון שמהם אף אחד לא יצליח להפריד אותי.

בתור נכדה בכורה במשפחה גדולה, מוקפת בפינוקים מעשרים דודים ודודות, הכול יכול היה להיות טוב. אני זוכרת את המתיקות של סבתא זוהרה ז"ל, אימא של אבא ממרוקו. היא הייתה דואגת לחיזוק האהבה והאחדות במשפחה. עד גיל 92 הייתה שרה מכל הלב שירי געגועים לארץ ישראל, לירושלים של זהב ולתורה, משמחת את כולם, ודואגת לכל אחד למה שהוא צריך. גם אם היינו מבקשים מופלטה או ספינג' (קינוחים מרוקאיים) באמצע הלילה, היא הייתה קמה ומכינה לנו בשמחה. ההורים של אימא הגיעו מפרס, וגרו לא רחוק מאתנו. סבתא הייתה באה לקחת אותי מהגן מדי יום, כשהוריי היו בעבודה, ולעתים קרובות הייתי נשארת לישון אצלם. כאב לי עליה, כי סבלה מאוד מבעלה, סבא אברם. אחד הסיפורים של סבתא, שגרמו לי סיוט, היה על סבא שהעמיד אותה ליד הקיר כשהייתה בהיריון בחודש התשיעי, וזרק על הבטן שלה תפוחים. כשסבא היה מתחיל לצעוק בבית ולקלל היא הייתה אומרת לנו הנכדים: "תלכו תלכו אתם מכירים אותו הוא רשע". הוא והבן שלו, דוד בני, עשו בי מעשים שהרסו את הילדות שלי, פגעו בתמימות שלי, וגרמו לי לפחדים, לחרדות וטלטלה עזה בנפש.

סבא שלי היה עובד אדמה והייתה לו ולבניו חברת טרקטורים וחפירות. מה שהיה חשוב לו זה רק כסף, כל השיחות שלו היו סביב כסף ומכוניות. הוא היה משפיל ומבזה את מי שאין לו כסף, ומתחנף לכל מי שחשב שהצליח. בכל הזדמנות היה שואל אותי את אותה שאלה: "מי יותר טוב חמור או מרוקאי?" זה כאב לי והכעיס אותי, כי הוא התכוון לאבא שלי, אך כל פעם מחדש, לא רציתי להאמין. לפעמים הייתי מורידה את הראש, מתביישת ושותקת, אך הוא היה ממשיך ושואל: "מי יותר טוב אבא שלך או חמור?" זה כבר היה יותר מדי. השאלה הזאת הרסה אותי. "אבא שלך חמור!" אני שומעת את הצחוק הטיפשי שלו בזמן שהוא אומר את זה. כל פעם שראיתי אותו קיוויתי שאולי הפעם הוא לא ישאל אותי את השאלה הזאת, אך לצערי הוא לא הפסיק. בכל מקום, בכל זמן, גם לבד, גם מול כולם, גם מול אורחים, ולצערי גם לנכדים אחרים. כשהיה נכנס לבית הכנסת היה מכריז: "כל הדתיים חמורים!" בשבילו זה היה כמו להגיד שלום. חשבתי שאם אומר לעצמי שאני צריכה להתרגל לזה שהוא מדבר שטויות, הוא לא יצליח לפגוע בי. בכל פעם זה דקר אותי מחדש. הוא היה מציע לי עשרה שקלים בשביל שאענה לו: "מי יותר טוב אבא שלך או חמור?" הייתי שותקת בבוז, בכוונה שירגיש מטומטם. כשהחלטתי לענות לו, פחדתי שירביץ לי, אבל כבר לא יכולתי לשתוק. ובהזדמנות, כששאל אותי עוד פעם, עניתי לו במהירות: "מי ששואל את השאלה הזאת הוא בעצמו החמור!" וברחתי, לפני שהספיק לתת לי סטירה. החלטתי שעל אבא שלי הוא לא ידבר עוד ככה. הספקתי לשמוע שצעק לעברי: "תלכי מפה חמורה, שאני לא אראה אותך יותר!"

את השבתות שהיינו עושים אצל סבא אברם במושב אני לא אשכח לעולם. ערב שבת אחד, אחרי הקידוש וארוחת הערב המשפחתית, סבא הלך לחדר שלו וביקש ממני, בתור נכדתו הדתייה שעלתה לכיתה א', לקרוא לו את פרשת השבוע. הוא נעל את הדלת, הוריד את המכנסיים והדליק את הרדיו בתחנת החדשות, נכנס למיטה וכיסה את עצמו בסדין. ישבתי לידו עם הספר ביד. הוא שאל אם אני מכירה את השיר "אש אש מדורה תחתונים של בחורה". הוא שר את זה כשהוא מקפיץ את הגבות בקצב השיר ופותח את העיניים בהתלהבות שהייתה מוזרה לי. הרגשתי לא בנוח, והחלקתי את עצמי מהמיטה לכיוון הרצפה, סובבתי את הראש לכיוון הדלת, ידעתי שהמפתח אצלו. הוא אמר לי להוריד את החצאית ואת התחתונים. חשבתי שאני צריכה לעשות מה שהוא אומר. הוא המשיך: "בואי אני אלמד אותך על איברי הגוף". הוא שלח ידו לאבר המין שלי, צבט לי את הדגדגן ואמר שלזה קוראים "דולדול". זה כאב לי נורא. הוא ציווה עליי לעלות על המיטה ולהוריד את התחתונים הגדולות הלבנות שלו. ניסיתי לקחת לו את המפתחות שהיו לידו כדי לברוח מהחדר, ולא הצלחתי. ידעתי שאין לי איך לברוח... משכתי לו את התחתונים ולא היה לי מושג מה אני עושה. הוא מיד לקח לי את היד, שם על האיבר שלו ואמר לי לעשות ככה... לא רציתי והוא הפעיל כוח כדי להחזיק לי את היד על האיבר שלו וכדי להראות לי מה לעשות. הוא התחיל להתרגז ואמר לי ללקק את זה כמו גלידה, ולתת לו נשיקות שם. נחנקתי, הלב שלי דפק עוד יותר מהר. נגעלתי והתאפקתי לא להקיא. כשלא הצלחתי לעשות מה שהוא אמר לי התחלתי לבכות, הוא הרים אותי על האיבר שלו ואמר לי: "תרכבי כמו על סוס". לא הצלחתי לעשות מה שהוא אמר, אז הוא הרים אותי בכעס על הכרס שלו, ואמר שאני צריכה לזוז קדימה ואחורה. הוא המשיך לגעת בעצמו ולהגיד בפרסית "קיר אחאר" (פירוש: זין של חמור) העלה את הגבות שלו והוריד אותם כאילו קורה לו משהו טוב, ואז השכיב אותי בכוח ועלה עליי. נמחצתי מהמשקל ומהכובד שלו, ולא יכולתי לזוז ולהתנגד, היה לי קשה לנשום. ניסיתי לדחוף אותו ולא הצלחתי. הרגשתי שהוא מנסה להכניס לי מוט ברזל, וזה כאב לי מוות. הוא קילל אותי וניסה בכל כוחו, עד שהצליח לחדור. אני לא יכולה לתאר במילים את הייסורים, הוא לא הפסיק להכניס אותו ולהוציא. כשצעקתי הוא שם לי שתי כריות על הפנים. אחרי שהפסיק לזוז הרגשתי תולעת כבדה מונחת על האזור התחתון שלי. לא הבנתי מה קרה ומה אני צריכה לעשות. המיטה הייתה רטובה, חשבתי שעשיתי פיפי מפחד. אחר כך הוא צעק עליי: "חמורה צאי מהחדר! את יודעת שאני סבא שלך ואני אוהב אותך, אני קונה לך בגדים, מביא לך ופלות וכסף. מי יותר טוב, אבא שלך או חמור? קחי חמישים שקל, תני לאימא שלך, תביאי את המכנסיים מהארון, אם תספרי למישהו, אני אהרוג את אבא שלך!"

התלבשתי במהירות ורצתי לשירותים. האסלה התלכלכה מדם. חשבתי שאני הולכת למות. נלחצתי וניקיתי מהר בלי לחשוב. פחדתי לדבר על זה עם מישהו כי פחדתי שהוא באמת יהרוג את אבא שלי.

מאז, כל ערב שבת הפך להיות סיוט. פחדתי מהרגע שיבקש שאקרא לו פרשת שבוע בחדר... הייתי כועסת על כל המשפחה שלי שלא היה שם אף אחד בשביל לעצור את זה. לפעמים אני חושבת שאם לא הייתי שותקת כל כך הרבה פעמים על זה שהוא קרא לאבא שלי חמור, אולי הוא היה מפחד לגעת בי. הוא לא פחד. זה חזר על עצמו בתדירות גבוהה, לא רק בשבתות אלא גם בימי חול. בפעמים הבאות שזה קרה, האיומים הלכו וגברו, ותוך כדי שהוא היה אונס אותי הוא היה מאיים עליי איומים מפחידים וקשים, בכל פעם יותר ויותר.

דוד בני, הלך בעקבותיו, והרגיש שהכול מותר לו. הוא היה משפיל מולי את אימא שלי, אחותו הגדולה, ואומר לה שבעלה הוא חמור. את גודל האכזריות שלו קשה לתאר במילים. הוא היה מבזה את כולם, חוץ מעשירים. הוא חשב שהכול שייך לו. התנהג כמו "שייח פרסי". האנשים במושב השתדלו לא להיתקל בו. כשהוא היה צוחק ומלגלג עליהם, הם היו על פי רוב שותקים, כי פחדו ממנו, וידעו שממילא אין עם מי לדבר. השומן של הגוף שלו נשפך לצדדים בדיוק כמו הפה המלוכלך שלו. כשהחליטו לשים מחסום בשער הכניסה למושב על מנת שלא יוכלו להיכנס רכבים בשבת למושב דתי, בני היה נוסע בשביל להכעיס את כולם, שבר את המחסום ואיים שמי שיעז לבנות אותו שוב ישלם על זה. הוא היה טיפוס אלים, חזק נגד חלשים. הוא היה מסתובב בבית בתחתונים גם כשאימא שלו התחננה שילבש מכנסיים.

שום דבר לא הרתיע את בני. אני הייתי בשבילו כמו צעצוע. כשהייתי בת שש הוא היה בערך בן 18. החדר שלו היה סמוך לחדר של סבא שלי. הרבה פעמים אני ובני דודים שלי היינו בחדר שלו כשהוא צפה בסרטים, שוכב על המיטה עם אחת החברות שלו ומתחת לשמיכה הם היו זזים ומשמיעים קולות מוזרים. באותו זמן לא הבנתי שמה שהוא עושה מולנו הילדים, זה לא בסדר. בני וסבא אברם הפכו להיות הטראומה של החיים שלי. כשבני היה בחדר שלו לבד הוא צעק לעברי: "כנסי מיד לכאן!" לא רציתי להיכנס. פחדתי ממנו. הוא המשיך: "מרוקאית אחת, חמורה דתייה, לכל שבת יש מוצאי שבת, אז אם לא תיכנסי אני אראה לך ולאבא שלך החמור מה זה!" אני זוכרת את החרדה שהרגשתי באותם רגעים, ידעתי שמשהו לא טוב עומד לקרות, אבל חשבתי שעדיף לי להיכנס ולשמוע לו מאשר שהוא יתפוס אותי, ואז אני גם אקבל מכות, והוא גם יעשה צרות לאבא שלי. כשנכנסתי, הוא הצמיד את רגלי המיטה לדלת וכבר לא היה אפשר לצאת. הוא היה שוכב על הגב ורק הרגליים שלו היו יוצאות מחוץ לשמיכה. זה התחיל כשאמר

לי לגרד לו את כפות הרגליים בין האצבעות עם הידיים. כשאמרתי שזה מגעיל אותי ואני לא רוצה, תכף היה מאיים שהוא יראה לי מה זה, לוקח נעל מהרצפה וזורק עליי בכל הכוח תוך שהוא צועק: "אני אחתוך לאבא שלך את הרגליים!" ידעתי שהוא מסוגל להזיק לאבא שלי. ראיתי אותו בבְּרֵכָה, מטביע ילדים עד שהם כמעט נחנקים ומשתעשע מזה. הוא היה מכאיב לנו האחיינים שלו בצביטות חזקות, ואם היינו בוכים הוא היה מרביץ לנו. הוא המשיך ואמר: "בסוף את עוד תנשקי לי את הרגליים ותגידי תודה". לקחתי מסרק וגירדתי לו את כפות הרגליים, הוא היה זז מתחת לשמיכה ולא הבנתי מה הוא עושה. אחר כך אמר לי לגרד לו את הגב וצחק עליי "אל תדאגי, על כל שעה תקבלי כסף". הוא שפשף את איבר המין שלו בידיו ואמר לי לעשות לו ככה. לא רציתי והוא נתן לי סטירה. כשהוא ראה שאני מתנגדת הוא תפס לי את הצוואר והכניס לי את איבר המין שלו לפה שלי. נכנסו לי שערות לפה ונחנקתי מזה. לא היה לי אוויר. הייתי בלחץ, רציתי שזה כבר ייגמר. לא יכולתי לנשום. אני זוכרת את עצמי נחנקת מהריח ומבקשת ממנו סליחה כי חשבתי שהוא מעניש אותי על משהו ולא הבנתי על מה. הוא התרגז כשלא עשיתי מה שהוא ביקש ממני, ואז הוא המשיך לשפשף את איברו ואמר: "ככה זה צריך להיות, את רואה? ככה תעשי לי בפעם הבאה, ואם תמשיכי לבכות אני אראה לך מה זה...!" ואז הוא תפס אותי והשכיב אותי על הגב, הראש שלי היה נחבט במוטות העץ של המיטה. הוא פתח לי את הרגליים בכוח לצדדים, ניסיתי בשתי ידיי הקטנות להדוף אותו ממני והוא אמר שאם אני לא אתן לו לגמור הוא ימשיך עם זה כל הזמן. לא ידעתי איך להפסיק את זה ומתי זה ייגמר. הוא נדחף לתוכי בכל כוחות האכזריות שלו. כשצעקתי "אימא!" הוא סתם לי את הפה ואת האף עם שתי ידיו, הוא אמר: "את חושבת שאימא שלך לא עושה את זה?" והמשיך. בדלת של חדרו היה ריבוע זכוכית מחוספסת וקיוויתי שמישהו יעבור שם ויציל אותי. הוא אמר שאם אני אפתח את הפה, הוא יהרוג אותי. כשהוא גמר חשבתי שאני כבר יכולה לברוח, אבל הוא היה תופס אותי חזק בין שתי הרגליים שלו וצוחק. הוא אמר: "את לא תצאי מפה עד שאני אגיד לך", היה מתלבש ויוצא מהחדר. יום אחד כשזה קרה, אחת האחייניות נכנסה לחדר ואמרתי לה שתברח מכאן שבני לא יתפוס אותה. אני חושבת שהוא עשה את זה לעוד אחיין, אבל ידעתי שאין לי למי לספר, כי הייתי בטוחה שכולם מפחדים ממנו. כשגמר הוא היה אומר לי: "לכי לסבא!".

האיומים וההתעללות הפיזית והנפשית של בני וסבא אברם השאירו בנפשי, שנים רבות, פצעים עמוקים, מדממים וכואבים ויצרו אצלי חרדות שהפכו למחשבות טורדניות. האבסורד הוא, שהייתי ילדה בת שש, ועד היום אני מאשימה את עצמי על כך שנכנעתי להם ופיתחתי בהם תלות. לפעמים אפילו הגעתי למצב שחשבתי שאני שותפה מלאה לזה.

כשהייתי בת עשר, בכיתה ד׳, לאבא שלי לא הייתה עבודה, המצב הכלכלי בבית היה קשה, הוא נאלץ לעבוד בחברה של סבא אברם ובני, אפילו שלא כל כך רצה. לא רק שהם היו מביישים אותו בלי סוף במכשיר הקשר, כשכל הפועלים שומעים ומכנים אותו 'חמור מרוקאי', הם גם הפסיקו לשלם לו משכורת, והכניסו אותו ליותר חובות וצרות. זה גרם לסכסוך בין ההורים שלי והיה בלגן שלא את כולו הבנתי. מה שהבנתי, היה רק שאימא שלי צועקת על אבא שלי שימשיך לעבוד אתם וייכנע לבני. היא בעצם הגנה על אחיה, במקום על אבא שלי. זה פגע בי עמוקות כי התלבטתי אם לספר להם על מה שבני וסבא אברם עשו לי, אבל ידעתי שכולם מפחדים מהם, והם לא ירצו לשמוע אותי. ועכשיו המצב הסתבך, כי בגלל מה שקורה בין ההורים שלי, אם אספר להם, זה יוכל לגרום לכך שאבא ואימא לא יחיו ביחד. אז החלטתי שאני לא אספר להם. מכל הסיפור הזה יצא דבר אחד טוב, בגלל המריבה הפסקנו ללכת לבית שלהם, סבא אברם ובני לא יכלו לגעת בי יותר.

לא הייתה לי ברירה אלא לחפש לעצמי איזשהו איזון לחיים במושב, עשיתי את זה בעזרת חברות, שכנים וקרובי משפחה מצד אבא. חוג הבלט הרגיע אותי ונתן לי להרגיש לכמה רגעים שאני כמו כולם. התנועה לצלילי המוזיקה יחד עם עוד בנות נתנה לי הרגשה שאני לא שונה מהן. הספורט, התחרותיות ב"התעמלות קרקע", השירה והריקוד הפכו לחלק בלתי נפרד מחיי היומיום שלי ועזרו לי להתגבר על העצבות ועל ההשפלה, אך הפחדים הלכו והתעצמו. אני זוכרת ששאלתי את דודה שלי, אחות של בני, שגדולה ממני בשנתיים: "אם אומרים לך לבחור, שאת תמותי או שההורים שלך ימותו, מי היית בוחרת?" היא מיד החזירה את השאלה אליי, ואני בחצי היסטריה עניתי לה: "שאני אמות ושלאבא, אימא ואחיות שלי לא יקרה שום רע". שאלות בנוסח: "מי עדיף שימות?" התחלתי לשאול בתדירות גבוהה. מאז החלטתי שאני צריכה לעשות מעשים שיצילו את ההורים שלי. המצאתי משחק, ושיתפתי את דודתי: כל אחת מאתנו בחרה מספר, אני בחרתי את המספרים הזוגיים, והיא בחרה את האי-זוגיים, ומאותו היום החלטתי שאני שותה, אוכלת ועושה רק דברים זוגיים. שתי כוסות מים, ארבע או שש, לא ממתק אחד ולא שלוש ואם אני מכבה את האור אני לוחצת פעמיים רצופות. הייתה לי תחושה מוזרה שאם לא אעשה זאת לפי המספר הזוגי, יקרה משהו רע. כך, אם בני יאיים עלינו שוב, על ידי המספר הזוגי, אציל מיד את המצב. פיתחתי לעצמי מנגנון הגנה.

כשהגעתי לגיל עשר כנראה שבני חשב שלא כדאי לו להמשיך את המעשים שהיה עושה לי, כי התחלתי להתפרץ ולהגיד לו דברים על המעשים שלו מול אנשים. אבל מה שעברתי מגיל שש עד עשר ממנו ומסבא אברם גרם לי לנזק גדול עם השלכות ארוכות טווח. בעקבות הפחד התפתחה אצלי מחלה. לא ידעתי מה יש לי, רק שתקפו אותי מחשבות כמו: "אם לא אקטוף עכשיו חמישה עלים אחותי תיפול..."; "אם לא אלך על הלבנים האדומות שעל המדרכה לא יהיה לאבא שלי כסף"; "אם לא אגע ברצפה ברגע זה יקרה אסון להורים שלי...". ההתמודדות עם המחשבות הייתה יומיומית, לקחה לי הרבה מגיל ההתבגרות, וגרמה לי לתסכול ולסבל.

האירוע שהייתה בו סכנת נפשות של ממש קרה כשנסעתי עם חברה שלי לבית הקולנוע. עמדנו על כביש מהיר כדי לחצות לתחנת האוטובוס. פתאום צעקתי לה: "רוצי!" והיא לא הבינה. תפסתי לה את היד ומשכתי אותה בכוח, אמרתי לה שאנחנו חייבות עכשיו לחצות את הכביש לפני שהמשאית הסמיטריילר האדומה עוברת. האמנתי, שאם לא נספיק לעבור את הכביש, אבא שלי ימות. המכוניות נסעו במהירות, ואני ראיתי לנגד עיניי רק איך מצילים את אבא שלי... חצינו בטירוף. כמעט נדרסנו... היא הייתה בהלם, ושאלה אותי מבוהלת מה קרה לי. התביישתי וכמעט בכיתי. עד אותו רגע שמרתי על הפחדים שלי בסוד. הרגשתי שההתנהגות שלי מוזרה אבל חשבתי שזה לא בשליטתי ושאין לי ברירה, כי רק ככה אני מצילה את המצבים.

חברה אחרת, בכיתה ו', העזה ושאלה אותי למה אני נוגעת ברצפה כל רגע. היא צחקה עליי מול שתי חברות נוספות, כשהיא מדגימה איך אני נראית כשאני עושה את זה. הייתי במבוכה, וניסיתי להסביר לה שיש לי פחדים שיקרו אסונות אם לא אמנע אותם. היא לא ממש הבינה. לא היה לי פשוט להסביר לה, אבל זה שחרר אותי וגרם לכך שסיפרתי לעוד חברה. לא ידעתי אם גם ילדים אחרים סובלים כמוני. אני לא יודעת למה ההורים שלי אף פעם לא דיברו אתי על זה. כשהייתי בת 15 בחדרי שבבית הוריי, כמו כל יום אחרי הצהריים שמעתי מוזיקה בווליום גבוה ורקדתי. המחשבות על מה שהיה מתחת לשמיכה של דוד בני ובמיטה של סבא אברם לא הניחו לי, ואז זה התחיל... מחשבה מטרידה אילצה אותי לגעת ברצפה כדי שלא יקרה משהו רע, ואז באה מחשבה נוספת שאם אני רוצה שהיא לא תתקיים אני מוכרחה לשים את האצבעות בדלת לנטרל את הסכנה. גל של מחשבות שליליות הציף אותי, דבר כזה לא קרה לי עוד מעולם. הטירוף עד כדי יאוש גרם לי להשתטח על המיטה עם הפנים תקועים במזרן, והתחלתי לצעוק ולבכות בחוסר אונים: "די... אין לי כוח יותר!" כבר הייתי ממש עייפה, ואז הגיעה עוד מחשבה: אם אני לא אגע עכשיו עם השיניים הקדמיות בקצה של מסגרת העץ של המיטה יקרה משהו רע לאחותי... בעייפות הזאת גררתי את עצמי לגעת ברצפה... כעסתי והתרעמתי: ריבונו של עולם, למה אתה עושה לי את זה?!

התחלתי לחפש אחר פתרון. אי-הצדק שחוויתי על בשרי הבעיר בי את האש לחפש שינוי. הבנתי שאני מוכרחה לאחוז באידיאלים האמתיים שבהם האמנתי, ולהילחם עליהם. זה מה שגרם לי להתנדב בהדרכה בנוער מולדת. רציתי לשנות את הסטטוס קוו במדינה, וכך הפכתי ללוחמת פוליטית. כשהקבוצה שלנו בתנועת הנוער הייתה בשיא פעילותה, גיבשנו תכנית: להקים קיבוץ התיישבותי ברוח חדשה. אך שוב כולם התפזרו, כי היה להם משהו חשוב יותר...

גם שכבר הייתי כבת 16, לא הפסיקו המחשבות לרדוף אותי. הרגשתי שאני זקוקה לאהבה, לתשומת לב, אבל לא יכולתי לחשוב על קשר עם בן, כי בשום אופן לא רציתי למצוא את עצמי במצבים כמו שהיו עם סבא שלי ועם דוד בני... אבא שלי באותה תקופה היה שומע כל מיני הרצאות של רבנים בקלטות. בנסיעות שלי אתו במשאית הקשבנו להם ביחד ואהבנו לשוחח עליהם. כדי שגם חברות שלי מהכיתה יתחזקו, הבאתי את הקלטות לבית הספר וניסיתי בהפסקות להפיץ אותן אפילו שהבנות לא רצו לשמוע אותם. למרות כל זאת, עדיין לא קיבלתי תשובה איך להתמודד עם הפחדים ועם המחשבות. התחלתי ללכת בערב לשיעורי תורה, אך גם שם לא מצאתי מענה. בכל זאת התאמצתי לדחוף את עצמי להמשיך ולחפש עצה.

יום אחד, השכנה שלי סיוון, חברתי ללימודים שהיא גם קרובת משפחה שלי, סיפרה לי שהיא קוראת ספר על תפילה ועל התבודדות. שמו של הספר היה "השתפכות הנפש, משיבת נפש". ביקשתי לשאול אותו ממנה, וכשקראתי אותו, כל פסקה הביאה אותי לידי בכי, התרגשות; או לקפוץ משמחה, לרקוד ובעיקר לדבר עם השם יתברך. זה הספר הראשון שבו קראתי על המחשבות:

> "...צריך לחזק את עצמו מאוד ולהאמין ולידע, כי כל נקודה טובה וכל איזה התעוררות דקדושא שהוא מתעורר בכל עת לנתק את עצמו ממחשבות רעות ולהמשיך על עצמו מחשבות קדושות וכל מה שהוא חותר בכל יכולתו לעשות איזה טוב אף על פי שבינו לבינו נעשה עימו מה שנעשה וכבר היה כן אלפים פעמים אף על פי כן שום נקודה טוב אינו נאבד..." (משיבת נפש סימן לא').

זה נתן לי תקווה שאוכל לשנות הכול.

סיוון התקשרה להזמין ספרים נוספים של רבי נחמן. כשהמפיצים הביאו לה את הספרים, הם הוסיפו לה סטיקרים של נ נח נחמ נחמן מאומן, פוסטר של רבי ישראל וכמה עותקים של הפתק הקדוש.

יום אחד סיוון הביאה לי קלטת וידאו. זו הייתה הפעם הראשונה שראיתי את רבי ישראל בער אודסר מדבר. נשבר לי הלב, התחלתי לבכות, הבנתי שרבי נחמן שכולם מדברים עליו הוא פה מולי. החלטתי לקרוא כל מה שרבי נחמן כתב. קניתי את כל הספרים מ״קרן רבי ישראל״, וגיליתי שהם מלאים עצות איך לשנות את ההרגלים שנקראים ׳מידות׳. לדוגמה: ״מי שמוחו מבולבל יהיה רגיל בתפילת חבקוק הנביא. גם אכילת חיטים סגולה לזה...״ (ספר המידות). שמחתי שמצאתי דרכים לצאת מהמבוכות שעוברות עליי. מעכשיו אני הולכת לחיות אחרת.

מכל הכסף שחסכתי בעבודה של שלוש שנים במלצרות ובייביסיטר, קניתי כמות גדולה של ספרים, והקמתי לעצמי מעין קרן קטנה להפצה. חשבתי על האנשים בבית החולים, וככה עלה בראשי רעיון, לנסוע לבית החולים קפלן, שהיה קרוב למושב שלי, ולהפיץ את הספרים. הייתי מפיצה סופר אנרגטית. התמכרתי להפצה, וזה הפך לסוג של תרפיה בשבילי. כמעט לכל מי שהכרתי; למורות, למנהל שלי בעבודה, לחברות, למורה נהיגה ולקרובי משפחה הבאתי ספר במתנה, עם הקדשה שהעתקתי מהספר אב״י הנחל.

יותר מהכול היה לי חשוב שהוריי יהיו ברסלבים נ-נחים. חלמתי ודמיינתי את אבא שלי חובש כיפת נ-נח, מפיץ את הפתק ואת הספרים בריקודים ברחובות... הייתי בת 17.5. בשבתות הייתי דואגת להביא לשולחן השבת מספרי רבנו כדי להסביר לכל המשפחה על השיר העשירי נ נח נחמ נחמן מאומן. ההורים שלי מהר מאוד הפסיקו אותי בטענה שהם הולכים לשיעורים של רבנים, ונותנים צדקה כל חודש, מתפללים בבית הכנסת ויש להם את הדרך שלהם. ניסיתי להסביר להם שהאמונה בנ-נח היא לא עוד דרך ביהדות, אלא הפתרון לכל הבעיות בדור שלנו. כאב לי שאין להם סבלנות לשמוע. ובכל זאת התעקשתי להוכיח להם שכבר בתהלים נאמר: ״ושם נשיר שיר חדש״, וכן בהרבה מקורות של חז״ל מדברים על השיר הזה. שאלתי את אבא שלי איך זה יכול להיות שכולם לומדים שרש״י כותב ב״שירת הים״ שנאמר ״אז ישיר״ בלשון עתיד, מכאן שמשה יחזור עם השיר שלעתיד וכשאני מספרת לך שהשיר הזה התגלה בפתק והוא כבר פה, אתה לא מתרגש? היה לי חשוב שהוא ידע מה שאני יודעת על ה״שיר חדש״. הצלחתי לעורר בו קצת עניין, והוא שאל: ״גם רבי נחמן מדבר על ה׳שיר חדש׳?״ פתחתי את התורה האחרונה שרבנו אמר לפני פטירתו, תורה ח׳: ״...לעתיד יתער (יופץ) שיר חדש של בחינת נפלאות, בחינת השגחה, כי אז יהיה הנהגה על ידי השגחה לבד. ושיר החדש הזה שיתער לעתיד, הוא בחינת שיר פשוט, כפול, משולש, מרובע...״. הראיתי לאבא שלי את החתימה בפתק בצורת השיר: ״פשוט-נ׳, כפול-נח׳, משולש-נחמ׳, מרובע-נחמן״.

״אבא, אתה קולט שרבנו הבטיח לפני הסתלקותו, וקיים את זה עכשיו! נ נח נחמ נחמן מאומן, זה השיר חדש!״

״יפה, אני גאה בבת שלי שהיא יודעת להרצות ככה!״

״אבא! תתעורר! זה לא צחוק! למה צריך להמשיך אותו דבר? אתה לא זוכר מה שלימדת אותי מהגמרא; שאנחנו סמוכים לאלף השביעי, סוף הזמן, שעוד אפשר לתקן משהו!?״

הוא התחיל לספר לי דבר תורה ששמע מאיזה רב. התעצבנתי ושאלתי אותו:

״הרב הזה או שאר הרבנים שאתה מכיר, ואתה מכיר הרבה רבנים, אמרו לך משהו על השיר חדש?!״

הוא מזג לי מיץ תפוזים קר והתחיל לזמר שירי שבת... אימא שלי ראתה שאני נסערת ואמרה בטון מתחנן: ״תעשי מה שאת רוצה, רק תעזבי אותנו״. זו לא הייתה הפעם הראשונה שהיא מבקשת שאעזוב אותם בשקט. כל פעם שהייתי נלחמת על העקרונות שלי, היא הביעה חוסר עניין. תמיד הייתי עקשנית ודומיננטית, ולאימא שלי זה הפריע. הפעם גם לי הפריעה ההתנהגות שלהם. כי הפעם לא היה מדובר באביב גפן ולא באידיאולוגיה של נוער מולדת, ואפילו לא על מה שעשו לי בני וסבא אברם מתחת לאף שלה, אלא על אפשרות לתיקון אמתי לכל הקלקולים מבריאת העולם. התקווה להתחלות חדשות. הם התייחסו אליי כאל ״ילדה קטנה״ ולא לקחו אותי ברצינות. חוסר האכפתיות שלהם גרם לי להפסיק לשתף אותם בהתלהבות שלי. הרגשתי שאין לי במשפחה עם מי לדבר. מה שהחזיק אותי עוד קצת במושב, היו הפרדסים והשדות היפים שאליהם הייתי מגיעה להתפלל. שם הייתי מספרת להשם את הסודות שלי, ומבקשת להכיר אנשים שמאמינים ברבי נחמן ולחיות אתם. לא שכחתי להגיד תודה שזכיתי לשמוע על רבי ישראל. גם בבית הספר ביליתי את רוב הזמן בתפילה, עד שנזכרתי שאני צריכה להפגין נוכחות בכיתה. בדרך כלל זה היה באמצע השיעור השלישי. בשיעור אנגלית התפתחה שיחה עם המורה, שהייתה קיבוצניקית לא דתייה. כששמעה ממני שאני רוצה להתחתן, היא לא הבינה למה כל כך מוקדם, ואיך אני חושבת להסתדר ולהעניק לילדים שלי מה שהם צריכים. לא חשבתי שתהיה לי בעיה ״להסתדר״ כי

במשפחה שלי כולם עוזרים אחד לשני ותמיד אפשר להשיג כל מה שצריך. התכנית שלי לחיי משפחה הייתה להתחתן עם מפיץ ספרים ולהוליד אתו ילדים, רק לא ידעתי איך לקיים את זה בפועל. בתום השיעור הקדשתי למורה את הספר אב״י הנחל ואיחלתי לה שתזכה להתקרב לרבי נחמן.

יום אחד תכננו אני וסיוון לנסוע לירושלים, להר המנוחות, לציון של רבי ישראל. ברכה, אימא של סיוון, הגיעה לבית הכנסת במושב שבו התפללתי, והתחילה לבכות לי בהיסטריה שאשכנע את סיוון לעזוב את רבי נחמן. היא אמרה שסיוון במין ״שיגעון״, ואינה שומעת לה, והיא מפחדת שכישפו אותה. היא עשתה הצגה שלמה ואף השתטחה על הרצפה. מיד עלה לי בראש סיפור ההתקרבות של רבי ישראל שמספר שאימא שלו יצאה לרחובות בצעקות כשהיה בן 17, והגיעה לרבי ישראל קרדונר ברסלבר, השתטחה לפניו בפישוט ידיים ורגליים ובכתה בכי תמרורים כבוכה על מת, וביקשה שירחיק אותו מרבי נחמן. חשבתי שזה מוזר, לא משנה לאיזה דור אנחנו שייכים, ההורים תופסים תפקיד של מניעה, ושמים את עצמם כתנאי ״או הם או הצדיק״. כאב לי שאימא שלה עושה לה את התרגיל הזה. חשבתי שזה לא ישר ולא אמתי להתנהג כך. ניסיתי להרגיע את אימא שלה, אבל בשום אופן לא הסכמתי למנוע מסיוון מלהתקרב לרבי נחמן. חזרתי לביתי, אימא שלי כבר נדבקה בהיסטריה והודיעה לי שהיא לא מסכימה שאסע לציון בירושלים. אימא שלי מעולם לא התערבה בהחלטות שלי, לכן שאלתי אותה מה יש לה, היא אמרה שברכה הייתה אצלה, והיא החליטה שהיא לא רוצה בעיות אתה. התחלנו לריב, והבהרתי לה שהיא לא יכולה לקבוע לי, אז שתעזוב אותי. אבא שלי הגיע וניסה לגשר בדיפלומטיה ביני לבין אימא. הוא הבטיח לי, בלי שאימא שלי יכלה לשמוע, שאם אוותר על הנסיעה בשביל להוריד את הלחץ של אימא, הוא בעצמו ייקח אותי לירושלים לציון של רבי ישראל. השתכנעתי, אבל כעסתי על אימא שלי שמושפעת ולא מסוגלת לחשוב בצורה עצמאית לטובתי.

ביום העצמאות שנת 1999 אבא שלי לקח אותי, כמו שהבטיח לציון של רבי ישראל. במשאית ה MAK הצהובה הישנה שלו. זו הייתה הפעם השלישית שזכיתי להגיע לציון של הצדיק יסוד עולם בירושלים. כשהגעתי לציון ראיתי בחורה צעירה מתפללת. התקרבתי, ושם היה מונח ספר ״ליקוטי תפילות״ בכריכה מיוחדת שלא ראיתי עד אותו יום, אפילו שכבר הייתי מפיצה מעל חצי שנה ספרים מ״קרן רבי ישראל״. על הכריכה היה צילום של הפתק הקדוש. שאלתי את הבחורה על אודות הספר, והיא התחילה להסביר לי שיש בנ-נח קבוצה של כמה משפחות מירושלים שמוציאות לאור ספרי רבנו עם הפתק, וזה היה חידוש בשבילי. כנראה שהיא הרגישה את ההתלהבות שלי, וניגשה לארון הספרים להראות לי ספרים נוספים עם הפתק על הכריכה. לאחר מכן הניחה בידיי בהתפארות ספר מיוחד מאוד, ואמרה שזהו ספר **״שיחות מתוך חיי הסבא״** שכולו שיחות מוקלטות, כתובות מילה במילה, של רבי ישראל. התיישבתי על המדרגה הצמודה לציון, פתחתי את הספר, התחלתי לקרוא. לא יכולתי להפסיק. התפעלתי מהפשטות שלו. בכל סיפור מרגישים את האכפתיות, את תשומת הלב. הרגשתי שאני חלק מהסיפור שהוא כותב, ושאני קוראת. שהוא שם לב אליי. הספר הזה הכניס בי כיסופים לעשות צדקה וחסד, והתעוררות מיוחדת לתפילה. התפללתי מכל הלב להקים משפחה עם בעל שיקדיש את חייו להפצת הספרים והפתק ובזה ראיתי את תכלית חיי. חיפשתי על הספר שם או מספר טלפון, אך לא הופיע לא שם ולא טלפון. שאלתי את הבחורה שהציגה את עצמה בשם צילה, אם היא יודעת איפה אפשר לקנות את הספר הזה, ועוד ספרים עם תמונת הפתק. היא ענתה: ״במחסן הספרים שלנו״. שאלתי אותה אם היא מכירה שדכנית בנ-נח, והיא סיפרה שיש להם בית מדרש ולומדים שם שני אחים מפיצים, שאחד מהם מחפש שידוך, רק שיש בעיה אחת, הוא לא עובד ואין לו ממש פרנסה. אמרתי לה שזה ממש לא בעיה, להפך, כל עוד הוא מפיץ, זה הברכה לכול. הלכנו יחד למחסן הספרים, וכל הדרך צילה סיפרה לי על רבי ישראל.

הגענו לבית אבן ירושלמי, שם גרו המפיצים, והוא שימש גם כמחסן ספרים. על הקירות היו תמונות מיוחדות ומאירות של הסבא, שנתנו הרגשה שהוא ממש כאן. כמויות של ארגזים מלאים בספרים נושאים ריח דפוס חדש. הרגשתי בבית. נדהמתי לראות שכל הספרים שהיו שם, הודפסו בכריכה ייחודית עם צילום הפתק, בצורה כל כך חדה וברורה. היה ניכר שמי שעשה את זה שם את כל לבו בכריכה הזו. כשעיינתי בהם, ראיתי שבכל ספר מודפס סיפור ההתקרבות של רבי ישראל לברסלב, וסיפור נס הפתק. קניתי בכל הכסף שהיה לי את הספר ״שיחות מתוך חיי הסבא״, והחלטתי שמעכשיו אפיץ רק את הספרים האלה. הצטערתי שנולדתי אישה, כי אם לא הייתי נשארת מרגע זה לחיות עם המפיצים. חזרתי למושב והבאתי לסיוון במתנה את הספר שידעתי שאין לה. היא התרגשה וחיבקה את הספר, והבינה שיש בידיה אוצר. לפתע, אחרי שלושה ימים היא החזירה לי את הספר ואמרה שהיא לא רוצה להוציא לשון הרע, אבל יש אנשים שמתנגדים להפצה הזו ולמפיצים מירושלים. הרגשתי פגיעה אישית, ואמרתי לה בצער: ״מה הבעיה עם ספר שאומר מילה במילה את הדיבורים המוקלטים של רבי ישראל?!״ אף שאז עדיין לא הכרתי באופן אישי את המפיצים הללו, הרגשתי צורך להגן עליהם. היא לא רצתה לספר לי מי דיבר אתה, ורק חזרה ואמרה שיש התנגדות. אמרתי לה שזו בדיוק הבעיה, שאם המתנגדים היו באמת בקיאים בדיבורים שכתובים בספר הזה, היו יודעים שרבי ישראל אמר: ״העיקר הוא אהבת חברים״. הוויכוח אתה כאב לי

מאוד, אבל חיזק את הבנתי שהסיבה לרדיפה של המפיצים האלו היא שהם היחידים שמפרסמים את דברי הצדיק כמו שהם בלי צנזורה. אני לעומתה, הרגשתי שזו המלחמה שאליה אני שייכת. חשבתי שמי שהוציא את הספר הזה לאור, הוא באמת אמיץ, כי העז לפרסם את הדיבורים של רבי ישראל על השקר של אותם הרבנים שמחפשים כסף וכבוד, וגונבים את דעת האנשים.

נסעתי עם סיוון להילולה של רבי שמעון בר יוחאי במירון. התארחנו אצל משפחות של נ-נחים. סיוון הכירה שם בחור וסיפרה לי שהיא עומדת להתחתן אתו. הרבה מבנות גילנו כבר התחתנו והרגשתי שאני מאבדת את החברה היחידה שנשארה לי, אמרתי לה: "למה צריך שניפרד, אי-אפשר שנחיה איכשהו ביחד? אפילו נתחתן עם אותו אחד". אני לא יודעת מאיפה זה יצא לי. היא לא לקחה את זה ברצינות, ואני נחרדתי מהמחשבה להישאר לבד. התחלתי לצאת לשידוכים, אבל זה לא הלך כמו שחשבתי. חיפשתי את מספר הטלפון של צילה. התקשרתי אליה וסיפרתי לה על השידוכים הלא מוצלחים שיצאתי אליהם. שאלתי אותה מה קורה עם השידוך שהיא רצתה להציע לי, ואם יש משפחה מארחת לשבת. קבענו שביום שישי אפגוש את ה"שידוך" – עזרא.

בפגישת השידוך עם עזרא, היה לי חשוב שנדבר על הערכים שעליהם היינו רוצים לבנות משפחה. על כל מילה שאמר, היה לי הרבה מה להגיד. נכון יותר: במשך שלוש שעות הסברתי לו איך צריך לחיות, למי הוא צריך להתחבר, וממי להתרחק, ובעיקר היה לי חשוב שיבין את העמדה שלי, כדי שלא יהיו טעויות בהמשך. הוא אמר שטוב שיש מפיצות חזקות לַסבא, וקבענו אירוסין למוצאי שבת. בוודאי לא התכוונתי לספר לו על מה שעברתי עם סבא שלי ודוד בני, ועל המצב הנפשי המורכב שלי, כי חשבתי שזה עלול לגרום לו להתרחק ממני. במהלך הריקודים במסיבת האירוסין בביתי, כי לא הייתי שלמה עם ההחלטה להתחתן אתו, נזכרתי בדיבורים שאמר לי בפגישה, וחשבתי שהוא לא ממש יקיים את מה שדיברנו. אחרי האירוסין הוא אמר שנעבור לגור אצל אימא שלו בתל אביב. לא הסכמתי בשום אופן. בכל מקרה בינתיים לא רציתי לבטל את השידוך, והחלטתי שאני נשארת בירושלים להפיץ. הגעתי למושב לקחת כמה דברים, סיפרתי לאימא שלי על השידוך שלי מירושלים, והופתעתי מהתגובה שלה כשאמרה: "המפיצים של ירושלים הם לא כמו מפיצים אחרים". ניסיתי לברר לאן היא חותרת, ועל סמך מה היא אומרת את זה. הבנתי שסיוון ואימא שלה דיברו אתה, והזדעזעתי שסיוון מעזה לבוא ולהסית את אימא שלי נגד אנשים שלא הכירה אף פעם. לא רציתי להתעכב יותר. אימא שלי ניסתה לשכנע אותי להישאר, הסברתי לה שאין לי עם מי לדבר פה, וחזרתי לירושלים.

הפצתי בבית החולים שערי צדק, וראיתי את אילנה, שאותה הכרתי בשבת עם צילה, שמחתי לראות אותה, היא הייתה בהיריון ואימא לשמונה ילדים. זה חיזק אותי לראות שאפשר להיות אימא ולהמשיך להפיץ. דיברנו על פסטיבל ערד הקרוב, וקבענו לנסוע ביחד ברכב הפצה של נשים, עם קארי ואדרת שגם אותן הכרתי באותה שבת. יצאנו להפיץ בפסטיבל ערד. כעבור שבועיים, בזמן שקניתי מטפחות ובגדים לחתונה, קיבלתי טלפון מהמשטרה להגיע מיד לבית המעצר בירושלים כי עצרו את עזרא, והם לא מתכוונים לשחרר אותו עד שאגיע. רצתי לתחנת המשטרה. השתוממתי כשראיתי שם את אבא שלי. מהר מאוד התברר שהמשפחה שלי עשתה תרגיל מלוכלך על מנת לסכל לי את החתונה. בני הנבל ושמונת חבריו הבריונים פרצו לבית של גילברגרוס, אחד החסידים, ולא נתנו לאף אחד לצאת. הם איימו עליו שיזרקו את אשתו מחלון הבניין ויהרגו אותה עם העובר בבטנה, אם לא ידאגו לביטול החתונה. גילברגרוס הצליח לחמוק ולהתקשר למשטרה, ולמרבה הפלא, במקום לעצור את חבורת הבריונים, המשטרה עצרה את החסידים המבוהלים. בני להגנתו המציא סיפור לא יאומן על חסידי ברסלב שחטפו אותי למערה כדי לחתן אותי בעל כורחי. מול חוקרי המשטרה אזרתי אומץ וסיפרתי בפעם הראשונה שבני אנס אותי מילדות, ושאני מתחננת שיגנו עליי כי גם ההורים שלי מפחדים ממנו ולא יודעים איך להגן עליי. הם חקרו אותי בקשר לאירוע שקרה עם החסידים והבינו מהתשובות שלי שבני שיקר להם ושחררו מיד את עזרא ואת גילברגרוס. לא הבנתי איך זה שהם בכל זאת מכריחים אותי לחזור עם בני ועם ההורים שלי למושב. סירבתי להיכנס לרכב שלו, וחוקרי המשטרה הזהירו אותי שרק עוד חודש אהיה בת 18, ועד אז אני חייבת לציית להורים שלי, כי אם לא, יאלצו להשתמש בכוח ולהחזיר אותי בניידת משטרה למושב. לבסוף בני דחף לי את הראש והכניס אותי בכוח מהדלת האחורית, בין אבא ואימא שלי. הרגשתי במלכודת. כשעברנו בכביש מול הר המנוחות בני אמר שיש לו שופל והוא יעקור את "הציון הקדוש", יחתוך לי את הילדים שייוולדו לי וישרוף "כל אצבע" של עזרא, בעלי לעתיד. הייתי מפוחדת ועצבנית, ונחרדתי מאבא ומאימא שלי שיושבים ושותקים, נותנים לבני אישור סופי לפגוע בי. לחשתי להם עם דמעות בעיניים: "איך אתם מעזים לתת לו להתערב, אחרי שהרס לי את החיים, איך יכולתם לפגוע באנשים שלא עשו לכם שום דבר רע, ולהפחיד ילדים קטנים ואישה בהיריון?" כשהגענו למושב, רצתי לחדר שלי שבו השארתי ארגזים של ספרים שהייתי מפיצה. לתדהמתי, הספרים לא היו שם. שאלתי את אימא שלי לאן נעלמו הספרים. היא רמזה שזה לא היא אלא אבא. משום מה תמיד חשבתי שלא מתאים לאבא שלי להתנהג ככה. במשך שבועות הוא לא הסכים להחזיר לי את הספרים שקניתי במיטב כספי, והכחיש את העובדה שהם אצלו. רק אחרי שאמרתי לו שאם

הוא לא מחזיר לי את הספרים הוא לא יראה אותי יותר, ומה שבטוח – בחתונה שלי הוא לא יהיה, הוא החזיר לי את הספרים. הסברתי להוריי שכדאי להם לקבל את העובדה שאני זאת שצריכה לבחור עם מי להתחתן, ושזה לא התחום שלהם. כדי לגשר על הפערים ועל מנת שדברים יסתדרו, רציתי לתת להוריי עוד הזדמנות, לכן ביקשתי מהמפיצים מירושלים, לדבר אתם בשבילי. גילברגרוס, עזרא ודניאל הגיעו למושב. עזרא חשש מהפגישה עם המשפחה שלי וחיכה בכניסה למושב. התרגשתי שהמפיצים טרחו להגיע לעשות שלום בית. השיחה הייתה נעימה, הגיעו עוד קרובי משפחה ושכנים, אך כשבני וסבא אברם הגיעו בלי הזמנה, התחילה התלחשות והאווירה נעשתה מתוחה. בני אמר בגסות מול כולם שעזרא מסומם וגנב ושהם לא ייתנו לי להתחתן אתו. חשבתי שאני יוצאת מדעתי, למה הוא ממשיך לרדוף אותי?! הצילו! איך יוצאים מזה?! רציתי לחזור לירושלים. בני גירש בהשפלות את דניאל ואת גילברגרוס. ואיים עליי שאם אני אסע הוא ישרוף את הילדים שלהם. סבא אברם צעק שהוא ישרוף את כל ברסלב. פחדתי. בני תפס אותי בכוח ביד, ודחף אותי לחדר, הפיל אותי על הרצפה ואמר: "את לא תצאי מפה, הבנת?! את לא תצאי מילימטר מהמושב! אם תעזי, אני אראה לך מה זה! חמורה!" זה היה מפחיד ששוב כל המשפחה שלי רואה בעיניים את האלימות שלו כלפיי ובכל זאת בוחרת להתעלם ולשתוק. נעלתי את עצמי בשירותים, והתחלתי לצרוח ולקלל אותו. הרגשתי שאני צריכה פשוט לברוח, כי הבנתי שבני בחיים לא ייתן לי להתחתן, רק כדי שלא אגלה את המעשים שעשה לי. כשיצאתי מהשירותים, הם התחילו לדבר אליי במילים רכות, אמרו שהם דואגים לי ושהם רוצים לעזור לי לערוך את החתונה. סבא אברם אמר שהוא רוצה להרים את הנכדה שלו על הכתפיים. הוא גם אמר שהוא ידאג שיהיה לי בית. אני מודה שהם הצליחו לשכנע אותי בהבטחות לביטחון כלכלי, שהם רוצים בטובתי. לא ידעתי שבזמן שהם מוליכים אותי שולל בדיבוריהם, בני וסבא אברם שלחו אנשים לעשות מארב על הרכב שבו היו דניאל, גילברגרוס ועזרא החתן המיועד שלי. בבית, אימא שלי התחילה להגיד לי שאולי אני צריכה לחשוב על הדברים מחדש, ולרדת מהרעיון של החתונה. קיוויתי שאולי הרב של המושב יעזור לי להסביר להורים שלי בשפה שהם יכולים להבין. ארגנתי להם מפגש בבית הכנסת הישן עם הרב, עם העובדת הסוציאלית ועם פקידת הסעד של המושב, ושוב הזמנתי את שני המפיצים מירושלים. המטרה שלי הייתה להקל על הוריי להבין שאיך שאני בוחרת לחיות הוא דבר בריא וטוב. זה כמעט הצליח. המפיצים סיפרו על רבי ישראל בער אודסר ועל רבי נחמן. הרב של המושב התעניין, וזה שימח אותי. העובדת הסוציאלית ופקידת הסעד הקשיבו קשב רב לסיפורים. הייתי מרוצה, חשבתי שהדברים הולכים להסתדר. לפתע, הופיע בני וצעק: "פה לא יספרו סיפורים על צדיקים!" הוא קילל את פקידת הסעד, וזרק כיסא לכיוונה. היא הייתה אישה מבוגרת, ובכל זאת בני לא פחד להרים עליה יד, וכמעט שנתן לה סטירה. העובדת הסוציאלית, שהייתה צעירה יותר צעקה על בני שזו שיחה בין בת להורים, והוא לא מוזמן בכלל. בני צעק שהוא יחתוך אותי ואת הילדים שלי אם אתחתן. העובדות הסוציאליות החליטו שהשיחה תמשיך במקום אחר. עברנו למועצה האזורית. בני נסע בעקבותינו, וניסה לתקוף עם עוד כמה בחורים מהמושב את הרכבים שבהם נסענו. קיימנו שיחה קצרה ומהירה בבניין המועצה. העובדות הסוציאליות החליטו, כיוון שרק עוד שבועיים אהיה בת 18, ובגלל הסכנה שמהווה בני, ובגלל חוסר היכולת של בני המשפחה שלי להגן עליי, שהן ישלחו אותי לשבועיים למשפחה מארחת במושב סוסיא. התעצבנתי מכיוון שאימא ואבא שלי לא מצליחים להגן עליי, אז מהרווחה כופים עליי איפה להיות. בני, שחיכה לי מחוץ למועצה, תפס את ידי וגרר אותי בחזקה מול העובדות הסוציאליות ועוד אנשי מועצה ואמר: "חמורה, לאן את חושבת שאת הולכת? את לא הולכת לשום מקום! את באה אתי!" הוא תפס אותי מהצוואר והכניס אותי בכוח לרכב שלו. בנסיעה המשיך לאיים: "אם תעזי לצאת מהמושב זה הסוף שלך!" עד היום אני כועסת על עצמי שנכנעתי לו, ושלא השתמשתי בכוחות שלי להגן על עצמי. למחרת, העובדות הסוציאליות העבירו אותי למשפחה המארחת. באחד הימים, האישה שאצלה התארחתי, הראתה לי שיש עליי כתבה בעיתון תחת הכותרת: "מוכת ירח". בכתבה בני מתראיין ואומר שברסלבים מירושלים חטפו אותי למערה כדי לחתן אותי. הוא לא נרגע והמשיך להגיד את אותם דברים גם בתכניות רדיו. לא די שבגללו איבדתי אמון בעצמי ובאנשים, אלא שהוא גם מצליח לעכב לי את החתונה, עושה לי בעיות עם ההורים שלי, ובגללו סגרו אותי במושב נידח בנגב; ועכשיו הוא גם מוציא דיבה ועלילות שווא על האנשים היחידים שבאו לעזרתי בזמן שההורים שלי לא עשו את זה. אבא שלי גם השתתף בכתבה, וזו הייתה מעילה נוספת באמון בינינו. ניסיתי ליצור קשר עם עזרא, הארוס שלי. הוא התחמק ממני, ואנשים אחרים ענו לטלפון שלו. בסופו של דבר, אחד החברים שלו הודיע לי שעזרא לא רוצה קשר למשפחה כמו שלי, ושהוא נפגע שפרסמו תמונה שלו על עמוד שלם בעיתון תחת כתבת שקרים על ברסלב שכולה חילול השם, ולפיכך הוא לא מעוניין בשידוך. ביטלנו את האירוסין.

השבועיים עד יום ההולדת ה-18 שלי נראו ארוכים במיוחד. חיכיתי בלי סבלנות להתחיל חיים חדשים בלי שיוכלו להפריע לי. ביום שעזבתי את המשפחה המארחת בסוסיא, הזדרזתי לנסוע לירושלים עם עוגת השוקולד שהכנתי כהפתעה לאילנה. בבית של אילנה ודניאל הרגשתי סוף סוף נחת ורגיעה. מהר מאוד הפכתי אותם להיות המשפחה שלי. בחג שבועות הראשון שעשינו יחד, הגברים והבנים היו בגבעת שאול, והנשים והבנות היו בבית של אילנה בשכונת בית וגן. קארי באותה תקופה התגוררה בשכונת בית הכרם. היא הגיעה בכניסת החג להדלקת נרות. אחרי ההדלקה ישבנו לדבר. היא סיפרה לי על מה שהיא עברה

בקהילות ברסלב השונות מצפת ועד ירושלים, על קהילה שלמה בצפת שנידתה אותה וקראה לה זונה, שהיא גידלה את ילדיה במסירות נפש, ולבסוף הגיעה לירושלים, ועכשיו היא מרגישה שהילדים שלה כבר לא סובלים מחיי טלטלה. הזדעזעתי לשמוע שהיא כבר הייתה נשואה שש פעמים, ושיש לה ארבעה ילדים מאבות שונים. שאלתי אותה על זה הרבה שאלות. חשבתי שמשהו לא בסדר אצלה. כשהיא סיפרה לי שדניאל הוא הבעל השביעי שלה, חשבתי לעצמי שאם היא הצליחה להתגבר על כל המשברים והצרות שהיו לה ולהתחתן שוב, אז גם אני יכולה. קינאתי בה שהיא עברה את החלק הקשה בחיים שלה, ועכשיו היא בפרק הטוב, וגם אני כבר רציתי להיות שם. התחלתי לחשוב על דניאל כאופציה, וזה עורר אותי, אבל לא דיברתי על זה עם אף אחת. הגיע זמן קידוש של ערב החג. אדרת עזרה לאילנה. הרגשתי לא בנוח שאני יושבת ומדברת בלי לעזור אחרי שאילנה טרחה והכינה את כל ארוחות החג. קארי אמרה שאני לא אדאג, כי חשוב יותר שאתרכז בהבנת הספרים, ותכננה שכולנו נעשה "לילה לבן" ונקרא תהלים עד הנץ החמה. שמתי לב שקארי נתנה לאילנה הרגשה שהיא מיותרת ועדיף שתטפל בילדים. אילנה נעלבה. הזלזול של קארי באילנה בסיטואציות שונות, יצר אצלי תחושת התנשאות כלפי אילנה, קלקל את החברות בינינו, וגרם לי לראות אותה באור לא נכון, עד כדי כך שרוב הזמן הייתי לצדה של קארי. עם זאת, היה לי מאוד קשה להסתדר עם קארי, כיוון ששתינו נשים כוחניות, והיו בינינו הרבה חילוקי דעות. מוצאי שבת, ישבנו כולנו בסעודה ודניאל ניגן בגיטרה לחן חדש למילים מתורה של רבי נחמן: "כי אין שום טבע כלל". תמיד אהבתי שירים מיוחדים, ומעולם לא שמעתי מילים ולחן כל כך עוצמתיים, שאלתי של מי הלחן היפה הזה, וקארי אמרה "של דניאל". הרגשתי שהניגונים האלה הם חלק ממני. שאני כדבורה שמצאה את הצוף של הפרח שהיא אוהבת יותר מכול, ורוצה להיצמד אליו. כך בעצם התחיל להתנגן פס הקול של סרט החיים הפלאיים שלנו. הסעודה נמשכה עד עלות השחר וכששטפתי את הכלים עם אילנה במטבח, ניצלתי את ההזדמנות לשתף אותה ברגשותיי כלפי הילדים וכלפי דניאל והיא קיבלה את זה יפה. רוחב הלב שלה נתן לי את האומץ לפנות לדניאל בבקשה להצטרף אליו לנסיעה לרבי ישראל עם הבנים הקטנים שלו. שם, כשמצאתי את הרגע הנכון, ביקשתי מדניאל תפילין על מנת לקיים את המנהג הברסלבי של "נקיטת חפץ". החזקתי את התפילין בשתי ידיים, עמדתי קרוב לציון ואמרתי לקב"ה בקול רם: "אני מבקשת לא להיפרד מרבי נחמן בעולם הזה ובעולם הבא ולהיות עם דניאל והמשפחה שלו כל החיים". דניאל נראה מופתע. כשיצאנו מהציון וחזרנו לבית, ביקשתי לדבר אתו לבד. הסברתי לו ארוכות על חשיבות ההפצה שהם עושים, על הספר של רבי ישראל שהוא הוציא לאור, שחיזק אותי, וכמה חשוב להמשיך ולהתפתח בהפצה. אמרתי לו שבאתי לעזור לו, ושאני מחפשת בעל שמאמין כמוני, ושיש לו התלהבות להפצה כמו שלי. בשלב מסוים לא יכולתי להתאפק ואמרתי: "עוד לא הבנת שאני רוצה בעל כמוך?!" כשדניאל הבין שאני רצינית, הוא אמר שצריך לשאול את אילנה וקארי. אילנה מיד אמרה בחיוך: "מזל טוב". קארי התרגשה מאוד. התחתנו לפי ההלכה היהודית. ב"שבע ברכות", דניאל ניגן בשבילי כמו שאהבתי וזה היה מרגש מאוד. יצאנו לטייל, אני ודניאל הגענו למעיין "מוצא", שם היה עץ זית עתיק ומיוחד. התיישבנו בצל תחתיו. התחלתי לשאול אותו שאלות אינטימיות שסיקרנו אותי בקשר לחייו ולעברו, עד שמצאתי את עצמי מצהירה שאני למעשה בתולה, ושאף פעם לא הייתי עם גבר. רציתי להאמין שאני יכולה להיות חדשה לבעלי, ולשכוח את המועקות. הוריי מעולם לא דיברו אתי על נושא הבתולים, ומעניין ששמעתי את זה רק מבני ומסבא אברם, שהיו משבחים את הנשים הפרסיות שהן טובות ובתולות, ושככה צריכה להיות אישה.

בחודשים הראשונים של הנישואין, אחרי שהילדים יצאו ללימודים, התיישבנו, הנשים ודניאל לארוחת בוקר והכנו תכנית להמשך היום. הייתה תקופה שכל בוקר למדנו ביחד מהספרים של רבי נחמן, שחיזקו אותנו בהפצה. הרגשתי שקיבלתי מתנה מרבי נחמן, בעל יקר מאוד, פיצוי על הצער שעברתי. אחרי ששמעתי שסבא אברם מת, העזתי להגיע למושב לספר להורים שלי מה עברתי. זה היה מאוד קשה לדבר על זה, בכיתי הרבה. על בני פחדתי לדבר כי הוא היה עדיין במושב, אבל ידעתי שיבוא יום ואני עוד אצעק את זה. ההורים שלי היו בצער לשמוע, אימא שלי הייתה ממש מבוהלת שהיא לא ידעה מכל זה, והם ניסו לחשוב מה יכול לעזור לי.

הוריי גם ביקשו סליחה על ההתנהגות שלהם עם המפיצים מירושלים, וסוף סוף יכולתי לספר להם שהתחתנתי עם דניאל! הם שמחו, ואבא שלי בירך אותנו. הם היו מגיעים לירושלים להופעות של דניאל עם הילדים, ואני מאוד שמחתי. כשהבת הראשונה של אילנה ודניאל התחתנה, הוריי הזמינו את כולנו לחגוג את "שבע ברכות" אצלם, בבית במושב. כשסבתא זוהרה ראתה את דניאל, היא התרגשה ממנו ואמרה: "יש לך בעל ג'ינג'י. הוא י פ ה! תביאו הרבה ילדים". לדניאל היא אמרה שכל החיים היא התפללה שהנכדים שלה והיא יפגשו אנשים טובים בדרך, והיא רואה שהתפילה שלה התקבלה.

<u>**ליפתא, חלקת גן העדן שלי**</u>

אחד התחביבים שלי היה לארגן ולסדר בתים. עכשיו היו לי כמה בתים להשתלט עליהם. התחלתי עם הבית של אילנה. אילנה שמה לב שאני נהנית להכניס הביתה חפצים ופריטים מיוחדים, וזה מצא חן בעיניה. מהר מאוד הרגשתי "בעלות" על עיצוב הבית, עד כדי כך שזה היה מעצבן אותי אם אילנה הייתה

מסגננת את הבד על הספה ולא אני. שיניתי כל הזמן את המקום הקבוע של פריטים שונים. הגענו למצב שזה חזר על עצמו עשרות פעמים, שאילנה רצתה לשטוף את הרצפה היא לא הייתה מוצאת את הדלי, ושאלה את כולם אם ראו אותו, ואני התחמקתי כי לא הרגשתי בנוח שלא החזרתי אותו למקום. כשראינו שתקלות מסוג זה חוזרות על עצמם, הבנו שצריך לתאם בינינו איך לכל אחת נוח להתנהל בבית. החלטתי לחשוב יותר על אילנה, ולהבין מה היא מרגישה ומה אני גורמת לה כשאני לא שמה לב לתכנית שלה. חיזקנו אחת את השנייה בכך שהחיים ביחד הם אפשרות נדירה ומיוחדת של עבודת מידות יומיומית, שבכל רגע נתון יש לנו אפשרות לעשות צדקה וחסד אחת עם השנייה, להתחזק בהכרת הטוב, ולרצות להשתנות לטובה. הגענו למסקנה שאם רוצים לזכות למתיקות של היחד, צריכים להתגבר על החיפוש אחר הכבוד, "שאני ואני ואני...עשיתי ועשיתי ועשיתי". היום, אחרי 15 שנה, כשאנחנו נזכרות וצוחקות על המריבות על הדלי אילנה אומרת: "איזה מטומטמת הייתי, למה לא השארתי לך את הדלי ואת הניקיונות ולא הלכתי לעשות משהו אחר? ולמה לא קניתי עוד דלי בשבילך? אולי בגלל שדניאל הוא מזל דלי, רצינו כל אחת להשתלט עליו בדרך שלה...

היחסים בין כולנו לא תמיד היו פשוטים. עם כל זה שהייתה לנו אמונה ואידיאל משותף, היו בינינו גם ויכוחים ומחלוקות על עקרונות ועל הרגלים שאף אחת מאתנו לא הייתה מוכנה לוותר עליהם. לא תמיד הצלחנו להתעלות על האכזריות, על הקנאה ועל הכבוד העצמי וכל אחת הייתה בטוחה שהיא צודקת. ועם זאת, השלמנו האחת את השנייה, והגענו לתוצאות יפות מאוד גם בבית, גם בהפצה וגם בעבודה האישית. הייתה אחווה מיוחדת, שהחזירה אותנו לשירים ולריקודים כמעט בכל ערב מחדש...

כשאדרת התחתנה עם דניאל, אני זוכרת את הפעם הראשונה שקלטתי שהיא הולכת להיות אתו בלילה, OK... אני מנסה לעכל מה קורה כאן. שדון קטן "מקפיץ לי את הפיוז", מחשבה מטרידה פולשת, אבל אני חושבת שאולי יש לי כלים, עם כל העבר שלי, להתגבר על הג'וק הזה. האמת היא שלא התגברתי. אך מה שניסיתי לעשות, זה להסתיר את זה באופן מוחלט מדניאל, ובטח מאדרת, שחס ושלום, לא יגלו שאני מקנאה. ומה באשר לאילנה? הרחקתי אותה מהמחשבה, הרי היא כבר זכתה לילדים והיא אתו שנים. קארי התפארה שהיא כבר עברה את הגיל של הקנאה, אז מה אכפת לה לוותר לי על כמה לילות אחרי ש"קברה" שישה בעלים?!

בשנה הראשונה לא שיתפתי את דניאל במה שעוללו לי בני וסבא אברם, והתביישתי להסביר לו את הקנאה שלי בנשים אחרות שלא חוו את הטראומה שאני סוחבת מגיל שש. הרגשתי שהעבר שלי חוסם אותי, ולא מאפשר לי להתפתח בקשר שלנו, אבל מדי פעם הרגשות שלי פרצו החוצה בהתנהגות מוזרה. יום אחד, בזמן שישבנו יחד לסעודת ערב, הרהרתי במה שסבא אברם ודוד בני עשו לי, וחשבתי שאם לא אעיף את קרטון החלב מהשולחן יקרה אסון. כשזרקתי את קרטון החלב בפתאומיות על הרצפה, כולם הסתכלו עליי, ולא הבינו מה קרה. מעשים מסוג זה חזרו על עצמם בתדירות גבוהה, בנוסף, הצטברו בי כל מיני כעסים קטנים, שהתבטאו במחשבות רעות כלפי דניאל, הנשים והילדים. ניסיתי לעשות הכול כדי שאף אחד לא ידע מזה. המחשבות שלי היו באותו נוסח האיומים והקללות של בני וסבא אברם. שהדהדו בראשי: "אני אחתוך כל אצבע של בעלך..."; "אני אשרוף לך את הילדים...". מצאתי את עצמי בהתקפה של מחשבות טורדניות על כל אחד מבני הבית. זה גרם לי להסתגר בתוך עצמי, ולהרגיש הכי רעה בעולם. חייתי בפחד אמתי, שבגלל המחשבות האלו משהו באמת יקרה. לא ידעתי איך כדאי לי להתמודד עם זה, בפרט שההתנהגויות האלה היו בולטות מדי וחסרות תועלת. כשהחלטתי שנמאס לי להתמודד לבד עם התסכול הזה, סיפרתי לדניאל ולנשים. זה כל כך שחרר אותי, שמאז, כל פעם שהותקפתי ב"מחשבות", הרגשתי צורך לספר למישהו. כל מה שלא יכולתי לשתף בבית הוריי כי התעלמו מהבעיה שלי, הצטבר בתוכי, ומצא עכשיו פורקן. המחשבות היו בעלות תוכן קשה וסבלתי מהן מאוד. דניאל והנשים ניסו בכל דרך אפשרית לעזור לי, אך היו חסרי אונים לראות ששום דבר לא מרפא מהשורש את החרדות ואת טראומות הילדות. דניאל הציע לי להיפגש עם איש מקצוע. אמרתי לו שאני באמת חושבת על זה כבר הרבה זמן. חיפשתי פסיכולוג באינטרנט, וגיליתי שלבעיה שלי יש שם: "הפרעה טורדנית כפייתית המכונה OCD". זה הפתיע אותי למצוא כל כך בקלות את ההגדרה, אחרי שנים שהתייסרתי מהמחשבה שאני היחידה בעולם עם הבעיה הזאת, גיליתי שאלפי אנשים ברחבי העולם, ואפילו רופאים, אקדמאים ואנשים בעלי אינטליגנציה גבוהה סובלים מזה. מצאתי פסיכולוג, והתוודיתי לפניו על כל מה שמטריד אותי. הוא הסביר לי שהמחשבות הטורדניות יכולות להיגרם גם כתוצאה מהתעללות מינית בילדות ובדרך כלל הסובלים מ-OCD משתמשים בפעולות טקסיות כפייתיות על מנת להפחית את החרדה. הוא גם אמר שיש שתי אפשרויות לטיפול: ספרי הדרכה, או טיפול תרופתי. לא האמנתי בטיפול תרופתי שרק מטשטש את המציאות, בחרתי להתמודד, לכן קניתי את הספרים. אדרת ישבה אתי ימים שלמים, קראנו וחיפשנו עצות מעשיות. נכתב שם על כמה שיטות התמודדות מעניינות ומאתגרות, וניסיתי ליישם אותן. דניאל עודד אותי שבוודאי אין שום ייאוש בעולם כלל, וביחד אפשר להתגבר על הכול. היו בספר גם תרגילים שדרשו עבודה קבוצתית. אחד מהם היה פסיכודרמה. התחלנו את סדנאות האלתור לפי הספר. הסדנה נפתחת לרוב בסבב

קצר שבו כל משתתף מספר בקצרה על אירועים משמעותיים שקרו לו בחיים בכלל, ובזמן האחרון בפרט, לאחר מכן חימום פיזי, ומשם מעבר לעבודה קבוצתית או פרטנית שבה משתתף אחד מציג נושא שברצונו לחקור ולהבין, ושאר הקבוצה מסייעת לו לגלם את הדמויות ואת האירועים. הסדנה מסתיימת ב״שרינג״, שבו כל אחד משתף באיזה אופן העבודה שנעשתה באותו יום נגעה בו. אהבתי את התרגיל הזה. היה לנו כיף ביחד, זה הביא אותנו לריקוד, לשירה ולמשחק, ועזר לחיזוק הקשר בינינו. זה הוריד ממני הרבה מהלחץ ומהפחד מהמחשבות.

בתחום של הרהורים על גברים, התמודדתי בתוכי עם שני צדדים מנוגדים, צד אחד שרוצה להתנזר לחלוטין ומפחד מכל אינטימיות עם גבר אפילו בדמיון, וצד שני שכולו התמכרות למחשבות על תאוות המשגל עם כל גבר שיכול להיות. רק המבנה המשפחתי של כמה חברות שחיות יחד, אפשר לי לדבר על הדברים. ראיתי שלכל אחת מהנשים יש משא שסחבה אתה מעברה, וזו לא רק אני. ויחד ניסינו להתמודד עם הכול על ידי שילוב בין האמונה והאמנות. דרך האמנות וסדנאות האלתור הצלחתי לחלוק את הרגשות האינטימיים, ולדבר על הכול. להפוך את כל האנרגיה הזאת לעשייה, ליצירה ולהפצה.

בספרים של רבי נחמן מצאתי את העצות שנותנות פתרון שורשי לבעיה, למשל, בליקוטי מוהר״ן, תורה נד׳:

״...והקדוש ברוך הוא... מזמין לכל אדם מחשבה דיבור ומעשה לפי היום ולפי האדם ולפי המקום, ומלביש לו בזאת המחשבה דיבור ומעשה שמזמין לו רמזים כדי לקרבו לעבודתו. בכן צריך להעמיק מחשבתו בזה ולהגדיל בינתו, ולהבין מה הרמזים בפרטיות שמלובש בזאת המחשבה דיבור ומעשה של זה היום, שהזמין לו השם יתברך...״

בתורה כ״ט רבנו כותב:

״...כי המחשבה שבמוח הוא כפי המידות שבאדם, וכפי המידה שהאדם אוחז בה, כן חולפין ועוברין עליו המחשבות שבמוח״.

עוד הבנתי מספרי הקודש שעיקר הבעיה היא הטקסים שעשיתי כדי לבטל את המחשבות הרעות, כמו לגעת ברצפה, או כל פעולה אחרת. וזה נקרא בלשון התורה ״דרכי האמורי״, שהוא איסור עבודה זרה. לפי הגמרא בסנהדרין פירוש ״דרכי האמורי״ הוא: ״..המשים לעצמו סימן אם יארע לי כך וכך אעשה דבר פלוני, ואם לא יארע לי לא אעשה״. המושג ״דרכי האמורי״ קיים כמעט 3300 שנה, מאז קיומו של העם האמורי, נינו של נוח. לפי רש״י האיסור נלמד מהפסוק: ״ובחוקותיהם לא תלכו״. גם קראתי אצל רבי נחמן שזה מה שנקרא ״אמונות כוזביות״.

כשהבנתי ששמתי את הדגש במקום הלא נכון, זאת הייתה התקדמות. תמיד הציקה לי עצם המחשבה, כי חשבתי שהיא המזיקה, ולכן ניסיתי להשתיק ולקבור אותה ולא הבנתי שהמחשבה היא הרמז שהשם שולח לי לאותו הרגע בשביל להתמודד, ושאני לא צריכה להילחץ ממנה ובוודאי לא להשתמש בטקסים. רבי נחמן אמר: ״אני הרופא הכי גדול מי שצריך רפואה שיבא אלי״. ואכן, בהתקרבות שלי לרבי נחמן, בלימוד מספריו ובהשתדלות לקיים את עצותיו, מצאתי את הרפואה לנפשי.

מסגרת החיים עם דניאל והנשים נתנו לי פתרון ומרגוע. הרגשתי שהמבנה הזה מתאים לי במיוחד. לא הייתי מסוגלת להיסגר עם גבר לבד ולהיות מחויבת. בסיכומו של דבר, האינטרסים האישיים של כל אחת מאתנו הסתדרו יפה ביחד. הבית פעל כמו קיבוץ וכלכל את עצמו. חיינו בביטחון כלכלי ובשפע. אנחנו יחד כמעט 16 שנים. 16 שנים של אהבה ושל עזרה הדדית, של אכפתיות ושל רצון להתפתח ביחד. החוויה של ״היחד״, ההפצה, הניגונים וההופעות, נתנו לי סיפוק אמתי. מאז ומתמיד חלמתי להתחתן עם גבר שמנגן ושר, שיחד נחיה את המוזיקה – גם זה חלום שהתגשם. השנים היפות של ההופעות של דניאל והבנים על הבמה, רוקדים ומשמחים, אין להם תחליף. גם הרצון להתגבר על כל הפחדים ולהביא ילד לעולם, ברוך השם התגשם.

אני זוכרת ערב שבת אחד, פנה אליי גיא-נועם הקטן בן החמש, הבן של אילנה, לבוש בחולצה לבנה, ג׳יקט ופפיון שחור והפאות הארוכות גולשות בצדי פניו המתוקות, בחיוך שאי-אפשר לסרב לו, וביקש שאשמע אותו מספר בעל-פה את הסיפור ״מאבדת בת מלך״. כשהוא אמר ברצף כמה עמודים, מילה במילה, חשבתי לעצמי: כזה ילד אני רוצה!

שנה אחרי שהתחתנו, נולד לנו בן יקר ולצורך הספר נקרא לו ידידיה. ידידיה נולד בלי מרפק. החן שלו היה כובש לבבות. מאז שהיה תינוק נראה היה שהוא מבין כל מה שקורה סביבו. בבית החולים ענדו לו צמיד זיהוי על היד. קרה דבר-פלא, על הצמיד היה כתוב: ״ידידיה בן של י-ה״, הרגשנו שהוא הבן של השם וכך קראנו לו. דניאל אהב אותו באופן מיוחד. הוא היה דואג להתפתחותו הפיזית של ידידיה, וחשב כל הזמן

מה יהיה אתו כשיגדל, ואיך הוא יסתדר, איך יתמודד עם כל הפעולות היומיומיות כמו לסגור כפתור או רוכסן, ואיך יהיה עצמאי ולא תלוי באנשים. לדניאל ולי היה חשוב מאוד שידידיה יקבל מאחיו את מלוא הביטחון והאהבה בבית ולא ירגיש חיסרון. ואמנם, כל האחים מהאימהות האחרות הרגישו אחראים לתמוך בידידיה ולחזק אותו. כשידידיה היה בן שלוש הוא כבר ידע לקרוא באופן שוטף, וידע לספר "סיפורי מעשיות" של רבי נחמן בעל–פה, והיה מרגש את כל האורחים שהיו מגיעים אלינו. בגיל שבע דניאל קנה לו גיטרה חשמלית אמתית שמתאימה לגילו, והם היו מתאמנים ביחד. בערבים, כשכל הלהקה ניגנה להנאתה, ידידיה היה הולך לפסנתר בסטודיו, וממציא לחן בהרמוניה חדשה. זה מאוד ריגש אותי, וחשבתי שיש לי מזל שיש לי בן כל כך מתוק ומשפחה כל כך תומכת. תמיד בסעודות הוא היה תופס את המקום ליד אבא, ולא מוותר לאף ילד ולאף אישה, ולא חסרו סעודות לוויכוחים. גם דניאל לא ויתר על הישיבה ליד ידידיה. ידידיה היה קופץ כמו תלמיד חכם להגיב לדברי תורה שלומדים בסעודה, היו לו חידושים הרבה מעבר לגילו והוא לא התבייש להתפלפל עם חברים של אבא שלו. הוא היה מתעקש ללכת עם אבא לכל מקום. בהופעות והילולות ידידיה ואחיו היו מפתיעים את הקהל כשהופיעו בביצועים יפהפיים של ברייקדנס על הבמה. אני ודניאל היינו הולכים עם ידידיה לבְּרֵכה ולים מאז שהיה בן שנה כדי להתאמן אתו, בשחייה ובפיזיותרפיה ותמיד בסופו של דבר זה הפך להיות בילוי משפחתי, כי כל הילדים רצו להיות עם ידידיה. ידידיה גדל עם הרבה שמחת חיים, אהבה וביטחון עצמי, הוא היה גאה מאוד במשפחה שלו והיה קשור מאוד לאביו.

כשרציתי להביא עוד ילד, אפילו שעם דניאל הרגשתי אהובה ובטוחה, לא יכולתי להימנע מהמחשבה שיש קשר בין זה שידידיה נולד בלי מרפק, למה שדוד בני וסבא שלי עשו לי. על מנת להיפטר מהבעיה שלי אחת ולתמיד, החלטתי לשבור את הפחדים האלה ואת הדאגות ולהפסיק להתחמק, לנסוע למושב בו גדלתי, ולחשוף את כל הסיפור בפני ההורים שלי. כשדיברתי על זה עם דניאל הוא חשב שזה רעיון טוב. השארתי את ידידיה אתו ועם האימהות האחרות, לקחתי תיק ונסעתי, לא ידעתי לכמה זמן. תקופה ארוכה הייתי שם, כשבשבתות, בחגים ובאמצע השבוע, הייתי חוזרת לירושלים, לדניאל ולידידיה, שהתגעגעתי אליהם מאוד, ואוגרת כוחות להמשיך את ההתמודדות עם הסיפור הלא פשוט הזה. כשסיפרתי להורים שלי שחוץ מסבא שלי, גם אח של אימא, במשך שנים בילדותי התעלל בי מינית, הם לא יכלו להתמודד עם זה: אימא שלי אמרה שהיא צריכה לשמור את מעט הכוחות שלה לטפל באחים שלי, שכבר היו גדולים ועצמאים; ואבא שלי אמר שהוא לא רוצה לשמוע דיבורים כאלה, ואם אני רוצה להישאר, שלא אדבר על זה... חשבתי שאם ידעו מזה עוד אנשים במושב, אולי ההורים שלי יתייחסו אליי יותר ברצינות. נשארתי בשבת במושב כי תכננתי משהו... בלילה לא הצלחתי להירדם, הייתי בסערת רגשות. בחמש בבוקר שכבתי על הרצפה ובכיתי. לקראת 10:00 התחלתי ללכת לכיוון בית הכנסת, הלב שלי דפק חזק, הסתובבתי והתחלתי לחזור לבית. כעסתי על עצמי, ושוב הלכתי לבית הכנסת. בקושי הצלחתי לנשום. כל הגברים של המושב היו בבית הכנסת לתפילת שחרית של שבת. אבא שלי היה בבית כנסת אחר ולכן הרגשתי שאני יכולה לעשות את זה. חיכיתי שיסיימו את קריאת התורה ואז נכנסתי ל'עזרת הגברים' התקדמתי לכיוון המרכז כשאני רועדת ואמרתי בקול: "אני רוצה שכולם פה ידעו משהו". נעשה שקט בקהל. הסתכלתי על בני, ראיתי שהוא נלחץ. הוא צחק צחוק מאולץ והסתודד עם מישהו. כבר לא היה לי אכפת מהבושה שכולם ידעו מה קרה... הגעתי קרוב לאיפה שישב בני והתחלתי לצעוק את כל מה שהוא עשה לי. הוא בתגובה השתגע והרביץ לי. המשכתי וצעקתי גם את מה שסבא שלי עשה לי... אנשים החזיקו את בני, והוא קילל ואיים שהוא עוד יתפוס אותי ויהרוג אותי. "ח-מ-ו-ר-ה!" הוא צעק לעברי. כולם התחילו לדבר על זה שבני הרס וסיבך הרבה משפחות, וניסו להרגיע אותי. כשההורים שלי שמעו מה שקרה הם אמרו לי: "תפני למשטרה". לא הייתי מסוגלת להגיע לתחנת המשטרה כי ריחמתי על אשתו של בני ועל ילדיו. ביום למחרת עזבתי את המושב. הרגשתי שעשיתי צעד גדול להשתחרר מהמועקה. הרגשתי כמה טוב שיש לי את דניאל ואת הנשים, החברות הכי טובות שלי, שאפשר לדבר ביחד על הכול מבלי לחשוש.

**<u>הערה:</u>**

בהכרעת הדין נגד דניאל התייחסו השופטים לביקור זה בבית הוריי, הם כתבו: "אזמרה שהתה במושב זרחיה לתקופה ארוכה כעונש הרחקה מהבית שניתן לה, בניגוד לרצונה, על ידי הנאשם".

והשופטים מסכמים:

"...מהאמור לעיל עולה מעורבותו הברורה והישירה של הנאשם בניתוק הקשרים בין נשותיו לבין משפחותיהן. הנאשם הסיט את הנשים כנגד בני המשפחות שלהן והשפיע עליהן לצמצם את היקף הקשר ובמיוחד את עומקו... ראיה ברורה למידת השליטה של הנאשם בנשים, אשר צייתו להוראותיו באמונה כה מוחלטת עד שהובילה אותם לנתק את קשריהן עם בני המשפחה (קשרים שהיו טובים ומבוססים קודם לכן)".

הנה לכם ראיה, קוראים יקרים, לדרך שהשופטים הופכים את הדברים, ומסלפים את העובדות, ולבסוף מעוותים את הדין ומרשיעים את הבן אדם הלא נכון.

כשבחדרי החקירות סיפרתי לשוטרים כל מה שדוד שלי בני וסבא אברם עשו לי, הם התעלמו, כאילו לא אמרתי כלום והמשיכו לנסות בכל הכוח לשתול בפי גרסאות נגד בעלי. משלא שיתפתי פעולה, הם המשיכו לאיים. מסתבר שמשטרת ישראל, שתפקידה להגן על האזרחים ולעזור להם, לא מתייחסת למצוקה שלהם, אלא פועלת אך ורק לפי המטרות שהיא מסמנת לעצמה.

סבא אברם מת. דוד בני מסתובב חופשי, מי יודע באילו ילדים הוא פוגע עכשיו.

ודניאל יושב בכלא.

---

ב-4.7.11 בערך ב-05:00 אחר הצהריים, ידידיה שהיה כבר בן תשע היה בבית ברוממה בירושלים עם אילנה ובתיה, אחותו בת השש. לפתע פרצו לבית שמונה גברים חמושים, באגרסיביות, באיומים ובקללות גסות. ידידיה היה מבוהל מאוד כשראה איך השוטרים דוחפים את אילנה לרצפה והופכים לה את הארון. הוא בכה בבכי היסטרי וצעק: "אבל למה, אבל למה, מה קרה?" שני עובדים סוציאליים תפסו את ידידיה, אחד בידיים ואחד ברגליים כשהוא נלחם וצועק: "למה אתם לוקחים אותי? אני רוצה את אבא!"

לא הייתי שם. לא ידעתי מה עשו לידידיה. כל מה שאני מספרת לכם נמצא בדפי החקירות. אותי עצרו באותו יום במרכז העיר, ואחרי חקירות אלימות שלחו אותי למקלט לנשים מוכות למשך שלושה חודשים. סגרו אותי ללא שום סיבה, כי לא הייתה להם כל טענה ואשמה כלפיי. הייתי בתנאי מעצר, בלי טלפון ובלי אפשרות לצאת החוצה, בהסבר שהם "מוכרחים לפרק את הכת". הם התחילו בכך שהפרידו בין כל בני המשפחה. במשך יותר מחודש נתנו לי לראות את ידידיה כלל, ואפילו לא לדבר אתו בטלפון.

שיחת הטלפון הראשונה עם ידידיה הייתה בפיקוח של פקידת הסעד נחמה ג'הסי. הוא סיפר לי במהירות איך שחוקר הילדים מיכה הרן קילל את אבא, אמר לו מילים גסות, שאל שאלות מוזרות ואמר לו שאנחנו משפחה לא נורמלית. העובדת הסוציאלית לא התחשבה בצער של הילד ובכאב שבו הוא חי כבר חודש לבד עם עצמו, וניתקה לנו את הטלפון באמצע השיחה. התקשרתי אליה בדאגה ושאלתי אותה למה השיחה התנתקה, היא אמרה לי בקרירות: "אסור לילד לדבר על זה". כשביקשתי שוב לדבר עם הילד, היא אמרה שאני צריכה אישור משופט.

בדיון הראשון בעניין הילדים, השופט קבע שהילד זקוק לי, והחליט שידידיה יראה אותי שלוש פעמים בשבוע. פניתי לפקידת הסעד, נחמה ג'הסי, כדי לקבוע את הימים של הביקור והיא אמרה לי שהיא החליטה שהביקור יהיה רק יום אחד בשבוע לשעה אחת בלבד. אמרתי לה: "אבל זו החלטה של השופט והילד זקוק לי, אין לו קשר עם אף אחד מהמשפחה, והשופט קבע שלוש פגישות בשבוע". היא עצרה אותי ואמרה: "תגישי לבית המשפט את הטענות שלך, ובינתיים זה כמו שאמרתי, פגישה אחת בשבוע לשעה אחת בלבד, הפעם הראשונה תהיה כשאני אודיע לך". חודש שלם בכיתי בפני מנהלת המקלט שאיני רואה את ידידיה, ושאני יודעת שהוא שבור. היא הבטיחה לי שהיא תעזור ותדבר עם פקידת הסעד. יום אחד המנהלת קראה לי וסיפרה שנחמה ג'הסי הודיעה שמחר יהיה מפגש עם הילד, אבל עליי לעמוד בשני תנאים: הראשון, שבשום אופן לא אדבר אתו על אבא שלו ועל המשפחה, ואם אדבר – יפסיקו את הפגישה בינינו, והוסיפה שלא אכפת לה שהוא זקוק לי. והתנאי השני, שאגיב נכון אליו. שאלתי אותה מה זאת אומרת, והיא ענתה: "פקידת הסעד סיפרה שידידיה לא רוצה יותר קשר אתך ועם המשפחה, הוא כועס על כל המשפחה, אל תכעסי עליו על זה, ותראי לו שאת מבינה אותו". צבט לי בלב, והיה לי קשה להאמין שידידיה, שכל כך אוהב את אבא ואימא שלו ואת המשפחה, ידבר כך, זה לא היה נשמע הגיוני. התרגשתי מאוד מהפגישה ובכל הכסף שחסכתי מעבודה בשביל נשים במקלט, קניתי לו מתנות. לא ישנתי כל הלילה מהתרגשות. לא ידעתי למה לצפות.

כשהגעתי לפנימייה ידידיה ראה אותי מרחוק. רץ, קפץ עליי וחיבק אותי, ולא רצה שאעזוב אותו. שנינו בכינו והתחבקנו חזק. הוא אמר לי: "את יודעת כמה ביקשתי שתבואי?" הוא ירד מהידיים שלי, הפך רציני ושאל: "איפה אבא?! תגידי לו שיבוא לקחת אותי מכאן, אני לא רוצה להישאר פה, אני רוצה לחזור לבית. איפה כל הילדים? הם גם בפנימייה?!"

פקידת הסעד, נחמה ג'הסי, הגיעה בצעדים גדולים והורתה לנו להיכנס לחדר קטן, חשוך ומחניק. שאלתי אם יש אפשרות לקיים את הפגישה בגינה, שיהיה נעים לילד, היא ענתה בקול צווחני: "לא, הפגישה בפיקוח". זה לא נעים, לא לי ולא לידידיה להיות תחת עיניהם הביקורתיות של אנשי הרווחה, במקרה זה, שלוש נשים, שש עיניים דוקרניות שמביטות בי ובידידיה משך זמן הפגישה, רושמות לעצמן על דף מה

שאחר כך יעבירו לשופט, עובדות שקריות ומעוותות, באופן שיטתי, על מנת להשאיר אותו תחת חסותם, וכך להפריד ביני לבין בני, למנוע ממני לקבל אותו בחזרה, ולמנוע ממנו אהבה אמתית של אבא ואימא. ידידיה שהיה עסוק בהתרגשות שהוא רואה אותי, אחרי חודש שלם שניתקו כל קשר בינו לביני ולשאר בני המשפחה, לרבות אחים ואחיות, חיבק אותי, הביט בי בעיניים מבריקות ומתוקות ואמר: "חלמתי שאני בסופרלנד ואבא מחכה לי בקצה המגלשה ואומר לי שהוא לא רוצה שאהיה עצוב, הוא רוצה שיהיה לי כיף, אימא איפה הוא?!! אני רוצה להיות אתו!" נחמה עצרה את השיחה ושאלה באיום, כשהיא מתעלמת לחלוטין מדיבוריו של ידידיה: "את רוצה באמת להפסיק את הפגישה? את לא עומדת בתנאי, הזהרתי אותך, אסור לדבר על אבא ועל המשפחה, שכחת?!" ידידיה החוויר, הוא התחנן אליה: "די בבקשה!". לא הבנתי איך שוב היא חותכת את דברי הילד בצורה כל כך בוטה וחסרת רגישות! מתעלמת מדבריו ופונה אליי בטענה שכזאת!

כשהפגישה הסתיימה שאלתי את נחמה, פקידת הסעד: "למה אמרתם לי שידידיה לא מעוניין לשמוע ממני?" היא לא ענתה לי. הבנתי באותו רגע שאם פקידת הסעד מסוגלת לשקר בעניין הצרכים הבסיסיים של ילד שמבקש לראות את אימא שלו, אז היא מסוגלת לשקר בכול.

משך שנה וחצי הפגישות עם ידידיה התקיימו פעם בשבוע למשך שעה אחת בלבד, בפיקוח של עובדת סוציאלית. בכל פגישה ידידיה היה שואל אותי מה קורה עם אבא, ואומר לי שהוא מתגעגע אליו ורוצה לחזור לבית עם אבא ואימא, ונמאס לו מהפנימייה. הייתי עונה לו ומנסה לחזק אותו, וכתוצאה מכך היינו מקבלים נזיפה מנחמה ג'הסי. בשלב מסוים ידידיה אמר לי שהסבירו לו שהוא יצטרך להישאר בפנימייה עד גיל 18, ושלא כדאי לנו לדבר על אבא, כי יבטלו את השעה שיש לנו ביחד. הרגשתי שהם מצליחים לשבור לו את האמונה ואת התקווה שהייתה לו. באכזריות הם לקחו ממנו את הזכות הבסיסית לרצות את אבא ואימא שלו. מאז, הוא לא דיבר על אבא ועל המשפחה, רק אם במקרה העובדת הסוציאלית השאירה אותנו לשתי דקות לבד, הוא היה מנצל את ההזדמנות לשאול על אבא. הפחד שגרמו לו להרגיש שאסור לדבר על אבא ועל המשפחה, חלחל לאט לאט כמו ארס של נחש, ועשה את שלו. השיא הגיע לפני שנה וחצי, אחרי שנגזרו על דניאל 26 שנות מאסר, קראה לי פקידת הסעד ושאלה אותי מה המצב אתי. חשבתי שהיא שואלת אותי כי היא דואגת לי ואכפת לה, וסיפרתי לה בתום לב שאני, אילנה, אדרת ושירן גרות ביחד, ואנחנו נלחמות לחשוף את השחיתות של החוקרים ושל השופטים. נדהמתי מגודל אדישותה למצב כשענתה לי בקרירות: "כל זמן שאת גרה עם הנשים האחרות ותומכת בדניאל, אין לך אישור לראות את הבן שלך. אם תתקרבי לאיפה שהוא נמצא אני אזמין לך משטרה מיד! את צריכה לבחור, הילד שלך או הנשים ודניאל!"

כבר כמעט שנתיים שאני לא רואה את הבן שלי, כעונש על כך שאני אוהבת את אבא שלו! כל ילד שאני רואה ברחוב מעורר בי רצון לבכות, זה צובט לי בלב. אני רואה בו את ידידיה, ואני חושבת כמה הוא מושפל כשאומרים לו ביזיונות על אבא שלו, וכמה הוא סובל. אני יודעת מה ילד מרגיש כשמקללים, מבזים ומשפילים את אבא שלו.

אי-אפשר יותר לסבול את המצב. איך ייתכן שנותנים לפקידת סעד סמכות להפריד בין אימא לבנה ללא שום פיקוח עליה, בזמן שאפילו את החלטת השופט היא לא מקיימת?! הרי היא יודעת שהבן שלי צריך אותי ולא מעניינת אותה באמת טובת הילד.

רק אחרי גזר הדין של דניאל קיבלתי מעוה"ד את הפרוטוקול של החקירות שעבר ידידיה אצל חוקר הילדים מיכה הרן, והזדעזעתי לראות איך החוקר התעלל בנפש של הילד שלי בן התשע!

החוקר מיכה הרן שאל את ידידיה למי הוא הכי קשור במשפחה, ידידיה ענה: "לכל האחים יש לי אותו קשר, ולאבא שלי הכי. כי אני הכי אוהב אותו". ידידיה היה במצוקה גדולה כאשר החוקר הסביר לו כבר ביום הראשון של המעצר שאבא שלו עשה פשעים שעליהם הוא צריך לשלם שלושים שנה בכלא, ושהוא לא הולך לראות אותו יותר בחיים, שהמשפחה לא תחזור להיות ביחד כי היא בעצם כת. ידידיה שלי עבר ייסורים מחוקר הילדים, שהטיח בפניו האשמות קשות נגד אביו ומשפחתו. הוא סיפר לילד סיפורים קשים שלא היו ולא נבראו, ואמר לו שזה מה שהיה בבית. הוא ציפה, כמו חיה רעה שאורבת לטרף, שידידיה יאשר שזה קרה. לידידיה כאב מאוד שמשפילים בשקרים עצומים את אבא שלו, ומקללים אותו. באומץ הוא ניסה להילחם בחוקר כדי להגן על אביו ועל משפחתו. ידידיה ביקש כמה פעמים במהלך החקירה לראות את אבא שלו, והחוקר התעלם ממנו.

אני מצטטת כאן מילה במילה מפרוטוקול החקירה הנבזי, שבו החוקר המשטרתי עורך חקירה של אש צולבת לילד בן תשע, בלי ליווי של מבוגר שיגן עליו, שזה כשלעצמו עברה פלילית:

"...מה שאתם עושים זה רק להתאכזר! זה לא פחות ממה שעושים ברוסיה לילדים שנותנים להם סרגלים ביד, זה ממש... בדיוק ככה אני מרגיש בלב שלי, שאתם צובטים לי את הלב, צובטים לי

את הלב! אתם תופסים אותו במקום ואתם אומרים לי: 'אתה מושגח במקום טוב..', ואתם צובטים לי את הלב ואוחזים אותו במקום שהוא לא שייך לו, כמו פאזל, אתם מחברים את הפאזל לא במקום הנכון".

החוקר ממשיך ושואל שאלות שידידיה מתלונן שמציקות לו, ובכל זאת מנסה להסביר: "אבא שלי, אני מפונק מאוד אליו, אין... אין פינוק כזה ואהבה כזאת...". ידידיה מתלונן בצער:

"איך היום בכלל העזתם לקחת אותי בכל כך צער, אחד מהידיים, אחד מהרגליים, אתם צריכים להגיד סליחה על הצער שעשיתם לנו. זה לא יפה, זה לא יפה, לעשות ככה לילד... וגם אני אומר לך עוד משהו, אני אגיד לך משהו עכשיו, שעדיף לי להישאר עם ההורים שלי, אפילו אם יהיה כעס הכי גדול בעולם. אבל אין כעס. אני מעדיף לא לעזוב את הבית הזה. אתם עושים לי סיוט. עוד יכול להיות שבעזרת השם אני אלך לבית שלי היום בלילה... זהו זה מה שיש לי להגיד. אני לא הייתי עושה כזה דבר, זה רק להתאכזר!"

ידידיה המתוק שלנו, התמים, בכל לבו ניסה להמשיך להסביר לחוקר למה המשטרה עצרה אותנו:

"אנחנו אנשים שמנסים לפרסם רק את רבי נחמן בניגונים, בגלל זה אנחנו עושים בלגנים... אנחנו באורות, אנחנו משוגעים. יש אפילו סיפור עם רבי נחמן על גנני, שהיה גן שהוא פרנס את כל המדינה, והיה הגן הזה כל כך יפה, והיה גנני... גנני מלשון ניגון... הוא היה מנגן ומחייה את הפרחים. פעם אחת בא מלך אכזרי והוא רצה להכניס שלוש כיתות לגן הזה, כדי שהגן ייהרס: ניבול פה ושוחד וניאוף. נכון כתוב שישוחד מעוור עיני חכמים'? אז הם כבר, כל האנשים, שכחו מי זה הגנני ולא היה מי שיפרנס את המדינה. פעם אחת בא צדיק ואמר: 'אם תחזירו את הגנני יחזור כל הפרנסה' אז אחד נזכר שהיה אחד שצעק ברחוב 'אני הגנני, אני הגנני' וכולם היו צוחקים עליו שהוא משוגע 'אתה משוגע'. ככה אומרים בדיוק עלינו, אנחנו המשוגעים משוגעים, אבל זה בסוף הגנני, רבי נחמן, שמתקן הכול ואנחנו מנסים לפרסם אותו".

החוקר לא מתייחס לשום מילה שהילד מתאמץ להסביר לו ורק שואל בקור: "האם קרה שמישהו הרביץ פעם לאימא שלך?"

ידידיה מניד בראשו לשלילה והחוקר חוזר על השאלה: "האם ראית שמישהו הרביץ לאימא שלך?" ידידיה עונה: "בטח שלא".

החוקר חוזר שוב ושוב על אותה השאלה, ידידיה עונה לו: "חס וחלילה". החוקר ממשיך עם אותה שאלה שוב "האם קרה שמישהו חנק את אחת הנשים?" ידידיה עונה: "די. חס וחלילה לגמרי, בכלל לא. אתה שואל שאלות ממש לא טובות. חס וחלילה שמישהו יחנוק אותם, מי שיחנוק אותם אבא שלי יפרק אותו. אבא שלי הוא איש טוב לנשים שלו". החוקר היה אדיש לראות את ידידיה מולו בלי מרפק אחת, מנסה להילחם בו כמו אביר קטן, בשארית כוחותיו.

בחקירות מאוחרות יותר, בדיוק באותו זמן שנחמה ג'הסי שיקרה לי והצהירה מול שופט שידידיה לא רוצה אותי ולא את אבא שלו, נכתב בפרוטוקול החקירות:

"צר לי בלי ההורים, צר לי בלי ההורים".

"אבל יש לך חברים".

"אבל חברים זה לא ההורים", וממשיך: "זה משהו פה שקר מאוד".

"לא, ממש לא, אני אומר לך את האמת".

"אם ככה למה אתם לא נותנים לנו להתקשר להורים שלנו!... לא רוצה להיות פה בפגישה הזאת!"

כשהחוקר שואל את ידידיה אם הוא יודע מה זה שוקר, ידידיה חושב שמדובר במצית, כשהחוקר מנסה להסביר לו שוב ושוב מה זה שוקר, ידידיה אומר: "בחיים בחיים לא שמעתי מילה כזו!"

"היו בבית עונשים לילדים?"

"האחים שלי היו נותנים עונשים קטנים לעמוד בפינה, אבא שלי לא נותן עונשים!"

החוקר מגיש דו"ח שקרי על ידידיה לבית משפט שבו כותב: "אין להעידו בבית משפט על מה שמסר לי בעדות, צעד אשר בכוחו לגרום לו לנזק נפשי נוסף, הן בשל התכנים הקשים עליהם דיווח והן בשל הקרבה המשפחתית לפוגעים". ואני שואלת את החוקר מיכה הרן, איך הוא מצליח לחיות כשהוא יודע שהילד התחנן לפניו לראות את אבא שלו, וסיפר לו כמה הוא מתגעגע אליו, וכמה הוא מפונק, וכמה אבא שלו אדם טוב שלא עשה רע לאף אחד ולא פגע בו אף פעם ולא באף אדם בעולם, ובכל זאת מגיש דו"ח הפוך ושקרי? ואני שואלת את השופטים האם זיהום עדויות כבר הפך לדבר חוקי? נראה שכן.

ב-6.2.2012 נסעתי לביקור אצל ידידיה. כשיצאתי מהביקור הזמנתי מונית. המונית נסעה עד שהגיעה לכניסה לעיר. לפתע עקפה אותנו מכונית לבנה בעלת לוחית אדומה וברמקול דרשה שנהג המונית יעצור בצד. זו הייתה משטרה. הודיעו לי שאני עצורה. הרגשתי שנופלת עליי פצצת אטום, אבל ניסיתי להתעשת מהר כי ידעתי מהחקירות שנערכו לפני חצי שנה שאני מתעסקת פה עם משטרה שהיא מעל החוק. לא היה לי מושג מה הולך להיות אתי מעכשיו, אבל ידעתי שיש לי ביקור ביום ראשון אצל ידידיה ואני לא מתכוונת לפספס את זה. תוך דקות ספורות מצאתי את עצמי במעצר, בתא קטן בלי חלון, ויש בו יש ריח עבה וכבד של דיכאון ושל ייאוש מאנשים ששהו בו לפניי, ובקושי היה אפשר לנשום שם. נאחזתי בסורגים של דלת התא לחפש אוויר. עוד לא קלטתי שאני הולכת באמת לכלא!

ביום שישי בבוקר אילנה, אדרת ואני מובלות באזיקים בידיים וברגליים לבית משפט השלום, מקוות להשתחרר.

להפתעתנו ראינו את שלושת הבנים הגדולים של אילנה, גם הם עצורים וכבולים באזיקים. היה נראה שהם מנסים לשמור על הגאווה המשפחתית גם במצב המשפיל הזה. הם קרצו לעברנו בחיבה כדי לחזק אותנו ואמרו לנו שנהיה חזקות ושלא נפחד, כי בקרוב נשתחרר כולנו. באולם בית המשפט היו ארבעה עורכי דין מהסנגוריה, אנשי ביטחון של בית המשפט, אנשי ביטחון של שירות בתי הסוהר ועיתונאים. האולם היה די מלא. עוה"ד שהמדינה מינתה עבורי משום מה לא הגיע. מצד התביעה הגיעו שני חוקרי ימ"ר שהיו בראש החקירה נגד המשפחה, אשר לַזמי ועמיתתו לילך רנן.

כשראיתי את החוקרת לילך רנן בבית המשפט, זיכרון המעצר לפני חצי שנה ב-4.7.11 – חזר אליי. שם היא תפסה לי את הצוואר כשהייתי אזוקת רגליים במסדרונות הימ"ר ודפקה לי את הראש בקיר בחוזקה עד כדי כך שנפלתי לרצפה מעולפת. כשהתאוששתי מאיבוד ההכרה, שמעתי שהיא ממשיכה לצרוח עליי בקללות גסות. אותה לילך רנן עומדת עכשיו בבית המשפט, מסתכלת עלינו בלעג, וצוחקת יחד עם החוקר אשר לַזמי. כשהשופט נכנס הם הפסיקו לרגע אחד, כולם עמדו לכבודו. מיד לאחר מכן החוקרת הציגה לפני השופט את הטענות להארכת המעצר שלנו, בביטחון שהשופט שם רק בשביל לאשר את מה שהיא רוצה. כשעורכי הדין מהצד שלנו התחילו לטעון שאנחנו בכלל לא צריכות להיות פה, לילך רנן ואשר לַזמי הסתודדו ביניהם ברעש וצחקקו. השופט ביקש שקט, אך הם המשיכו לדבר ביניהם והיה נראה שהשופט מתבטל בפניהם. פתאום התחלתי לקלוט שיכול להיות שאני הולכת להישאר פה ויש סיכוי שלא אגיע לביקור אצל ידידיה. המחשבה על זה גרמה לי להתחיל לבכות. הסתכלתי על שני החוקרים, והם הביטו בי והתלוצצו. פניתי לעו"ד של הבנים ואמרתי לו בבכי: "תסתכל איך הם מתעללים בנו בנפש". עוה"ד שמע אותי ופנה לשופט: "מה זה ההתנהגות הזאת של החוקרים? זה ביזיון לבית המשפט!" השופט אמר באדישות: "אבקש שקט", אך החוקרים לא התייחסו לבקשה. הייתי נסערת והתחלתי לבכות, ולצעוק לשופט: "איך זה יכול להיות שנותנים להם לצחוק מאתנו מולך ומול כל הנוכחים?!" השופט לא ריחם, וסימן לאנשי הביטחון להוציא אותי מהאולם. אנשי הביטחון הגיעו אליי, סגרו אותי באזיקים בידיים וברגליים. לא האמנתי שזה קורה לי! מוציאים אותי עוד לפני שהתקבלה החלטה, רק בגלל שנשברתי ובכיתי מההתנהגות המשפילה של החוקרים?! בכיתי לשופט: "למה? למה?..." כשהובילו אותי אנשי הביטחון לכיוון היציאה מהאולם, רפ"ק אשר לַזמי סינן לעברי בחיוך ערמומי: "את לא הולכת לראות את הבן שלך בקרוב..." הבנתי שאם אגיד בקול רם את מה שאני חושבת זה לא יעזור, הדבר היחיד שיכולתי לעשות כשהידיים והרגליים שלי כבולות זה לירוק לעברו בבוז. ירקתי לכיוונו, והיריקה נדבקה לעינו השמאלית. הדם עלה לו לראש. הפנים החומות שלו קיבלו גוון אדום מכעס, המשכתי ללכת אחרי איש הביטחון עם הגב אליו, רציתי להראות לו שעם כל הכוח שיש לו הוא לא שווה כלום! לפתע הרגשתי מהלומות חזקות בעמוד השדרה, בעורף ובראש, ויד חזקה מכופפת את ראשי לכיוון הרצפה. לקח לי זמן-מה לקלוט שזה היה הרפ"ק אשר לַזמי, שלא היסס לתקוף אישה חסרת ישע אזוקה בידיים וברגליים, מול השופט והעיתונאים. כשאנשי הביטחון ההמומים הבחינו במצוקה שלי הם קפצו עליו וניסו להרחיק אותו ממני וקראו לעברו: "אשר מה אתה עושה, זה לא מתאים, אתה מרביץ לבחורה עם אזיקים". אבל הוא המשיך בהתקף זעם לצרוח ולקלל בהתלהמות ולא נרגע. הוציאו אותי במהירות ונעלו אותי בתא מעצר. מאוחר יותר התברר לי שהשופט אפילו לא נזף באשר לַזמי על האלימות שלו כלפיי בבית המשפט. למזלי, עוה"ד של הבנים הזדעזע ואמר שלא ראה מימיו מקרה שכזה שהשוטרים לא מפחדים אפילו בפרהסיה ומול השופט לפגוע בחסרי ישע דרש מהשופט שהאירוע יצוין בפרוטוקול. במשך יומיים שלמים ביקשתי

מהסוהרים ומהקצינים לראות עו״ד, והתעלמו ממני. בינתיים סבלתי מכאב חד לכל אורך עמוד השדרה. מה שלא אפשר לי לישון. ביום השלישי לקחו אותי שוב לחדרי החקירות של הימ״ר. החוקר שישב שם התחיל להשפיל אותי ולהגיד שאני זונה ומוכה וסוסה ושאני משוגעת ושאני אוהבת מכות ושאני חולה שטופת מוח ועוד. אמרתי שאני רוצה להתלונן על אשר לזמי שהיכה אותי בבית המשפט. הוא צחק באדישות ושאל אותי בקרירות אכזרית: ״את יודעת למה את בכלל פה?״ אמרתי: ״לא״. הוא ענה: ״את פה בחקירה תחת אזהרה על תקיפת שוטר בעת מילוי תפקידו!״

זה היה כבר יותר מדי. אמרתי לו: ״אתם עושים מה שבא לכם בלי גבולות?!״ ״נכון״, הוא ענה בחיוך. ״אבל את צריכה לדעת שברגע זה כותבים לך כתב אישום. יש לך מה להגיד? אני מזכיר לך שכל מה שתגידי ומה שלא תגידי עשוי לשמש נגדך״. ״אין לי מה להגיד, אתם במילא תעשו מה שאתם רוצים״, עניתי. הובלתי חזרה לתא במגרש הרוסים, ומשם לכלא לנשים נווה תרצה.

בכלא נווה תרצה מצאתי את עצמי בחדר בגודל של שלושה מ״ר עם עוד חמש נשים מעמים שונים ומדתות שונות. בבת-אחת נזכרתי בפעמים שלא הערכתי את חברותיי לחיים. אין לי את אילנה שדואגת לי לנעליים, אין לי את אדרת שמוכיחה אותי בלי סוף, ואין לי את שירן שתצחיק אותי, ואפילו אין לי את קארי לריב אתה. השנה בכלא גרמה לי להתגעגע ל״יחד״. הבנות בנווה תרצה היו מאוד סקרניות לדעת איך אפשר לחיות יחד שש נשים. חלקן גם היו מאוד תוקפניות דווקא בעניין השאלה הזו. עניתי להן: ״כאן בכלא בתא אחד חיות ביחד שש נשים ומסתדרות עם כל הקושי. אז כשנשים חופשיות ועצמאיות, ולא חסר להן כלום, ואין להן את הצמצומים של הכלא, לא כל שכן!״

הסיבה האמתית שבגללה ישבנו בכלא נווה תרצה במשך שנה הייתה שהחוקרים ראו שמולם נשים חזקות, שלא מוכנות לשקר, ושלא נכנעות לשוחד ולאיומים שלהם, ותכננו לשבור אותנו במעצר כדי שנהיה מוכנות להגיד הכול נגד דניאל, רק בשביל להשתחרר. כך הם הצליחו לשבור את עליזה, האישה החמישית.

במשך שמונה שנים הייתה ביני ובין עליזה חברות קרובה מאוד. שתינו היינו באותו הגיל. לי היה בן אחד, ולה בת אחת. עברנו בילדות הרבה דברים דומים, והיינו עוזרות אחת לשנייה להתמודד אתם. שמחנו ביחד מאותם הדברים ובילינו ביחד את רוב שעות היום. הגענו לקרבה כזאת שהיינו משתפות אחת את השנייה בסודות האישיים ביותר שלנו. כשדניאל נעצר, חצי שנה לפני המעצר שלי, החוקרת שאלה אותי בחדרי החקירות: ״את מי הייתי רוצה לפגוש?״ עניתי מיד: ״את עליזה״. אז קראו לעליזה לבוא. כשהיא נכנסה לחדר כל כך התרגשתי לראות אותה אחרי תקופה ארוכה שהפרידו בינינו. התחבקנו. נתתי לה צמיד מיוחד שהיה לי על היד, שהכנתי אותו בחוג במקלט, וענדתי אותו כדי לתת בהזדמנות הראשונה לאחת מהנשים. שמחתי שהיא קיבלה את זה. היא נתנה לי עגילים שהיא ענדה. היא אמרה לי: ״אזמרה, את לא מבינה, החוקרים הסבירו לי שדניאל לא הולך להשתחרר עכשיו לפחות עשרים שלושים שנה לא משנה מה שאנחנו נגיד, אם ננסה לעזור לו או לא, המצב כבר אבוד! צריך להציל את הילדים. אסור שיהיה להם טראומה שלא יהיו להם גם אבא וגם אימא, חייבים להציל את המצב ולעזור להם לפחות לקבל את האימהות שלהם בחזרה. ואם את רוצה לעזור לידידיה תאשרי לחוקרים כל מה שהם אומרים לך להגיד, תאשרי להם את כל הסיטואציות שהם מתארים לך ותראי שתקבלי את ידידיה בחזרה, וגם תמיכה כספית. ידידיה צריך את אימא שלו, ואני בטוחה שדניאל עכשיו דואג לילדים והיה רוצה שנחשוב עליהם ולא עליו״.

לא הבנתי מה יש לה. כל זה היה מול חוקר ולא רציתי לבייש אותה אבל פשוט אמרתי לה את זה ישר בפנים: ״עליזה, את מוכנה לשקר על דניאל כדי לקבל את הבת שלך בחזרה?! את חושבת שבתיה, שכל כך אוהבת את אבא שלה תהיה מוכנה לגדול אתך בידיעה שהיית מוכנה ׳להציל׳ את החיים שלך ולסגור את אבא שלה? אל תספרי לי שזה בשביל הבת שלך, אנחנו מכירות לא מהיום״. היא לרגע התבלבלה. ואז היא התקרבה אליי לאוזן ולחשה לי: ״אזמרה אני עושה רק תחבולה כדי לקבל את הילדה. כשהילדה תהיה אצלי אני אתרכז להוציא את דניאל״. לא הייתי מוכנה לקבל בלב שזה מה שהיא אומרת לי. לא האמנתי למה שאני שומעת, שבסופו של דבר היא תהיה מוכנה לשקר שקרים על בעלה שהצהירה תמיד שהיא אוהבת כשהיא יודעת שבתמורה היא תקבל את הבת שלהם, אבל 13 ילדים יישארו בלי אבא שלהם בגללה. החוקרים נכנסו לחדר וקטעו את השיחה בינינו, ואני נשארתי עם חץ בלב.

חששתי מה יהיה על דניאל אם עליזה מדברת ככה. שנה לאחר מכן, כשהפרקליטות זימנה אותה כעדת תביעה הייתי בטוחה שהיא לא תעז להגיע לבית המשפט לדבר נגדו. כששמעתי איך היא הגיעה ושפכה את דמו בשקרים מזעזעים, בעזות מצח, בלי לפחד שיש בורא עולם. לא יכולתי לנשום מרוב כאב על דניאל שאהב אותה כל כך. הרגשתי שהיא כמו דלילה ששולחת להורג את שמשון.

חוקרי המשטרה לא הסתפקו בהסתת עליזה נגד דניאל, חצי שנה לאחר מכן הם גם דרשו שהיא תעיד כעדה מרכזית נגדנו הנשים. אחרי כמעט שנה שהיינו במעצר התנהל סוף סוף המשפט, והוזמנו לדיון שבו עליזה

היתה צריכה לבוא להעיד נגדנו. ידעתי שאין לה גבולות, ובכל זאת לא האמנתי שהיא הולכת לסגור אותנו, החברות שלה, בכלא לפחות ל-14 שנה. קיוויתי שתזכור כמה ידידיה זקוק לאבא ולי, ושיהיה לה לפחות טיפה אחרונה של מצפון בשביל ילד נכה שזקוק לאימא ולאבא שלו.

נכנסנו לאולם בית המשפט, אילנה, אדרת ואני באזיקים בידיים וברגליים, לבושות במדים של בית הסוהר, ומלוות בכמה "נחשונים" שחלקם הרגישו בעוול שנעשה לנו וניסו לחזק אותנו. התיישבנו בספסל הנאשמים, ולתדהמת כולנו עליזה הגיעה. היא נעמדה בדוכן העדים והחלה לספר כל מיני סיפורים על דניאל. עוה"ד שלי עצר אותה ואמר לה שהדיון הוא לא על דניאל, ושכדאי שתתרכז בעניין. בחקירה הנגדית התגלה השקר שלה בצורה שגרמה אפילו לשופטים להיות במבוכה. בסוף הדיון שאל עוה"ד שלי את עליזה אם יש לה משהו להגיד לנשים שיושבות באולם בספסל הנאשמים. עליזה, בפעם הראשונה מתחילת הדיון העזה להסתכל לי בעיניים, ואמרה לי בדרמטיות כמו שחקנית בתיאטרון: "תאמיני לי אזמרה, אני עושה את זה לטובתך! את חייבת להתעורר ולעשות כל שביכולתך לקבל את הבן שלך בחזרה, כי הילד צריך להיות יותר חשוב לך מאבא שלו!" כל הדרך חזרה לכלא הצטערנו שלא מחאנו לה כפיים בסוף ההצגה.

בהדלקת הנר השמיני של חנוכה התקשרתי מהכלא לעוה"ד שלי כדי לדעת מתי הדיון הבא. הוא הודיע לי שנארוז את הדברים, כי מחר אנחנו משתחררות מהכלא! לרגע התבלבלתי ושאלתי: "באמת? איך אתה יודע את זה?" הוא אמר לי: "אחרי שתמנע, עליזה וסמי סיימו להעיד בחקירה הנגדית והשופט ביקש שתצאו שלושתכן מהאולם, השופט נזף בפרקליט והבהיר לו שלא הייתן צריכות לשבת בכלא בכלל!, ושכדאי שיגיע מהר להסדר שתשתחררו, כי המצב בתיק הוא לזיכוי". למחרת השתחררנו מהכלא. אני זוכרת את הצעדים הראשונים מחוץ לכלא, מלפניי החופש, אך מאחוריי הרגשתי שנשארו נשים, שלחלקן נעשה עוול גדול ושמקומן הוא לא בכלא. קיוויתי שהמלחמה שלנו תעזור לעוד הרבה אנשים, ושהמכונה הדורסנית שבשם החוק מפרקת משפחות בלי שום אמת וצדק, בזמן הקצר שיש לאדם לחיות, תפסיק את מרוץ הדמים שלה.

הבית היה הרוס, ולא רצינו לאבד זמן. ראינו מול עינינו רק את השחרור של דניאל. התחלנו במלחמה. פניתי מיד למחלקת חקירות שוטרים, הגשתי תלונה על האלימות בחקירות, צירפתי את הפרוטוקול שבו השופט מציין את האלימות של השוטר כלפיי, וגם כתבה ב-YNET המתארת את מה שקרה בבית המשפט, משום מה כל זה לא עניין את מח"ש (המרכז לחקירות שוטרים). וכשהתקשרתי לשאול מה קורה בקשר לאותו חוקר שהיכה אותי מול שופט, ובקשר לאותה חוקרת שהכתה אותי בחדרי החקירות, המזכירה אמרה שהתיק נסגר "מחוסר עניין לציבור". פניתי לתקשורת, אך גם שם הבנתי שאין עניין לציבור בדברים שהם לא הוצאת דיבה. חיפשתי עו"ד פרטי, אבל גיליתי שגם להם אין עניין במי שאין לו כסף או דירה למכור כדי לשלם לו. מה שחיזק אותנו היה ההתחזקות של הילדים כתוצאה מהמאבק שלנו. הם התרגשו והתחזקו מאוד מהשחרור שלנו מהכלא כי זה נתן להם תקווה שגם את השקר במשפט של אבא יגלו וישחררו אותו הביתה. במשך כל השנה שהיינו בכלא, קארי גרה אצל בנה יאן ואשתו מארי (הבת הגדולה של דניאל ואילנה). כשהשתחררנו, יאן ומארי ביקשו מאתנו שנגור אצלם כולנו יחד, ושהם רוצים לדאוג לנו בתקופה הקרובה. הם שכרו בית קרקע בגבעת שאול כי דאגו לכולם, וכאב להם שהמשפחה הולכת לאיבוד. הם רצו לקבל את כל האחים אליהם הביתה, ושהמשפחה תחזור להיות יחד. בבית היו שלושה חדרים, והם פינו עבורנו חדר אחד. אילנה, קארי, אדרת שירן ואני ישנו באותו החדר. היינו מטפלות בנכדים, בחשבונות ובניקיונות לפסח. מארי הייתה בהיריון של הבן השלישי, ולכבוד הלידה דאגנו לה לחדר במלון קרוב לבית החולים. פעם בשבועיים באופן קבוע יאן היה לוקח את קארי לבקר את דניאל בכלא ושמחנו שלפחות היא יכולה להיכנס אליו, כי היא לא ישבה בכלא. מארי באה לבית המשפט להעיד לטובת אבא שלה, ודיברה בטלוויזיה, ברדיו ובעיתון על העוול שעשו לאבא שלה, השופטים התעלמו מעדותה. שוש בת ה-16 ברחה מהפנימייה כדי להגיע לבית המשפט, שם אמרה לשופטים: "חשוב לי שישמעו שאבא שלי יושב על חינם כבר שנה וחצי ואני מתגעגעת אליו אישית מאוד, למה מקשיבים לאנשים שבאים לשקר אנשים שאני לא יודעת מה הם מחפשים?!" השופטים התעלמו גם מעדותה, והרשיעו את דניאל גם בהאשמה לגביה. היא נשברה מכך והלכה להתראיין בערוץ 2, סיפרה מה שהיה בבית המשפט ודיברה על מה שעשו לאבא שלה, וערוץ 2 החליטו לא להעלות אותה לתכנית. כששידרו את התכנית וראתה שהיא לא מופיעה שם ושמדברים נגד אבא שלה, היא התייאשה ובכתה: "אתם רואים שכלום לא עוזר?" גם סמי שהיה עד תביעה וחזר בו מעדותו רצה להתראיין באותה התכנית בערוץ 2 אך הם לא הסכימו.

כשהגעתי לבית המשפט להעיד לטובת דניאל ועמדתי על דוכן העדים, עדיין קיוויתי בלבי שהשופטים יהיו מספיק ישרים לשמוע אותי בלי דעות קדומות. השופט צבן אמר לי שעליי להגיד את האמת וכל האמת ורק את האמת אחרת אהיה צפויה לקבל את העונשים הקבועים בחוק. משך כשלוש שעות סיפרתי על החיים שלנו יחד. השופט שאל אותי אם דניאל עשה לי פעם משהו נגד רצוני, עניתי לו:

"מה זה השערורייה הזו? כשמגיל שש עד עשר עברתי אונס מדוד שלי וסבא שלי ודיברתי על זה עם חוקרי המשטרה, לאף אחד זה לא הזיז. דניאל הוא היחיד שהיה אכפת לו ממני ועזר לי עם הרבה אהבה וסבלנות לצאת מהפוסט טראומה שחייתי ועכשיו, אותו אתם רוצים להאשים באונס?! דניאל הוא הבן אדם הכי קרוב אליי, הכי עדין והכי רחוק מלהיות טיפוס כזה, כמו שהשאלות שלכם מנסות לרמז. חשוב לי שזה יהיה ברור שדניאל מעולם לא פגע בי בשום צורה ואופן, מעולם לא אנס אותי וזה פשוט לא מתקבל על הדעת שיש כתב אישום שדניאל אנס אותי על סמך דברים שמישהו אחר אומר עליי?!"

כשראיתי בהכרעת הדין שאותם שופטים הרשיעו את דניאל בטענה שאנס אותי שש פעמים, ועל זה הוא יושב בכלא, גיליתי שבית המשפט מושחת ו"מכור מראש". כשקראתי שכתבו השופטים שדניאל יצר מציאות שבה הנשים חייבות להתוודות לפניו על מחשבות, הבנתי שהפכו את המציאות על פניה, ואת הצורך שלי לשתף את בעלי, החבר הכי טוב שלי, במחשבות איומות שרדפו אותי כשאף אחד אחר לא היה מוכן לשמוע אותי, אפילו לא ההורים שלי, הפכו בן-רגע לתשתית שעליה מבוססים כתב האישום וההרשעה.

אותם שופטים שדרשו ממני לומר רק אמת, הרשיעו את דניאל ב-18 סעיפים של שקר, עשו משפט שקר וקיבלו עדויות של עדי שקר, ובעצם הם אלו שאנסו אותנו הנשים להיות עבדים של מערכת שלא נותנת לחיות יחסים אישיים לפי בחירה חופשית. חשבתי: האם אותם שופטים גם צפויים לקבל את העונשים הקבועים בחוק על עיוות הדין? האם הם ישלמו על מה שהם עשו לנו? מי יצליח לפצות אותנו על החורבן הנורא הזה? מי יחזיר לילד שלי את השנים הכי יקרות שאיבד עם אבא שלו?

גזר הדין המעוות גרם לי להאשים את כל מי שהביא אותנו למצב הזה. בראש ובראשונה חשבתי על דוד שלי בני. לא הבנתי איך יכולתי כל השנים האלה, במקום להאשים אותו במה שעשה לי, להאשים את עצמי ולחשוב שאני, ילדה בת שש גרמתי לו לעשות לי את כל מה שהוא עשה, ושביקשתי ממנו את זה. החלטתי לנסוע חזרה לזרחיה לראות את בני ולבקש ממנו שייקח אחריות על כל מה שעשה לי ועל ההשלכות של זה על חיי ועל חיי משפחתי. הגעתי לשם, וכשהייתי מולו, במקום לצרוח עליו, כמו שתכננתי, ולהתעמת אתו על החיים שהוא לקח ממני, מצאתי את עצמי מרחמת עליו, בטון ילדותי ממש התחננתי ממנו שרק יבקש סליחה, כי מישהו אחר יושב במקומו בכלא.

בס"ד

**מכתב אישי לעליזה מאזמרה**

אני כותבת לך את המכתב הזה ברגשות מעורבים. הייתי רוצה לרחם שהגעת לאן שהגעת אבל הלכת רחוק מדי.

את זוכרת שגרנו בליפתא ואמרת לי שאת מקנאה בי שיש לי אמביציה ואהבה לרבי נחמן ולהפצה, והיה לך רעיון ששתינו נתחזק; ניקח את הרכב וניסע לכל קברות הצדיקים בצפון הארץ, את זוכרת שבנסיעה כל הדרך היינו שומעות את השירים שאנחנו אוהבות ומדברות על כל מה שכל אחת עברה בחיים לפני שהכרנו את דניאל, וסיפרת לי המון דברים חדשים שלא ידעתי עלייך שגרמו לי לרחם עלייך, כמו על זה שלא הייתה לך אף פעם חברה טובה כי חשבת שכולן מקנאות בך ויותר מהכול הצטערתי על האונס שסיפרת שעברת מאח שלך. רציתי להיות בשבילך חברה טובה אמתית.

כשהיית בצבא, הייתה בבסיס שלך חיילת שידעת שהיא לסבית וצחקת כשסיפרת לי את התרגיל שעשית לה: "תשמעי מה עשיתי לה". אמרת ותיארת לי איך התאפרת והתלבשת בשביל למשוך אותה וכשהיית אתה לבד והגעתם למצב מאוד קרוב, כשהיא פשטה את החולצה והתחלתן להתנשק, בפתאומיות עצרת ואמרת לה "מה את חושבת שאני לסבית כמוך?! וצחקת עליה בצחוק גדול, פתחת את דלת מגורי הבנות וצעקת לכולם: "בואו תראו יש פה לסבית!" מעניין אותי אם זה נשמע לך נורמלי הסיפור הזה...

והסיפור שלך על ההפלגה לספרד לאיביזה לשבוע שלם עם עוד שתי חברות שעל חשבון אחת מהן נסעת וגם שילמה לך בית מלון וכשהשתמשת לה בסבון פנים היוקרתי שלה והיא צעקה עליך שגנבת לה ולמה לקחת בלי רשות, החזרת לה בחוצפה: "קמצנית כאילו זה מה שחסר לך.." ומאותו רגע לא דיברת אתה. גם ציערת אותה שלקחת אתך את החברה השנייה ויצאתן לבלות, הכרתן שני בחורים שאתם העברתם את הלילה ארבעתכם יחד במיטה אחת ולא בשינה. אפילו התפארת שיום למחרת נשארת עם שני הגברים האלה לבד במיטה. כשראית שאני קצת בהלם אמרת "מה את מתרגשת הייתי בת 18". כבר אז היית מוכשרת להוציא את החברה

ששילמה עלייך הלא בסדר. גם אז אמרתי לך מיד שאת הלא בסדר בסיפור הזה ועכשיו אני רואה שהייתי צריכה להבין שמה שעשית בקטן לאותה חברה את עוד עלולה לעשות בגדול. וזה בדיוק מה שעשית למשפחה. עד מתי תמשיכי לנצל אנשים?! היה עדיף שתעשי אתנו מה שעשית עם הגברים שסיפרת לי שהיית מתחברת אתם ליום אחד רק בשביל שיקנו לך בושם ועוזבת.

למה אותנו לא עזבת אחרי שלקחת כל מה שרצית?

כשהגענו לחיפה למערת אליהו הנביא הייתה שם אישה זקנה ונחמדה שטיפלה בנרות ואמרת לי "בואי נלך אליה נבקש ממנה ברכה" והיא בירכה אותנו "שתזכו לגדל את הילדים שלכם בנחת" את בכית ואמרת לה שיש לך מחשבות רעות על הבת שלך ועל ילדים של אימהות אחרות וגם על הבן שלי... והיא אמרה לך: "תעשי מעשים טובים". התחלנו לקרוא תהלים ואז אמרת לי בהתרגשות: "אזמרה, בואי נצום שלושה ימים" האמת שלא התחשק לי לצום אבל רציתי להשתתף בהתלהבות שלך. משם נסענו לאלישע הנביא, התלמיד של אליהו הנביא ומשם לרבי שמעון בר יוחאי במירון ולרבי מאיר בעל הנס בטבריה ועוד. הייתה לנו מפה של קברות הצדיקים וראינו שאסתר ומרדכי קבורים לא רחוק מטבריה בשפרעם. אני אף פעם לא הייתי שם ומאוד רציתי שנגיע אליהם.

מזל שנסענו עם ה–**GMC 4X4**, כי הדרך הייתה מלאה אבנים גדולות. באיזה שהוא שלב היינו צריכות להתקדם ברגל ורק בעזרת סימוני הדרך בצבע כחול לבן על הסלעים הצלחנו להגיע. כשהיינו שם אמרת שאת כמו אסתר המלכה שלקחה על עצמה שלושה ימים לצום. איך העזת בבית המשפט להאשים את דניאל כאילו שהוא אמר לך לצום?! אם העולם היו שומעים את הקללות שאת מקללת את הבת שלך היו מבינים את כל הסיפור שלך.

כשגרנו בפוריה חשבת שזה יעזור לך להשתנות, להיות בן אדם טוב יותר, לקבל יראת שמים אם תיקחי אותנו בלילה ליער וכל אחד בתורו ישכב על האדמה לבד ויחשוב על זה שהזמן הוא מאוד יקר ובשביל שננצל אותו טוב כדאי לעשות טוב. כמה שילמו לך השוטרים בשביל שתהפכי את כל הסיפורים והחוויות להאשמות והתעללויות?!

איך יכולת להשוות את עצמך לאסתר המלכה כשעשית הפוך ממנה ולקחת את כולנו לשמד?!

את דומה לזרש אשתו של המן שנתנה לו את העצה לתלות את מרדכי היהודי ורעה ממנה ואני בטוחה שאת יודעת את זה.

אני שמחה שאין לי יותר חברה כמוך.

**<u>הסיפור של אילנה האישה הראשונה, חלק שני:</u>**

אני בוכה וצועקת שיחזירו לי את דניאל ואת כל הילדים.

ב-2011 ילדיי: זלמן היה בן 22, בועז בן 20, גיא-נועם בן 18, מארי בת 19, ציפי בת 16, שוש בת 15, עקיבא בן 13.5, קטי בת 12, נוריאל בן 11 ובלה בת תשע. בלי שום אזהרה או התראה מוקדמת, בלי לאפשר לי להגן עליהם, בפתאומיות נלקחו ממני; וכך גם ילדיהם של דניאל ונשותיו האחרות: יהונתן בן עשר וחצי, ידידיה כבן תשע ובתיה בת השש, שהיו קוראים לי אימא, שאתם לא אפשרו לי לקיים שום סוג של קשר – לא שיחות ולא ביקורים; צילה בת 26, יאן בן 24, אנסטסיה בת 19 וסמי בן 14, הילדים של קארי, עם הזמן הפכו להיות כזרים, כאילו שלא גידלתי אותם והשקעתי בהם במשך 11 שנה לא פחות ממה שהשקעתי בילדים שלי. בכל אחד מהם המדינה פגעה בצורה עמוקה. הפכו ילדים תמימים ושמחים לילדים שמחפשים איך לשרוד ולהינצל מהרדיפה הבלתי נסבלת של המשטרה ושל אנשי הרווחה. המשבר שעברו בארבע השנים האחרונות, כשעקרו אותם מההורים ומהאחים שלהם וערערו את כל עולמם, גרם לכך שהבנות נפלו לסמים קשים, וכמה אפילו איימו ואף ניסו לשים קץ לחייהם. על עקיבא, הבן שלי שהיה בזמן המעצר בן 13.5, איימו שאם לא יעיד נגד אבא שלו הוא ישב בכלא בעצמו. הם הפעילו עליו לחץ בלתי נסבל והשתמשו בשיחות ובכדורים פסיכיאטריים, עד שהצליחו לגרום לו להיות עד תביעה נגד אבא שלו. מיד לאחר מכן עקיבא ניסה לבצע שלושה ניסיונות התאבדות, ואושפז לתקופה ארוכה בבית חולים פסיכיאטרי.

בבית, עקיבא רצה לעשות לנו נחת, והיה תמיד מתעניין במה אפשר לעזור. כבר לפני בר-המצווה שלו, הוא החליט לטפל בידידיה בן התשע, וביהונתן בן העשר. הוא היה אומר לי: "אימא אל תדאגי, אנחנו נטפל בכביסות שלנו, בקיפול הבגדים ובגיהוץ, והכול יהיה פיקס". יחד עם סמי הם היו קבוצה של ארבעה אחים משלוש אימהות בגילאים קרובים, שהיו עושים הכול ביחד. עקיבא אהב לקבל על עצמו אחריות, והיה נראה שהוא משפיע עליהם בצורה חיובית. האחים שמחו שהוא דואג להם.

כשהכנו את אלבום הלהקה של המשפחה שלנו: "הבעטלירס", זו הייתה חוויה משפחתית יוצאת מן הכלל. באחד הסרטונים ב-DVD, עקיבא מספר בעל-פה את הסיפור "מבן מלך ובן שפחה שנתחלפו". דניאל הכין רקע מיוחד של סרטון מצויר בליווי של מוזיקה לסיפור. כשעקיבא ראה את הסרטון בפעם ראשונה הוא התרגש מאוד, שימח אותו שזה יצא כל כך יפה, אני זוכרת איך הוא חיבק את אבא. הוא חיכה בקוצר רוח להכין דיסק נוסף עם שאר הסיפורים בעל-פה.

עקיבא היה קשור לאבא שלו מאוד. תמיד רצה ללכת אתו לכל מקום, לכותל, לבית הכנסת ולבית המדרש. כשהיה לומד תורה עם אבא ועם האחים שלו היה מצטיין בלימוד בעל-פה. בשבילו זה היה כמו משחק תחרות עם האחים שלו, מי לומד יותר דפים בעל-פה, והיה נהנה להרשים את המשפחה ביכולות שלו. הוא גם היה מוכשר במוזיקה, ואהב להתלוות לאבא לאולפן ההקלטות. הוא היה שר במיקרופון כשדניאל ניגן באורגן לכל המשפחה, יחד הם עשו לנו הופעות נחמדות. היה לו כיף לרכוב על סוסים עם אבא בחופי הים של נתניה וטבריה, ולשחק אתו טניס וכדורגל על החוף, ואפילו ניסה לנצח אותו בשחמט.

בשבוע האחרון לפני שנעצרנו הרגשתי שעקיבא מוטרד מאוד, ושמשהו מציק לו. ובאמת קצת אחר כך הוא סיפר לי ולדניאל שמהיום של בר-המצווה שלו, הוא התחיל לשחק עם האחים שלו יהונתן וידידיה שהיו בני תשע וחצי ועשר במשחקים מיניים. הוא התבייש בזה מאוד ואמר שהוא מתחרט על הכול ומצטער.

הוא סיפר שכשהיה מבקש להראות לאחיו סרטי ילדים במחשב הנייד, הם נעלו את עצמם בחדר והיו גולשים באינטרנט באתרים אסורים. האשמתי את עצמי שהאמנתי שהם רק רואים סרטי ילדים, כפרס על הכנת שעורי בית. לא יכולתי לדמיין שזה סוג המשחקים שהם משחקים מאחורי דלת נעולה.

איך לא הרגשתי שמשהו קרה מתחת לאף שלי כבר ארבעה חודשים? פתאום נזכרתי שאדרת התלוננה שהיא דופקת להם על הדלת רבע שעה עד שהם פותחים, ולא הבינה למה לקח להם כל כך הרבה זמן.

שאלנו את יהונתן וידידיה אם זה נכון מה שעקיבא מספר, והם היו נבוכים ואמרו שכן, זה נכון. לא ידעתי איך להגיב לכזה דבר, הייתי המומה שלמרות כל השמירה שלנו עליהם, הם מצאו דרך להיחשף לכזה חומר תועבה. אנחנו בית דתי, והחינוך אצלנו אמנם לא היה סגור וקפדני כמו אצל החרדים האדוקים, אבל תמיד דאגנו שהחינוך יהיה לפי כללי הצניעות של התורה. מיד ששמענו ממה שעשו, חיפשנו אנשי מקצוע להתייעץ אתם איך להתמודד עם הבעיות של גיל ההתבגרות, ואיך למנוע כאלה משחקים ביניהם. נסעתי לירושלים כדי לדבר עם הפסיכיאטר החרדי ד"ר כ' אך כשהגעתי לירושלים, הגיעה אלינו המשטרה, ובאלימות קשה לקחו את כל המשפחה לחקירות.

עקיבא היה עד למעצר של אבא שלו. השוטרים לא גילו שום רגישות לעובדה שהבנים הקטנים נמצאים יחד עם אבא שלהם בזמן שהם עצרו אותו בצורה משפילה. הם קיללו וביזו אותו מולם. אסרו אותו באזיקים, ונתנו לו לחכות שעות במכונית בחום הקיץ של טבריה. הם לא נתנו לו לשתות מים גם כשהילדים התחננו שאבא צמא וביקשו מהשוטרים מים בשבילו. האכזריות של השוטרים כלפי אבא השאירה רושם טראומטי על כל הילדים, ובפרט על עקיבא. עקיבא סיפר לעובדת הסוציאלית שהוא חי מאוד קשה את המעצר של אבא, ושהוא כועס מאוד על המשטרה שלקחו לו את אבא שלו שהוא הכי אוהב בעולם.

סמוך למעצר שלחו את עקיבא לבדיקה פסיכיאטרית אצל ד"ר פ' שקבע שהילד מתגעגע למשפחתו, ללא מחשבות אבדניות, אינטליגנציה תקינה, אין לו פוסט טראומה (P.T.S.D) אין דיכאון או חרדה, ללא פלשבקים, אין בעיות שינה ואין תחלואה נפשית ממשית נכון לעת זו...

עקיבא היה נסער מהמצב, ואפשר לראות בתמלולי החקירות איך הוא צעק על החוקר מיכה הרן: "המשטרה הזאת שתלך לעזאזל אני רוצה לחזור לאבא שלי ולאחים שלי". כשהחוקר אמר שהוא רוצה לברר אם אבא שלו פגע בו, עקיבא ענה לו: "אבא שלי הוא אבא טוב ולא עשה שום רע... אני לא מבין מה אתם רוצים ממנו". וכשהחוקר המשיך להציק ולקלל את אביו, עקיבא התפרץ לעברו בזעם: "אני אתאבד בסוף בגללך אתה עושה לי סיוט".

במשך תקופה ארוכה, אנשי הרווחה מנעו ממני לדעת מה קורה עם כל הילדים ועם עקיבא. יחד עם המשטרה הם הפעילו כוחות אדירים כדי להפריד בין כולנו על מנת לנתק את הקשר בינינו הנשים, ובין האימהות לילדים. הלב שלי נקרע מגעגועים ומדאגה. הייתי חרדה לשלום כולם, מנסה למצוא דרך לדעת מה קורה עם דניאל ועם כל ילד וילד, וכמובן עם עקיבא, שאותו לא ראיתי מאז שנסעתי לירושלים. לא ידעתי מה מעוללים לו בחקירות המשטרה, לא ידעתי גם שהוא איים להתאבד. העובדה הזו הגיעה לידיעתי רק לאחר שמימש את איומו מאוחר יותר עם כמה ניסיונות התאבדות, כפי שתקראו בהמשך...

אחרי כארבעה חודשים שהיינו במעצר, העבירו את עקיבא לכפר הנוער "בית חגי". פקידת הסעד לא עדכנה אותי שזוהי פנימייה טיפולית. הוא הועבר לטיפולה של עובדת סוציאלית בשם שרית ורד, שפעלה בכל הכוח ובשיטתיות כדי לנתק אותו ממני.

אפשרו לי לבקר אותו רק שלוש פעמים לחצי שעה בלבד, תחת הפיקוח של העובדת הסוציאלית שרית ורד. בפגישה האחרונה עקיבא ביקש: "אימא, אני רוצה שתבואי ליום ההולדת שלי", אני בתמימות הבטחתי לו שאגיע, ואז אמר בתחנונים: "אימא, תיקחי אותי מכאן, אני רוצה לחזור הביתה! תשכירי מקום, אני רוצה להיות אתך" מיד העובדת הסוציאלית התערבה ואמרה לי מול הילד, כשהיא מתעלמת לגמרי מהרגישות ומהעדינות של המצב: "זה לא טוב שאת באה כל שבועיים, זה מבלבל את הילד, אנחנו התחלנו טיפול, אני מרשה לך לבוא רק פעם בחודש, וזה לא מתאים שתבואי בתאריך של יום ההולדת, תבואי שבועיים אחרי כן!" עקיבא הסתכל עליי בפנים מבוהלות ופחד לדבר מול העובדת סוציאלית, המבט החיוור שלו חרוט בלבי, אני לא הבנתי איך ייתכן שעובדת סוציאלית מעזה לדבר כך בנוכחות הילד, בפרט שדבריה היו מנוגדים להסכמת השופט, שאישר לי פגישות בתדירות גבוהה יותר עם עקיבא. זו הייתה עוד התמודדות לא קלה בשביל עקיבא, בנוסף לכל מה שחווה עד אז. בשבילי זה היה אסון. אני הרגשתי שהעובדת הסוציאלית מנסה לגנוב ממני את המקום שלי כאימא, ולא מנסה לעזור לו.

ביום ההולדת שלי, עשרה בטבת תשע"א (2011) הייתי סגורה במקלט לנשים מוכות כשקיבלתי שיחת טלפון מעקיבא. השיחה הייתה בפיקוח מהפנימייה. אני זוכרת את המועקה בקולו כשאמר: "את יודעת אימא, הם רוצים לתת לי פה כדורים פסיכיאטריים ואני לא יודע מה לעשות, אני לא רוצה לקחת אותם". נבהלתי מאוד. איך ייתכן שלא מבקשים אישור מאימא כדי לתת לילד שלה כדורים פסיכיאטריים? מה הם עושים לו? מי יודע איזה השפעות יש לכאלה כדורים, ומי לקח כזו אחריות ללא ידיעתי, ולמה? כשעקיבא שאל אותי: "מה שלום אבא", עניתי: "הורידו אותו לצינוק". עוד לא הספקתי לסיים את המשפט וכבר אב הבית והעובדת הסוציאלית ניתקו את השיחה לאחר שהספיקו לזרוק לעברי את האיום: "את עשית שגיאה חמורה ביותר להתייחס לשאלה של עקיבא, את לא יודעת שאסור לך לדבר על דניאל? מעכשיו לא תדברי עם עקיבא בטלפון עד להודעה חדשה!" לא יכולתי להאמין שהם יקיימו את האיום. כל יום חיכיתי לטלפון מהפנימייה, כשהתקשרתי לעובדת הסוציאלית היא הייתה מנתקת את הטלפון. בודדו את עקיבא בפנימייה. לא הייתה לי אפשרות לדבר אתו, לא לראות אותו, לא להעביר לו מכתבים ולא מתנות. פקידת הסעד מסרה לי שהוא לא מכיר בי יותר.

כחודש לאחר אותה שיחה, בתאריך 31.1.12, חצי שנה לאחר פירוק כל המשפחה, קראו לי לפתע לתחנת המשטרה לחקירה. לא הבנתי מה קרה. הגעתי לחקירה ונדהמתי לשמוע מהחוקרת לילך רנן שאני עצורה. החוקרת טענה שהפרנו הוראה חוקית כיוון שאסרו על הנשים להיפגש מאז החקירות הראשונות ויש בידיה מידע שמוכיח שנפגשנו. אמרתי לחוקרת: "נפגשנו בבית החולים שבו אבא של דניאל שכב באשפוז, השגחנו עליו במשמרות, זו לא סיבה לשים אותי במעצר, הרי הזהירו אותנו שאם ניפגש נצטרך לשלם קנס כספי של 7000 ₪, מדוע אם כן את עוצרת אותי? ואיך את יכולה להשאיר אותי על חינם במעצר כשעשרה ילדים צריכים אותי אחרי שלקחתם להם גם את אבא שלהם?" החוקרת לא הקשיבה לדבריי, היא אמרה: "הם כבר לא יותר הילדים שלך, בעוד מספר ימים תקבלי כתב אישום ואז תביני, את הולכת להירקב בכלא".

כשקיבלתי את כתב האישום הבנתי הכול. זו הייתה עלילה, פשוטו כמשמעו. טכסיס נבזי שמטרתו להפעיל עליי לחץ להעיד נגד בעלי, ולנתק אותי מהילדים שלי. הנזק שגרמה הפרקליטות בתקופה הזו לי, לילדים ולדניאל הוא מעוות שלא יוכל לתקון.

הייתי בכלא במשך שנה, בלי שום אפשרות לדעת מה קורה עם עקיבא. כל תקופת המעצר הייתי בצער גדול שלא נתנו לי לראות אותו, ידעתי שהוא מחכה לי, נשארתי עם הרושם של הפגישה האחרונה שלי אתו, לפני שנעצרתי, הפגישה נחקקה עמוק בזיכרוני כיוון שאחריה, במשך שלוש שנים, לא נתנו לי אישור להיפגש אתו. מהכלא התקשרתי לעובדת הסוציאלית שרית ורד, לבקש לדבר עם עקיבא ולאחל לו מזל טוב ליום ההולדת. גם ביקשתי שהוא יבוא לבקר אותי פעם בחודש, כמו שניתן לכל אימא בכלא. היא התעלמה ממני ואפילו לא הודיעה לעקיבא שנעצרתי ושאני בכלא, ולא הסבירה לו שזו הסיבה שבגללה לא הגעתי לביקור ביום ההולדת שלו שכל כך חיכה לו. היא בשום פנים ואופן לא אפשרה לי לדבר אתו בטלפון והסבירה לי שעקיבא החליט שהוא לא רוצה לדבר עם אימא. רק חמישה חודשים לאחר מכן, בתי הגדולה מארי, קיבלה אישור חד-פעמי לבקר את עקיבא. הדבר הראשון שהוא שאל אותה היה: "למה אימא לא מתקשרת אליי? למה היא לא באה לבקר אותי? למה היא לא הגיעה ליום ההולדת שלי?" והוסיף: "העובדת הסוציאלית אמרה לי שאימא ואבא וכל האחים שלי שונאים אותי". היא ענתה לו "אתה לא יודע שאימא בכלא...?" הוא הסתכל עליה בהלם, לא האמין למשמע אזניו, וענה לה בשקט: "מה?! באמת?!" העובדת הסוציאלית כעסה על מארי מאוד וביקשה שתעזוב את הפנימייה מיד. היא לא התחשבה בכך שמארי הייתה בהיריון ועם תינוק בעגלה, ושעשתה מאמצים גדולים כדי להגיע באוטובוס עד לאזור חברון לכפר הנוער. מארי יצאה, המומה ומבוהלת, ובדרך החוצה הצליחה לצעוק לעבר עקיבא: "אבא, אימא וכולנו אוהבים אותך מאוד!"

המדריכים של הפנימייה אמרו לעקיבא שוב ושוב דברי הסתה ונאצה נגד משפחתו. עקיבא סיפר בחקירתו: "הם הסבירו לי ימים ולילות שגדלתי בכת ושמה שחייתי זה לא נורמלי".

את התיק הרפואי שלו הצלחתי לקבל מבית המשפט רק אחרי הרבה מאוד חודשים.

לפי הדיווחים של הפסיכיאטר ד"ר ויינשטיין באותה תקופה שהייתי בכלא, עקיבא נכנס לדיכאון ואמר שהוא סובל מהבידוד מבני משפחתו, ושאין לו יכולת להתמודד עם המציאות הזאת שאין משפחה... כשכל הילדים היו יוצאים לחופש הביתה, עקיבא היה לבד בפנימייה. התחילו לתת לו כדורים פסיכיאטריים בלי ידיעתי, ומאז החלה הידרדרות דרסטית במצבו.

העובדת הסוציאלית לא ענתה לי לטלפונים מהכלא. התקשרתי למנהל של הפנימייה, חיים כהן, והוא אמר לי: "אין מה לעשות, עקיבא לא רוצה לראות אותך". אמרתי לו: "אני רוצה לשמוע אותו בטלפון אומר לי את זה", הוא ענה: "אי-אפשר" וניתק.

לא סיפרו לי מה הילד עבר בחקירות המשטרה. רק חודשים מאוחר יותר קיבלתי מעוה״ד שלי את הדו״חות של החקירות שעבר עקיבא במשך כל אותה שנה מאז שפירקו את המשפחה. אז הבנתי שאנסטסיה, הבת של קארי סיפרה למשטרה על המשחקים שעקיבא שיחק עם האחים שלו בתקופה שלפני המעצר, והחוקר השתמש בזה כנקודות לחץ נגדו. החוקר שיקר לו שהאחים שלו התלוננו עליו בחקירות שהוא אנס אותם ולכן יש לו אפשרות להיות נאשם על מה שעשה לאחיו ולשבת בכלא לפחות עשר שנים או להאשים את אבא שלו ולקבל מהם את כל התמיכה. עקיבא אמר לחוקר שזה לא נכון, הוא לא אנס את האחים שלו. החוקר התעלם ממנו והמשיך ואמר לו שהוא עוד פחות מחודש בן 14... ואם הוא לא ישתף אתו פעולה, ייקחו אותו למשטרה, ובתנאים של משטרה יחקרו אותו... דרך אגב, ציין: ״יש לי פה שתי עדויות של אחים שמספרים בדיוק מה עשית להם...״.

עקיבא בהתחלה לא האמין לחוקר והיה תקיף נגדו אך לבסוף נכנע לאיומים ואמר לחוקר: ״תסביר לי מה שאתה רוצה שאני אגיד לך...״. כך הצליחו לגרום לעקיבא להפוך לעד תביעה נגד אבא שלו.

בתאריך 4.9.12 מטעם הפרקליטות לקחו את עקיבא לפגישה לצורך רענון העדות שלו נגד אביו. יומיים לאחר מכן ב-6.9.12, הוא לקח סכין וחתך את עצמו כמה פעמים בגופו, באותו יום הופנה לחדר מיון פסיכיאטרי בבאר שבע. אני הייתי עדיין בכלא. מהרווחה לא הודיעו לי על מצבו הנפשי של הבן שלי שניסה להתאבד, גם לא הודיעו לשופט בבית משפט לנוער וכתבו בדו״ח הסוציאלי ש״מצבו תקין״. רק לאחר שלושה חודשים, עוה״ד מהסנגוריה לתיק הפלילי שלי, הודיעה לי על ניסיון ההתאבדות שלו ועל כך שהיה יום אחד במיון בבית חולים פסיכיאטרי ושחררו אותו על אף שחתך עצמו בזרועות ובבטן. קשה לתאר את תחושת חוסר האונים, הצער והדאגה שהייתה לי, מאחורי מנעול ובריח, בלי רשות להיות בקשר עם הבן שלי, ובידיעה שהוא מנסה לשים קץ לחייו! קשה מאוד לסבול את העובדה שהמדינה הפכה את הבן שלי לאמצעי כדי להשיג הרשעה של אביו. איך שיחקו עם הנפש של הילד שלי, מוטטו אותו נפשית, ואחרי שהשיגו את מבוקשם התנערו מאחריות על מצבו.

באחד מימי דצמבר 2012 בשעה 5:00 לפנות בוקר, לקחו אותי באזיקים מכלא נווה תרצה לבית המשפט לנוער, לדיון על הילדים. הגשתי לשופט את הטופס של הדו״ח הסוציאלי שהוגש לו גם על ידי פקידת הסעד שטוען שמצב הילדים תקין, ולעומתו הצגתי את טופס האשפוז במיון בית חולים לבריאות הנפש. השופט נדהם שפקידות הסעד הסתירו ממנו את העובדה הזו, ובפרט שדיווחו שמצב הקטינים תקין בזמן שהילד ניסה להתאבד והובא למיון פסיכיאטרי. השופט אמר לפקידת הסעד שתוך חודש האימא צריכה לקבל את כל התיק הפסיכיאטרי של עקיבא.

שבוע לאחר מכן, כשהשתחררתי מהכלא, התקשרתי לפקידת הסעד לחוק נוער, יעל בן דוד חלימי, שהייתה אמורה לפי הוראת השופט, להעביר לי את התיק הפסיכיאטרי. היא אמרה לי שהיא משאירה לי במשרד מעטפה אצל השומר. כשהגעתי למשרד השומר נתן לי את המעטפה אך בתוכה היה רק דף אחד בקשר לעקיבא, שלא קשור בכלל לניסיון ההתאבדות שלו. התקשרתי שוב לפקידת הסעד וביקשתי פגישה. חיכיתי הרבה זמן לפגישה הזו, וכשסוף סוף, אחרי כחודש היא הזמינה אותי לפגישה, במקום לעזור לי להבין מה קורה עם הבן שלי, היא שאלה אותי מאיפה קיבלתי את המידע שהילד ניסה להתאבד. הראיתי לה בתמימות את הטופס מהמיון של בית החולים הפסיכיאטרי שקיבלתי מעוה״ד שלי. היא חטפה לי את הנייר מהידיים ויצאה בחיפזון מהמשרד. נשארתי בהלם מהתגובה שלה. קיוויתי שהיא הלכה להביא לי את התיק. כרבע שעה לאחר מכן היא חזרה. שאלתי אותה: ״את יכולה להשלים לי את התיק הפסיכיאטרי של עקיבא?״ היא הסתכלה עליי במבט קר ואמרה: ״אין לנו שום דבר! הפגישה אתך הסתיימה״. אמרתי לה: ״אבל יש צו מהשופט שאת צריכה להביא לי את התיק הרפואי שלו״. היא אמרה: ״הטופס שהבאתי לך במעטפה הוא המסמך היחיד שיש בעניין עקיבא, וכפי שאמרתי, הפגישה הסתיימה״. יצאתי בצער ובכאב מהמשרד כי הבנתי שאין לי עם מי לדבר. חצי שעה אחר כך, עוד לפני שהספקתי להגיע הביתה, צלצלה עוה״ד שלי, היא נשמעה מאוד לחוצה ואמרה לי ש עכשיו צלצל אליה הפרקליט, שגיא אופיר, התובע נגד דניאל, שנזף בה על כך שהעבירה לי את האינפורמציה שהבן שלי ניסה להתאבד, ועל כך שהיה במיון של בית חולים פסיכיאטרי. היא ביקשה ממני להשמיד את המסמך שנתנה לי כדי שלא יעשו לה בעיות.

בתאריך 16.12.12, לאחר שהיה מנותק כבר שנה וחצי ממשפחתו, הביאו את עקיבא לבית המשפט המחוזי בירושלים להעיד נגד אבא שלו. התובע שגיא אופיר ביקש מהשופט שהילד לא יראה את אביו בזמן העדות, השופט הסכים, ודניאל הועבר לחדר אחר, שם היה צריך לראות על גבי מסך טלוויזיה את הבן האהוב שלו, ממציא סיפורים שקריים עליו. אני לא הפסקתי לבכות. אחרי העדות, העובדת הסוציאלית שרית ורד שמרה עליו שאפילו לא יתקרב לאימא של דניאל, סבתו, בת ה-84. עקיבא היה מאוד קשור אליה מאז שהיה קטן. גם כשנכנס לכפר הנוער ושמע שסבא שלו נפטר, היה לו מאוד חשוב לבקר את הסבתא. הוא נלחם להגיע אליה לנחם אותה, ביקור שנערך תחת פיקוח. לעומת זאת, עכשיו, בבית המשפט, כשעקיבא

ראה את סבתו, העובדת סוציאלית שרית ורד אמרה לסבתא: "את מחפשת מלחמה?! תתרחקי מעקיבא!" זאת בזמן שהסבתא כלל לא התקרבה אלא רק נשענה על הבת שלה שהייתה עדה למחזה. הסבתא והדודה נבהלו ונדהמו מהאגרסיביות ומהאלימות המילולית של שרית ורד ואמרו לי שעקיבא נראה מסומם. לפי הדו"ח הרפואי של ד"ר וינשטיין. עקיבא קיבל כדורים פסיכיאטריים בדיוק עד אותו היום שהעיד נגד אביו, ומיד לאחר מכן הפסיקו לתת לו את הכדורים.

הפרקליט שגיא אופיר העלים מהשופטים את האינפורמציה החשובה על מצבו הנפשי של הילד, על הכדורים הפסיכיאטריים ועל ניסיון ההתאבדות. בהכרעת הדין קבעו השופטים שעקיבא, בניגוד לשאר העדים, הוא העד האמין ביותר.

ב-19.12.12 שלושה ימים לאחר שהעיד עדות שקר נגד אביו בבית משפט מחוזי, לפי הדיווחים של ד"ר וינשטיין. עקיבא ניסה לתלות את עצמו. אך גם בניסיון התאבדות זה לא עדכנו אותי ולא את בית המשפט.

בתאריך ה-2.5.13, יום חמישי בלילה, אשפזו את עקיבא בבית בריאות הנפש בבאר שבע, לאחר שאיים להתאבד עם חבל. ורק חמישה ימים לאחר מכן התקשרה אליי עובדת סוציאלית ודיווחה לי על המצב של עקיבא. דניאל ואני היינו חרדים לשלומו. נסעתי מיד מירושלים לבית החולים בבאר שבע לראות את הבן שלי, אבל לא נתנו לי בשום פנים ואופן לראות אותו. העובדת סוציאלית שרית ורד אמרה לי שעקיבא לא רוצה לראות אותי. בכיתי במסדרונות בית החולים, אך לא היה לי למי לפנות.

בדיון בבית המשפט לנוער, פניתי בבקשות ובתחנונים לשופט שיעזור לנו להציל את הבן שלנו כי הוא במצב של פיקוח נפש, וכל המצב הזה נגרם מאז שהוא בכפר הנוער. אמרתי לשופט שאני כל כך דואגת ומרגישה חסרת אונים, התחננתי לקבל אישור לראות את עקיבא, ידעתי שהוא זקוק לאימא. השופט לנוער אישר לי להביא חוות דעת פרטית של פסיכיאטר מטעמי שיפגש עם עקיבא. הוא קבע שזה מאוד חשוב להחזיר את הקשר בין אימא לבן, וביקש שעוה"ד שלי תיפגש עם עקיבא כדי לבדוק אם באמת הוא לא רוצה לפגוש אותי. לאה אליאב, עוה"ד האפוטרופוס לדין שמינתה המדינה עבור כל הילדים שלי, סירבה לאפשר את הפגישה אתי בתירוץ שזה יגרום לו טראומה.

הייתי מגיעה כמעט מדי יום מירושלים לבית החולים בבאר שבע כדי לשאול לשלומו, ובתקווה שירשו לי לראות אותו, אך כל יום התאכזבתי מחדש שלא קיבלתי אישור. כתבתי לו מכתבים, והוא החזיר לי מכתבים דרך העובדת הסוציאלית. ב-25.6.13 הוא שלח לי מכתב: "... אני מעדיף שלא יהיה בינינו קשר...". הלב שלי נצבט, איך זה יכול להיות?! שאלתי את עצמי האם הוא כתב את המכתבים בעצמו או שהכתיבו לו?!

הזמינו אותי מטעם בית החולים לבריאות הנפש לוועדה רפואית באישור השופט. הוועדה החליטה שצריך להאריך את תקופת האשפוז שלו, בטענה שעקיבא מבקש להישאר בבית החולים הפסיכיאטרי. עדיין לא נתנו לי לראות אותו, ולא יכולתי לשאול אותו אם זה נכון. רק ב-11.7.13, חודשיים וחצי לאחר שאושפז, הצלחתי לאשר ביקור של פסיכיאטר ילדים פרטי בבית החולים בבאר שבע שבדק את עקיבא. הופתעתי כששמעתי שעקיבא התלונן לפניו שהוא רוצה מאוד להשתחרר מהמחלקה, ואמר שהוא ביקש ממנהל מחלקת נוער, ד"ר ר' שישחררו אותו, והוא לא מבין למה משאירים אותו שם כל כך הרבה זמן. מיד פניתי במכתב לשופט לבקש שיעזור לבן שלי.

בחוות הדעת הפסיכיאטרית כתב הרופא:

"הילד אומר את הדברים הקשורים לעדות נגד אביו כמנותק מהם רגשית, נראה מדקלם דברים, כשכמובן אמינותם של הדברים נפגעת באופן זה".

כאב לי הלב בשל המצב שלו, רציתי לחזק אותו, קניתי לו מתנות: את משחק השחמט האלקטרוני שידעתי שהוא מאוד רצה וספרים מיוחדים. אחרי כמה שבועות הרופאה החזירה לי את כל המתנות ואמרה שעקיבא ביקש שלא אביא לו יותר מתנות.

כעבור זמן-מה עקיבא שוחרר מבית החולים וחזר לכפר הנוער.

ב-17.10.13 חיכיתי בכניסה של בית המשפט המחוזי כדי להיכנס לדיון שבו היו צריכים להודיע מה גזר הדין של דניאל. לפתע ראיתי מולי את עקיבא. לקח לי כמה רגעים עד שזיהיתי אותו. לא הבנתי איך קיבל רשות להסתובב בלי פיקוח ולהגיע לדיון. הוא לא היה דומה בכלל לילד שלקחו לי לפני שנתיים וחצי. הוא גבה, גזר את הפאות והוריד את הכיפה והיה נראה לי קצת מבולבל. הוא התקדם במהירות לכיוון שלי. התרגשתי כל כך, קראתי לעברו: "עקיבא!" אך הוא חלף על פניי בלי להביט לעברי, והלך ישירות לעבר

הפרקליט שנלחם לסגור את אבא שלו בכלא. הוא שוחח עמו ארוכות, והיה צמוד אליו עד הדיון. כשהשופטים נכנסו לאולם לגזור את הדין, זה לקח להם בדיוק שתי דקות להגיד באדישות שהם שולחים את דניאל ל-26 שנה לכלא. כשיצאנו מהאולם, ראיתי את עקיבא מוקף בצלמי טלוויזיה, מדבר נגד אביו. הרגשתי כאילו תקעו לי חץ בנשמה. בסיוט הכי מצמרר לא יכולתי לדמיין מציאות שכזו. ב-17.12.13 התקשר אליי עקיבא ואמר לי: "האבא שלי זה הפרקליט שגיא אופיר".

יומיים לאחר מכן עקיבא התקשר אליי ושמעתי שיש מישהו לידו שלוחש לו מה להגיד לי. שאלתי אותו: "יש מישהו לידך?" והוא ענה: "כן, אבל אני רוצה להגיד לך משהו חשוב: אני לא יכול להיות בקשר אתך אם את עם אבא! את מבינה? לא מרשים לי! אני לא יכול! אסור לי! אני רוצה שתבחרי, זה או אני או אבא!".

כשאמר לי שיש מישהו לידו, הבנתי מיד שמשתמשים בילד ובאהבה שיש לי אליו כדי לגרום לי לנתק את הקשר עם אהבת חיי, דניאל קודם ניסו דרך השיחות עם העובדות הסוציאליות במקלט ועם הפסיכולוגים הקליניים מטעם הרווחה, דרך החוקרים בחדרי החקירות ואפילו על ידי הלחץ של מעצר לשנה בכלא, כשבכל יום אמרו לי: "תעזבי את דניאל, תגידי שאת קרבן ותשתחררי מיד", וכשראו שלא הצליחו, ניסו כעת להפעיל את הילד, להשפיע עליי לעזוב את אבא שלו. חששתי שהילד נמצא תחת איומים.

זמן קצר אחר כך עקיבא התקשר ואמר לי: "אימא, ברחתי אתמול מהפנימייה. חשוב שתביני, אני או אתך, או בבית חולים, או בקבר. העובדת הסוציאלית שרית ורד שקרנית. היא משקרת לי והיא משקרת לך, בבית החולים רציתי להתקשר אלייך והם חטפו לי את הטלפון מהיד, גם שלחתי לך מכתב שאני רוצה לפגוש אותך". אמרתי לו: "לא הגיע לידי כזה מכתב, ולהפך, קיבלתי מכתב שאתה לא רוצה לראות אותי", הוא אמר שהוא שונא את מה שעושים אנשי הרווחה. הוא סיפר שחוקרי המשטרה הגיעו לבית החולים בבאר שבע ואמרו לו שאם הוא יהיה בקשר עם אימא שלו או יקבל מתנות ממנה זה יפגע בעדות שנתן בבית המשפט, והפחידו אותו שהם עוקבים אחריו ויודעים כל מה שהוא עושה, ואיימו עליו שישימו לו אזיקון אלקטרוני באוזן. הוא סיפר שהיה בצער כשהיה צריך להחזיר לי את המתנות, ואמר: "העובדת הסוציאלית שרית ורד ופקידת הסעד שרית אשורי אמרו לי שאת באה להזיק לי, אני מטומטם שהאמנתי להן, הייתי תחת השפעת כדורים פסיכיאטריים".

מאז, החל להתקשר אליי עשרות פעמים ביום, כי רצה לפגוש אותי. התייעצתי עם עוה"ד שלי מה לעשות, בפרט לאור העובדה שעוקבים אחריו, עוה"ד אסר עליי להיענות לבקשתו, ואמר שייתכן שזוהי מלכודת מהפרקליטות, שמחפשים שוב איך לתפור לי כתב אישום חדש. נאלצתי להסביר לעקיבא שעוה"ד שלי אמר לי שאסור לי להיפגש אתו כי הוא עד תביעה מרכזי, והם יכולים להחזיר אותי לכלא ולהעליל עליי שאני מטרידה עד תביעה. אמרתי לו שהגשתי בקשה לשופט לקבל אישור להיפגש אתו בצורה חוקית ומסודרת בפיקוח, ובינתיים השופט עוד לא אישר כי העובדות הסוציאליות אומרות בבית המשפט שעקיבא לא רוצה לפגוש אותי.

עקיבא לא הסכים לחכות לאישור של שופט. הוא כעס מאוד שסירבתי להיפגש אתו לאחר שברח מהפנימייה, והתקשר להודיע לי שהוא מחכה לי בקניון מלחה בירושלים, ומתעקש שאגיע עכשיו. כל כך רציתי לראות אותו אך היה לי מאוד חשוב לא לחזור לכלא, כדי שאוכל לטפל בשאר הילדים שלי ובנכדים. אמרתי לעקיבא שאני אוהבת אותו מאוד אבל אני מאוד מצטערת שאני לא יכולה לקחת כזה סיכון. כששוב התקשר, שוב הסברתי שגם שיחות הטלפון שלו מסכנות אותי. אבל עקיבא כנראה לא הבין שאני באמת מפחדת מהעלילות שיכולים לתפור לי, או שכעס שאני לא סומכת עליו. בכל מקרה הוא לא היה יכול לסבול את הסירוב שלי לפגוש אותו, ואת העובדה שלא עניתי לו לטלפונים. באותו הלילה ב-1.1.14 הוא הגיע עם הבן של האישה השנייה – סמי, שהשפיע עליו לזרוק אבנים על הבית, ולשרוט את הרכב של האנשים שבאו לקנות מזגנים שמכרנו כדי לשלם חובות. סמי ועקיבא התנהגו באלימות רבה. לא הכרתי את הבן שלי. לא הבנתי איך הוא הגיע למצב כזה. סמי בא מולי והתחיל להקניט אותי ולצחוק שהם הולכים להתחלק ב100,000 ₪ שיקבלו פיצויים כי העידו נגד דניאל, ולמה אני פראיירית שלא רוצה להתחלק אתם בכסף. כעסתי מאוד על ההתנהגות שלהם, וביקשתי שיעזבו את המקום. בלילה שמעתי צעדים על הגג של הבית. בבוקר יצאתי מהבית. כשחזרתי, הפועל הערבי שבונה בבניין לידינו סיפר לי שהוא ראה בלילה נערים על הגג. הדוד החשמלי כבר לא היה שם. ניסיתי לפתוח את דלת הבית, אך לא הצלחתי. הסתכלתי מהחלון לתוך הבית, וראיתי שסתמו את הכניסה של הבית עם ארון שהזיזו לכיוון הדלת, וכל הבית היה מפורק כמו אחרי פוגרום. הלכתי למשטרה וביקשתי ששוטר יבוא לקחת בדיקת תביעות אצבע כדי להבין מי הפורץ. כשהגעתי לדירה עם השוטר, ראיתי את שני הילדים קופצים מהחלון ולוקחים אתם ציוד יקר של אולפן המוזיקה מהבית. הם תלשו ספוגים של האולפן מהקירות, הוציאו חלונות מהמקום, זרקו את כל מה שהיה בארונות המטבח על הרצפה, הוציאו את הדלתות של ארון הקיר מהמקום. נבהלתי כשראיתי את הילדים ואת הבית במצב הזה. היה בי צער גדול. ניסיתי לעצור את עקיבא, ולתדהמתי, הוא

השתמש נגדי בכוח. הייתי המומה מהעובדה שהשוטרים עמדו והסתכלו על הילדים שמרוקנים את הבית, וכעסו עליי שאני מונעת מהם לקחת דברים. אני יודעת שזה נשמע הזוי, אך חברה שלי שהייתה אתי צילמה והקליטה, והכול מתועד. הגיע טנדר גדול וחנה ליד הניידת של המשטרה, ומול עיני השוטרים ובעידודם הילדים מילאו את הרכב ברכוש. חשבתי שאני בתוך סיוט.

למחרת הגשתי תלונה במשטרה, וחוץ מצו הרחקה לשלושה חודשים, המשטרה לא חקרה את האירוע, וסגרה את התיק מיד.

לאחר שעקיבא ברח מהפנימייה בחברון, מצאו אותו, ופקידת הסעד הכניסה אותו לפנימיית "נירים" בעכו. דאגתי לו והתגעגעתי אליו מאוד.

ב-9.5.14 פקידת הסעד ציפי לוי הודיעה לי שעקיבא ברח מפנימיית נירים, מצאו אותו על פסי הרכבת בעכו, בניסיון התאבדות, ואשפזו אותו בבית חולים לבריאות הנפש בחיפה טירת הכרמל. נשברתי. הייתי בחרדות ובפחד לשלומו. כשדניאל התקשר מהכלא וסיפרתי לו שעקיבא שוב ניסה להתאבד, דניאל היה מזועזע מהבשורה והיה בצער גדול.

אחרי שבוע, ברוך השם, הילד שוחרר מבית החולים וחזר לנירים. הופתעתי לקרוא בדו"ח הרפואי שהפסיכיאטר כתב שהילד "שולל כוונות אבדניות". אז שאלתי את עצמי, אם כן, למה סגרו אותו בבית חולים פסיכיאטרי...?

אחרי שנתיים וחצי שניתקו אותי לגמרי מעקיבא, שלוש שנים אחרי המעצר של דניאל ופירוק המשפחה, יום אחד בספטמבר 2014 התקשרו אליי מהמשרד של עוה"ד אבי כהן מהסנגוריה הציבורית, שהיה עוה"ד של דניאל, והודיעו לי שהם קיבלו מכתב מעקיבא. נסעתי מיד למשרד לראות במה מדובר. כשאחזתי בידי את המכתב בכתב ידו של בני והתחלתי לקרוא, לא יכולתי לעצור את שטף הדמעות:

*לכבוד עו"ד אבי כהן* 9.9.14

*רציתי לשתף אותך על מה שעובר עליי בתקופה הזאת, ובכללי מה שעבר עליי מתקופת החקירות. אני לא יכול יותר לסבול את השקרים ששיקרתי בבית המשפט ועל האבא שלי בעיקר.*

*אני רוצה שתדע שבגלל זה התחילו לי המחשבות האבדניות וניסיתי להתאבד כמה פעמים בגלל שלחצו עלי כל האנשים הטיפוליים שעבדו מולי בפנימיות, כגון שרית העוסית, מדריכים, חוקרים ועוד...פחדתי מאוד. וגם הייתי פחדן בגלל שהחוקר הראשון מיכה הרן איים עלי שכדאי לי לשתף פעולה אתו ואם לא החקירות יעברו לידי המשטרה ויוציאו נגדי כתב אישום, והחוקרים של המשטרה יכולים בסמכות שלהם להפעיל אלימות נגדי. הוא אמר לי שאם אני רוצה שהשופטים יחוסו עליי כדאי לי לשתף פעולה ולהוכיח שפגעו בי בבית, כי נערים אלימים הם נערים שחטפו בבית שלהם מכות ואמר לי שהייתי קרבן.*

*אבל אני לא קרבן של אף אחד.*

*בגלל ששיקרתי ושיתפתי פעולה עזבו אותי לתקופה. אחר כך שוב חזרו אליי הודעות מהמשטרה דרך הפנימייה, ובחנופה אמרו לי שזה לא מספיק וניסו לגרום לי להעיד בבית משפט נגד אבא שלי. ושלא רציתי, אז שגיא (הפרקליט) אמר לי: "תשמע אתה תצטרך להיות בכלא במקום אבא שלך, אנחנו לא רוצים שתפגע, ושיהיה לך רע, אך זה תלוי בך ואם תשתף פעולה ותעיד לא יקרה לך כלום". ולפני העדויות כל פעם ניסו לרמוז לי וגם אמרו לי, להודות בשקר שאנסתי את יהונתן ואת ידידיה, על מנת להוכיח שהעדות שלי אמינה (למרות שהאשמות נגדי בחלקם הגדול היו נכונות שעליהם גם שיקרתי לחוקרים ולבית המשפט המחוזי בירושלים שלא היו). שגיא הסביר*

לי שבמידה וההגנה תוכיח שכן אנסתי אז העדות שלי תיפסל, כי אני משקר לבית המשפט. הביאו לי נגד רצוני כדורים פסיכיאטרים עד ליום המשפט. אמרו לי: "מה אכפת לך, תגיד שאנסת, מה זה משנה לא נעשה לך שום דבר רע". והפריע לי שיגידו עלי סתם שאנסתי ולפני העדויות בבית משפט נפגשתי עם ליזו וולפוס והיא הסבירה לי מה להגיד ובאיזה דרך להגיד כל דבר.

כששאלו אותי השופטים אם מישהו הדריך אותי ואמר לי מה לומר, שיקרתי ואמרתי שלא הכינו אותי מראש.

אני רוצה לכתוב לך בקצרה על דברים ששיקרתי בבית משפט:

שיקרתי על אבא בנושא ההחדרה של המקל לפי הטבעת שלי 20 30 פעמים. גם במקרה שאמרתי שבצפון ראיתי את אבא מחזיק את המקל או ששמעתי אותו, שיקרתי ואני מצטער ששיקרתי.

שיקרתי על אבא שהוא אמר לידידיה וליהונתן שהם עבדים שלי וכל הסיפור שסיפרתי סביב זה היה מצוות (ברוממה ובצפון). שיקרתי שהוא אמר לי לתת מכות להם. כל ההאשמות עלי לגבי יחסי המין שלי אתם היה נכון הכול חוץ מאונס. לכן האשמתי את אבא וכיסיתי על עצמי ובכלל כל מה שסיפרתי על זה היה שקר. אבא שלי לא ידע ולא תמך במעשים המגונים שנעשו ביהונתן ובידידיה שיקרתי על אבא בנושא של ק. אבא לא היה שם כשק. הכניס מקל לסמי והתעלל בו. אבא היה ברופא שיניים והוא בכלל לא היה בבית בזמן ההחדרה של המקל לפי הטבעת של סמי ושיקרתי בבית המשפט ואמרתי שהמשטרה לא איימה עלי.

אני גם מרגיש רע ששיקרתי בקשר לשוש שאמרתי על הטבעה בג'קוזי ועוד וגם העדתי בשקר שאבא היה שם.

בסיפור עם הים בגיל 10 בצפון שיקרתי על שאבא הכריח אותי לשכב מחובק עם אסא ערום ושאדרת נכנסה ערומה. ומה ששיקרתי על אסא לגבי ההתעסקות המינית. ומה שאמרתי שכל הזמן אבא הכריח את הנשים ואסא לעשות דברים ביחד, כגון יחסי מין ועוד...

לגבי העבדות שלפתי המון המצאות שלא היו מעולם. שיקרתי לבית משפט גם שכמעט כל יום היה שוקר חשמלי, ושוט ותעניות, ויש עוד מלא שקרים באותם נושאים ואני רוצה לדבר איתך עליהם כי לא הספיק לי המכתב.

וכל זה כדי לרצות את שגיא והתביעה על מנת שישמרו עלי ויעשו לי פרוטקציה, אבל עכשיו אני כותב לך מרצוני החופשי את האמת. תודה.

כשאישרו לי להיפגש עם עקיבא בפעם הראשונה, נסעתי לעכו. עקיבא שמח מאוד לראות אותי וסיפר לי בהתלהבות על הפנימייה החדשה, על הלימודים, על הטיולים בהרים. הפנימייה נמצאת קרוב מאוד לחוף הים ואישרו לנו ללכת על החוף בליווי עובד סוציאלי. אמרתי לעקיבא שמאוד דאגתי לו כשסיפרו לי שהוא ניסה להתאבד על פסי הרכבת לפני ארבע חודשים, וציער אותי שלא הרשו לי להיפגש אתו. עקיבא אמר לי:

"אימא, זה שקר! הם משקרים! בכלל לא רציתי להתאבד! ברחתי מהפנימייה ולא רציתי שיראו אותי על הכביש אז הלכתי במקביל לפסי הרכבת. אני יודע שהסיבה שהם סגרו אותי בבית חולים לחולי נפש היא בגלל שהתקשרתי לפרקליטה ליזו וולפוס ואמרתי לה שיש לי מצפון על ששיקרתי על אבא שלי בעדות, היא הבינה שאני רוצה לחזור בי מהעדות, אז סגרו אותי בבית החולים, שיקרו שרציתי להתאבד ותפרו לי תיק שאני פסיכוטי ובעל שיפוט פגום, כדי שלא תהיה אפשרות להתייחס ברצינות למה שאני אגיד".

מצד אחד שמחתי מאוד שהבן שלי בריא בנפשו, מצד שני הייתי בחרדה כי הבנתי שהוא בסכנה ודאגתי לו מאוד. "עוד הוכחה שאני צודק", הוסיף עקיבא להסביר:

"זו העובדה שבשנה שעברה, כשכן ניסיתי לחתוך את עצמי, וזה היה לפני העדות נגד אבא, הם הביאו אותי למיון, ולא אשפזו אותי כי פחדו שזה יפגע להם בעדות, באוזניים שלי שמעתי אותם מדברים עם הרופא שלא יאשפז אותי". עקיבא היה מאוד נסער והוסיף: "ואת יודעת שבכלל לא אכפת להם ממני, כי אני הזהרתי אותם שאני אתאבד בסוף בגללם ומי שהביא לי את האולר שאתו חתכתי את עצמי זו האפוטרופוס לדין – לאה אליאב".

"איך זה ייתכן?!" נדהמתי.

"לכבוד פורים הייתה הגרלה בפנימייה של כל מיני פרסים, ואני קיבלתי מהמדריך אולר. בשלג, כשהתארחתי אצל לאה אליאב איבדתי את האולר והיא אמרה לבעלה להביא לי את האולר שלו". עקיבא העביר לי מעטפה עם תמונה שלו ואמר לי בשקט, תפתחי את זה בבית, כתבתי לך משהו. כשהפגישה הסתיימה, העובד הסוציאלי אמר שרק בעוד חודשיים אולי יהיה לי עוד ביקור אצלו. הם הלכו ונשארתי על חוף הים עם הרגשה של נחת שלפחות הוא אוהב את הפנימייה, ושמחתי בעיקר לשמוע שעכשיו אין לו שום בעיה נפשית. אבל כשפתחתי את המעטפה עם התמונה וקראתי את המכתב שכתב לי צרחתי להשם, הבנתי שהסיוט שעושים לו ממשיך, הוא כתב:

*"אתמול ביקשו ממני לדבר עם פסיכיאטר ואמרו לי שאני רואה שדים בחושך וכל מיני הזיות, בקיצור ניסו לשכנע אותי שאני זקוק אולי לכדורים פסיכיאטריים ושהם דואגים לי... (בטיפול פסיכולוגי) בספסל, אפילו בנושא על אימא והפגישות איתך, הם קשקשו קווים כך שמסמלים פחד ופחד, בטוח הם עובדים עם המשטרה... והכי חשוב להאמין בהשם שהוא שומר עלינו, אוהב ונתראה בפגישה הבאה".*

בתחתית הדף הוא צייר לב גדול שלידו ארבע פרחים, ומעליו לוח שחמט, והתרגשתי מאוד לראות שכתב:

*"אז בסיום בהצלחה לנו בהמשך הדרך, כאן המלחמה שלי מתחילה באמת. ושלכם מזמן. נעשה להם שחמט!"*

שבוע לאחר מכן, שוב הודיעו לי שאשפזו את עקיבא בבית חולים לבריאות הנפש, בצו חירום של עובדת סוציאלית שרית אשורי, גם הפעם לא בגלל כוונות אבדניות אלא בגלל שסירב לקחת כדורים פסיכיאטריים מהפסיכיאטר בפנימייה, התחצף למדריכה, וכשהיה בחצר זרק אבן קטנה שהתגלגלה לכיוון המדריכה. עקיבא אושפז בבית חולים לבריאות הנפש "טירת הכרמל" במחלקה סגורה.

לא האמנתי באיזו קלות סוגרים ילד בבית חולים פסיכיאטרי, ועוד במחלקה סגורה! אשפוז שעלול להשאיר על נפש הילד רושם ללא תקנה, סיוט נוסח "קן הקוקייה", טראומה לכל החיים. וכל זה רק בגלל התנהגות חצופה...! מי מושך כאן בחוטים?!?

התקשרתי לרופאים של המחלקה וביקשתי להגיע לשיחה אתם. המנהל של המחלקה קבע אתי פגישה יחד עם הרופאה. בפגישה הוא הסביר לי שהילד שלי סובל ממחלה חדשה: "פרנויה מהמשטרה ומהרווחה ומהמדריכים בפנימיות!". ניסיתי להסביר להם מה הילד עבר מאז שלקחו אותו בכוח מהבית, על הטראומה שהייתה לו מהמעצר של אביו, על האיומים והמכות שקיבל משוטרים, על העובדות הסוציאליות שהפרידו וניתקו אותו בכוח ממני ומכל המשפחה ועל חוקרי המשטרה שהפחידו אותו כשאמרו לו שהם עוקבים אחריו ושישימו לו אזיקון באוזן. אמרתי להם שאם יש לו פחד מהמשטרה והרווחה הרי שלפי כל מה שהוא עבר, זה בטוח לא פרנויה אלא עובדה, זו מציאות. ניסיתי להבין למה מאשפזים את הילד במחלקה סגורה, הרי הוא לא ניסה להתאבד, הרופא ענה שבכל מקרה הוא לא רוצה שהילד יישאר במחלקה כי היא עמוסה מדי, והוא מעדיף להעביר את הילד לבית חולים לבריאות הנפש בירושלים. היה לי אישור מהשופט לבקש חוות דעת נוספת של פסיכיאטר, הרופא בא לבקר את הילד, ובחוות הדעת אמר שהילד לא צריך אשפוז.

בדיון בבית משפט לנוער ביקשתי מהפסיכיאטר לבוא ולהעיד. בעדותו הוא אמר לשופט שהילד לא צריך אשפוז בכפייה ולא כדורים פסיכיאטריים, אך פקידות הסעד נלחמו נגדו וטענו שהן רוצות שתהיה ועדה

רפואית שתקבע בנושא האשפוז שלו, ובינתיים, עד החלטת הוועדה הילד צריך להיות מאושפז במחלקה הסגורה של בית החולים.

ב-1.10.14 העבירו את עקיבא לאשפוז בכפייה באיתנים, בית חולים לבריאות הנפש בירושלים. הגעתי ל"מפגש הורים", ופגשתי לראשונה את ד"ר טניה שכטר, הפסיכיאטרית של הילדים. ביקשתי לשוחח אתה על המצב, והסברתי לה שהרופא שקבע שיש לעקיבא פרנויה מהמשטרה ומהרווחה טועה, כיוון שהוא לא לוקח בחשבון את מה שהילד עבר בשנים האחרונות מהרווחה ומהמשטרה, וביקשתי שתדאג לשחרר אותו מבית החולים, כי הוא לא צריך להיות מאושפז. בסוכות קיבלתי אישור לפגוש את עקיבא בפיקוח. הגעתי לבית החולים עם ארבעת המינים, עם בגדים, נעליים וממתקים לחג, בדיוק בזמן שעקיבא התפלל תפילת שחרית. עקיבא היה לבוש בבגדים של המחסן של בית החולים. לא הבנתי למה פקידת הסעד שדאגה לאשפז אותו לא דאגה להביא לו חלק מהבגדים שלו מהפנימייה, בפרט שהוא כבר כמה שבועות שם. הוא שמח מאוד לראות אותי. הוא ביקש שאני אחכה לו כמה דקות שיסיים את התפילה ויברך על ארבעת המינים, ואז נוכל לדבר. כשחיכיתי לעקיבא, ד"ר טניה שכטר עברה שם, ושאלה אותי: "מה קורה, איפה עקיבא?" עניתי לה שהוא הלך להתפלל ותכף יחזור. בפגישה עקיבא סיפר לי איך לקחו אותו מפנימיית נירים לאשפוז בטירת הכרמל בתוך ניידת משטרה, ושהשוטרים היו מאוד אלימים אתו, שהוא שמח שלא נשאר במחלקה הסגורה של טירת הכרמל כי היה לו מאוד קשה שם, ולא הרשו לו לצום ביום כיפור. סיפרתי לו שכשנפגשתי עם הרופאים בטירת הכרמל, שמעתי מהחצר ילדים שרים בחוג מוזיקה, וקיוויתי שגם הוא שר, ושצעקתי מהחצר לכיוון החלון הגבוה שהיה פתוח: "עקיבא, אימא אוהבת אותך". הוא ענה לי: "אימא, לא היה שום סיכוי שאני אשיר בחוג או שאשמע אותך צועקת לי, אני הייתי במחלקה נעולה במקום שלא יורדים אפילו לחוגים", הוא אמר:

"שתדעי אימא שהכדורים הפסיכיאטריים שנותנים לי כאן עושים לי לחץ בלב וגורמים לי לכאב ראש, לסחרחורות ולחלישות נוראה שאני צריך לישון כל שאר היום. הם איימו עליי שאם לא אקח אותם יעשו לי 'החזקות' ויזריקו לי את החומר בישבן כמו שכבר עשו לי קודם בבית החולים טירת הכרמל".

ביקשתי מהרופאה ד"ר טניה שכטר שתוריד לילד את המינון של הכדורים לפחות לחצי. היא הבטיחה לי שתוריד את המינון ותעשה א.ק.ג לילד, אך בביקור הבא עקיבא סיפר לי שבמקום להוריד את המינון הכפילו לו את המינון, והמשיכו לאיים עליו ב"החזקות" וזריקות.

הבנתי שהילד בסכנת נפשות. הוא אמר לי שהוא לא מוכן להישאר שם דקה אחת יותר, ואם השופט לא ישחרר אותו הוא יברח מבית החולים. לא ידעתי מה לעשות. לא רציתי שהוא יברח ויסתבך שוב עם המשטרה ויקבל מכות משוטרים, רציתי להצליח לשחרר אותו דרך בתי המשפט. הזמנתי שוב את הפסיכיאטר המחוזי של תל אביב, שיתן חוות דעת ויהיה נוכח בוועדה הרפואית של הילד. ד"ר טניה שכטר מאוד לא אהבה שרופא חיצוני מתערב בעבודה שלה, ומאז שינתה את היחס שלה אליי ואל עקיבא, ונהייתה מאוד תוקפנית. ביום הוועדה הגעתי עם הפסיכיאטר לבית החולים והוא שוחח עם עקיבא שיחה ארוכה. עקיבא סיפר לו כל מה שהוא עבר: מההתעללות במשטרה, בחדר חקירה, בפנימיות ובבית החולים הפסיכיאטרי, והקריא לו את המכתב שהכין כדי להגיש תלונה למח"ש. הפסיכיאטר דיבר בוועדה ואמר שעקיבא לא צריך להיות מאושפז ושיש לשחרר אותו מבית החולים. הוא כתב בחוות הדעת לבית המשפט:

"...עסקינן בחוות הדעת בשאלה האם מצבו הנפשי של עקיבא מחייב אשפוז בכפייה. להערכתי לא. עקיבא אינו במצב המסכן את עצמו, אינו אבדני ואף אינו פסיכוטי. ואם הטענה שמחוץ לכותלי בית החולים לא יגלה את התובנה שבנטילת טיפול תרופתי, הרי אינני סבור שעקיבא זקוק לו".

הוועדה הרפואית קבעה לאשפז את עקיבא בכפייה לעוד שלושה חודשים. הייתי בהלם כשקראתי בדו"ח של הוועדה שאותה ד"ר טניה שכטר שיקרה לוועדה שעקיבא לא שמח לראות אותי כשבאתי לבקר אותו, ואמרה שהוא התעכב לבוא לפגישה עם אימא, אף שידעה שהוא התעכב כי היה צריך להתפלל ולברך על ארבעת המינים. עוד יותר מפתיע היה לקרוא שהיא כתבה בדו"ח שיש כאן מקרה של "פולי-אדו" כלומר שיגעון משותף עם האם... לא הבנתי איך ייתכן שרופאה מומחית מדברת על פולי-אדו כשלא הייתי בקשר עם הבן שלי במשך שלוש שנים. מה היא רצתה להמציא עוד?! רק מאוחר יותר, כשראיתי את סוג הקשר שלה עם פקידת הסעד, הבנתי הכול...

התקיים דיון בבית המשפט לנוער על החלטת הוועדה. הביאו גם את עקיבא לדיון. כשראיתי אותו הוא נראה מאוד מתוח ואמר לי: "אימא, אני לא חוזר לבית חולים פסיכיאטרי יותר!". נבהלתי מאוד. דאגתי, מה הולך לקרות? שלא יעשה שטויות, שלא ינסה לברוח... איך הוא יתמודד אם השופט יחליט להשאיר

אותו באשפוז? באולם הדיונים של בית המשפט בזמן ההמתנה לשופט, עקיבא פנה לאפוטרופוס לדין לאה אליאב, ואמר לה: "איך את משאירה אותי באשפוז כפוי? את אומרת שאכפת לך ממני, אבל את בתור אפוטרופוס לדין לא עושה כלום לטובתי". הוא ביקש ממנה שתעזוב את התיק שלו ותתפטר. לאה אליאב צעקה על עקיבא: "אתה מושפע מאימא שלך, יש לך אימא שטן, אתה יודע שהיא עשתה תלונה עליי לשופט?" לא יכולתי להאמין שאני שומעת אותה מדברת כך לעקיבא. הרי היא זו שאחראית על כך שהבנות הגדולות שלי הגיעו לבית סוהר לעברייניות צעירות והידרדרו למצבים קשים ולא דאגה לקחת את הבת הקטנה שלי למעקב רפואי בבית חולים שנידר אחרי שעברה צנתור בגיל שבע, ועל כך התלוננתי לשופט, איך היא לא מתביישת להסית את עקיבא נגדי, ועוד מולי ? עקיבא הרגיש מאוד לא בנוח מהביזיון שעשתה לי. כשהשופט נכנס, התחיל הדיון. העובדות הסוציאליות טענו שהוועדה הרפואית קבעה שצריך לאשפז את עקיבא לעוד שלושה חודשים לצורך אבחון, עוה"ד מהסיוע המשפטי אכזבה מאוד את עקיבא, כי לא התאמצה בכלל להילחם מול השופט כדי לשחרר אותו, הפסיכיאטר המחוזי שהזמנתי בשביל חוות דעת, הסביר לשופט שהוא מכיר את עקיבא מאוגוסט 2013, עוד מהאשפוז בבאר שבע, ושבהתאם למה שהילד עבר בשלוש השנים האחרונות מהמשטרה ומהעובדות הסוציאליות אין שום סיבה לאשפז אותו והוא בהחלט לא פרנואיד. היינו במתח גדול לשמוע מה החלטת השופט. ואז, ברגע שהשופט אמר: "אני מסכים עם החלטת הוועדה הפסיכיאטרית, עקיבא יישאר בטיפול בבית החולים לעוד שלושה חודשים..." עקיבא כבר לא יכול היה יותר לשמוע כלום, הוא זינק מהכיסא וברח מאולם בית המשפט. פקידת הסעד שרית אשורי צעקה: "הוא בורח! משטרה! שומרים! תעצרו אותו! תתפסו אותו!" רצתי אחריו אל מחוץ לבית המשפט וראיתי איך השומרים תפסו אותו ברחוב והחזירו אותו לדיון. הוא היה שבור מאוד. כאב לי לראות אותו במצב הזה, בכיתי וניסיתי להרגיע אותו, ושמעתי ברקע את פקידת הסעד שרית אשורי צועקת לשופט: "עקיבא ברח בגלל אימא שלו! היא משפיעה עליו רע...!" עקיבא היה בסערת רגשות, הוא לא יכול היה עוד לסבול, הכול כבר היה יותר מדי, ולפתע מול כולם הוא זרק לכיוון השופט שקית שבתוכה היה המעיל שלו. הייתה סערה באולם. שרית אשורי שוב צעקה: "תעצור אותו! תקראו למשטרה!" השופט אמר שהילד חוזר עכשיו לאשפוז לשלושה חודשים. כשראיתי את עקיבא עם אזיקים בתוך ניידת משטרה, שלוקחת אותו חזרה לאיתנים, ראיתי איך הילד שלי מושפל. בכיתי בצער מעומק הלב.

שאלה שמאוד הטרידה אותי היא איך ייתכן שכשהגיע בפעם הראשונה למיון בבאר שבע, אחרי שחתך את זרועותיו ואת בטנו עם סכין והיה עם כוונות אבדניות, יומיים אחרי פגישת הריענון עם הפרקליטות, לפני שהעיד בבית המשפט נגד אבא שלו, שחררו אותו מיד מהמיון לפנימייה, לא עשו לו אבחון, העובדות הסוציאליות העלימו את המקרה מבית המשפט ודיווחו שהמצב תקין, ולעומת זאת עכשיו, כשאין לו כוונות אבדניות, העובדת הסוציאלית מוציאה צו חירום ומאשפזת אותו לכמה חודשים...? משהו פה לא מובן!

בתאריך 2.12.14 עקיבא מתוך בית החולים הפסיכיאטרי, כתב מכתב לשופטים ב"עליון", כדי לצרף אותו לערעור על הרשעתו של אביו. המכתב בן 11 עמודים, ועולה ממנו זעקה של ילד שסגרו אותו כמו חיה פצועה בכלוב כדי להשתמש בו לכלוא את אבא שלו, הוא כותב מתוך הכאב העמוק שבלבו: "ברצוני להתלונן על כל מה שפגעו בי במשך השלוש וחצי שנים האחרונות המשטרה הרווחה פנימייה ועוד..", וזו לשון המכתב:

**בס"ד**

***לכבוד בית משפט עליון***

*אני עקיבא אמבש, בן 16 וחצי ת.ז...*

*ברצוני להתלונן על כל מה שפגעו בי במשך השלוש וחצי שנים האחרונות המשטרה הרווחה, פנימייה ועוד.*

*הוציאו אותנו מהבית, הפרידו בינינו.*

בהילולא של רבי נחמן הורודענקר, נסענו לקבר שלו בטבריה להתפלל ובחזור לקראת היציאה מבית הקברות עלינו על הרכב ופתאום נשמע רעש חזק מאחור על הרכב כי המשטרה דפקו עליו.

עצרו את אבא שלי, שמו עליו אזיקים והכניסו אותו לניידת. עיכבו אותנו עד מאוחר בלילה ליד הניידת שבה הוא ישב. דאגנו לשלומו, חששנו שלא נראה אותו יותר ואפילו שהשוטרים אסרו להתקרב אליו עקפתי אותם ודפקתי על החלון להגיד לו שלום והוא עשה לי שלום בחזרה. שרנו כל האחים נ-נח בתפילה לשלומו ולשלום כולם. היינו רק הבנים ביחד וגם לא כולם ואת שאר המשפחה גם הוציאו מהבית. התברר שהעיכוב היה בגלל שהמשטרה של טבריה חיכו שיגיעו ניידות מירושלים לאסוף אותנו וכשהגיעו נסענו בניידות לירושלים לתחנת המשטרה במגרש הרוסים..

הגענו למגרש הרוסים בסביבות שלוש וחצי לפנות בוקר. את אבא שלי הכניסו למעצר ומאז לא ראיתי אותו יותר. חקרו אותנו ולאחר מכן הכניסו אותי ואת אח שלי למרכז חירום מבטח עוז שברמת שלמה ושם נפגשתי עם אימא פעם בשבועיים בפיקוח של המדריכים. עשו לי אחיזות כואבות במשק שעות. כלומר, תופסים לי ידיים במשך שעתיים על הרצפה כשהידיים משולבות כמו X תופסים לי את שני הידיים מאוד עד שאני נרגע. עשו לי את זה בדרך אלימה וגם המדריך מוטי מלכה הפיל אותי בבעיטה לרצפה ואחז אותי. ועשו לנו גם שיחות וטיפול הרסני. מהמשטרה חקר אותנו חוקר ילדים בשם מיכה הרן ששיקר לנו בחקירה ואמר לנו "נכון שנפגעתם נכון שאבא שלך היה כך וכך". ורצה שאאשר לו דברים וגם איים שאם לא אשתף פעולה אצטרך להיחקר עם מכות בידי חוקרי המשטרה.

לאחר ארבעה חודשים של סבל וגם דאגה לשלום כל המשפחה כי ידעתי שכולם סובלים לאחר פירוק הבית, העבירו אותי משם ל'בית חגי' אני חשבתי שאולי יהיה לי טוב ושאוכל להיות סוף סוף בקשר עם המשפחה ושיתנו לי יציאות לאמא, אבל כשהתקבלתי הבנתי שטעיתי ורק סגרו אותי יותר ואחרי קצת זמן לקחו לי את הפלאפון וכל דרך להיות בקשר עם אמא שלי והמשפחה ובלי פגישות. פגעו בי גם הצוות וגם הנערים במכות השפלות ובסחיטות כסף. באחד המקרים כשיצאנו, אני והמדריך משה חסין ועוד נער, חנינו ב"גן החיות התנ"כי" על מנת לאסוף את המדריכה ושם המדריך הרים עליי ידיים והרביץ לי ברכב וכן היו עוד כמה וכמה פעמים שהרביץ לי בפנימייה, בעט חפץ לעברי, דחף אותי ועוד, וכשהייתי במקלחת הוא חיבק אותי מאחורה. את הכסף שבשבילו עבדתי בפינת חי למשך תקופה מאוד ארוכה לא שילמו לי ורק כשאיימתי בתלונה ועשיתי בלגן שילמו לי וגם גנבו ממני כסף הנערים והצוות. עשו לי גם טיפול הרסני שגרם לי הרבה כאב והרס; שהרס לי את כל העולם הפנימי. ד"ר ויינשטיין, הפסיכיאטר של 'בית חגי' שיחק לי עם כדורים פסיכיאטרים ובכלל לא הקשיב לי ושמע רק לשרית ורד העובדת סוציאלית שטענה עליי דברים שיקריים. ויומיים לאחר העדות הוא הפסיק לי את הכדורים. ויש עוד דברים שעברתי בפנימיית "בית חגי" סבל. אבל הדברים הקשים ביותר שעברתי זה שהכריחו אותי באיומים להעיד נגד אבא שלי ונתנו לי כדורים פסיכיאטרים על אף שהבטיחו לי שאחרי החקירות עם החוקר ילדים מיכה הרן הכל יסתיים.

כשהיינו עוד בבית עם המשפחה ,בחמישה חודשים האחרונים שלפני המעצר של אבא שלי הייתי בן 13 וחגגו לי בר מצווה. חבר של אבא שלי שאמר שהוא סופר סת"ם הכין עבורי את התפילין. הבת שלו היתה בת שבע והיינו חברים וכשאבא שלי גילה שהוא כומר מסיונר שמתחפש למפיץ הם רבו ונחתך הקשר ביניהם ומאז לא יכולתי לראות אותה יותר. הקשר שהתחלתי איתה של נשיקות וחיבוקים היה מאוד חסר לי כשהיא עזבה, גם הייתי גולש באינטרנט מה שהתפתח לאחר מכן להתעסקות מינית עם יהונתן וידידיה האחים שלי שהיו בני 9 ו-10 שנים וגם בהמשך השתלטתי עליהם ונתתי להם פקודות למלא את צרכי האישיים ולעשות עבודות וגם הייתי נותן להם מכות ,אבל לא אנסתי אותם. אף אחד במשפחה לא ידע מזה ולא ראה.

ביום ההילולא של רבי יונתן בן עוזיאל ,כ"ו סיון 28.6.11 הרגשתי חרטה גדולה על מה שעשיתי לאחים שלי ודיברתי איתם .חמישה ימים לאחר מכן פירקו את המשפחה, המשטרה רצו שאעיד שקרים נגד אבא שלי ולא הסכמתי לזה בהתחלה.

שגיא אופיר וליזו וולפוס התובעים מהפרקליטות נגד אבא שלי, אמרו לי לפני העדויות "תגיד שאנסת ,לא נעמיד אותך לדין ,מה אכפת לך ,גם אם זה שקר" גם אמרו שהעדות שלי לא תצא אמינה במידה ויוכיחו ההגנה שכן אנסתי .והוסיפו שגם את שלך סמי אמר שאנס את בתיה ולא עשינו לו כלום כי רצו שאשקר על מנת שאוכל להכניס את אבי לכלא ולהשיג את שמם.

שיתפתי פעולה ושיקרתי.

רק בדבר אחד לא הסכמתי לשקר: להגיד שאנסתי.

גם ליזו וולפוס עודדה אותי שאני יכול להיות העו"ד הכי טוב.

בשביל להוריד מעצמי את הלחץ שעשו לי שגיא אופיר וליזו וולפוס וכדי שלא אצטרך לשקר שאנסתי, סיפרתי מציאות אחרת: אמרתי שאבא היה אחראי על הכל ,על כל הדברים שכן עשיתי ליהונתן ולידידיה ובכללי - שיקרתי. שרית ורד העו"ס היתה אומרת לי: "אתה צריך להציל את המשפחה שלך שלא יסבלו" והיא וכולם גרמו לי להבין שאולי מישהו מת או ימות אם לא אשתף פעולה עם התביעה ושיתפתי פעולה ואף כדי להוכיח שהעדות שלי אמינה נגד אבא מרוב שפגעו בי ושיגעו לי את השכל שגיא אופיר וליזו וולפוס ומיכה הרן והפנימייה נאלצתי לפגוע בעצמי לפני בדיקה רפואית ודחפתי לעצמי מקל לישבן על מנת להוכיח את האשמות נגד אבא שלי ולגרום שהשופטים יחוסו עליי.

הם גם השתמשו באותם הדברים שאמרתי והכניסו את אמא שלי לכלא נווה תרצה לשנה כי שיקרתי שאמא שלי היתה קורבן ושעודדה את אבא שלי לפגוע בנו ,אבל כבר לא היה איכפת לי. הרסו אותי ואף גרמו לי להרוס במו ידיי את עצמי, כבר לא היה איכפת לי להעיד גם נגדה כל כך שיחקו בי המשטרה והרווחה בעזרת הפנימייה...

אבל היו אנשים בתוך הפנימייה שתמכו בי ועזרו לי אבל הם היו רק מיעוט .ובכללי הייתי בדיכאון בעיקר סביב העדויות שרצו שאעיד נגד אבא והצרות שעשו לי בפנימייה.

חתכתי ידיים וחלה והוצאתי דם ובקושי התייחסו לזה. כי כשחתכתי, צוות הפנימייה פחדו לפגוע בקשרים המשותפים שלהם עם המשטרה סביב העדות שלי נגד אבא ושאר הנאשמים ולא חיפשו את טובתי האישית בשיקולים שלהם ודאגו שאהיה רשאי להעיד גם אם ישלחו אותי לבדיקה פסיכיאטרית. שמעתי בבית חולים את המנהל מעונות בפנימייה, קובי אייל, משכנע את דוקטור בוש שישחרר אותי ושמדובר במקרה חד פעמי. וכך עברתי בדיקה פסיכיאטרית בבית החולים בבאר שבע ולאחר הבדיקה הם הסכימו ביניהם לשחרר אותי, ושיחררו אותי באותו יום.

בעדויות סבלתי מאוד.

לאחר התקופה של העדויות וכשהעדתי נגד אבא ושאר הנאשמים שקרים רציתי לעזוב את הפנימייה ואת החיים.

מרוב הדיכאון לא השלמתי עם הכאב הנפשי, ולא הרגשתי כאב פיזי. כיביתי סיגריות על הידיים וביקשתי מהנערים בפנימייה בתור משחק מצידם, שיתנו לי סטירות.

ושוב איימתי להתאבד גם סביב זה שסבלתי מאוד בפנימייה, אבל הפעם, זה כבר לא היה משנה להם כל כך כי כבר העדתי ונגמר שלבי העדויות וזה כבר לא יזיק לעדויות, ושלחו אותי לבדיקה והתאשפזתי בהסכמה. שמחתי שסוף סוף הצלחתי לצאת משם כי רק רציתי לצאת משם בכל דרך והצלחתי ולכן שמחתי, אבל נפלתי לגהנום חדש. ושם נתנו לי כדורים והכניסו אותי סתם ל"חדר הרגעה" וכשהתנגדתי פעם אחת לכדור הביאו לי את זה בזריקה בישבן ובדרך אלימה, דחפו אותי, תפסו לי את הידיים והרגליים בכח ודפקו לי את הראש במיטת הברזל שזרקו אותי עליה. וגם בנוסף לזה גם שם שיקרו לי מהפנימייה, בעיקר העובדת סוציאלית שרית ורד, שאמא רוצה לפגוע בי. ושיכנעו אותי שלא אפגוש אותה, מה שעשו והצליחו דרך שקרים ומניפולציות כל השנים שהייתי שם. בנוסף מהפנימייה באו אליי גם המדריכים ושרית ורד העו"סית כדי לחזק את המחשבות האובדניות שלי כי העדיפו אותי בקבר. ממש כך הרגשתי כי פחדו שאתלונן עליהם ובפרט כששמעו גם מהבית חולים שיש לי מטען גדול עליהם ושאני לא רוצה לחזור לשם.

ורק בסוף אחרי שבאו ושיכנעו אותי הרבה עם שקרים וממתקים ועוד, נתתי בהם אמון וחזרתי לפנימייה. שוב התעללו בי ואפילו שגם ידעו שסבלתי בבית חולים כי שיתפתי אותם השתמשו בזה כדי לאיים עליי שיחזירו אותי לשם ופעם אחת ניסו להחזיר אותי לשם וברחתי. חזרתי באותו יום לפנימייה בתקווה שיניחו לי עם הבית חולים פסיכיאטרי, כי חשבתי שאם אחזור אפתור בעצם את הבעיה שהם חשדו בי שאברח מהפנימייה וקרה שהניחו לי. בפרט כי ידעו שלא יוכלו להכניס אותי כשהרופאה ד"ר מרינה המליצה עליי טוב. לאחר מכן, ביום הגזר דין של אבא שלי ואסא, לא הסכימו שאלך לשם הסירוב שלהם הראה לי שלא איכפת להם ממני ושיקרו לי שרוצים בטובתי, כי לעדויות נגד אבא שלי והנאשמים הסכימו שאלך ומה קרה הפעם שלא הסכימו?

אני הייתי סקרן לדעת מה קורה עם הגזר דין, היו לי רגשות מעורבים שמצד אחד היה חשוב לי לדעת מה קורה ומה יקרה עם אבא שלי ודאגתי ומצד שני היה חשוב לי לדעת שהצלחתי להציל את המשפחה בזה שישב בכלא כמו שהסבירו לי ושיקרו לי.

ברחתי בלילה. יצאתי בלי כלום רק עם עצמי וכסף לאוטובוס. הייתי בתחנה מרכזית חיכיתי לאוטובוס ונסעתי, כיוון שהיה קר בחוץ אז היה לי רעיון להיות בכותל המערבי ושמה התפללתי שיהיה טוב. ביום נסעתי לבית משפט מחוזי ופגשתי בחוץ את אמא שלי ואת אחותי... בפעם הראשונה לאחר תקופה ארוכה כל כך. מחוץ לבית המשפט פגשתי גם את שגיא אופיר וליזו וולפוס והם אמרו לי שאתעלם מאמא ומכל הנשים.

בגזר הדין שלא בצדק אבא שלי קיבל 26 שנים ואסא קיבל 6 שנים ודיברתי בתקשורת שטויות על אבא שלי.

באותו היום, לאחר הגזר דין נפגשתי עם אחותי (שוש)... והיא התחילה לספר לי על כל הסבל שסבלה בשנים האלה מהמשטרה והרווחה וגם סיפרה לי על שאר האחים שסבלו ונתנה לי איזו שהיא פרספקטיבה שונה, אמיתית ונפתחו עיניי ובנוסף גם בפנימייה כשחזרתי לאחר הבריחה לא הענישו אותי על הבריחה וגם לא הפעילו את המשטרה באותו יום שברחתי עד כמה שידוע לי. עם זאת כששאלתי את המנהל חי כהן על כך ומה הסיבה שלא הסכימו שאלך לגזר הדין, הוא לא ידע לענות לי, נסתם פיו, הוא התחמק.

את סמי פגשתי פעם ראשונה קצת לפני העדות נגד אבא כששגיא אופיר התובע הזמין את שנינו למשרד שלו וגם נתן לנו לצאת ביחד לבחוץ כי סמי רצה לעשן. בפעם נוספת שראיתי אותו היתה אחרי הגזר דין, באחת הבריחות שלי, סמי סיפר לי שסבל וגם שאיימו עליו החוקרים ושקנו לו דברים בסך של 800 ₪ כמו בושם ועוד כדי שהוא ישתף פעולה איתם וסיפר לי על אותה התנהלות של השוטרים גם מול אנסטסיה אחותו. ושעד היום החוקר אשר לזמי עושה לסמי ולאנסטסיה פרוטקציות. הדברים התבררו לי יותר על השחיתות שעשו גם מולי. אז התחלתי לברוח הרבה ולחזור. זה חזר על עצמו ובהמשך גם ניסיתי לעזוב את הפנימיה דרך הפקידת סעד החדשה שהחליפו לי, שרית אשורי ולא עזר, היא רק היתה אומרת לי שאוכל צפרדעים ואבלע רוק. היא מאז היתה שותפה וניהלה את כל מה שפגעו בי. אז ברחתי וחזרתי.

אחרי יום טוב של ליל הסדר של פסח 2013 התקשרתי לפרקליטה ליזו וולפוס ושיתפתי אותה במצפון שיש לי על השקרים ששיקרתי בעדויות בבית משפט המחוזי בירושלים. היא אמרה לי שכדאי שאני אתחיל דף חדש ושאעזוב את זה. ועל החלקים שאני אשם כלפי יהונתן וכלפי ידידיה שלא אדאג כי אני לא אשם שהובילו אותי לעשות את זה ואמרה עוד שקרים שאבא שלי הוביל אותי וכפה עליי דברים ולהתנהג כך. אני יודע שהיא יודעת שהיא משקרת, כי היא אמרה לי לשקר בעדות, גם ברענון שלפני העדות היא באה ל"בית חגי" כדי להזכיר לי את מה שהתביעה רצו שאגיד שקרים ונתנה לי ממתקים. בכל זאת בפסח אחרי השיחה איתה בפלאפון הרגשתי הקלה שסוף סוף הוצאתי את האמת והתנקיתי קצת מהשקרים.

הבריחות מהפנימייה חזרו על עצמם וגרמו לשרשרת של אירועים עם המשטרה שבה המשטרה של חברון נכנסו לתמונה והיו מאיימים עלי. שוטר בשם אבי איים עליי שיתלוש לי את הביצים ויתן לי מכות אם אברח שוב וישים לי שבב באוזן כמו שעושים לבקר וצאן...

אחרי הרבה פעמים שטורטרתי ברחתי וחזרתי ושוב המשטרה ושוב ברחתי וגם המשטרה העלו לפייסבוק תמונה שלי מה שלא רציתי וכתבו שם שיש נער נעדר ויש חשש למותו וכל מה שרצו זה שיסגירו אותי אנשים ואולי אם אמות אז אמות כבר בפנימיה עם כל ההתעללות שלהם ושל המשטרה והרווחה שמארגנת וארגנה וניהלה הכל. ופקידת הסעד שרית אשורי לא התייחסה כשאמרתי לה שפוגעים בי שם ורק עודדה אותם שינסו בדרכים מניפולטיביות יותר כדי שאסבול ולא אברח. והיתה מבטיחה הבטחות שתעזור והיתה חדשה בתקופה הזאת אבל שקרנית כמוה אין ולפחות לא פגשתי. כל פעם שיקרה ובקיצור שיחקה בי ובאחד הפעמים שחזרתי ונעצרתי בוריס החוקר בחברון לא נתן לי להגיש תלונה על מה שעשו לי ולאחר שישנתי לילה במעצר השופט שמעון לייבו שיחרר אותי בערבות עצמית של 1000 ₪ והסכים לבקשה שלי שאשהה בהוסטל זמני עד שיסתדרו הדברים.

עברתי להוסטל "מבשר טוב" שם הזמינו אותי לחקירה מתחנת מוריה על פריצה שהיתה באחת הבריחות, כשהסתובבתי ברחוב, התגעגעתי לאמא, ניסיתי לקבוע פגישה איתה. התקשרתי וקבעתי איתה פגישה והיא לא באה. כשזה קרה פעם שניה והיא לא באה, אז מרוב שהתגעגעתי אליה, הלכתי לבית בגבעת שאול ולא היה שם אף אחד.

באותו זמן הייתי בקשר עם סמי שהיה מגיע לבקר אותי בהוסטל. סמי ניסה עם תוכנית משלו ושל עוד אחרים לשכנע אותי שאפרוץ יחד איתו לבית בגבעת שאול ואגנוב להן דברים. גם כשהלכתי לבקר את אחי זלמן ואשתו צילה היתה שם קארי אמא שלה שעזבה את אבא שלי אחרי הגזר דין והיא ניסתה להשפיע על כולם ולשכנע אותי שאמא וכל הנשים גונבות לה כסף ומוכרות את חפצי הבית ועודדה אותי לגנוב להן אני האמנתי לה, כי כשבאתי עם סמי לגבעת שאול ראיתי אנשים שאני לא מכיר מוציאים את המזגנים מהבית וסמי ואני רבנו איתם. לא ידעתי שבשנה שהנשים ישבו בכלא קארי גרה בבית והשאירה להן חובות גדולים של חשמל ולכן נאלצו למכור את המזגנים כי כשעזבה ניתקה להן את החשמל והמים. למחרת כשלא היה אף אחד פרצנו לבית בגבעת שאול ועשינו שם נזק. אמא הגיעה ונבהלה והתקשרה למשטרה. כשהשוטרים הגיעו באחד הפעמים כשנכנסנו הם עזרו לנו לגנוב כי שמעו מאיתנו על גזר הדין.

בקיצור התנגדתי לחקירה אמרתי שאני בהוסטל, שאל החוקר איזה הוסטל עניתי "תחפש..." ושוב טורטרתי כי האמנתי וסמכתי עליהם וחזרתי לבית חגי וממבשר טוב עברתי ל"אתנחתא" שזה גם הוסטל זמני ואחרי תקופה של שקט מהמשטרה ברחתי מאתנחתא בעקבות ריב שטותי של מכות שבו האשימו בעיקר אותי.

כשברחתי, ישנתי בגן הפעמון נגנב לי תיק עם תעודת זהות וכסף ולמחרת בבוקר שאלתי את האחראי שם והוא אמר לי שיחפש והוא לא מצא הוא הסביר לי שאני יכול

לבדוק את המצלמות ביפו ועזר לי ונתן לי כסף לנסיעה. כשנסעתי ליפו הם אמרו לי שבשביל לפתוח את המצלמות צריך שוטר אז הלכתי למגרש הרוסים ושם כשהגשתי תלונה עצרו אותי והעבירו אותי לתחנת מוריה ועשו לי חקירה סביב הפריצה הבריחות ועוד דברים שהוסיפו. שתקתי בחקירה ולא אמרתי כלום. שאלו אותי שאלות ולא עניתי, אז הקצין שחקר אותי זרק לי משפטים כמו: "נראה לך מה זה! על כל דבר הכי קטן נכתוב לך תיק כי אתה לא משתף פעולה" וגם לא רציתי לחתום על החקירה אז הכריחו אותי באלימות הקצין צעק ודחף אותי לקיר ולשולחן. ובאו שלושה שוטרים או יותר ועיקמו לי את הידיים והאצבעות ולקחו לי טביעת אצבע בכח ובכללי קיללו והתייחסו מאוד מגעיל כמו בחברון. לקצין נראה לי קוראים איציק. בלילה שלחו אותי למגרש הרוסים ולמחרת הנחשונים שיקרו לי כשהייתי בהמתנה שלא אשתחרר במידה ולא אדבר עם פקידת הסעד שרית אשורי ולאחר שעתיים שיחררו אותי. אם אני לא טועה השופט הפלילי החליט לשחרר אותי לפני.

מ"אתנחתא" עברתי ל"נירים" אחרי שהמנהל של "אתנחתא" ירון ושרית אשורי המליצו לי עליהם. אבל לא אמרו לי שמדובר ברמה כזאת אינטנסיבית של טיפול נפשי כי לא רציתי ואני לא רוצה פנימיה טיפולית אבל זו האופציה הטובה שהיתה וגם זה בסך הכל מקום טוב עם לימודים גבוהים. כשהתקבלתי ל"נירים" בהתחלה היה מאוד טוב ולאחר תקופה קצרה התחילו בעיות בפנימיה ורציתי בגלל זה לברוח. לא ידעתי את הדרך להגיע לתחנת רכבת כי הייתי חדש ולא רציתי לבזבז כסף על מונית או אוטובוס כדי שיהיה לי מספיק לרכבת. אז חשבתי על רעיון פשוט ללכת ליד פסי הרכבת עד לתחנת עכו. יצאתי ברגל והמדריכה יעל נסעה אחרי עם אופניים ודיברה איתי וניסתה לשכנע אותי לחזור בדרך בכביש וגם ליד פסי הרכבת עד שנהיה לה פנצ'ר בגלגל של האופניים והיא הלכה איתי ברגל וניסתה עוד לשכנע אותי לחזור לפנימיה, עד שהסכמתי וחזרתי איתה ועם המנהל אמנון בתוך רכב משטרה. כשחזרתי ניסיתי שוב לברוח ונעלו אותי במשרד ולא נתנו לי לצאת עד שהצלחתי לברוח מהחלון ושוב דיברו איתי ושוב חזרתי. ולמחרת הם התעקשו שאבדק בבית חולים פסיכיאטרי ושלחו אותי לבדיקה בבית חולים פסיכיאטרי מעלה הכרמל. הם אמרו לרופאה שהכניסה אותי שקרים בקשר אלי. אמרו שעליתי על פסי רכבת ושרציתי לשרוט את עצמי עשו לה הכנה וכרגיל עושים הכנה לרופאים ולכולם. בהתחלה ברחתי, כי לא רציתי להתאשפז סתם וחשבתי שאם אברח לא יכניסו אותי שוב, כמו שהיה בבית חגי, אבל טעיתי, ברחתי ולמחרת "נתנו לי מילה" שזו רק בדיקה. שוב האמנתי להם והם איימו שאם לא אשתף פעולה יעיפו אותי מהפנימייה. שיקרו לי ונכנסתי לשבוע הסתכלות לבית החולים הפסיכיאטרי. לאחר מכן ד"ר דניאל הרופא שהיה לי כתב בהמלצה שאין לי שום מחלת נפש ושיחרר אותי מבית החולים. וחזרתי לנירים.

לאחר תקופה ארוכה של ארבע או חמש חודשים שהיה לי טוב שלמדתי ועשיתי בגרויות, שוב חזרה הפקידת סעד שרית אשורי מהרווחה, בניסיון להכניס אותי לבית חולים פסיכיאטרי בטענה שקרית שאמא משפיעה עליי לרעה ושאנו נפגשים ומדברים ללא פיקוח. היא ניצלה את המצב הרגיש שלי ושוב חזרה עם טענות שקריות בנוגע

לעבר שלי והסיתה נגדי את יעל המדריכה האישית וגרמה לה שתסית עוד אחרים בפנימיה נגדי, מה שהוביל אותי בסוף לברוח, אך תוך דקות ספורות המנהל של כל הכפר מצא אותי דיבר איתי וחזרתי איתו.

נתנו לי פגישה אחת עם אמא בפיקוח אחרי שנתיים וחצי שלא נפגשנו וכיוון שחשדו שדיברתי עם אמא גם בלי פיקוח ,תפרו לי תיק והאשימו אותי בהאשמות שלא היו. כשזרקתי אבן בתור משחק לכיוון אחד העמודי בטון של החצר בלי נסיון לפגוע באף אדם ובלי שפגעה ,המדריכה יעל עמדה בחצר בשיחה עם אחד הנערים ועל אף שהאבן לא פגעה בה ,ניצלה את המצב ואירגנה לי ביחד עם הפקידת סעד שרית אשורי בלגן גדול .הייתי ב"ספסל", "ספסל" זהו צריף שמשמש לענישה על ידי חשיבה על המעשים דרך שאלות במחברת. הם שאלו אותי כמעט רק סביב הנושא של השיחה שאמרו שהיתה עם אמא וסביב זה רצו לתפור תיק – גם לי וגם על אמא שלי שטענו שהסיתה אותי והוציאה אותי משפיות. גם ניסו בשיטות פסיכולוגיות לשכנע אותי שהם צודקים ושאני לא שפוי. בועז, מנהל הצוותים, אמר לי בביטחון שבוודאי ברחתי מהפנימיה כי אני מפחד מהחושך בלילה בספסל ובגלל שאני רואה שדים ויש לי הזיות. ביום כשחזרתי מהספסל לחדר שלי ראיתי פתאום שמונח אצלי בארון שרוק חדש בודד בתוך ניילון זה היה לי מוזר וכששאלתי את החברים שלי שם: "מי שם לי ושל מי השרוק הזה?" אף אחד לא ידע, נכנסה בי דאגה שמישהו מנסה להגיד עלי שיש לי כוונות אובדניות והיו עוד דברים שקרו מאותו סוג שעוררו בי חשד הם גם החליטו שאני צריך להיבדק אצל הפסיכיאטר של הפנימיה ורציתי שבוע לחשוב, כי לא סתם שולחים לבדיקה לכן ביקשתי שאולי שבוע הבא אבדק אצלו, ובפרט כי שמעתי שתכננו להכניס אותי לבית חולים פסיכיאטרי. בסוף באמת החליטו שאני אעבור להיבדק בבית חולים פסיכיאטרי "מעלה הכרמל".

לפני שלקחו אותי לבית החולים "מעלה הכרמל" הלכתי למנהל של הפנימיה לראות אם יש לי אופציה אחרת כי כבר חיכו לי ברכב לבית חולים ולא הסכמתי לעלות עם יעל אז נתנו לי את האופציה ללכת למשרד של המנהל ובועז המנהל דיבר איתי בכעס, אמר לי שאני לא שפוי ושאם לא אשתף פעולה, עוד שעתיים אני אצטרך לעזוב את הפנימיה ואם לא אלך יפנו לי או יזרקו לי את הדברים מהארון . אז לקחתי את התיק של מישהו מהם חשבתי שהתיק של המנהל וברחתי ,אך התברר שזה היה של העובד סוציאלי, יהודה. הוא רץ אחרי ואמר לי שיש בתיק דברים חסויים של הנערים, אז החזרתי לו את התיק. אז אמרו לי לחזור בטוב למשרד וכשהסכמתי וחזרתי לא נתנו לי לצאת. לאחר שכמה שעות ניסיתי לברוח ולא נתנו לי, כשניסיתי שוב לברוח מהחלון התנפלו עלי. החזקתי במשקפיים של העובד סוציאלי כדי שיפסיקו להרים עלי ידיים ושייתנו לי לצאת וזה לא הפריע להם, הם ניסו לקחת לי את המשקפיים בכח מהיד ועיקמתי אותם קצת. הם מהבוקר ניסו להזמין את המשטרה אבל חיכו לצו של הפקידת סעד לבינתיים מהפנימיה סיפרו למשטרה על עוד כמה תקריות קטנות שלי איתם שהיו באותו שבוע סביב הנסיון שלהם להכניס אותי לבית חולים פסיכיאטרי בכפיה ושיקרו שעשיתי ונדליזם ואמרו עלי שאיני שפוי ושאני מהווה סכנה ועוד שקרים, בקיצור שיקרו לשוטרים. באו חמישה שוטרים לקחת אותי קיללתי אותם אז שוטר בשם רפי עיקם לי את שורש כף היד וכמעט שבר אותה

ובניידת קיללתי אותו וקילל אותי בחזרה ותפס לי יד אחת וביד שנייה שלו נתן לי מרפקים לחזה והשוטר שישב בצד השני שלי בשם יעקב, תפס לי יד שניה וגם קילל אותי. בדרך הם עצרו בתחנת משטרה בעכו ושמו לי אזיקים בידיים וברגליים ושאלו אם אני מעדיף שיאזקוני מאחור ושם ירדו שני שוטרים ועלתה לניידת יעל המדריכה והכניסו אותי לבית החולים הפסיכיאטרי "מעלה הכרמל".

יעל עשתה הכנה לרופא ד"ר ציברי, כמו שעשו בשאר הפעמים לפני שנכנסתי לבית החולים ולמוסדות אחרים והוא אישפז אותי. בשיחה איתו הסברתי לו שהרווחה והמשטרה עושים יד אחת כדי לפגוע בי והוא הסיק מכך שיש לי מחלה של "פרנויה". נפגשתי עם ד"ר ינקו פסיכיאטר פרטי והוא לעומת זאת איבחן שאני בריא ושאין לי שום מחלה, שלא צריך לאשפז אותי, שאני לא אובדני ולא פסיכוטי ולא זקוק לתרופות.

כשנתנו לי כדורים אנטי פסיכוטים ב"מעלה הכרמל" נמנעו מלתת לי את השם של הכדורים, בקיצור מושחתים. היחס שם היה מאוד מגעיל ואפילו שהתלוננתי שיש לי כאבי ראש וכאבים בלב מהכדורים לא החליפו לי אותם .הייתי מאושפז שם במחלקה סגורה במשך שבועיים והיה לי מאוד עצוב לחגוג שם את ראש השנה. לאחר מכן ד"ר ציברי החליט לשלוח אותי לבית חולים "איתנים" כי קבע שיש לי מחלה ושכנע אותי וכמעט התחנן שאשתף פעולה עם ד"ר מיגל מ"איתנים" ושאדבר איתו כי הם חברים טובים, כי רצה שבבקרים וברמאות אקבל עוד חוות דעת של רופא אחר מבי"ח אחר שיש לי את אותה מחלת הפרנויה שהוא איבחן.

העבירו אותי ל"איתנים". שמחתי שביום כיפור אני לא צריך להיות ב"מעלה הכרמל" כי ידעתי שב"מעלה הכרמל" לא היו מרשים לי לצום ולא לצאת אפילו לחצר ובכללי בית חולים איתנים יותר פתוח .בסוכות היה לי קשה להיות בלי המשפחה בחג. שמחתי כשאמא באה לבקר אותי. גם שם שיחקו בי ועם הכדורים ולא הורידו לי אותם כמו שהבטיחו ולא התייחסו גם כשהתלוננתי שיש לי כאבים בלב וכאבי ראש ועוד הרגשות רעות מהכדורים, במקום להוריד את המינון כמו שאמרו, העלו לי אותו בעוד חמש מיליגרם

בדיון בבית משפט השלום בירושלים ביקשתי מהשופט שמעון לייבו שישחרר אותי מהאשפוז הכפוי. אמרתי לו שאני לא חושב שאני צריך טיפול ושאני מרגיש שהכדורים מזיקים לי. הוא איים עלי שאם אסרב לקחת כדורים יאריכו לי את האשפוז ונחזור לתקופה של "בית חגי" והתכוון לתקופה שסבלתי. באותו דיון האפוטרופוס לדין לאה אליאב צעקה על אמא שלי בבית המשפט: "אמא שטן".

בדיון שאחריו הגעתי לבית משפט בתקווה שהשופט שמעון לייבו ישחרר אותי מהאשפוז. כשהבנתי שהשתכנע מהצד של הפקידת סעד שביקשה להאריך את האישפוז הכפוי, יצאתי מהאולם של בית המשפט והתחלתי לרוץ החוצה ולברוח. תפסו אותי השומרים של בית המשפט והחזירו אותי לאולם. השופט שאל אותי בלעג: "למה זה היה?" אז התעצבנתי וזרקתי עליו שקית. בפרט שראיתי שאמא שלי בוכה והמצב לא טוב. הרגשתי שאנחנו חסרי אונים, אז זה מה שעשיתי.

אח שלי (גיא-נועם) בא לבקר אותי ב"איתנים" ואמר לי שהאפוטרופוס לדין לאה אליאב סיפרה לו באותו יום, שכל הענין סביב הבית חולים הפסיכיאטרי לא היה קורה אם הייתי משתף פעולה איתם ולא עם ההגנה על אבא שלי.

הבנתי עוד מזה שרוצים לתפור לי תיק פסיכיאטרי כדי שלא אוכל לחזור בי מהעדות נגד אבא שלי ולכן מנסים להגיד שאני פראנויה, פסיכוטי, דלוזיה, פוסט טראומה ופוליאדו עם אמא שלי...

לכן לא רציתי לעשות את האיבחונים הדידקטים פסיכולוגים של בית החולים. כשד"ר טניה קראה לי לעשות איבחון שאלתי אותה: "למה חייב?"

היא ענתה: "כי בית משפט החליט".

אמרתי לה: "אולי בית משפט לנוער, אבל עכשיו עושים עוד ערעור במחוזי".

ד"ר טניה אמרה בכעס: "אני כותבת לבית משפט שאתה לא מסכים! אתה מעכב את כל הדברים שבא לי לעשות! כשלא יהיה אבחון אתה תשאר פה לעוד זמן, יש פחות סיכויים שאתה תקבל ערעור חיובי, אתה לא מבין את זה?!"

פחדתי ממנה ועניתי לה: "טוב אני אעשה את האבחון".

אז היא ענתה: "אל תעשה לי טובות".

התייעצתי עם עו"ד והוא אמר לי שאני אבקש שיביאו לי עו"ד שיהיה נוכח באבחון. כשביקשתי מהם שיביאו לאבחון עו"ד, המאבחנת הודיעה לד"ר טניה על זה אז ד"ר טניה שאלה אותי:

"עקיבא, איזה עו"ד אמר לך? מי העו"ד?"

עניתי לה: "עו"ד".

אז איימה עליי: "עכשיו הוא חתם על ההמשך שלך חבל על הזמן... אני סיימתי!"

שאלתי אותה: "למה...מה?..."

היא ענתה בלעג: "גם לי עו"ד אמר לא לדבר איתך..."

אמרתי לה: "לא... הוא אמר שאני כן אעשה אבחון אבל עם עו"ד".

היא ענתה: "עם עו"ד לא עושים שום דבר!"

שאלתי: "למה לא?"

אמרה: "אתה בבית חולים יש פה רק רופאים ולא עורכי דין".

עניתי: "אז אי אפשר לעשות את זה".

ואמרה: "כן מאוד חבל אי אפשר לעשות את זה" והוסיפה בשיחה אחר: "אני לא מרשה לך קשר איתו, הוא מציק לך ומחר ניקח לך את הטלפון", כי לא נתתי לה את המספר שלו.

התקשרתי שוב לעו"ד והוא אמר לי שאבקש שיעשו לי את האבחונים רק אחרי שיומיים לפני לא יתנו לי כדורים כי אחרת התוצאות יוצאות על הפנים ומאוד נמוכות כשמטושטשים מהכדור. למחרת בבוקר כשראיתי את ד"ר טניה אמרתי לה מה העו"ד אמר, היא כעסה ואמרה שהיא לא מוכנה לשמוע הוראות מילד ושהעו"ד שלי הוא שטן.

כבר חודשיים שאני סגור נגד רצוני בבית החולים "איתנים" והסיפור שלי עדיין לא נגמר וממשיך עד עצם היום הזה ה-2.12.14 כיוון שאני עדיין כאן סגור במחלקת "נוער" בית חולים פסיכיאטרי "איתנים".

באינטרנט שהשופטת בדימוס חנה בן עמי מזהירה נגד השחיתות של עובדי הרווחה. התקשרתי אליה וביקשתי עצה מה לעשות. היא הפנתה אותי לכמה גורמים, וכך בחסדי השם הגיעו עו"ד מתנדבים שראו את המצוקה של הילד והשתדלו מכל הלב לעזור.

יום אחד קיבלתי הודעה מבית המשפט שהשופט נוער אישר בקשה של העובדת סוציאלית שרית אשורי לקחת מעקיבא את הטלפון הנייד שלו, כי הרופאה ד"ר טניה שכטר התלוננה שהוא מתייעץ בטלפון עם עו"ד. כעסתי מאוד. איך שוללים מהבן שלי את הקשר עם עו"ד? לא די בכך שסוגרים אותו בכפייה, אלא שגם לא נותנים לו להגן על עצמו? למה לא עוזבים אותו בשקט? הגשתי ערעור למחוזי על החלטת השופט. השופטת שטיפלה בערעור הייתה אחת מהצוות של שלוש השופטים שכלאו את דניאל ל-26 שנה. קיוויתי שכשהיא תקרא במכתב של עקיבא שהפרקליטים שגיא אופיר וליזו ולפוס איימו עליו שישקר ויעיד נגדו אחרת ישב בכלא, ולימדו אותו כל מה שהוא צריך להגיד – ייפתח לה הלב והיא תבין שטעתה בגזר הדין שבו שלחה יהודי חף מפשע לכלא ל-26 שנה על עלילות שווא שתפרו לו. חיכיתי לדיון.

בתחילת הדיון השופטת חייכה לעקיבא ואמרה לו משהו בשקט, ראיתי שעקיבא זז בספסל בחוסר נוחות ומביט בה במבט כועס. לא הבנתי מה קרה. גזר הדין שלה היה קשה ואבסורדי במיוחד. היא אסרה על עקיבא להחזיק טלפון או ליצור קשר עם כל עו"ד אחר מלבד האפוטרופוס לדין עו"ד לאה אליאב, ומעוה"ד שהוא קיבל מ"הסיוע המשפטי" שממשיכה להגיע לדיונים על אף שביקש ממנה להתפטר.

זו הייתה מכה כואבת.

אחרי הדיון שאלתי את עקיבא, מה לחשה לך השופטת בתחילת הדיון? עקיבא חשב לרגע ואז אמר: "האמת שלא הבנתי על איזה משקפיים היא מדברת, אבל היא אמרה לי: "עקיבא אתה זוכר אותנו...? הבאתי לך את משקפי השמש היקרות ששכחת אצלנו..!" היא נתנה לי להרגיש שכדאי לי לזכור שאני בצד שלה, אבל לא הבנתי על מה היא מדברת, לא שכחתי אצלה שום משקפיים! כששמעתי את זה מעקיבא, לא יכולתי להאמין למשמע אוזניי! מה שעקיבא לא ידע זה שאת משקפי השמש האלה אחיו החורג, סמי בן ה-15 הביא לבית המשפט כשחזר בו מעדותו נגד דניאל, כי רצה להראות לשופטים באילו משקפיים יקרות שיחדו אותו החוקרים... כל מי שהיה בדיונים של דניאל ראה שאותה שופטת הייתה נרדמת במהלך הדיונים, זו כנראה הסיבה שהיא התבלבלה בין סמי ועקיבא...!

עקיבא גם סיפר לי שבזמן שישב על הספסל באותו הדיון ישבה לידו מישהי מהפרקליטות והראתה לו תוך כדי דיון שהתובעת ליזו ולפוס שלחה בשבילו s.m.s וכתבה: "אל תדאג, הפרקליטות לא תעשה לך כלום, אנחנו דואגים לך, תתקשר אליי". הוא אמר שאחרי הדיון הוא התקשר לליזו ולפוס ושאל אותה אם היא זוכרת ששנה שעברה בערב פסח הוא התקשר אליה כדי להגיד לה שהוא מרגיש רע מאוד מהשקרים ששיקר נגד אבא שלו, היא אמרה לו שהיא זוכרת אבל שלא ידאג, הוא עשה טוב שהעיד נגד אבא שלו והם ישמרו עליו ולא יושיבו אותו בכלא על מה שהוא עשה לאחים שלו... עקיבא הקליט את השיחה והגיש אותה למבקרת על הפרקליטות, ליועץ המשפטי לממשלה ולמבקר המדינה.

בינתיים עורכי הדין המתנדבים הגישו ערעור לבית המשפט המחוזי על החלטת הוועדה הפסיכיאטרית לאשפז את עקיבא למשך שלושה חודשים לצורך אבחון.

בעיקרי הטיעון שהגישו עורכי הדין בערעור למחוזי, כתבו:

"... פקידת הסעד מועלת בתפקידה ולא מוצאת לקטין מקום לגור בו עם מיטה אוכל ולימודים. פקידת הסעד מפחדת שכל התזות שבנתה לעצמה על "כת מסוכנת" שבה גדל הקטין יתנפצו, והיא עוד תקבל תביעת רשלנות גדולה, לפיכך עושה פקידת הסעד כל שביכולתה על מנת לנעול את הקטין, להשתיק אותו ולסתום לו את הפה באמצעות תגית פסיכיאטרית. מדובר בקטין שהפרקליטות הפלילית ושירותי הרווחה השתמשו בו כדי להפליל את אביו, על מעשים שלא היו. הקטין נתפש בפעולה משטרתית ברוטאלית ונאלץ לדקלם עדות שנתפרה מראש, אין פלא שהוא כעת סובל. תלשו אותו ממשפחתו, זרקו אותו לפנימיות, מנתקים אותו מאחיו ואימו מסיתים אותו נגד אימו ואחר כך מצפים שהוא לא יתעצבן? את העצבים או הכעס המוצדק הזה מתרגמים במילים יפות ל"חשד להפרעה דלוזיונלית". לסיום יצויין שניהול ההליך בבית משפט לנוער כאשר העו"ס שרית אשורי מדברת, אבל לא נחקרת, גורם להשתלטותה של העו"ס על הפרוטוקול כאשר בית המשפט לנוער הופך חותמת גומי שלה. עו"ס שרית אשורי לא הכינה בכוונה כל תכנית טיפולית חלופית וזאת כדי להשאיר את הקטין בכוונה באישפוז: כמו שאמרה: "אנחנו בשלב זה לא מוצאים לו מסגרת וטרם נערך לו איבחון".

עקיבא התקשר מבית החולים לאפוטרופוס לדין לאה אליאב, לשאול למה היא לא עוזרת לו להשתחרר מבית החולים. הוא הקליט את השיחה והגיש אותה אחר כך לשופט בבית משפט מחוזי, יחד עם התמלול הבא שבו תיאר את השיחה:

"עקיבא, אימא שלך באה והסיתה אותך נגד כולם כדי לכתוב מכתב שקר לבית המשפט העליון".

"סליחה, אם זה מכתב שקר אז את מושחתת! סליחה אם זה מכתב שקר אז את מושחתת, כי אני לא חושב שכתבתי שם משהו שהוא שקרי! גם אם יש לך טענות נגדיות, זהו!"

"חבל שאימא שלך מעמידה אותך במקום הזה! אני אוציא אותך מאיתנים בדקה, אני יכולה בדקה להוציא אותך מאיתנים, אני לא מוכנה לקשר ההרסני הזה עם אימא שלך, אימא שלך הורסת לך את החיים, ותמיד אמרתי לך, אימא שלך פגעה בך, אימא שלך... אני אעזור לך, אני אמצא לך מסגרת ואתה תצא מאיתנים, אתה לא צריך להתחבר לכל חבורת הפשע שפגעה בך, אתה יודע את זה...".

"את מדברת על פושעים? את מדברת על פושעים? את מדברת על פושעים? אני חושב שפושעים, פושעים זה אתם! מי שעובר על החוק זה אתם! מי שתומך בפגיעה הזאתי זה אתם!"

"עקיבא, נשמה שלי, אימא שלך הרסה לך את החיים וממשיכה להרוס לך, וחבל".

"אני מבחינתי רוצה שתרדי לי מהחיים, זהו, זה מה שאני רוצה!"

הדיון בבית המשפט המחוזי התקיים בתאריך 23.12.14, שלושה וחצי חודשים מאז שעקיבא אושפז בכפייה. עקיבא הכין מכתב שבו הוא מתאר את השחיתות שהייתה סביב המשפט של אבא שלו. השופט דרורי, סגן הנשיא, אמר שהוא מאוד מצטער שהוא לא יכול להתערב בכל מה שקרה בחדר הסמוך לשלו עם שופטים אחרים בדיון של אביו, אבל שהוא קרא את המכתב שעקיבא כתב ל"עליון" והוא מבין ללבו, ולכן הוא רוצה לשמוע מעקיבא מה הוא מבקש ולפי זה להחליט. זה היה שמיני של חנוכה. הרגשתי שמול עיניי מתרחש נס חנוכה. בשמיני של חנוכה שנתיים קודם לכן השופטים במחוזי שחררו אותי ואת הנשים מהמעצר, ואמרו שלא היינו צריכות להיות סגורות בכלל, ובשמיני של חנוכה 26 שנים קודם לכן היה יום הנישואים שלי עם דניאל.

השופט הורה על שחרור מידי של עקיבא מבית החולים לבריאות הנפש איתנים. עקיבא ביקש לקבל חזרה את הטלפון הנייד שלו והשופט אמר: "כמובן", והוסיף: "מכל מקום, ברצוני להבהיר, ולכך יש חשיבות לצורך המשך חייו של הנער, כי אין להטיל על הנער סטיגמה כלשהי של מי שסובל מבעיות פסיכיאטריות כלשהן".
היועמ"ש של משרד הרווחה עו"ד דברה הירש לב רן ופקידת הסעד שרית אשורי לא יכלו לסבול את הכישלון שלהן, וכשראו שהשופט עזב את בית המשפט וגם עורכי הדין המתנדבים של עקיבא נסעו מחוץ לעיר, ניצלו את ההזדמנות ופנו לשופט תורן לדיון חירום, כדי לשנות את תנאי השחרור. עוה"ד דברה הירש לב רן ניסתה ב"דיון המחודש" לפתוח את כל הנושאים שנדונו בערעור אצל השופט דרורי, ולנסות לשנות

בכוח את ההחלטה שלו. פקידת הסעד התלהמה מול השופט וטענה שעקיבא מקליט אותה, היא ביקשה מהשופט התורן שיאסור עליו להשתמש בטלפון הנייד. זה היה תעלול נבזי, אך שוב קרה נס חנוכה, השופט התורן קבע שכל מה שפסק השופט דרורי נותר על כנו, והוסיף שגם ההחלטה של השופטת מהמחוזי לשלול את הטלפון לעקיבא הסתיימה כיוון שזה היה מוגבל לתקופה שהוא היה מאושפז.

עקיבא המתין בבית המשפט כדי שהמאבטח שהביא אותו מאיתנים ייסע לבית החולים להביא לו את הציוד ואת הבגדים, אך המאבטח עזב ולא דאג לו. שרית אשורי שכל כך צעקה בבית המשפט שצריך לשמור על הילד מפני אימא שלו, לא דאגה אפילו להביא לעקיבא את הציוד שלו או להתקשר אליו לראות שקיבל את כל מה שצריך.

כחודשיים לאחר ששוחרר מבית החולים לבריאות הנפש, בתאריך 17.2.15 נערך דיון בבית משפט לנוער על הארכת צו נזקקות, וברוך השם, השופט הורה להסיר את הצו בעניינו של עקיבא, כלומר עקיבא שוחרר מדי הרווחה.

אני דואגת, מה יהיה השלב הבא. אני מאוד מפחדת באשר לעקיבא. קשה להבין מי עומד מאחורי כל הסיוט הזה. מה יהיה עם דניאל? מה יהיה עם הילדים? נחמה אחת מחזקת אותי להמשיך להילחם ולשרוד, והיא הידיעה ש״נצח ישראל לא ישקר״, ושעוד יבוא היום שהשקר ייפול והעולם ידע את האמת.

---

הבת שלי ציפי הייתה רק בת 16 בזמן שנעצרנו. בת שחונכה בדרכי הצניעות, למדה רק עם בנות ולא היה לה שום קשר עם בנים. בתכנית טלוויזיה שעשו עלינו ושאלו אותה: ״מה את רוצה להיות כשתהיי גדולה?״ ענתה: ״אני רוצה להיות בדיוק כמו אבא שלי!״ החוקר איציק לוי בחדר החקירות הסגור פגע בה פיזית ונפשית וגרם לה לנזק קשה, אחרי הטראומה שעברה היא פנתה נסערת וכועסת לעובדת הסוציאלית שלה והגישה יחד אתה תלונה למח״ש, וזו לשונה:

״הוא אמר לי מפגרת, דפוקה תתחילי לדבר. את לא יודעת אפילו לשקר. אז אמרתי לו אפשר חוקר אחר? ואז אמרתי לו שאני צריכה שרותים והוא לא נתן לי, אז התחננתי ממנו שהוא יקח אותי לשרותים, ואז הוא לקח ובדרך לשם היה שוטר ואמרתי לו תחליפו לי חוקר הוא אכזר... אחר כך לא רציתי להכנס לחדר, כי רציתי שיביאו לי חוקר אחר, כי הוא מדבר בגסות, ושואל אותי בצורה לא יפה ומנומסת. הוא שאל אותי את חומר החקירה בצורה של אלימות, כגון - תתחילי לדבר מפגרת. אחר כך הוא מול האנשים דחף אותי חלש לחדר, אבל את הצביטה לא ראו ולא נכנסתי, והוא אמר לשני אנשים: ״אל תתייחסו אליה היא סתם מפגרת״. אחר כך הוא ראה שאין אנשים בחוץ, אולי רוסיה אחת שאחר כך ראיתי שהיא באה.

האלימות: הוא תפס אותי בשיער ומשך אותי לרצפה ונתן לי מכה בראש ואז הרגשתי מסטולה. ואז אמרתי לו שלמדתי במרכז חרום שזה אסור לו להרביץ לי. והוא אמר מותר לי אני שוטר-חוקר... הוא אמר לי שאני מכוערת שמנה ומפגרת. ואז אמרתי לו אתה יודע שלמדתי שזו הטרדה מינית להגיד לאישה שהיא מכוערת (למדתי במרכז חרום) והוא אמר לי: ״סתמי״ ונתן לי סטירה חזקה בפה כמעט נזל לי דם. ואז הוא אמר: ״אפשר להרביץ לך יא בת זונה, יא זונה. את רגילה למכות בבית, זה קטן עליך. את רגילה לשוקר חשמלי, שוטים ברגליים. את רגילה בשביל להגיד את האמת לקבל מקל בתחת בגלל זה את מפגרת, מפגרת אחת, אמר לי. מפגרת, אבא שלך זיין אותך בתחת כי הבתולים שלך חשובים אז במקום זה זיינו אתכם בתחת. וכשהוא אמר לי את זה הוא הזיז את כל החלק התחתון שלו כלפי הביצים שלו. הוא אמר ״הזין של אבא שלך לא עומד, אני אפרסם את זה בטלוויזיה שהזין של אבא

*שלך לא עומד ולא עובד" ... ואז הוא אמר לי בגלל זה את לא מדברת כי בטח גם את מצצת את הזין של אבא שלך". ואז הוא שם את הידיים שלו, ליד, קרוב ממש לציצים שלי, כמעט נגע בי. ואמרתי לו: "תעיף את האצבעות שלך ממני" ואמר: "לא רוצה". ואז הוא אמר לי: "אבא עשה ככה בציצים" והזיז את האצבעות שלו. והוא אמר לי: "צריך לזיין אתכם כדי שתתחילו לדבר" והזיז את האגן שלו החלק התחתון שלו בצורה מאוד גסה ואמר לי "מצצת לאבא שלך את הזין ובטח אנסת את האחים שלך, זונה! סתומה!". וכל הזמן היה מאיים עלי מכות. וכתב במחשב כל מיני דברים שלא אמרתי וכעסתי עליו ואמרתי לו תן לי למחוק. ואז הוא אמר: "באת לשבור את המחשב וזה אוכל בשבילי לבית משפט", "ככה לא תוכלי להגיד אותי". אמרתי לו: "תן לי לדבר עם העורך דין שלי" הוא אמר לי: "לא". אז אמרתי לו : "אל תדאג אני אכתוב את הכל, כל מה שאמרת לי" אמר לי: "אם את מדברת יש לי עדים שאת ירקת עלי ודחפת אותי". והייתי בהלם כי זה בכלל לא קרה. והתחלתי לבכות וחשבתי למי אני יכולה להעביר את הדפים. "אם לא תתן לי להביא את הדפים לבית משפט אני אביא את זה לעורך דין שיביא לבית משפט" והוא אמר שהעורך דין לא יבוא.*

*ובאמת עד עכשיו לא נתנו לי לדבר עם העורך דין. הוא כתב במחשב שהרבצתי לו וירקתי עליו וקיללתי אותו עשרות פעמים. ואמר שאני אמרתי שאמא שלי זונה והייתי בשוק כי בחיים לא אמרתי את זה. הוא אמר לי: "בת זונה, פוסטמה אחת". הוא אמר לי: "אני מחכה שתשברי את המחשב ותקרעי את הדפים ותקללי אותי, זה בשבילי אוכל לבית משפט, כדי להאשים אתכם. אני מאוד מתחנן שתעשי את זה. אמרתי לו שאני לא אעשה את זה אבל קרעתי לו דף אחד מהחקירה ...הוא הביא לי את הפרצוף שלו ואמר לי: "תני לי סטירה. אני מחכה שתיתני לי סטירה. זה טוב. אני רוצה שלך יהיה אשמה בבית משפט." ויותר שתקתי כבר לא רציתי לדבר. הוא כתב במחשב: "זה מוזר, היא*

*שותקת".*

*ציפי אמב"ש*

כעבור חצי שנה מח"ש סגרו את התיק. שנה לאחר מכן, כשהשתחררתי מהכלא פניתי למח"ש להגיש ערעור על ההחלטה כי זו הייתה שערורייה שלא מתייחסים לפגיעה חמורה כל כך בקטינה שלי. באותו זמן עוד לא הבנתי שמח"ש, היא מחלקה מטעם פרקליטות המדינה בעצמה, ושאין עם מי לדבר. גם את הערעור הם דחו. החמור ביותר היה שבדיון בבית המשפט המחוזי בתיק הפלילי, כשעוה"ד של דניאל שאל את איציק לוי בחקירה נגדית: "האם מח"ש באו אליך לחקור אותך?" ענה בספונטניות: "כן", ומיד תיקן ואמר: "אה.. אולי בעצם לא". השופט נחלץ לעזרתו וסגר את העניין בקביעה: "אולי הילדה בכלל לא הגישה תלונה". כך נתן השופט לאיציק לוי לצאת נקי מהסיפור ואת האו.קיי להמשיך באותה צורה בחקירות הבאות. את הילדה ואותי השאירו בתחושת חוסר אונים קשה שהכול מושחת, שאף אחד לא מחפש אמת, ושאין למי לפנות.

שוש, הבת הקטנה יותר שהייתה רק בת 15, ילדה שחונכה על ערכי הצניעות, מאוד חכמה ומסודרת, הייתה לבושה תמיד בחולצות שרוול ארוך, בחצאיות ארוכות ובגרביונים, אוספת את השיער לצמה. בזמן החקירות אחד מהשוטרים הפיל אותה לרצפה וצעק עליה: "אני אזיין אותך בתחת כמו שעושים לך בבית!"

את שתי הבנות שלי, ציפי ושוש, שלחו בהתחלה לפנימייה בצפון. היה דיון בבית משפט לילדים בקשר אליהן. ביקשתי מהשופט לקבל את הילדים חזרה. עוה"ד האפוטרופוס לדין, לאה אליאב, קמה במהלך הדיון וטענה שהילדים לא רוצים לשמוע, לא על אימא ולא על אבא, והם רוצים את העזרה שלה רק כדי להתכונן למבחני הבגרות. הרגשתי חץ בלב. שלושה ימים אחר כך הבנות ציפי ושוש התקשרו אליי בפיקוח

של העובדת הסוציאלית שלהן ושאלו אותי: "אימא, מתי חוזרים הביתה? מתי את באה לראות אותנו? נכון אימא שזה לא נכון מה שאמרו לנו, שאת לא רוצה לראות אותנו?" הייתי בהלם, אמרתי להן שבוודאי שזה לא נכון, אני נלחמת לראות אתכן, ומנסה להשיג אישורים.

הכול היה יותר מדי בשביל ציפי. החורבן של המשפחה, ההתעללות של החוקר, ההשפלות בפנימייה, האכזריות של הצוות, ועכשיו השקר של האפוטרופוסית לדין. היא טיפסה על גדר גבוהה מאוד של הפנימייה וברחה לרחוב. זה היה ביום שבת, בקיץ, ביולי 2011. אני הייתי סגורה במקלט. אחרי שש שעות של שוטטות ברחוב בחום ובצום ציפי חזרה לפנימייה. המנהלת לא רצתה לפתוח לה את הדלת. אחותה שוש עשתה תחבולות והצליחה אחרי כמה שעות לפתוח את השער. ציפי, שלא אכלה ולא שתתה עד אותו רגע, רצה לברז לשתות מים. המנהלת אסרה עליה לשתות ואמרה לה: "לא תאכלי ולא תשתי. אם את רוצה לשתות תשתי מהמים של מכבי האש". לציפי נשבר מהכול, היא לקחה את הצינור של מכבי האש והשפריצה מים על המנהלת. כל המדריכות תפסו את ציפי, הפילו אותה לרצפה, גררו אותה והרביצו לה. המנהלת החזיקה בכוח בזרועות של ציפי ונעצה את ציפורניה בבשרה. זרועותיה ובטנה של ציפי היו מכוסות בסימנים כחולים ובשריטות עמוקות של ציפורניים. שוש רצתה לתמוך באחותה ולהיות אתה, וכיוון שלא הרשו לה וסגרו אותה בחדר אחר, היא שברה את החלון הקטן של הדלת והצליחה לצאת. ציפי ושוש השתוללו ולא נתנו לאנשי הצוות לתפוס אותן. בדרך שברו והעיפו כיסאות ושולחנות. הפנימייה הזמינה משטרה עבורן. הן עברו חקירות משטרה קשות בהאשמה של השחתת רכוש ואלימות כנגד המנהלת.

הצוות של הפנימייה לא עדכן אותי בכלל במה שקורה עם הבנות שלי. למחרת הגעתי עם הרבה מתנות לבקר בפנימייה את הבנות, בלי לדעת מכל מה שקרה. נסעתי 300 ק"מ עד אליהן. כשכמעט הגעתי צלצלה אליי המנהלת ואמרה לי: "תחזרי הביתה, את לא תראי אותן היום, הן בעונש בגלל ההתנהגות שלהן". שאלתי: "מה קרה?" היא ענתה: "הן שברו הרבה דברים והן בעונש". אמרתי למנהלת: "אני כבר פה ואני מגיעה. אני רוצה לדעת מה קורה עם הבנות שלי". היא אמרה: "את לא תראי אותן". אמרתי לה: "ציפי אחרי ניתוח ברגל ולא קניתם לה נעלי ספורט ומדרסים. היא מסתובבת עם נעלי אצבע והתלוננה שכואב לה, קניתי לה נעליים ומדרסים ואני רוצה להביא לה". המנהלת לא הסכימה. הגעתי עד הפנימייה, השארתי את המתנות וחזרתי בשיברון לב ובדאגה רבה לשלומן.

כתוצאה מהמקרה הזה הפרידו בין הבנות והענישו אותן בעונש חמור ביותר: את ציפי שלחו למעון סגור לבנות –"מסילה", ואת שוש – ל"צופיה" באשדוד.

כשהגעתי למסילה וראיתי את המקום זה הכביד על לבי. האווירה הייתה מפחידה. את המקום מקיפה גדר תיל, וצריך לעבור כמה דלתות ברזל נעולות על מנת להיכנס. ציפי הייתה נסערת מאוד. היא הראתה לי את כל סימני המכות שהיו על גופה וסיפרה לי מה באמת קרה. הזדעזעתי. גם העובדת הסוציאלית של ציפי במסילה הייתה בהלם מהמכות שציפי קיבלה בפנימייה ונתנה לי רשות לצלם את סימני המכות והשריטות שעל גופה. הראיתי הכול לשופט בבית המשפט ולאחראים ברווחה. לצערי, התעלמו מהתלונות שלי על ההתנהגות של המנהלת, שלא הייתה לה כל רגישות למצב של הבנות.

ההשפעה של המעון הסגור על הבנות שלי הייתה הרסנית. לראשונה הכירו בנות בנות גילן שהגיעו ממשפחות הרוסות, והרווחה, במקום לעזור להן ולמשפחתן מבחינה כלכלית, סגרה אותן וגרמה להן ליפול לזנות, לשתייה ולסמים. בנות חמודות שיכלו להצליח אם המדינה הייתה משקיעה בהן, ולא מפקירה אותן. הבנות שלי הידרדרו למקומות שבסיוטים הכי נוראים שלי לא הייתי חולמת שהן יגיעו לשם. הן איבדו את התמימות. הייתי חסרת אונים ובוכה להשם שיציל את הבנות האלה. הייתי מחכה בקוצר רוח ובדאגה רבה לכל שיחת טלפון אתן שהייתה בפיקוח עובדת סוציאלית. באחת הפעמים שביקרתי את ציפי במסילה זה היה בזמן שהיה חוג שירה באולפן עם מורה שליווה בפסנתר. והיא שרה עם מיקרופון, מכל הלב, בצורה מרגשת מאוד את השיר: "הו אבא", של שלומי שבת. אני התאפקתי לא לבכות מולה.

כשהסבא שלהן, אבא של דניאל, נפטר לא הרשו להן להגיע להלוויה. הן היו בכעס גדול על כך אך לא היה למי לפנות ולבקש קצת הבנה והתחשבות בנפש של הבנות.

ממסילה ציפי הועברה להוסטל, ולאחר זמן-מה גם שוש הועברה להוסטל אחר. אני הייתי סגורה בכלא והן היו מספרות לי בטלפון על קשרים מסוכנים שיצרו עם אנשים מפוקפקים מהעולם התחתון, ואני לא יכולתי לעשות כלום כדי לעזור להן, כדי לשמור עליהן או בשביל להגן עליהן מהאכזריות שיש בעולם. כדי לדבר אתן בטלפון – מכרתי לאסירות את החפצים שלי, את סיר הבישול, את הכיריים ואת מנורת הלילה, כדי שאוכל לקנות כרטיסי טלכרט לשמוע אותן. התחננתי אליהן שיחזיקו עוד קצת מעמד וינסו לא לעשות שטויות, שאני מבינה שקשה להן בלי המשפחה אך שיחזיקו אחת את השנייה.

באחד התאים שאליהם הועברתי ישנתי באותו החדר עם עוד חמש אסירות, שאחת מהן הייתה טרנסג'נדרית ערבייה. היא הייתה מאוד אלימה. פעם אחת היא לא רצתה לתת לי את התור שלי בטלפון לכן סגרה אותי בשירותים ולקחה מכסה של קופסת שימורים, דחפה אותי לכיוון האסלה, שברה את הצינור ואיימה לחתוך לי את הפנים. לא רציתי להגיב כי לא רציתי שיסגרו אותי בבידוד ואז לא תהיה לי אפשרות לדבר עם הבנות שלי. הקצינה החליטה להעביר אותי לאגף סגור במקום להעביר אותה. למחרת היא חתכה אוזן של אסירה אחרת, ובכל זאת השאירו אותי באותו האגף עוד חודש. שם הייתה אפשרות לצאת לחצר רק שעה אחת ביום ובאותה שעה להתחלק עם עוד כעשרים אסירות בטלפון אחד. הלחץ על הטלפון היה עצום. איך יכולתי לדבר עם הילדים? התנאים באגף הסגור היו מאוד קשים. לא יכולתי לטפל בכאבים בכתפיים שלי שנפגעו מעט לפני כן כשסוהרת דחפה אותי במעבר מפוסטה לפוסטה כשהייתי עם אזיקים בידיים וברגליים. גם באגף הסגור הייתי מתחננת לפני האסירות שיחליפו אתי את הדבר היחיד שהיה לי, הסיגריות, תמורת שיחת טלפון. דאגתי מאוד לבנות ולכל הילדים. ציפי הייתה בוכה לי מדי יום על ביזיונות נוספים שחטפה בהוסטל מהבנות ומאנשי הצוות. היו מבזים אותה ואמרו לה שבגלל שהיא "אמבש" אין לה סיכוי להצליח בשום מקום, ואפילו אם תתגייס לצבא יתנו לה רק לנקות שירותים. בהתחלה היא הייתה מתווכחת ורבה עם הבנות, אך לבסוף החליטה לצאת לעבוד ולהיות פחות בעימותים אתן. כשהתחילה לעבוד הכירה בחור ערבי שחיזר אחריה והחליטה שהיא רוצה להיות מוסלמית. היא התלבשה כמו ערבייה ונסעה אתו לכפר ערבי. אני הייתי חסרת אונים מאחורי סורגים. כששמעתי ברדיו ששוב נדקרו יהודים במזרח ירושלים על ידי נער ערבי, דאגתי מההידרדרות המסוכנת של הבת שלי, לא ידעתי איך להציל אותה. התחננתי שתעזוב אותו, אך ציפי לא רצתה לשמוע אותי. התפללנו הרבה עליה דניאל ואני והאימהות האחרות, ובנסי ניסים ברחמי השם היא ניתקה את הקשר עם הבחור. כשהשתחררתי מהכלא היא אמרה לי שזה נס שיצאתי מהכלא כי היה סרסור שכמה ימים לפני כן הציע לה עבודה, ואם לא הייתי יוצאת היא הייתה מתחילה לעבוד אתו מתוך דיכאון.

מצב הרוח של ציפי היה קשה מאוד. היא באה לבקר אותי כשהשתחררתי מהכלא והראתה לי איך הזרועות שלה מלאות חתכים של סכין מרוב שלא רצתה לחיות יותר כי לקחו לה את אבא ואימא ואת כל האחים. המשברים שעברה מאז שפירקו את המשפחה, הפכו אותה להיות עצבנית וחסרת מנוחה, כאב לי לראות אותה מחפשת מרגוע לנפשה במסיבות טבע ובסמים. כל לילה עד 2:00 לפנות בוקר הייתי הולכת לחפש את ציפי בפאבים כדי להחזיר אותה הביתה, גם בלילות גשומים. והייתי בוכה ברחובות מדאגה לשלומה.

כשהייתה מגיעה אליי הביתה, היא סיפרה איך העובדות הסוציאליות ניסו להשפיע עליה להתנתק מהמשפחה ולשכנע אותה שהיא מסכנה, שנולדה בכת ושרק להן אכפת ממנה באמת, והייתה גורמת לאזמרה, לאדרת ולשירן לבכות מתוך הזדהות עם הסיפורים שלה, שהזכירו לנו את השיחות עם העובדות הסוציאליות מהמקלטים. היא הייתה כותבת יומנים מלאים במכתבי געגועים לאבא שלה בכלא, באחד המכתבים כתבה לדניאל:

*"אבא אני אוהבת אותק מאוד. מרגש אותי לחשוב עליק, להיזכר בק. אין לי מילים. באמת הלב שלי מתפוצצ. אתה חיים שלי. אין לק מושג כמה אני אוהבת אותק. רק אהבה בליבי ודמעות חמות נשפכות מליבי מגעגועים. כמה אתה חסר לי. אני מנסה לחשוב שאחרי הרבה זמן שלא דברתי איתק, לשחק עם עצמי טלפון ולדבר איתק ואני לפחות מקווה שהלב שלק מקשיב ושלא רק אני מדברת לעצמי.* I love you*. אין, אין מי שאוהב אותק כמוני. בשבילק כל העולם אהפוק".*

ציפי הכירה בחור אתיופי שהיה רגיש וסבלני אליה, הוא היה מבוגר ממנה ב-11 שנה. באחד הימים היא עלתה לבניין גבוה והתחילה לחתוך עמוק בזרועה. הוא עצר אותה ולקח אותה למיון. רק למחרת הם הגיעו אליי הביתה ונבהלתי מהמצב שלה. לקחתי אותה מיד עם ההפניה של המיון לרופא בקופת חולים, ולקנות אנטיביוטיקה. החבר אמר לי שכשהיא שותה היא מדברת על אבא שלה ובוכה שהיא זקוקה לו ומתגעגעת אליו, הוא שיתף אותי שהוא מרגיש שהיא אתו כי היא מוצאת בו את הדמות האבהית שלקחו לה. ציפי נכנסה להיריון. תמכתי בה לכל אורך הדרך. לקחתי אותה לאולטרא סאונד, לבדיקות ולעמותות שיעזרו לה מבחינה כספית למשך שנתיים אחרי הלידה. במהלך ההיריון, אולי בגלל המשברים שלה שגרמו לה לחוסר יציבות, נפרדה מהחבר שלה, והתמודדה לבדה עם הלידה.

היא חיכתה בקוצר רוח להיות בת 18 כדי שתוכל לבקר את אבא בכלא. בדיוק ביום ההולדת היא הגיעה בפעם הראשונה לביקור. היא התרגשה מאוד לראות אותו. בפעם השנייה שהיא באה כבר לא נתנו לה להיכנס.

ציפי כתבה ביומן:

*"אלוקים, תן לי לחלום הלילה שאני מחבקת את אבא, אני מתגעגעת אליו. תלטף אותו מהאהבה שלי. תאמין לי אבא, כל זמן שאני מתדרדרת ונופלת חלישות, זה מההרס של האויבים. אבא, תחבק אותי חזק ואל תעזוב אותי. אני פוחדת לבד. כשאתה לא נמצא הכל חושך ואני כמו פרח בלי שמש ומים. אבא תכניס אותי ללב שלך ותחבק אותי שם. אני בסכנה, רוצים להרוג אותי, אבל אני כבר לא פוחדת כי אתה כבר שומר עלי. אין לי מילים רק תודה ואהבה, ושום דבר לא יפריד בינינו. אם שואלים אותי מה יקר לי מכל וכל זה האהבה שלי אליך".*

יום אחד ציפי התקשרה אליי והזמינה אותי לבית קפה. הסתובבנו במשביר. פתאום היא שאלה אותי: "את עדיין עם אבא?" שאלתי אותה: "מה זה השאלה הזאת?" היא הרגישה לא בנוח ואמרה: "אין לי ברירה, את צריכה לבחור, או שאת אתי או שאת אתו, כי העובדת הסוציאלית בהוסטל הזהירה אותי שאם את בקשר עם אבא ואני אשאר בקשר אתך לא יתנו לי לגדל את התינוק אז תבחרי: זה או אני או אבא!"

גם מצבה של שוש הלך והידרדר. הגעגועים לאבא, הדאגה לאחים שלה, התסכול מהמצב, ההשפלות והביזיונות היומיומיים שספגה היו קשים מנשוא. השבירה מכך שהמצב הקשה לא נגמר ואבא עוד לא חוזר הביתה הייתה כואבת בעצמות שקשה היה לה לסבול. יום אחד גם היא הראתה לי את זרועות הידיים שהיו מלאות בסימנים לניסיונות חיתוך ורידים בעזרת סכין, על הזרוע למעלה היא חרטה את המילה "אבא" במספריים חדות. היא אמרה לי כשכולה נסערת: "קשה לי אימא, אני מתגעגעת לאבא". חיבקתי אותה חזק וניסיתי להרגיע אותה: "עוד הכול יהיה טוב, אבא יחזור ויהיה אתנו כאן". בכינו אחת על כתפי השנייה.

כשהייתי בכלא, הבת הגדולה מארי, סיפרה לי ששוש הגיעה אליה בלילה אחרי שבילתה והשתכרה עם סודנים בתחנה המרכזית בתל אביב, ושעוד מעט יגיעו לקחת אותה למסילה. הייתי בחרדה, לאן המצב עוד עלול להידרדר?!

להפתעתן, הגיעו שוטרים לקחת אותה. שוש הייתה במיטה עם דלקת גרון וארבעים מעלות חום. השוטרים צעקו עליה שתקום ותבוא אתם. הם הפילו אותה לרצפה על הבטן, ישבו על הגב שלה, סגרו את הידיים שלה מאחורי הגב באזיקים. אחד השוטרים נתן מכה עם המרפק שלו בגרון שלה, והיא דיממה. את כל זה הם עשו בבית של אחותה הגדולה, שהייתה חודש אחרי לידה, וזרקו לה: "תגידי תודה שאת לא מקבלת סטירה", או כמו שאחד מהם אמר לשוש אחר כך: "הייתי צריך להעיף לאחותך חמישיה לפרצוף". שוש הייתה נסערת מאוד והתלוננה לפני העובדת הסוציאלית שלה, וזו פנתה אתה למח"ש עם מכתב מפורט המתאר את התעללות השוטרים בה. כשהגעתי לבקר אותה וראיתי את כל הסימנים הכחולים על גופה, נחרדתי. היא סיפרה לי שהשוטרים קראו לה: "זונה של ערבים, מזדיינת עם ערבים, זונה, שרמוטה גדולה, מוצצת כוס, לסבית, שמנה, מכוערת, תרנגולת...", ועוד בלי סוף כינויי גנאי. בנסיעה למסילה הם דפקו לה את הראש בחלון, נתנו לה בעיטות וסחבו אותה בכוח. כשביקשה לשחרר קצת את האזיקים המהודקים, הם הידקו אותם חזק יותר לידיה, וסובבו לה את הידיים עם האזיקים. הרכז במסילה שיצא לפגוש את שוש מספר בדו"ח למח"ש שראה אותה יושבת אזוקה בניידת כאשר אחד השוטרים מחזיק אותה באזיקים ומצמיד את המרפק שלו לגרונה. אפילו מולו התנהגות השוטרים כלפיה הייתה אלימה ותוך שימוש בשפה בוטה ותוקפנית.

אחרי חודש במסילה שוש שוב ברחה. היא הגישה את המכתב הבא לשופט בבית משפט לנוער:

*"עוד חודש אני בת 17. בשלב זה אני נמצאת בבריחה ממעון מסילה כי לא טוב לי שם. הצוות שם מעניש על כל דבר בהחזקה או 'חדר' או 'פסקי זמן' (חדר מבודד) והסברתי להם שזה לא עוזר לי להירגע רק מכעיס אותי וגורם לי להגיע להתנהלויות שעשיתי שם. בהחזקות שלהם הם לא נזהרים, הם מכאיבים בכוונה. תמיד אני יוצאת עם כחולים בכל הגוף וזה לא מפריע להם. אני תמיד שם יוצאת בהרגשה שמחפשים אותי ורוצים שאני אגיע להתנהלות בשביל לעשות לי החזקה. הם היו אומרים לי: "התפקיד שלנו זה לעצבן אותך והתפקיד שלך זה להירגע". ואם הם אומרים שהם באים לעזור*

*לי זה ממש שקר כי תמיד הייתי אומרת להם שיש דרך להסביר לי את הדברים וזה לא בדרכים שלהם. אני מבקשת ממך שתיתן לי להוכיח את עצמי בבית. ללמוד. לא להסתכן, לא לשוטט ברחובות.*

*ודרך אגב, אני צריכה לשוטט ברחובות בגלל הרווחה והמשטרה ומשם זה לוקח אותי למקומות מסוכנים. אם יתנו לי לחיות בבית של אמא שלי זה לא יקרה.*

*כל מה שעשיתי היה או מהגנה עצמית או מאי הסכמה על זה שאומרים לי שעברתי התעללות במשפחה שזה שקר שבגללו החיים שלי נהרסים".*

*תודה רבה - שוש.*

באחת הפעמים שפגשתי את שוש היא שאלה על אח שלה עקיבא. סיפרתי לה שנותנים לו כדורים פסיכיאטריים. היא סיפרה לי שהייתה תקופה שהעובדת הסוציאלית לקחה אותה לפסיכיאטר, וגם לה נתנו כדורים פסיכיאטריים. היא אמרה שההשפעה של הכדורים כל כך הרסנית שאם היו אומרים לה באותו הזמן לאכול עץ היא הייתה עושה את זה.

כששמעה שבכתב האישום בשני סעיפים מאשימים את אבא שפגע בה, היא הזדעזעה, והחליטה לברוח ממסילה כי רצתה בכל כוחה לצעוק את האמת בבית המשפט. היא ידעה שהמשטרה תחפש אותה ושיעשו הכול כדי למנוע ממנה לבוא להעיד, היא גם ידעה שיש להם את הכלים להפעיל עליה לחץ כדי שלא תעיד, לכן הייתה משוטטת מעיר לעיר כדי שלא יתפסו אותה, והייתה ישנה בחדרי מדרגות. היא לא יכלה להיות אצלי כי פחדה שיתפסו אותה. אחרי שעברה ימים קשים ומרים ברחובות, בלי מקלחת, בלי בגדים להחלפה וכמעט בלי אוכל, היא הצליחה סוף סוף להגיע לבית המשפט ולהעיד לטובת אביה. בבית המשפט היא אמרה לשופטים: "מאוד חשוב שכולם ישמעו את האמת שאבא שלי חף מפשע, אבא שלי לא עשה שום רע לאף אחד וכל מה שמאשימים אותו זה שקר גמור. הבית היה מלא אהבה ושמחה ואבא תמיד היה שם בשביל כולם. זה עוול נורא מה שהמדינה עשתה לאבא שלי ולמשפחה שלי". במסדרון של בית המשפט אחרי העדות היא צעקה לדניאל שהיא אוהבת אותו ושיהיה חזק: "אנחנו לא נוותר, אנחנו ננצח!

השופטים התעלמו מכל מה שאמרה והרשיעו את דניאל גם בשני הסעיפים המתארים התעללות בה על אף שלא היו להם שום הוכחות לכך, ועל אף שהיא עצמה הגיעה במיוחד לבית המשפט להעיד שזה אף פעם לא היה!

כששוש שמעה שבהכרעת הדין השופטים הרשיעו את אביה ב-18 סעיפים, שמתוכם שני סעיפים הם בקשר אליה, היא הייתה ממש נסערת. היא החליטה להצטלם יחד אתנו הנשים, לערוץ 2 ולהודיע על השקר הנבזי של הכרעת הדין בתקשורת. כשרואיינה היא דיברה על העוול ועל עיוות הדין, ועל התנהגות השוטרים ועל השקר של השופטים. אך ערוץ 2 החליטו לא לשדר את הריאיון אתה בתוך הכתבה, ובמקום ערכו כתבה משמיצה. שוש הייתה במשבר גדול. היא הכינה סרטון שבו היא אומרת: "בגלל שלאבא שלי היו כמה נשים והיו לנו כמה בתים קינאו בנו, גם אני הייתי מקנאה, היו לנו חיים הכי טובים שיש, הכי כיפיים...".

חודש לאחר מכן השופטים גזרו על דניאל 26 שנה. מאז שוש החלה להשתתף בטיפולים פסיכולוגיים מטעם הרווחה וכתוצאה מכך ניתקה גם היא את הקשר אתי. יום אחד התקשרה ואמרה: "אימא, את צריכה להבין, אם אדם מקבל 26 שנה, בטוח שיש לזה סיבה. לא יכול להיות שהשופטים טועים. שכל המדינה טועה".

---

בכלא, אפילו לרוצחות נותנים פעם בחודש ביקור ילדים. העובדות הסוציאליות שאמורות היו להביא לי את הבנות הקטנות, קטי, מוריאל ובלה, לא אפשרו לי לראות אותן, אפילו שהבנות התחננו לראות אותי. גם האחראיות של השב"ס לא הבינו למה מונעים ממני ביקורים. רק אחרי חמישה חודשים אישרו באופן חד-פעמי ביקור אחד ויחידי שלהן אצלי, ויותר לא ראיתי אותן בכל אותה שנה של מאסר. גם כשיצאתי מהכלא נתנו לי לחכות ארבעה חודשים עד שקיבלתי אישור לבקר אותן בפיקוח במרכז קשר, פעם בשבועיים לשעה וחצי בלבד. לפני כל ביקור הייתי צריכה לשוחח עם שני פסיכולוגים קליניים במשך שעה ולאחר מכן שתי עובדות סוציאליות הביאו אותן לפגישה ונשארו לפקח עלינו יחד עם הפסיכולוגים הקליניים. שיחה טלפונית של מקסימום עשרים דקות עם כל אחת מהן התקיימה רק פעם בשבוע, כשהטלפון אצלן על רמקול, ועובדת סוציאלית משגיחה על השיחה. בפגישות ובשיחות הטלפוניות עם

הילדים אסרו עלינו לדבר על אבא ועל המשפחה וכל פעם שחרגנו מהכללים, העובדות הסוציאליות ניתקו את השיחה ואיימו לבטל את הפגישה הבאה. על הבנות הקטנות שלי הפעילו מניפולציות פסיכולוגיות, ביזו והשפילו אותן, וגרמו להן להתבייש במשפחה, הסבירו להן שהמצב בלי תקווה, והן לא תראינה את אבא שלהן לפחות עשרים שנה, ושהדרך היחידה להתחיל חיים חדשים זה לתת אמון במערכת. עם הזמן הבנות הבינו שאם לא ידברו על אבא יקבלו תשומת לב ומתנות מהצוות של הפנימייה, ולאט לאט, ככל שהזמן עבר, הן הפסיקו לשאול אותי מה שלום אבא.

העונשים שהבנות מקבלות בפנימיות של הרווחה הם בלתי נסבלים. שלושת הבנות הקטנות שלי היו סגורות בחדר שלושה ימים, בלי ללכת ללימודים, ורק בליווי מדריכה יכלו לצאת לשירותים. אני לא מבינה איפה הצדק במדינה שלנו, כשאנחנו שלחנו ילד להירגע בחדר כעונש חינוכי, הרשיעו את דניאל באישום שנקרא "כליאת שווא", וכשעובדות סוציאליות כולאות למשך שלושה ימים את הבנות שלי, כל אחת בחדר נפרד, למה אותן לא סוגרים בכלא על כליאת שווא?

---

יהונתן, שאסרו עליו לדבר עם דניאל בטלפון, רצה לשלוח לו מתנות ואהבה. הוא היה משקיע ומכין ציורים יפים, או מעתיק מציירים גדולים ורושם עליהם הקדשה לדניאל ומנסה, בלי שהעובדת הסוציאלית תראה, להעביר אותם לקארי כדי שתעביר אותם לאבא בכלא. באחד הפעמים כשהוא שאל: "מה אבא אמר על הציור?" הוא היה שבור מכך שקארי בישרה לו שהסוהרת לקחה ממנה את הציור שהוא הכין לאבא, וקרעה אותו מול עיניה של קארי לחתיכות קטנות.

---

ב-5.7.11, ביום שלאחר הפירוק של המשפחה על ידי המשטרה, הבנים הגדולים שלי: זלמן (22), בועז (21) וגיא-נועם (18); הבת הגדולה של קארי – צילה (26) והבן של קארי – יאן (24), מצאו את עצמם בלי בית. אבא במעצר, אני וכל הנשים במקלט לנשים מוכות כחלופת מעצר, ואת האחים הקטנים פיזרו בפנימיות של הרווחה. תקופה ארוכה המשטרה אסרה עליהם להיכנס לבתים שבהם גרנו. הם היו בהלם מהמצב, והיו בטוחים שבכל רגע המשטרה תבין שעשתה טעות, ישחררו את אבא שלהם והמשפחה תחזור לחיות ביחד. כל שעה שזה עוד לא קרה הייתה קשה מנשוא. הדאגה לאבא שלהם כרסמה בלבם ולא נתנה להם מנוחה. לפתע כל האחריות לגורל המשפחה ולעתידה נפלה על הכתפיים הצעירות שלהם. כשחיכו לאבא מחוץ לכותלי בית המשפט היו מדברים עם העיתונאים ואפשר לראות ולשמוע אותם מדברים בחדשות ומנסים לחזק את דניאל במסדרונות של בית המשפט וקוראים לעברו: "אבא תהיה חזק אנחנו ננצח, אוהבים אותך אבא".

בועז אמר לכתבים: "קודם כול אבא הוא הבן אדם הכי פשוט שיש. כל העניין הזה של הרב של המנהיג זה בדיוק ההפך, זה פשוט לא הבן אדם" ; על השאלה: "הוא לא היה מעניש אתכם?" בועז ענה: "אני לא מבין, אני כבר לא אתפלא אם תשאלו אותי אם רצחתי! זה כל כך לא נעים כל השאלות האלה, זה דברים שהומצאו מאיפה שהוא ואנחנו צריכים לבוא ולהתעמת אם רצחנו או לא רצחנו?! הדברים האלה לא היו ולא נבראו!".

גיא-נועם מתפרץ לדבריו ואומר לכתבים: "שקרים! כזבים שלא היו" [...] "אם האנשים היו יודעים באמת איך היינו חיים, כולם היו רוצים לחיות כמונו".

זלמן אמר לכתבים: "נוח להלביש עלינו דברים, אנחנו מעט שונים מהנורמה הציבורית הישראלית ולכן היה נוח מאוד להלביש עלינו דברים שלא היו ולא נבראו... אלו טענות שקר... וגם לא יודעים באמת איך אנחנו חיים. כל כך כיף לנו. הם חושבים שבטח הוא שולט עלינו. אולי אני מכושף גם?!...".

צילה אמרה לכתבים: "העדות הכי יפה שהייתה יכולה להיות לכולכם זה שתלכו לילדים ותשאלו מה יש להם על הלב, תראו איך הם מדברים, איך הם נראים, מה יש להם להגיד... ובקשר לאבא, אם תסתכלו בעיניים שלו תגידו אם באמת... אם זה יכול להיות שבן אדם כזה עושה דברים כמו שמספרים עליו!"

אחד הילדים הוסיף: "אני גדלתי בהתחלה עם אימא אחת ובשלב מסוים זה עבר לכמה אימהות. לי היה טוב עם זה... לא הייתה שום התעללות...".

מארי אמרה לכתב: "אבא לא התעלל בנשים ובילדים שנולדו להם, הוא אוהב אותם ומביא להם אהבה. לכל בן אדם חילוני יש פי כמה נשים! אם אישה העידה נגד זו עדות שקר, הפחידו אותה כדי שתדבר".

("להאשים גם את הנשים", YNET; "שכניו של מנהיג הכת", וואלה חדשות; "ביתו של מנהיג הכת – לא הייתה שום התעללות", נענע10).

הילדים גם פנו לעיתונים שונים על מנת לפרסם כתבות ולהודיע על העוול ועל השקר הנורא שנאמר על המשפחה שלנו. הם התרוצצו בין משרדי עו"ד כדי לחפש מי ייצג את אבא שלהם בצורה הטובה ביותר. המחירים שדרשו עורכי הדין עבור ייצוג היו מאות אלפי שקלים. הלחץ היה בלתי נסבל. הם ניסו לגייס כספים מבני משפחה בכל הארץ כדי לשלם לעו"ד, חיפשו מקום למעצר בית לדניאל למקרה שבית המשפט יסכים לחלופת מעצר ודאגו לכל אחד מבני המשפחה. הם כל היום נסעו ממקום למקום, וכשהיו מתמוטטים מעייפות, היו נרדמים בתוך הרכב בצדי הכביש. הם רצו בכל נפשם ומאודם להציל את המצב ולהחזיר את אבא הביתה. בהתחלה לא היה לי קשר אתם כי הייתי במקלט. כשראיתי אותם לראשונה ראיתי את האש בעיניים שלהם. הם היו חדורי מוטיבציה ואמונה שיצליחו במשימה. כשראו שהעו"ד שייצג את דניאל בתקופת הארכת המעצרים לא הצליח להשיג עבורו מעצר בית ולא עשה את עבודתו כראוי, הם חיפשו מיד עו"ד שייצג אותו, ואתו הם היו בקשר יומיומי ודאגו להעביר לו כל אינפורמציה שיכולה לעזור לשחרר את דניאל. הם היו מחזקים את אבא בשיחות הטלפון באהבה, וגיא-נועם היה לומד אתו מדי יום בחברותא בטלפון. הם היו מסיעים את אימא של דניאל לכלא לבקר אותו, והיו מגיעים גם הם באופן קבוע לביקורים. הם היו אומרים לי שהם יהפכו את העולם בשביל להוציא את אבא שלהם מהכלא. הם לא נרגעו בשל העובדה שהמשטרה פוגעת באבא ומשפיעה על עדים לשקר, ועדיין היו מזועזעים מהתנהגות השוטרים כלפיהם בחקירות. הם נלחמו בשיניים, ימים ולילות.

כל ארבעת עדי התביעה יצרו אתם קשר בדרכים שונות וביקשו מהם עזרה להיחלץ מהאיומים של חוקרי המשטרה שהפעילו נגדם אולטימטום. על עדת התביעה המרכזית, עליזה, איימו שאם לא תעיד נגד דניאל ייקחו לה את הבת לאימוץ בחו"ל, והיא לא תראה אותה יותר; על אחרים איימו שאם לא יאשימו את דניאל, יהיו הם במעצר לכמה שנים טובות. עדי התביעה היו מבוהלים וביקשו מהבנים הגדולים עזרה כדי לצאת מהמצב שנקלעו אליו נגד רצונם. אחת מעדי התביעה – תמנע, ביקשה עזרה לטוס לחו"ל ולהיעלם עד אחרי המשפט. סמי היה כל הזמן בורח מהפנימייה שאליה שלחו אותו, מחפש את האחים שלו, ומתחנן אליהם שימצאו לו מקום להיות בו כדי שהשוטרים לא ימצאו אותו. עדת התביעה אנסטסיה, אחרי חודשים רבים ששילמו עבורה שכר דירה, ביקשה שהם ישכרו לה ולבעלה דירה במקום רחוק, שלא ידעו איפה היא ושלא תצטרך לבוא להעיד. במשך חמישה חודשים אחרי המעצר של דניאל עליזה הייתה בקשר עם הילדים, מחפשת פתרונות למצב ומבקשת מהם לחשוב על דרך כדי שתוכל להיות עם הבת שלה, ולא תיאלץ להעיד נגדו. היא גם ביקשה מהם עזרה כספית, כדי שלא תהיה תלויה בחסדי החוקרים של המשטרה, והציעה שאולי הפתרון הטוב ביותר יהיה אם ימצאו לה מקום שתוכל להיעלם מעיניהם המאיימות של החוקרים עד אחרי המשפט. הבנים והבנות הגדולים שלי היו אובדי עצות וחיפשו מה הדרך הטובה ביותר לשנות את המצב כך שיהיה טוב לכולם ושהם יצליחו להוציא את דניאל מהכלא.

יום אחד הם הגיעו לעו"ד בצפון הארץ. הוא גבה מהם **60,000** ₪ תמורת עצה גרועה שייעץ להם, שסיבכה אותם וגרמה לכל ההידרדרות של המצב שלהם לאחר מכן.

כיוון שהבנים שלי ידעו שכל עדי התביעה לא רוצים להעיד נגד דניאל ומשוועים לעזרה, אותו עוה"ד הציע שישכרו מקום, יאבזרו אותו ויציידו אותו במזון ושאר מצרכים נחוצים שיספיקו לשנה, וכך יעזרו לכל עדי התביעה להיעלם מהמשטרה עד שיעבור זמן המשפט. הוא הסביר להם שזו דרך מאוד "בטוחה" להצליח להציל את אבא שלהם, ושרק כך יש סיכוי שאבא ישתחרר באופן מידי. הוא גם הדריך אותם בכל הפעולות שעליהם לעשות. הבנים שלי, מרוב רצון להציל את המצב החליטו שזה מה שהם יעשו, בפרט שעדי התביעה לחצו עליהם למצוא מהר פתרון עבורם. הם הלוו כספים, שכרו וילה גדולה ביישוב קרוב לטבריה כדי שהעדים יוכלו להתחבא שם מהמשטרה עד אחרי המשפט. הווילה הכילה חדרי אירוח, ובכל חדר יש ג'קוזי וטלוויזיה. הם דאגו למלא את הבית בכל טוב, בשפע של אוכל: שני מקררים תעשייתיים מלאי בשר, כמויות אדירות של חמאה, שתי חביות של גרעינים, מחסן מזון של קופסאות שימורים, חלב עמיד שמספיק לשנה, קמח ושמן לאפיית לחם, בקבוקים גדולים של תרכיז מיץ פטל, בגדים, תרופות, חומרי ניקוי ועוד. הם גם קנו תרנגולות שיטילו ביצים, ושקים של אוכל לתרנגולות – דוחן, בכמות שתספיק לשנה. על מנת שהעדים ירגישו טוב בבית הם דאגו עבורם למסך פלזמה עם חיבור לכבלים, לכמות גדולה של ספרים בנושאים שונים, מילאו ארון בכמויות אדירות של סיגריות מהסוג שהם ידעו שהעדים מעשנים, אפילו דאגו

לחדר כושר מאובזר בהליכון, במשקולות ובמכשיר לכפיפות בטן. הם שכרו שולחן סנוקר, קנו משחקים שונים. הציבו בכניסה כלב רועה גרמני לשמירה. וכל זה בסודיות גמורה, וכמובן בלי לשתף בזה את אבא שלהם, כי ידעו שכל השיחות לכלא מוקלטות, והם לא רצו לסכן את התכנית שתלו בה הרבה תקוות.

אחד העדים שהפך לעד תביעה כתוצאה מהלחץ האדיר שהפעילה עליו המשטרה הוא סמי בן ה-16, הבן של קארי. סמי חי בפחד ובטראומה מהשוטרים, וסיפר לבנים איך התנהגו אליו בחדרי החקירות, ואיך איימו עליו כדי שישקר, והחתימו אותו על עשרות דפי חקירה שלא ידע מה כתוב בהם. עם הזמן הבנים סמכו עליו, האמינו ברצון שלו לעזור להם ושיתפו אותו בתכנית ההצלה שלהם. הם הביאו אותו לבית ששכרו וגילו לו את כל התכנית שלהם. יום אחד סמי ביקש מבועז סיגריה, ובועז לא רצה להביא לו, סמי התעצבן ואיים שעכשיו הוא יספר למשטרה על כל מה שתכננו.

למחרת ב-31.1.12 המשטרה עצרה באופן מפתיע את הבנים ואותי. בחקירות המשטרה סמי סיפר לשוטרים על הבית שהבנים שכרו וכולנו נדהמנו לגלות שכתב האישום שהוגש נגד הבנים היה על "חטיפת עדים", כשבאמת אף פעם לא דובר על חטיפה ולא בוצעה שום חטיפה. להפך, העדים ביקשו עזרה והתכנית אפילו לא הצליחה לצאת מהכוח לפועל!

נגד האחים הגדולים של סמי, צילה ויאן, הילדים של קארי מנישואים קודמים, שפעלו יחד עם הבנים שלי כדי להציל את המצב וגם נגד קארי לא ננקטו שום הליכים והם לא ישבו בכלא. רק מאוחר יותר הבנו שאנסטסיה הבת שלה שהפכה להיות אחת מעדי התביעה, השיגה עבור כל בני משפחתה חסינות בתמורה להפללת דניאל. יש הקלטה של אנסטסיה שמספרת שהיא הלכה לחוקר אשר לזמי לבכות לו שלא יפגע באימא שלה ובאחים שלה, כי אם הוא יסגור אותם בכלא היא לא תעיד נגד דניאל...

עליזה התגלתה כנוכלת. סחטה את הילדים בכספים וביקשה מהם עזרה בלי סוף ואמרה שאם לא תקבל מהם עזרה היא תלך לקבל עזרה מהשוטרים שהבטיחו לה כספים. היא גרמה לילדים להתרוצץ כמו משוגעים כדי לספק לה את כל מה שביקשה, ובכל זאת, בכתב האישום התברר שהיא פנתה למשטרה בתלונה נגדם ונגדנו הנשים, וטענה שהם שיחדו אותה כדי שלא תעיד נגד דניאל, וגרמה למעצרם ולמעצר שלנו הנשים.

כך קרה ששבעה חודשים לאחר המעצר של דניאל, כשהמשטרה עצרה את זלמן, בועז וגיא-נועם, הם עברו שוב חקירות מתישות שבמהלכן הציעו להם השוטרים שאם הם לא רוצים להיות מואשמים בחטיפה ובהטרדת עד ובהאשמות נוספות, עליהם להאשים את אבא שלהם. הבנים שלי היו חזקים בדעתם לא להיכנע לפיתויים של השוטרים. זלמן היה בהתחלה בכלא ואחר כך עבר שנה שלמה במעצר בית ובעבודות שירות, ובכל התקופה הזו ניסו נציגי הפרקליטות לשבור אותו שיאמר שהוא קרבן של אבא שלו, אך הוא היה חזק מול כולם, והגיע להעיד בבית המשפט לטובת דניאל. לבסוף אחרי שנה וחצי של מלחמה חזקה נגד המערכת, הוא ואשתו צילה נאלצו להשתתף כל שבוע בשיחה עם פסיכולוג קליני ועם עובדות סוציאליות שהסבירו להם בכל שיחה שהם צריכים להיכנע למערכת ואיימו עליהם שאם ימשיכו לשמור על קשר עם המשפחה, ייקחו להם את הילדים. מאז הם ניתקו אתי את הקשר לגמרי. דרך אגב, אותו תהליך עבר גם על יאן ומארי, מאז שאנשי הרווחה איימו עליהם שהם לא ראויים לגדל את הילדים שלהם אם הם קשורים ל"כת של אמבש", גם הם ניתקו את הקשר אתי.

את בועז כלאו לשנה בכלא באר שבע, על מנת להפעיל עליו לחץ. גם הוא החזיק מעמד הרבה זמן, אך כשיצא מהכלא לא הכרתי אותו. הוא גזר את הפאות והוריד את הכיפה וטס להודו.

את גיא-נועם לקחו באזיקים לחקירות קשות יום אחרי יום ואיימו עליו: "או שאתה מאשים או שאתה נאשם". הוא שאל את החוקרים: "כל יום אתם תביאו אותי עם אזיקים לחקירה?" החוקרים ענו לו: "אנחנו יותר חזקים ממך ובסוף נשבור אותך, אבל אם אתה מתחיל לשתף פעולה אתה לא תהיה צריך לחזור יותר לפה". אחרי תקופה שישב בכלא הוא הועבר למעצר בית אצל משפחה של פסיכולוגים. בשלב מסוים הוא בלע עשרה כדורים פסיכיאטריים במטרה להתאבד. אני לא ידעתי כשזה קרה. הייתי בכלא במשך כל שנת 2012, ואף אחד לא עדכן אותי מה קורה עם גיא-נועם. דאגתי לו מאוד. המרכז הישראלי לנפגעי כתות ניצל את מצבו הנפשי המעורער בלי אבא, בלי אימא, בלי אחים ובלי כסף, וכשניצל מניסיון ההתאבדות, הסבירו לו בשיחות ובמפגשים שהוא גדל בכת, והבטיחו לו כספים ותמיכה בתמורה לכך שידבר בטלוויזיה ובעיתונות נגד אבא שלו. הם שילמו לו על לימודים במכינה לבגרות באוניברסיטה בירושלים, וגרמו לו להרגיש שהוא יכול לסמוך עליהם. הוא טופל גם כן בכדורים פסיכיאטריים, עד שיום אחד, לאחר גזר הדין של דניאל, הודיעו לי שגיא-נועם הולך לדבר בתקשורת נגד אבא שלו. לא האמנתי למשמע אוזניי. בתכנית הטלוויזיה שבה השתתף והתראיין, הרגשתי שהיה לי הרבה יותר קל אם הוא היה מגיע עם אקדח ויורה בי למוות. כל מילה שלו בתכנית גרמה לי עינויים וייסורים קשים ומרים מגיהינום.

הבן שילדתי במטרה שיפיץ ויפרסם את שם הצדיק בעולם, משקר בפרהסיה ומוציא שם רע על אבא שלו, תוך שהוא מפיץ את "החברה נגד כתות" שמטרתה לקבור את אביו חי.

גם נדהמתי לשמוע אותו אומר בתכנית שאבא גונב לו את אימא. מאז ומתמיד השקענו בו המון תשומת לב ואהבה, וגם כשיצאתי מהכלא דאגתי לו מאוד והייתי אתו בקשר טלפוני יומיומי. הייתי מדברת אתו שעות, הולכת אתו לבית קפה, רואה אתו סרט, הייתי מכבדת מאוד את החברה שלו ומארחת אותה אצלי. אבא שלו תמיד דאג לו וטיפל בו במסירות מאז שהיה קטן, איך זה ייתכן? הוא קיבל באולפן הקלטה חדר פרטי לאימונים בתופים מקצועיים הטובים ביותר שיש, ומערכת נוספת של תופים אלקטרוניים. הסאונדמן שהיה מלמד את הבנים ונמצא כל יום אתם אמר שהשקעה כמו שהשקיעו בגיא-נועם במוזיקה מגיל כל כך צעיר, הוא לא ראה בשום מקום.

כחודש אחרי התכנית, גם גיא-נועם, כמו כולם, התקשר אליי ואמר לי: "אימא, את צריכה לבחור, זה או אני או אבא!"

אימא של דניאל, הצליחה להימלט מזוועות השואה בבולגריה כי התחבאה עם כל משפחתה מאחורי ארון בביתו של רופא בולגרי, אבל מהשואה שעשתה מדינת ישראל לבן שלה ולכל המשפחה שלה, היא לא הצליחה לשרוד. היא הלכה לבית עולמה בצער גדול, אחרי ארבע שנים שדניאל היה במעצר, לאחר שאיבדה את בעלה ואת בתה היחידה. היא לא זכתה לראות את הבן שלה משתחרר מהכלא.

כשהייתה נזכרת בתקופה שהילדים היו מגיעים אליה לבקש כספים בשביל המאבק לשחרורו של דניאל, הייתה מספרת בהתפעלות על המרץ, על ההתלהבות ועל האמונה החזקה שהייתה להם שיצליחו להחזיר את אבא שלהם הביתה. היה לה קשה מאוד לראות את ההידרדרות שלהם אחרי שהיו בכלא, והיו לה רצונות חזקים שהאהבה שיש להם בלב תנצח. היא הייתה בהלם וכאב לה מאוד שהם הפסיקו לבוא לבקר אותה ולהתעניין בשלומה. הם התקשרו אליה פעם בכמה חודשים. היא לא הבינה איך הם השלימו עם זה שאבא שלהם בכלא, שהם זנחו את אימא שלהם לאנחות, והפכו להיות החברים הכי טובים של סמי, אותו ילד שאמם גידלה מאז שהיה בן שנתיים, והפך לעד תביעה שהכניס אותם ואת אבא שלהם לבית האסורים.

אני זועקת בלב כואב של אימא, וצורחת עד לב השמיים, ממררת בבכי על העוול הנורא ואיום, הרצח לאור יום שמבצעת המדינה שלנו. הילדים שלי היו חזקים מול המערכת המקיאוולית לפחות במשך שנה וחצי מהזמן שפירקו את המשפחה. המערכת (חוקרים, משטרה, עובדות סוציאליות, פקידות סעד, מדריכים, מנהלים בפנימיות, התקשורת, פסיכולוגים קליניים, פסיכיאטרים...) נתנה להם להבין היטב שהיא יותר חזקה מהם. המערכת פעלה באיומים חזקים נגד כל אחד ואחד על אבדן הדבר שהכי יקר לו, עד שהצליחה לגרום לכל אחד מהם להשתעבד למדיניות שלה.

איך ייתכן שלקחו ילדים תמימים ואהובים, ובצורה שיטתית לימדו אותם לשנוא את הוריהם ולהתבייש במשפחתם? הילדים לאט לאט התייאשו מהתפילה, וזרקו את הכיפה והפאות. סיפורים שמזכירים את סיפורי קרבנות האינקוויזיציה הקתולית בספרד, שגרמו לילדים יהודים להוציא להורג את הוריהם על עלילות דם. המשטר ידע להמריד ילדים כנגד הוריהם עד כדי כך שהילדים האמינו שזו מצווה לרדוף ולהרוג את ההורים שלא רצו להמיר את דתם.

בכל זאת אני מודה להשם שהם בריאים. הם הסתדרו מבחינה כלכלית, פתחו כל אחד עסק משגשג ומצליח משלו, למשל, מכון כושר, חברת מזגנים, חברת הפקות אירועים, קבלני בניין, קנו מכוניות מפוארות ובנו לעצמם כלים להישרדות.

אני לא מוותרת, לא על בעלי ולא על אף אחד מהילדים שלי, ואני מקווה שגם הילדים יפסיקו לפחד ממה שחושבים האנשים, ושיהיה להם את האומץ לבחור באבא שלהם ובי.

## הסיפור האישי שלי – שירן

אם הייתם שומעים סיפור על נשים שלא וויתרו על האהבה שלהם,

אפילו לא כשנעצרו על ידי משטרת ישראל שלקחה מהן כל מה שהיה אפשר לקחת,

אפילו שחטפו מכות, קללות והשפלות בחדרי חקירות כשלא שיתפו פעולה עם התכנית הזדונית לכלוא עד מוות את האדם שהן אוהבות, על מעשים שהן יודעות ועדות שלא ביצע!

אפילו כשהציעה להן המשטרה שבתמורה לשיתוף פעולה כעדות שקר בזאת העלילה, יקבלו הטבות רבות מהרשויות במדינה ויזכו למקלט מדיני, לחיסיון ולהגנה, למגורים ולטובות הנאה, לתמיכה מהרשויות ולהכרה כ"נפגעות". הכרה שתעניק להן "כל מה שהן צריכות"; ואם ימשיכו בעקשנותן, ולא יסכימו לשתף פעולה באחת מהדרכים שלעיל, יצטערו על כך שנים רבות מאחורי סורג ובריח, ויבכו על ילדיהם שיעברו למשמורת המדינה, ולא בטוח בכלל שיזכו לראותם עוד.

במשטרה היו בטוחים (כנראה לאור הצלחות בשחיתויות קודמות...) שיצליחו לסחוט מהן חתימה או הודאה, וכך בקלות יתרה יכריזו בכותרות, שכל סיפורי הזוועות, שהם פיתחו ללא לאות, הם אמת לאמתה, וכך לא תתגלה התרמית שמוטטה והמיתה בדם קר משפחה של 25 נפשות.

מיד פרסמו בכל כלי התקשורת שנתפס "הפושע של המדינה"; "שדבר כזה לא ראו במשטרה זה שלושים שנה"; "ראש כת סדיסטית שמעביד בפרך את בני ביתו!"

אבל מי מבני ביתו אמר שכן?! מה זה משנה?! מגישים כתב אישום רשום וחתום! מארגנים מסיבת עיתונאים עם הראשים המרכזיים; ברווחה, במשטרה, רות מטות פקידת הסעד שבלי להניד עפעף מצהירה בביטחון ובגאון שנציגי הרווחה נפגשו עם כל אחת מהנשים והילדים ושמעו את התלונות, כשבפועל יש הוכחות על כך שמעולם לא נפגשו, לא עם הנשים ולא עם הילדים, וכך במהרה מציגים בגאווה ליושבי הכורסה שמול הקופסה תיק מופלץ ארוז כמפץ!

בלי לבדוק עובדות בסיסיות, ובמכוון, לא נבדק שום דבר ולא הביאו ממצאים מלבד אלו המומצאים מהזירה השזורה...

מהסיבה הברורה שאז היה מתגלה; ש"לא דובים ולא יער", אלא רק עלילות חסרות שחר, והעולם היה מבין שבישראל המשטרה אינה ישרה, והיו מוכרחים לבצע שינויים דרסטיים לאור תאוות הבצע שהקפיצה את המשטרה למבצע הפשע!

מאחר שהנשים מסיפור האהבה הזה סירבו בתוקף לכל ההצעות המגונות של המשטרה, הן נשלחו מידית לחלופת מעצר במקלטים לנשים מוכות בכפייה ובהפרדה, כל אישה במקלט בעיר אחרת לחודשים ארוכים, הן ספגו את המכה הכואבת להיות תחת ההגדרה של "אישה מוכה", בעוד המכות היחידות הן המכות הטריות מחדרי החקירות בידי שוטרות אכזריות (הסיפור המלא בהמשך תחת הכותרת "אישה מוכה").

כל זאת ועוד, לאור המצלמות הנסתרות, שעל פי חוק חייבות להקליט ולתעד את כל מהלך החקירה, מה שלא נעשה במקרה שלפנינו.

ומה הסיבה? רפ"ק אשר לזמי, ראש צוות החקירה, נאלץ להודות, ובלי בושה, מול חבר השופטים ב"משפט הזוטא", שאכן נתן הוראה מפורשת לא לתעד התנהלויות מכוונות בחקירה. במקרה או שלא, בדיוק בנקודות שבהם הפכו אנשי משפחה אוהבים לעדי תביעה מפוחדים. כשנשאל על ידי הסנגור "אתה יכול להסביר לנו?" ענה השוטר לזמי: "אין לי תשובה באמת בדוקה למה, מה עמד לנגד עיניי באותו רגע, אני לא יודע...יש אמרה כתובה". הסנגור: "אבל העד אמר תיעוד מאוד חשוב, כי לפעמים ההודעות יכולות להיות ערוכות מחוכמות לכן חשוב לראות את התיעוד, נכון?" השוטר לזמי: "נכון". הסנגור: "למה לא מצלמים?" השוטר לזמי: "א' אין חובה". הסנגור: "אין חובה? למה אין חובה?" השוטר לזמי: "חקירות של עדים אני לא חייב לצלם".

כך ללא מאמץ הפכו השוטרים-חוקרי הימ"ר את כל זיהום העדויות ושיבושי החקירה החמורים להתוויית דרך קלה לשופטים.

התלונות שהוגשו למח״ש על האלימות המינית והמילולית שעברו בני המשפחה בחודשים הארוכים של חקירות המשטרה, נדחו על הסף בתואנת ״חוסר עניין לציבור״.

כשהסתיימו חודשי החקירות שממילא היו מיותרים כיוון שכתב האישום הוגש עוד הרבה לפני כן, שוחררו הנשים מהמקלטים. ותוך זמן קצר הוזעקו שוב לחדרי החקירות כדי לברר אם הן עדיין לא מוכנות לוותר על אהבת חייהן; אם כל האיומים והייסורים שעברו במשטרה והשיחות עם העובדות הסוציאליות שהפחידו אותן שלא יקבלו את ילדיהן בחזרה הצליחו להשפיע עליהן ״להתפכח״ ולהבין שבמצבן הנוכחי רצוי וכדאי להן לשתף פעולה עם הגורמים השולטים במדינה, ואם לא ישתפו פעולה יימחצו כמו מקק תחת הסוליה העבה של המגפיים האימתניים של המערכת הכבדה.

בבידוד כמעט מוחלט, בתחושת ניכור ותחת איומים בלתי פוסקים התחזקו הנשים באמונה שהאמת והאהבה מוכרחות לנצח! על זה נזרקו ל-11 חודשים בבית סוהר. על מה? ובעצם, מה זה משנה?! בהאשמות חמורות על מעשים אבסורדיים שלא ביצעו! אחרי כמה דיונים מתסכלים, שבהם לא נתנו להן לדבר ולהביע את עמדתן, טענה התביעה טענה הפוכה: הן ללא ספק ״שטופות מוח, קרבנות״.

עד למועד שמיעת העדים – ההוכחות – אילנה כמעט נרצחה על ידי אחת האסירות, אזמרה חטפה צעקות ורדיפה מבוקר עד לילה מאסירה אחרת שדקרה אדם למוות, ואדרת הייתה בתא עם אישה שלא יכלה לסבול את רחש הדף שהופכת אדרת ב״ליקוטי תפילות״.

עדי התביעה נבראו מאלה שבחרו לקבל את טובות ההנאה מהמשטרה כדי להגן על עצמם, לאחר שנאמר להם (על ידי חוקרי המשטרה כמובן) שאם לא ישתפו פעולה לסגירתו הנצחית של האדם שסומן כמטרה (דניאל – הנאשם) בכך ש״יאשרו״ את הסיפורים שמכתיבים להם בחדרי החקירות, ישבו בכלא במקומו, ויכתבו להם כתבי אישום חמורים שיסתמו להם לנצח את החיים. כל זאת ועוד מתועד בדפי החקירות והפרוטוקולים.

עורכי הדין שמונו לייצג את הנשים מטעם הסנגוריה הציבורית נדהמו לגלות שכל אחד מעדי התביעה מגבב גרסה שונה מחברו, מלאה בסתירות! בית המשפט היה נבוך לשמוע את עדי התביעה מעידים עדות שקר בצורה בוטה נגד הנשים, ושום סעיף לא נשאר עומד כשעד אחד מעיד על דבר שכביכול קרה בשנה אחת, ועד שני מעיד שהדבר היה בשנה רחוקה אחרת, ועד שלישי נותן מיקום של עיר שונה, ועד רביעי שכח מה הפרקליט לימד אותו להגיד ובאיזה טון, וגרסתו לגמרי תלושה, והפרטים שונים וכן הנפשות שבסיפורים... ובקיצור... באותו יום שיחררו את הנשים.

אבל על האיש שהן אוהבות, עדות ויודעות עד כמה התיאורים הגרוטסקיים נגדו בכתב האישום ובהכרעת הדין הם הפך האמת! גזרו השופטים 26 שנה, והוא כמעט בן 60!

סיפור האהבה שנגדע במעצרים, באיומים, במכות ובכתבי אישום לחפים מפשע וביניהם ילדים, לא מיועד לבעלי לב חלש. ואם בכל זאת לב פועם בקרבכם ולא אבן, חשוב שתדעו מה נעשה ממש פה על כדור הארץ הזה שבו אנו, היחידים שברא השם יתברך עם יכולת בחירה, לבחור בטוב ולסור מרע, האמורים בניגוד לשאר היצורים על פני הכדור להיות ״אנושיים״.

בזמן ארוחת הצהריים שלכם, בזמן שיצאתם לקניות, בזמן שבילית‍ם עם יקיריכם, בזמן שהשכבתם את ילדיכם לישון והערתם אותם בבוקר, בזמן שהכנתם להם כריך לבית הספר ושטפתם להם פרות, בזמן ששילמתם חשבונות, בזמן שהסתכלתם במראה, בזמן שצחצחתם שיניים, בזמן שנסעתם וחזרתם וחייגתם ועניתם וחשבתם והלכתם ועליתם והתקדמתם ואיחרתם.... קרו דברים איומים לאזרחי מדינת ישראל שלא פשעו ולא עברו על החוק. בחדרי חדרים, במסמכים סודיים לשופטים שבולעים את הכדורים שמגישה להם המשטרה עם כוס מים צוננים, במילים חמות... אתם מקבלים את התוצאה הסופית, מעובדת היטב על ידי התקשורת ועל ידי הגופים המדיניים הפועלים בעזרתה כדי לתעתע בכם. בכל רגע.

זה היה יכול לקרות לכל אחד מכם, וגם עכשיו. תאמינו לי. אני לא האמנתי במשפט הזה עד שזה הגיע אליי, עד הבית.

תחזיקו חזק ותישארו איתי עד הסוף. אפילו שהוא לא ידוע עדיין, אפילו אם לפעמים תרגישו כבמרוץ מכוניות ולפעמים על ספינת שודדים בלב ים, וגם אם תרגישו את הסיבובים החדים, ואת הלופים ב-360 מעלות, כשהרגליים בעננים והראש בתחתונים, אם הלב מכוון לדעת האמת, נגיע בדיוק לאן שהיינו צריכים, אפילו אם זה ממש לא מה שחשבנו. הדרך היא חלק מכלל התמונה, ולא פחות חשובה.

כיום, אוקטובר 2015, כבר עברו 4 שנים **ועדיין לא נותנים** לנשים הללו שעוברות גיהינום בארץ מולדתם ועל לא עוול בכפם; לא לראות את האיש שהן אוהבות, לא ללדת ילדים ולא לחיות כרצונן כמו לפני המהומה על לא מאומה שעוררה בחורה אחת מפוקפקת שיצאה לנקום בהשראת תכנית טלוויזיה בדיונית אחת, שהתחפשה לתכנית תחקירים. לנקום במי? בדניאל שהעז וסירב להצעות הפיתוי האובססיביות שלה, פעם אחר פעם, ונמלט בחיים מאצבעותיה הלהוטות...

אני, שירן אמבש, בת 32 הייתי האישה השישית, עכשיו אני הרביעית. פחות שתיים; עליזה (החמישית) שאותה תוכלו לראות ולשמוע ב-youtube (https://youtu.be/qAZ-L6pXxJo) מצלמת את עצמה כשהיא בתנאי מעצר במקלט לנשים מוכות מספרת על איומי המשטרה והרווחה שייקחו לה את הילדה אם לא תעיד עדות שקר נגד בעלה דניאל אמבש. היא מודה שעשתה זאת תחת לחץ בחקירות המשטרה, ומביעה חרטה. חודשיים אחר כך, כלומר חמישה חודשים מיום המעצר, שינתה את גרסתה לפי מה שהכתיבה לה החוקרת לילך רנן, שהבטיחה שתחזיר לה את הילדה ותעניק להן הטבות לחיים שקטים ונוחים. חמישה חודשים שבהם היא נלחמה, וביקשה מהילדים הגדולים של דניאל שהיו היחידים בקשר אתו שימסרו לו את אהבתה, דרשה שיתקשר אליה כל יום, כי אחרת היא תחשוב שוויתר עליה וזה עלול לשבור אותה. ניסתה לחבר בינינו הנשים בכל תוקף, גיבשה אותנו לתפילה אצל הצדיק רבי ישראל בעל הפתק בירושלים, אפילו שהיה אסור לנו לראות זו את זו ולדבר אחת עם השנייה, ניצלה כל הזדמנות, כשאישרו לה לנסוע לנתניה לבקר את בתיה, הילדה המשותפת שלה עם דניאל, בדרך חזור קבעה עם כולנו מפגשים סודיים בתל אביב: בתחנה מרכזית בקומה תחתונה; צילה, זלמן ובועז, גיא נועם ואנחנו כמובן, ישבנו וחשבנו על תכנית איך לצאת מהבוץ. היא ביקשה בכל פעם שנחזיק מעמד אפילו כשאנחנו רחוקות, ושנתפלל עליה שלא תיכנע ללחצים של אימא שלה ושל אחיה שתתגרש ותצא עם השכן העשיר שבא לארץ מארצות הברית ולפתוח אתו דף של חיים חדשים. שאלתי אותה אם היא חושבת על זה ברצינות, היא אמרה שזה לא היא, זה הלחץ שמפעילים עליה מכל הכיוונים, ושהיא מרגישה שזו מלחמה רוחנית. היא אמרה שהיא נחלשת כשאנחנו לא ביחד, ושהדיבורים הרעים שסביבה, והשיחות עם העובדות הסוציאליות מחלחלות, מעקמות לה את הלב ומשפיעות עליה בכל פעם יותר ויותר. כשעלתה לאוטובוס חזרה למקלט בירושלים, לא נכנסה מיד לתפוס מקום, היא נשארה עומדת ליד הנהג וסימנה בידיה לבבות, בחיוכים גדולים ועצובים כשהאוטובוס התרחק באטיות מהמדרכה. משהו בלב שלי הרגיש בעלי הכותרת שנושרים מהפרח שלה, משהו בלב שלי לא רצה להכיר בדעיכה שלה.

בימים גשומים הצליחה לחמוק לפגישות שקיבצה את כולנו במרכז המסחרי הקרוב למקלט שבו היא שהתה. הכינה לכל אחת מתנה מיוחדת, לי ולאזמרה היא הביאה עגילים, לאדרת – שרשרת, ולאילנה ואסתר – צעיפים ממשי בצבעים שאהבו במיוחד. במפגש מיוחד שארגנה בתל אביב בדירה של רינה, חברת ילדות שלי, הביאה לכל אחת מגנט עם תמונה של זוג ציפורים, שעליו כתוב "פשוט סיפור אהבה" ובעיטור לבבות אדומים. ולראש השנה הכינה לנו תפוח מלא בתבונניירות, וחילקה לנו ציפורי פורחץ על מקל ארוך. היא גיבשה את כולנו להצטלם לתכניות טלוויזיה ועיתונות כדי שנספר על השקרים של המשטרה ועל מה שהם מנסים לעשות לנו, כדי שכל עם ישראל וכל העולם ידע, לדבריה, על העלילה שהם מנסים להלביש על דניאל, רק משום שהעז לפרסם ש"סבא המלך ואומן עכשיו בירושלים". היא הדריכה כל אחת מאתנו לספר מה שעשו לה בחדרי החקירות, האיומים, השוחד (https://youtu.be/jlhws1p7MZA) ובעיקר איך העזו לשבור משפחה של עשרות נפשות, רק בגלל שהיא לא מתאימה לפס הייצור "הארי-בורגני" של מדינת ישראל בשנת 2011. ביום ההילולה של שמואל הנביא הרגישה כמנצחת כשהצטלמה עם הכתב רביב דרוקר, כדי לתקן את העוולה שאימא שלה עשתה, כמה שנים קודם לכן בכתבת לשון הרע, רק בגלל שעליזה הפסיקה להעביר לה כספים לחובות שהיו להם בשוק האפור. יומיים לפני יום ההולדת שלה התקשרה להזכיר לנו שהיא רוצה לחגוג אתנו, ואמרה שהיא מקווה שתצליח להתחמק מהמקלט ומבני משפחתה ולהיות אתנו לפחות כמה שעות. כבר באותו ערב היא הגיעה לדירה של קארי ברחוב נחום בשכונת גאולה, שם היינו כולנו הנשים וגם סמי שהיה בורח תדיר מהפנימייה שבה נעלו אותו השוטרים. היא הביאה וודקה להרמת כוסית, ודיברה על המניעות ועל הקשיים שנערמים מכל כיוון. וזה לא נהיה קל יותר... ביום ההולדת שלה שחל יומיים לאחר מכן הזמנו אותה לספא בבית מלון יוקרתי לטיפול פנים ומסגי מפנק, ואחרי הטיפול הפתענו אותה במסיבת יומולדת ועוגות קטנות ומעוצבות כמו שהיא אוהבת, והשתדלנו לשמח אותה. היא עצרה רגע אחרי כיבוי הנרות ואמרה בדרמטיות שחלמה חלום שאריה, אבא של דניאל הלך לעולמו... לא מובן מאיפה זה בא לה. תמיד בשיא של שמחה היא הייתה חייבת לקלקל ולהכניס עצבות ומרירות אל הלב, בעיניה הגדולות, סמוכות ובטוחות שאמרו דבר מה נפלא, היא לא מתבלבלת וכמו לא שומעת את עצמה, ממשיכה. היא אמרה דברים קשים מאוד, ולא היה נראה שהיא מרגישה את המשקל של הדברים שהיא אומרת בקלות דעת ושהיא מייחסת רצינות רבה מדי למחשבות שלה או לחלומות, שהם רק דמיונות. באותה נשימה היא פותחת בספר "שיחות שאחר סיפורי מעשיות", ומתחילה לקרוא:

"על ידי הריחוק כל שהוא, אפילו פחות מחוט השערה שנתרחק והלך ממקום שהיה בתחילה. שם בעולמות עליונים נתרחק כמה וכמה אלפים עולמות ופרסאות. מכל שכן וכל שכן כשאדם הולך פרסה או כמה פרסאות בעבודת השם. עין לא ראתה וכו׳."

כשעמדה מולנו לפני שנפרדה מאתנו אמרה: "אתן לא צריכות לקנא בי". זה הצחיק אותי שזה מה שיש לה להגיד, אני גם די בטוחה שכולנו הרגשנו כלפיה רחמים יותר מכל דבר אחר, ולקנאה לא נשאר מקום כבר באותם ימים... היא נשארה להביט בנו עוד קצת לפני שמיהרה לחזור למבצר הנעול תחת הפיקוח של העובדות הסוציאליות.

יום אחד, כשחזרה מעוד ביקור אצל בתיה, ביקשה שנחכה לה בתחנת הרכבת בתל אביב. כשראתה אותנו היא רצה לקראתנו וכשפרשה את זרועותיה סביבי החלה לבכות ולספר שבתיה שואלת איפה אבא, שהיא מתגעגעת אליו ומבקשת אותו. עליזה אמרה שכמעט נחנקה מדמעות, ולא ידעה מה לענות לילדה. היא הביטה בי בעיניה הגדולות, כמו מחכה לבשורה שהכול השתנה, שהמלחמה נגמרה וניצחנו, חוזרים הביתה... לא הייתה לי עבורה כזו בשורה, והיא הרגישה שאני קצת מתפתלת באי-נוחות כי אני מאוד רוצה לחזק אותה, ולא יודעת במה... היא אמרה שהיא לא עומדת בניסיון, והכל קשה מדי... היא הפחידה אותי, כי בסרט הזה מי שמרים ידיים לא נשאר במקום, אלא עובר לצד האויב שמשתמש בו לתקוף אותנו לחיסול סופי. אמרתי לה: "את לא מתייאשת עליזה, זה לא סוף הסיפור!" היא הגבירה את קצב צעדיה לכיוון האוטובוס ושלחה נשיקות באוויר. היא אמרה שחבל על כל רגע שבזבזנו על מריבות טיפשיות, היו לנו את החיים הכי יפים שיש ואיך יכולנו להרשות שדבר כזה יקרה?! היום אני חושבת שהייתי צריכה לומר לה שגם מה שקורה לנו עכשיו, זה חלק מהחיים, וזו עוד התמודדות בדרך שצריך לעבור, למה חיפשתי תשובות אחרות שחשבתי שימצאו חן בעיניה יותר, ובסוף לא מצאתי מילים... ניסיתי להדביק את הקצב שלה בצעדים גדולים יותר (היא גבוהה ממני לפחות בעשר סנטימטר), אמרתי שעכשיו בטוח נהיה החברות הכי טובות. היא רימזה שזהו זה, נגמר. שאלתי אותה: "אבל את אוהבת אותו". היא אמרה: "בטח שאני אוהבת אותו, הוא הדבר הכי טוב שקרה לי בחיים. ואין דבר שישנה את זה". היא הייתה רצינית ואז חייכה במרירות.. ניסיתי להזכיר לה דיבורים שלה: "אבל את כל הזמן מספרת שיש שני ציפורים, אחד זכר ואחת נקבה, והם רק זוג אחד בעולם... והם היו מחפשים הרבה זה את זה עד שטעו וראו שאינם יכולים למצוא אחד את השני. ואז כל אחד בנה לו קן שהשני יוכל לשמוע את הקול, זוכרת? וכשמגיע הלילה, אזי אלו הציפורים מתחילים ליילל, כל אחד על זוגו, והקולות נשמעים למרחוק... הגעגועים נשמעים בקול, זוכרת? סיפרת לי שביום מתקבצות הציפורים ואומרות להם דברי תנחומין, שעדיין אפשר שתמצאו זה את זה... ואת השמחה שביום יש שם לא שומעים למרחוק רק את קול היללה של הזוג שומעים.. את שומעת עליזה?" דמעות כבדות זלגו מזוויות עיניה ושטפו את פניה שנראה כי איבדו את התקווה... למה לא מצאתי מה להגיד לה? דברי תנחומין, אחרי כל הקולות שהיא שלחה... רציתי לרוץ אחריה ולא לתת לה ללכת, אבל הרגליים שלי הפכו כבדות כמו שתי משקולות, ולא נתנו לי לזוז. התאבנתי כמו פסל. לא ידעתי מה לעשות, מה היא עושה? מה קורה? זה לא יכול להיות, אני בחלום בלהות... פתאום הציפו אותי הזיכרונות, כאב חד חתך אותי, הצטערתי על כל רגע שלא הייתי לצדה, שחשבתי על עצמי מעל הכול, ובמקום לקנא לנסות יחד להשתנות, להיות ולעשות קצת אחרת... היא סיפרה לי איך הגיעה לראשונה בתחפושת של כיפה אדומה, וכשראתה את דניאל עם ידידיה התינוק בידיו, היא אמרה שהרגישה את החום, את האהבה, האור הזה היה חסר לה בבית שבו גדלה והיא התרגשה מהלב הרחב של דניאל לילדים ולמשפחה. היא אמרה שאהבה כזאת היא רוצה בשבילה. לפעמים היא הייתה אומרת שהיא רוצה לחיות אתו לבד, שיתגרש מהנשים האחרות, ובכל זאת לא ויתרה עליו אפילו כשאף אחת אחרת לא ויתרה על המקום שלה. עם זאת האמינה מאד במבנה הזה שחיים יחד כמה נשים, כי בכל מקרה דניאל הוא הבעל הכי טוב שיש. היא הייתה עושה לו הצגות ומפתיעה במחוות רומנטיות. כשהם היו רבים, הייתי רוצה להיות שם כי זה היה כמו סרט מרתק שאיש עוד לא צילם. לראות אותם מהצד בשבילי זה היה כמו לצפות הכי מקרוב במה שתמיד חלמתי שיהיה לי עם מי שאני אוהבת, אפילו שדרך הפילטרים שלי היה נראה לי שיש לו חולשה אליה. קינאתי בהשפעה שהייתה לה עליו, אחרי שהייתה צועקת ובוכה בדיאלוג דרמטי שהייתה גוררת אותו אליו, הוא היה סולח לה על הכול. היא הייתה מְמסה אותו ומתמרנת אותו בכל פעם כרצונה. היא עשתה רושם שהיא יכולה לשלוט בטבע, שיתבטל בפניה. ועכשיו מה?! רוח סערה פיזרה את הכול. כאוס אחד גדול.

אספר לכם קצת יותר על עצמי כדי שתבינו מהיכן באתי ולאן אני הולכת...

נולדתי בטבריה כבת בכורה להורים צעירים ואמידים. יש לי אחות שצעירה ממני בשלוש שנים, ואח שצעיר ממני בעשר שנים.

בכיתות א׳-ג׳ למדתי בבית הספר בטבריה. המחנכת שלי, חנה מרום, אמרה לאימא שצריך "לשים לי פלפל חריף בטוסיק", שאני "מרחפת"... השיעורים לא עוררו בי עניין. הייתי עסוקה בעיקר בציור. יום אחד, בהפסקה הגדולה, כשכל הילדים משחקים מחוץ למבנה הכיתות, מצאתי את עצמי במרכז המגרש, מציירת

בגירים צבעוניים על משטח האספלט השחור, שהיה נדמה בעיניי כלוח ענק הממתין שיכניסו לו צבע לחיים... מרוב שהייתי שקועה בציור, לא שמעתי שהיה צלצול וכל התלמידים חזרו לכיתות. לפתע נעלי עקב קשוחות נעמדו בגובה ידיי כשאני על הברכיים... הרמתי את ראשי, ונבהלתי כהוגן מפרצופה החמור של המנהלת. לא חשבתי שאני עושה משהו שאינו כשורה. רק התגובה שלה, והעובדה שלפתע מצאתי את עצמי לבד מחוץ לבניין הכיתות הלחיצו אותי מאוד, עד שהתחלתי למחוק את ציור הגיר מהאספלט החם בשפשוף האגודל, עד שחרכתי את העור לכדי כאב נורא, שגרם לי לברוח בריצה, בהרגשה איומה ובבכי לכיוון ביתה של סבתא ויולט, שגרה במרחק שני רחובות מבית הספר. כשהגעתי, התקשרתי לאימא בבכי שאני לא רוצה לחזור יותר לבית הספר. אימא דאגה לי וניסתה לנחם אותי, אבל מיד גם הוסיפה שאין ברירה וזו חובה ללכת לבית הספר עד גיל 18.☹

המשפט הזה ליווה אותי, הרבה מאוד פעמים אימא שלי אמרה אותו במהלך השנים, עד שהגעתי לגיל המיוחל...

הייתי ילדה מלאה בביטחון עצמי. אולי בגלל ההערצה של אימא שלי שהתלהבה שהבת שלה מעוררת עניין רב בכל מקום שאליו מגיעים, סוחפת אחריה את כל הילדים, מפיקה הצגות, פנטומימות, תיאטרון בובות ולהקות. מארגנת קבוצות ומרימה "מחנות". בעלת יכולת מופלאה לחקות שפות ודמויות, שגרמה לאנשים להחזיק את הבטן מרוב צחוק ולהיות מקור לגאווה רבה בשבילה... אימא אמרה שאפילו החברים שלהם היו באים לבית רק בשביל לראות את הילדה המיוחדת, רבת-הכישרונות, שאף אחד לא נשאר אדיש אליה, ובקלות מתאהבים בה. אבא שלי, שאינו מרבה לדבר, תמיד נהג לקום מוקדם לעבודה ולחזור בערב. עם זאת, היה מפצה אותי על הזמן שהוא לא נמצא בהרבה מותרות ומתנות. רק בגיל הרבה יותר מאוחר שמעתי מחברה, שלהורים שלה אין כסף, וצריך לחכות לחודש הבא כדי שאבא שלה יקנה לה משהו שרצתה. אני זוכרת שלא ידעתי שיש כזה דבר שלהורים אין כסף לקנות לילדיהם מה שהם רוצים. גדלתי בעושר ואושר. הייתי ללא ספק הבובה של אימא שלי. היא עשתה לי תסרוקות בשֵׂער כל יום, עם סיכות וגומיות מיוחדות, בבגדי נסיכה, שאפשר לראות בעשרות האלבומים שאימא שלי מחזיקה בכספת עד עצם היום הזה, ומתאבלת על הרגע שכיסיתי את הראש במטפחת, ואת הפופיק בשמלה. היא העדיפה שאהיה שחקנית פרובוקטיבית על במות, מתחככת בחברת ה"עשירון העליון" ונישאת לאחד מהם שיפתח לנו, לי ולה, כך בפנטזיה שלה, חנות שבה נמכור את החפצים שהיא מקשטת וצובעת, את פסלי החֵמר שלה ואת התמונות שלמדה להכין בבית הספר "אורנים", כשלמדה שם "תולדות האמנות" (מיותר לציין שהתכניות שלי היו אחרות...).

בתום בית הספר היסודי, בחופש הגדול, בכיתי בכל הכוח שאני רוצה ללמוד בבית ספר לאמנויות התיאטרון, לפחות שיהיה לי מעניין, כי הכביד עליי מאוד שלאימא היה חשוב שתהיה לי תעודת בגרות, ולא הצלחתי להבין למה. בעיתון הילדים "כולנו" התפרסמה כתבה עליי עם תמונה על חצי עמוד תחת הכותרת: "שירן אסלן סופרת צעירה בת 11".

אימא ניסתה לפייס אותי באומרה שבתי ספר לאמנויות יש רק במרכז הארץ, והיא לא תשלח אותי לגור רחוק ממנה, כך שעד גיל 18 אני ברשותה. שוב המשפט הזה... לא יכולתי לדמיין לעצמי איך הזמן הזה הולך לעבור. ניסיתי לנתק את עצמי מהמציאות, וחייתי בין עולם של ספרים שקראתי וסיפורים שכתבתי, לבין "חבורות" שהקמתי עם ילדים מהמושב והדרכתי אותם למסעות על כנפי סיפורים דמיוניים שהמצאתי, כי הייתי מוכרחה להאמין שהכול אפשרי, אחרת לא הייתי מצליחה לדלג על כל השנים האלו בשמחה. השיטה שלי הייתה בעיקר: לחשוב שאני בסרט, ואין לי ברירה אלא לשחק את התפקיד הראשי בצורה הטובה ביותר.

כשהגעתי לגיל 18 והתכוונתי להיפרד מבית הוריי לטובת העיר הגדולה, שלה חיכיתי וציפיתי, וידעתי שתקבל אותי בזרועות פתוחות ללא דעות קדומות, ותיתן לי להרגיש חופשיה להיות איך שאני, ולבטא את עצמי כרצוני.

אימא לחצה עליי להתגייס לצבא ולא היססה להשחיל הערה: "לפחות את זה תעשי כמו כולם", כדי לרמוז שעד עכשיו לא הייתי כמו כולם. רק כדי שלא יהיו לה טענות כלפיי יותר, הודעתי לה שזה הדבר האחרון שאני עושה בשבילה, ואחרי זה, היא לא מבקשת ממני כלום יותר! עשרים שנה לחכות כדי לחיות כמו שאני רוצה – זה לא מעט! והימים היו ארוכים ומייגעים בהמתנה לחיות את החופש שלי...

לא רציתי שהיא תהיה גאה ובכוונה תחילה בחרתי להיות "שק"מיסטית"! שק"ם צה"ל הוא מעין "כלבו" לחיילים בבסיסים השונים, ולא נחשב לתפקיד פטריוטי במיוחד, בלשון המעטה, אלא די בזוי. שלחו אותי לטירונות ולקורס משק"ית שק"ם (שזה כמעט שווה ערך למנהלת קיוסק!). אחרי שלושה שבועות ב"שבירת דיסטנס" עם המפקדים (מפגש של החיילות עם המפקדים בסיום הקורס, בלי המשחק הקשוח ובלי הפער

בין מפקד וחיילת, ובלבוש "אזרחי" ולא "על מדים"), הם הודו שהתפוצצו מצחוק מהשטויות שהייתי עושה, ויוצאים מהכיתה כדי שלא נראה שהם לא מצליחים להישאר רציניים וקשוחים כששירן מגיבה במופע "סטנד-אפ" על כל דבר... בשבילי, כמו שכבר אמרתי, זו הייתה הדרך היחידה לשרוד, לאו דווקא מצורך בתשומת לב או באהדה.

שובצתי בבסיס בחרמון. השק"ם שניהלתי היה בתוך חלון קיר במועדון החיילים של הבסיס המבודד, וכמעט כל מי שהגיע, קיבל חיקויים של כל המוצרים בשק"ם. בכל זאת לא החזקתי מעמד וברחתי. הסגרתי את עצמי למשטרה הצבאית, ולקחו אותי להישפט בכלא 400 לבנות בצריפין. בכיתי בפני השופט שהתגייסתי רק בשביל לרצות את אימא שלי, ואני מרגישה שאני נחנקת ואני לא מסוגלת לקבל מרות ובטח שלא פקודות! הוא הצטער כשראה שלא הצלחתי להתאפק מלבכות... הוא כל כך הצטער ואמר: "אפילו אם אני רוצה לתת לך פחות אני לא יכול. את על תנאי 15 יום! אני לא יכול לתת לך פחות!"

כך חטפתי 15 יום כלא צבאי. ראיתי חושך. אני לא יכולה להישאר פה, הסתכלתי סביב למצוא דרכי מילוט. אין. הכול גדרות וחוטי תיל. רק כשאמרתי לעצמי שקיבלתי תפקיד בסרט על נערה בצבא שהתגייסה רק כדי שאימא שלה תניח לה לחיות את שארית חייה לפי רצונה החופשי ולפי הבחירות העצמאיות שלה, ולא להיות יותר הבובה שלה, והיא בכלא צבאי, רק אז יכולתי לחשוב שאני צריכה לעבור את זה. אחרי כמה ימים, מפקדת "המתקן" עשתה לנו (האסירות) שיחה ואמרה שיש אפשרות לכתוב לה מכתב. שמחתי ומיד קפצתי על ההזדמנות להיחלץ בעזרת כישרון הכתיבה שלי. השתחררתי אחרי תשעה ימים. אבא הרים טלפונים ועברתי לתפקד כמדריכה באתר ההנצחה של גולני, בסיס "פתוח", חמש דקות מהבית, קל"ב (קרוב לבית), 11 חיילים ומפקד אחד. כך העברתי את השנה האחרונה. כשהשתחררתי, אבא שלי תפס אותי ואמר שעבודה מועדפת מהצבא תיתן לי מענק כספי ועוד הטבות, ומדובר רק על 150 שעות או 150 יום, לא זוכרת. אמרתי שאני לא מתכוונת לעבוד בשום עבודה מסוג העבודות שמציעים לחיילים משוחררים לצורך קבלת ההטבות.. אבא שלי, במיוחד, החליט לנהל תחנת דלק, כדי שאוכל לעבוד אצלו בתור מתדלקת, וכך הצליחו ההורים להשאיר אותי עוד חצי שנה בבית. ביום ה-150 פשטתי את הסרבל, ובג'ינס וגופייה עליתי לאוטובוס הישיר לתל אביב, עם תיק גב ענק מהצבא שעכשיו הוא עמוס במה שהכנסתי כדי להתחיל את החיים החופשיים שלי.

בתל אביב חיכה לי חצב, בן זוגי, שהכרתי בחופשת השחרור כשהתארחתי אצל חברה בתל אביב. הוא אמר שזו אהבה ממבט ראשון. אפילו שהצהרתי שאני לא רוצה בן זוג, ושאני רוצה להתחיל את החיים לבד, הוא היה יפה ורומנטי ועשה רושם שהוא מעריץ אותי, הוא היה שחקן מנחה ומתופף, ועזב חיים דתיים, מתאים לי. עברתי לגור אתו בדירה שחלק עם שותפה ושותף, ומהר מאוד עברנו לדירה משלנו. הוא גדל בבית דתי וסיפר לי איך ברח מפנימיית "כפר חב"ד". ריחמתי עליו ורציתי שיחד נתחיל חיים חדשים. חיזקתי אותו להצליח במה שהוא אוהב, והוא האמין בי ודחף אותי לעבודה במשחק, בהנחיה ובדוגמנות. אני מצדי לא תכננתי לעבוד, חשבתי שהגעתי עם מספיק כסף, ורק רציתי להיות משוחררת מכל החובות וההתחייבויות, ופשוט לחיות.

לפעמים היינו נוסעים לשבת אצל ההורים שלו. הייתי אנטי-דתית וכדי לא ליצור סנסציות ולהתאים את עצמי לנוף, חיפשתי במשך שעות שכבות של בגדים כדי להצניע לכת והורדתי את הנזם מהאף. בנסיעה באוטובוס הממוגן, המלא בחרדים לבושים חליפות שחורות וכובעים, בדרך לבית הוריו, נכנסה בי חרדה שלא יכולתי להסביר, ולא יכולתי להפסיק לבכות עד שהאוטובוס עצר וירדנו. לפני שעלינו על האוטובוס הבא, רציתי להגיד לחצב שאני חוזרת, אבל לא יכולתי לעשות לו את זה. הכרזתי בהפגנתיות שאני מחזירה את הנזם ולא מעניין אותי כלום. חצב שלח לי חיוך עקום והתאפק מלהגיב, כי פחד שאעשה סקנדל מול כל ה"דוסים" השחורים. ההורים שלו היו מאד נחמדים אליי, מה שלא מנע מאתנו ללכת לעשן סיגריה אחרי סעודת שבת. נשארתי בעמדתי האנטי-דתית, ולא הבנתי כלום בענייני תורה ואמונה בהשם, וגם לא ניסיתי להבין.

כשהכסף שחסכתי אזל, התחלתי לעבוד בחברות הפרסום הגדולות בארץ בתור "פרילנסרית" בפרויקטים מעניינים שבחרתי, והרבה מהם יחד עם חצב. הצטלמנו יחד גם לכמה סרטים קצרים. חצב עבד יום ולילה, וגם למד "משחק מול מצלמה", התאמן בחדר כושר וערך חזרות לתיאטרון גם בבית. אני עסקתי בעיקר בכתיבת נבכי נפשי, שעדיין מחפשת את מקומה ואת ייעודה בעולם; ובהליכות ארוכות בעיר המישורית, כשהמפגשים האקראיים עם טיפוסים מעניינים בדרך הופכים לסיפורים קצרים בספר התובנות שלי מהעיר הגדולה. אהבתי גם לצייר, אף על פי שרוב הציורים היו מסתכמים ברישומי דוגמניות ונשים ערומות. הרישום שציירתי את חצב כמודל היה אולי הרישום הטוב ביותר שלי.

לחצב לא היה כסף. הוא היה בחובות עצומים. כשאימא שלי הייתה מתקשרת ואומרת שאולי כדאי שאעבוד כמנהלת משרד או שתממן לי לימודים בבית ספר גבוה למשחק, הייתי מתרגזת, ומבהירה לה פעם

אחר פעם שאני לא רוצה מהם כסף, בעיקר כדי לא להיות תלויה באף אחד, וכדי שלא יגידו לי מה לעשות. זה היה מוציא אותי מדעתי שהיא ניסתה להתערב לי בחיים ולשלוט בהם, וזה גרם לי לתפוס מהם מרחק...

אחרי שנה עברנו לדירה חדשה ברחוב שינקין. חצב דרבן אותי להירשם ללימודי משחק והנחיה, שהתנהלו ברחוב בלפור, הקרוב לדירתנו מרחק דקות הליכה.

בשיעור שהנחה אחד הבמאים הטובים בארץ, הוא חילק לנו מונולוגים קצרים ללמוד בעל-פה. המונולוג הראשון שקיבלתי ללמוד בעל-פה היה המונולוג של "מורפיוס" מהסרט "המטריקס". בסצנה הזאת מורפיוס נותן ל"ניאו" לבחור בין הגלולה הכחולה או האדומה, כלומר להישאר בעולם השקר שהוא חי עד היום או לעבור לממד אחר, שאין חזרה ממנו, והוא ממד האמת (https://youtu.be/9a9B1qO6ihA).

האמת באמת הכתה לי בפנים כשגיליתי במקרה, שחצב בקשר עם לא אחרת מאשר טרנסג'נדרית, עטורת קעקועים צבעוניים, לבושה בלבוש מינימלי. יצא לי לראות אותה כמעט בכל יום ברחוב דיזנגוף, וכולם ידעו שהוא נערת ליווי... כבר לא הייתי בטוחה שאני מכירה את חצב כמו שחשבתי... ואחרי שנים של חיים מלאים יחד, התחלתי להבין מאין שאבו, הוא והשותף שלו, השראה להצגה, שלשמה הם הצליחו לשכנע מחזאי נודע לכתוב ולביים ולתת להם תפקידים ראשיים בתיאטרון מכובד, מחזה על החיים הכפולים של שני חרדים, שנשותיהן אינן יודעות היכן ועם מי בלילות הם מבלים... הרגשתי מטומטמת, "נפל לי האסימון". בכל מקרה, בסופו של דבר, סלחתי לו.

באשר למערכת היחסים עם חצב, אולי בגלל שזה היה בגיל כזה, אחרי הצבא, אחרי העזיבה של בית הוריי, עם המעבר לתל אביב, לימודי המשחק והמגורים המשותפים, היה בזה משהו נוח לאותה תקופה, והוא השתדל לרצות אותי, ועמד פחות או יותר בכל הקפריזות שלי... פעם אחת, כשחזר מאוחר מדי הביתה והתחלתי לחשוד, נעלתי אותו מחוץ לדירתנו המשותפת. במשך שעות ישבנו כל אחד בעבר השני של הדלת, לא נתתי לו להיכנס. בכיתי שהוא בטח לא מסופק וכבר מצא אחרת. הוא כתב לי מכתבי פיוס בלי חרוזים, ומכתבי אהבה בלי רומנטיקה ובלי משחקי מילים, שלח אותם תחת הדלת ובכה. יכול להיות שהוא עשה הצגה לכבודי, שזו גם כן מחווה יפה ואני מעריכה אותו על זה, ובכל זאת לא היה כה משכנע... אחרי כמה שעות של שיחות מעבר לדלת נאלצתי להתרצות ולפתוח לו. ובכל זאת, לא חדלתי להיות טראגית, ולהשאיר אותו בהרגשה מבישה.

אחרי יותר משלוש שנים שגרנו יחד, עבדנו יחד ועברנו הרבה יחד, כשדיבר על חתונה ושהוא כבר בן 26, לא יכולתי לחשוב על זה בכלל. עדיין הייתי כמגששת באפלה בנוגע לקשר הזה ולאימות המושג שנתפס כשקרי בעיניי: "זוגיות". נפרדנו.

מצד אחד הפרדה הקלה עליי. תמיד היה לי צורך להיות חופשיה, ואולי משהו בקשר הזה חסם אותי. לאו דווקא בגללו. המשכתי להרגיש את זה בכל מערכות היחסים הזוגיים שהיו לי. ההגדרה התבניתית לקשר של "זוגיות" הפריעה לי, הרגשתי שזה מגביל את חופש התנועה שלי במרחב, ומצמצם לי את הדעת, בסופו של דבר תמיד, "שברתי את הכלים", והעדפתי להמציא את עצמי מחדש, ולהתקדם כרצוני ללא מחויבות לשום אחד. לא רציתי לחיות תחת שום הגדרה, אלא רק לפי בחירה של אותו רגע.

עברתי לסטטוס של "רווקה" בעיר הגדולה, ואהבתי את זה. שכרתי לעצמי דירת סטודיו גדולה ויפה, בבניין מיוחד של אמנים. כל קומה היא מסדרון ארוך שמשני צדיו 9 דירות סטודיו. בבניין היו לפחות שלושה שחקנים, מוזיקאי, צייר וכותב. כולם היו מוזמנים אצלי. בכניסה לדירתי, על מתלה מעץ היו כובעים שונים ומשונים, לגברים ולנשים, מעילים מיוחדים לדמויות ובמידות שונות, עניבה, פאה ונעליים. כל מי שנכנס מוכרח היה לשים על עצמו לפחות אחד מהאביזרים ולהיכנס לדמות. כך זרמנו באימפרוביזציות ארוכות ואפילו הכנו מערכון קומי, השכן ממול (שהיה ידיד קרוב, שגר שם לפניי ובעקבותיו הגעתי) היה הקופירייטר; הכותב, אני והשכן מלמטה היינו השחקנים. ההיכרויות המהירות והמזדמנות עם גברים שונים, כמו: הרוסי, היפני, הרקדן האפרו-אמריקני, גרוסמן המרוקאי, המוזיקאי השרמנטי, המקסיקני הרומנטי, השרירן עם הבולדוג, הפנקיסט מבן יהודה, הברמן מ"היהושע", הג'ינג'י עם השֵׂעָר הארוך על החוף, הקיבוצניק, הירושלמי, כולם, כחלק מרשימה ססגונית, נוספו לספר הזיכרונות שעמד לצאת לאור כיומן הרפתקאות של סיפורים קצרים, המגלים חלק מעולמה של בחורה, חלק שבדרך כלל רבות מעדיפות להסתיר...

כשעבדתי 15 יום בתור דיילת תצוגה למכונית יוקרתית בקניון רמת אביב הגיעה משפחה; אבא, אימא וילד. כשהצגתי להם את הרכב, התיישבנו במושבים הקדמיים, אני והאבא, כשאשתו והילד מעבר לשמשה הקדמית, האבא, שהיה קרוב לגיל 80, התחיל לפלרטט אתי ושאל שאלות שגרמו לי להחליף צבעים... מנהל

העבודה שלי בדיוק הגיע, וכנראה זיהה את המצוקה על פניי, הוא התנהג כמו ג׳נטלמן כשעט לעברי והכריז ״אשתי!״ במהירות חילץ אותי מתוך המכונית היוקרתית שבקניון, למכונית הפרטית שלו שבחניון. הוא המשיך והציג אותי במשרד החברה ולכל מכריו באותו הכינוי, התעצבנתי והודעתי לו ש״אני לא אישה של אף אחד...״. לאחר כמה שבועות, כשקרקע אותי לדירתו וניסה לעשות ממני משהו שאני לא. בזמן שהיה בעבודה, נתקפתי כאב חד ועמוק במרכז הבטן. מיהרתי לדירה שלי כדי לקבור את עצמי מתחת לשמיכות; לצרוח מכאבים בלי להטריד את השכנים. אימא שלי התקשרה ואמרה שהם באים לקחת אותי לבית חולים. כשהוא הגיע לדירתי עם כבד עוף ממסעדה, והכריח אותי לאכול, הקאתי, וכששמע שההורים שלי מגיעים מהצפון במיוחד כדי לקחת אותי לבית החולים התרגז שאני קוראת להורים כשהוא בשבילי הכול, וכבעלי – הוא האבא והאימא שלי, ושאתקשר להודיע מיד שלא יבואו חלילה! לא התקשרתי. הם באו ולקחו אותי לבית החולים. שם עשו לי את כל הבדיקות האפשריות. אחרי אשפוז לילה הכריזו הרופאים כי ״לא נמצאו תסמינים...״ אין שום דבר. כשהוא בא לקחת אותי אמרתי לו שאני מרגישה ש״זה פסיכוסומטי, אני יודעת שהנפש שלי זועקת, אני לא במקום שאני צריכה להיות״. הוא צחק ממני. שנאתי את זה שהוא לא מבין אותי. עצבן אותי עוד יותר כשהמשיך ואמר: ״תתחתני אתי, יהיו לנו ילדים בלונדינים קטנים, את תהיי מלכה! לא תצטרכי לעשות כלום, אני אבנה לך ארמון על הר ויהיו לנו סוסים...״. זה היה נחמד שהוא חשב עליי בתור האחת בשבילו, אבל לא יכולתי לסבול את המחשבה אפילו לרגע אחד בדמיון: להיות כלואה בחיים של מישהו אחר... רציתי להמשיך לחפש את החיים שלי. בשישי בצהריים, המנהג הקבוע שלו חזר, הייתי בדרך מהעבודה כשהוא צלצל להודיע לי: ״אני אוסף אותך לשניצלים אצל אימא שלי, מחכים לנו״. אזרתי אומץ – ויתרתי על טירות, סוסים וארמונות, ועניתי: ״לא, די! אני רוצה ללכת עם חברות, אל תגיד לי מה לעשות!״ מהעבר השני של הקו: ״אם ככה, תיקחי את הדברים שלך מהבית, אני לא רוצה לראות אותך יותר״. הפעם, חשבתי, אני לא מתכוונת להיכנע לא לשקר החן ולא להבל היופי, לא לשרמנטיות ממגנטת ולא לקישוטי ממון ללא דופי! זה לא מה שאני מחפשת! אני לא מסוגלת לשמוע את המילה ״חתונה״, זה עשה לי בחילה. בכל פעם מחדש. אמרתי לעצמי, מעכשיו אני רוצה להיות לבד, לא בן זוג ולא גבר, זה רק מעכב אותי בדרך למצוא את מה שאני משתדלת כל כך לחפש... ושוב מצאתי את עצמי במערכת יחסים שתוקעת אותי, עם גבר שמבקש לשתול אותי בחלקת קרקע להתרבות. אני מוחה! לא עוד!

כעבור חמש שנים של מגורים בעיר הגדולה, על חוף הים ״on the rocks״ כשהחברים מהבר סביבי, גמעתי עוד כמה בקבוקי שתייה חריפה. גלים של הגיגים הציפו אותי, אני בעצם מרגישה בודדה. כשכולם התקפלו ושאלו: ״את באה?״ שיקרתי שאני רוצה להישאר לראות את הזריחה... כשנותרתי לבדי, נתתי לראשי להישמט לתוך החול וביקשתי מהמלאכים בשמים שייקחו את הנשמה שלי מהעולם הזה, שאני לא מסוגלת יותר לחיות בו... היה נדמה לי שהרגשתי איך הנשמה שלי נשאבת ממני והלאה, אל האין-סוף... לפתע בקעה ממני צרחה ללא קול ״לא! אני רוצה להגשים את המשימה שבשבילה נבראתי מלכתחילה״, הרגשתי שיש בי יכולות שאמורות להגיע ליעד מסוים, לא ידעתי לאן לנתב את כל הרצונות האלה... צלצול הפלאפון קטע את מחשבותיי, רינה, חברתי מהגולן מעבר לקו, היא אומרת שהיא אצלי ומחכה לראות אותי. אמרתי לה שאני לא במצב להראות את הפרצוף שלי... היא הגיעה לחוף ואספה אותי עם עוד כמה מיליוני גרגירי חול זהובים שנאספו יחד אתי... היא נבהלה מהתפזורת שהייתי, ואמרה שמעולם לא ראתה אותי ככה, ושקשה לזהות אותי...

״זהו!״ סיננתי בהחלטיות על ספל הקפה: ״אני חייבת להיגמל מהעיר הזאת!״

שכרתי חדר קטן עם גינה בקיבוץ על שפת הכנרת. בהרגשה שברצוני לעשות ההפך מכל מה שעשיתי עד עכשיו (פירוט בבלוג האישי). לא רוצה גברים יותר. התחלתי לחשוב על זוגיות עם אישה, אבל לא הייתי מספיק אמיצה לממש את זה.

חיפשתי עבודה ברפת. הרגשתי שהגעתי להתנשאות כזאת, שאני מוכרחה לעשות קפיצת ראש לתוך החרא של הפרות, ולהתחיל משם.

לפני הצום של יום כיפור הייתה לי הרגשה מוזרה. כאילו יצאתי מהגוף של עצמי וריחפתי מעל שנות קיומי על פני האדמה. ראיתי סצנות אמתיות מחיי, שבזמן אמת לא שמתי לב למה שראיתי עכשיו, הפגיעות שגרמתי, בכוונה או שלא בכוונה ולא הרגשתי, עד כמה הכאבתי, לאלו שאהבו אותי ולאלו שלא. במבט לאחור לא הבנתי איך אפשר היה לאהוב מישהי כמוני. הצטערתי על כל מה שעשיתי, והצטערתי על מה שהייתי צריכה לעשות ולא עשיתי. הרגשתי שקלקלתי, ורציתי לתקן. רציתי למצוא את כל מי שסבל מההתנהגויות הגועליות שלי, מההתנשאות שבה נהגתי ומהמעשים האנוכיים שליוו את יישותי החצופה, ולהגיע לפייס אותם. פתאום קלטתי שעד היום השארתי מאחוריי נפגעים, שנשארו עם צלקות, או כמו ששני, חברה שלי הייתה אומרת, השארתי מאחורי גופות אדם... איך יכולתי להתקדם עם אות קלון מובהקת שכזו! הרי זה בלתי אפשרי. ככל שחשבתי על זה, נזכרתי בעוד ועוד סיטואציות שבהן נהגתי

בחוסר רגישות, ולא חשבתי על איש מלבד עצמי. כשהכאבתי ועזבתי, בעודי ממשיכה לחפש מי ימלא את מבוקשי כרצוני וכאוות נפשי. כתבתי מכתבים וצלצלתי כדי להביע את צערי בפני כל אותם "קרבנות" הגאווה הסרוחה שלי...

לראשונה, אני צמה ומתייסרת מעוונות ומעברות, ומבקשת מחילה, מצפה לכפרה, לישועה, משמים...

ברפת הקיבוץ לא היו צריכים עובדים. מצאתי עבודה בבית אריזה, ועבדתי 11 שעות ביום, בחברת תאילנדים ודרוזיות עם מנהל עבודה קשוח בעל עבר צבאי מפואר שצרח עלינו כאילו שהיינו חיילים בצבא שלו. חשבתי שזה יעזור לי להרגיש קצת השפלה... לא היה לי קל, לקום כל יום ב-4:00 בבוקר ולעבוד על פס ממונע שמוביל ארגזים חדגוניים, שבהם עליי לסדר קלמנטינות, תמיד באותה הצורה... במשך שעות רבות כל כך...

למזלי, אימא של חברה טובה שלי (שהכירה אותי מאז שהייתי בת 15 וניהלה את חנות המזכרות בקיבוץ) התקשרה אליי עם הצעת עבודה. שמחתי שההשגחה מציבה אותי בחנות נקייה וממוזגת, והתחלתי לעבוד בחנות המזכרות של הקיבוץ. בכל זאת ניסיתי להתבודד. משום דבר לא להתבלבל, להקשיב לרחשי הלב. כשסביבי רק הטבע במלוא עצמתו והדרו, מה הלב שלי אומר לי?! לאן הוא נושא אותי...?!

תיירים רבים הגיעו מכל העולם לחנות המזכרות והתרגשו מהארץ ומהיהודים. באחת השבתות עבדתי בחנות שבכפר הנופש של הקיבוץ (היו שתי חנויות, אחת בקיבוץ על שפת הכנרת, ואחת בכפר הנופש – מול חדר האוכל), תיירת מגרמניה הניחה על שולחן הקופה טליתות, כיפות, מזוזות, תהלים ועוד מיני סממנים יהודים. היא שאלה אותי על כל דבר מהו ומה הוא מסמל. אני, שלא ידעתי מה לענות, הרגשתי שאני מביישת את העם היהודי. אחרי המשמרת הזו, וכשהצטברו עוד כמה מקרים מביכים בפני מבקרים מהארץ ומחו"ל, ששאלו שאלות על התורה, על מנהגים מאבותינו הקדושים ועל סיפורי התנ"ך, ולא היו לי תשובות עבורם... פתחתי את המחשב בדירת החדר הקטנה שלי, והתחלתי ללמוד יהדות. אמרתי למנהלת החנות שלא אוכל לעבוד עוד בשבת כי אני מרגישה שזה עושה לי רע. בפרט חשבתי לעצמי, שאני עלולה לבלבל את הגויים שהגיעו עד הקיבוץ מארצות שונות בקצווי תבל, וחלקם יודעים שלפי התורה – יהודי לא עובד בשבת. הם גרמו לי לשמוח בהיותי יהודייה, ולרצות להוות דוגמה חיה שהתורה ניתנה לנו על מנת לחיותה, אז למה שלא אקיים אותה? ומה עשיתי עד עכשיו?! מנהלת החנות הסבירה לי שתאלץ למצוא לי מחליפה, כי הרבה פעמים שיא העבודה שלנו היא בשבת. התחילו לבוא מתלמדות שיוכלו להחליף אותי. הרגשתי שמחה בלב, והתרגשתי מהמחשבה: לאן הרוח תישא אותי, מה היעד הבא שלי...? מצאתי ספר שנקרא "יהדות הלכה למעשה", וחיפשתי בו הלכה לאישה, שאוכל לקיים מיד. קראתי על הלכות טבילה. כשירד הלילה והחושך בחוף היה כהה במיוחד, השארתי את הבגדים על סלע קרוב למים, ונכנסתי מתחת למי הכנרת המתוקים. ירדתי לאט ואז עליתי מעל המים בבת-אחת, וירדתי שוב פנימה בתנופה. מתחת למים התחלתי לצעוק: "ראש בני ישראל! תראו לי את ראש בני ישראל תראו לי את משה רבנו".

באותה תקופה הייתי בקשר טוב עם טל שלמד קונדיטוריה בטבריה ושכר דירה באזור. הכרתי את טל דרך חצב, גם הוא ברח בתור נער מפנימיית "כפר חב"ד". טל היה ידוע בחכמתו ובידיעותיו הרבות בתורה ובתחומים נרחבים. באחת הפעמים שהייתי בחנות והתיירים שאלו על אברהם אבינו ושאלות נוספות, התקשרתי אליו ולחשתי בתוך השפופרת: "טל, תלמד אותי את כל התורה, מהר!" הצעתי לו שנעשה עסק, אני אחפש לו אישה, והוא ילמד אותי תורה. כשנסע לראות את אבא שלו, שהיה חסיד ברסלב (לא שידעתי מה זה חסיד ומה זה ברסלב), חזר אליי עם מתנה בהשאלה מאביו: "סיפורי מעשיות של רבי נחמן". הוא אמר שסודות גדולים צפונים בפנים, והקבלה טמונה בכל אות ובכל מילה. סגולות רבות לסיפורי מעשיות אלו והוא ביקש שאשמור על זה כמו על אוצר כי זה הדבר שיקר לאבא שלו מכול, והוא הבטיח שיחזיר לו. הוא אמר שגם אם אני לא מבינה, שאקרא בכל זאת, כי הנשמה יודעת. וככל שאקרא ואתפלל ואתחזק, אוכל להבין יותר, וגם דברים שונים, כי בכל פעם אפשר לגלות, מה שצריך כל אחד עצה לנפשו. במעשה א – מאבדת בת מלך – השני למלכות היה נחוש למצוא את בת המלך שנאבדה, בכל מקום, משך שנים רבות, ולא התייאש אפילו שמכל עבר אמרו לו שיניח לזה, ושהמקום שהוא מחפש לא נמצא ולא קיים בעולם. הוא המשיך להתעקש, לא התבלבל ולא התייאש, גם כשנודע לו שכבר הגיע עד אליה לבת המלך והפסיד אותה והיא כבר נתרחקה ואיננה, ועוד ושנים יעברו עד שיגיע אליה שוב... המשיך והתאמץ בחיפושים אחריה, עד שמצאה. הסיפור חיזק אותי, כי ידעתי שאני בתהליך של חיפוש של מה שנאבד לי, אולי בעולמות מקבילים, אולי בגלגולים קודמים. חיפוש אחר הדבר שבשבילו אני נבראתי. לא יכולתי להתייאש, כי הרגשתי שאני מוכרחה למצוא דרך אמתית לחיות, וכמו שרבי נחמן אמר: "מי שמחפש באמת, בוודאי ימצא...". רציתי לחיות את סיפורי מעשיות במציאות היומיומית, וזה עורר בי כיסופים למצוא אנשים להקמת תיאטרון נודד, מעין קרקס נייד, שיורכב בצורת מגן דוד, ונעלה הצגות מהסיפורי מעשיות ובכל פעם יצטרפו אלינו עוד אנשים, ויחד נפיץ את דברו של רבי נחמן ברחבי הארץ, וכך ייראו החיים שלנו.

ובחזרה לקרקע; בשביל לשמור את השבת ומאחר שלא הכרתי אף אחד דתי, נרשמתי לסוף שבוע של הרצאות למשפחות שרוצות להתחזק במצוות בבית מלון בדרום הארץ. באחת ההרצאות, אולי האחרונה, המנחה הזמין לבמה את כל מי שרצה לקבל על עצמו התחזקות באיזו מצווה ושמירה. אני הרמתי את היד חזק כי רציתי שיאשרו לי לעלות, וכשעליתי, התרגשתי להגיד במלוא הכוונה: "אני מקבלת על עצמי לחזור בתשובה שלמה!" ...משם, מצאתי את עצמי במדרשה בירושלים. שכרתי דירה עם עוד חמש בנות שלמדו במדרשה והתחלתי ללמוד מה שצריך בשביל לחזור בתשובה, להבדיל בין טומאה לטהרה, להיות יהודייה כשרה, וכן הלאה. הלימוד עם בנות בלבד, הקסים אותי, בשבת כלה במדרשה, בכיתי מהתרגשות, הרגשתי בחלום, איך יכולתי לעבור חיים שלמים בעולם מקביל בלי לדעת שאפשר אחרת! כמה צער היה יכול להיחסך לי אם מגיל צעיר לא הייתי לומדת עם בנים... הייתי יכולה להיות בן אדם אחר לגמרי...

מה שלא התיישב בדעתי הוא שיש כל כך הרבה סוגים של יהדות, ולכל סוג – רבנים שונים, שהקהל שלהם שומע להם בעיניים עצומות. לא הבנתי איך זה יכול להיות! הרי השם בחר במשה רבנו שהיה 'עניו מכל אדם', ולימד אותו את כל התורה, ונתן לו את התורה, ואפילו קרא לה "תורת משה" כדי שאנו נקבל אותה ממנו, ושהוא ילמד אותנו לקיימה ולחיות על פיה, וזו הדרך שהשם נתן לכל היהודים. על כן חשבתי, אני מוכרחה למצוא את משה רבנו, כי בלעדיו הכול תוהו, כמו שנוכחתי ב-25 שנותיי. וכמו שנאמר "ויאמינו בהשם ובמשה עבדו", אין דרך להבין את התורה בלעדיו, ומי שבכל זאת מנסה, ממילא מבין הכול הפוך, והולך נגד מה שהשם קבע. כשהבנות בדירה רצו להדליק נרות לעילוי נשמת הצדיקים, שאלתי למי הן מדליקות, והן הראו לי תמונות של רבנים מפורסמים (שלא הכרתי), לא יכולתי להסתכל בפניהם. נבהלתי. הם היו נראים לי זרים, ולא הרגשתי שייכת לזה. אמרתי שאדליק לנשמת אבותינו הקדושים, אברהם, יצחק ויעקב בזכות משה רבנו. יום אחד, אחת השותפות שלי בדירה, לקחה אותי להרצאה של פרופ' לאפנה ב"בצלאל" (בית ספר גבוה לאמנות, שבו היא למדה). שלוש שעות הרצאה, ופרט לצעיף האדום שאתו התבדרה ופלירטטה במשך כל ההרצאה, איני זוכרת אלא משפט אחד שאמרה: "**השינוי אף פעם לא בא מהרוב**". באוטובוס, בדרכנו חזרה, נזכרתי שזהו יום החופש במדרשה ואין לימודים; אמרתי לשותפתי שאני צמאה לשיעור תורה. היא אמרה שארד בתחנה המרכזית ולא רחוק משם, מתקיים שיעור בעוד שעה וחצי, על ידי רב חסידי. כשאמרה לי את שמו, נזכרתי שזה אותו הרב שהרצה באותו סופשבוע במלון בדרום, וזו הייתה הפעם הראשונה ששמעתי אדם דתי שסיפר שאם יראה אישה ערומה טובעת בנהר, הוא לא יחשוב להתחסד כדי לשמור על צניעותו ולתת לה למות, אלא יקפוץ למים לעשות הכול כדי להציל אותה, והרי היא בת ישראל, כאחותו. זה שינה בי מאוד את ההתנגדות שהייתה לי כלפי אנשים דתיים, שלא חשבתי שאי-פעם אוכל לדבר אתם או להבין איך הם חושבים... (דאז לא ידעתי שכתוב בגמרא שמי שלא קופץ למים במצב כזה נקרא "חסיד שוטה"). ירדתי בתחנה המרכזית, ובזמן שהיה לי חיפשתי ספר על חנוכה. היינו לפני החג וחשבתי שהגיע הזמן שאדע למה בכלל מדליקים נרות ומה משמעות החג. בעודי ליד דוכן הספרים בלי שמצאתי שום ספר לגעת בו... פנתה אליי אישה נחמדה ודקה, ומטפחת לראשה, אדרת. היא שאלה אותי אם ראיתי את הפתק הזה. מה זה? שאלתי בסקרנות לנוכח מה שהחזיקה בידיה; פתק, שנראה בעיניי כמגלת סתרים, כמפת אוצר עתיקת יומין. "זה הפתק משמים ששלח רבי נחמן 111 שנה לאחר פטירתו לרבי ישראל בער אודסר, שלמד אז בישיבה של רבי מאיר בעל הנס בטבריה". לא קישרתי את רבי נחמן הזה לרבי נחמן שכתב את הסיפורי מעשיות שקראתי בקיבוץ. בטבריה? נולדתי בטבריה! זה הזכיר לי ש"הטבריינים" תמיד אהבו להתפאר שטבריה היא עיר קודש מלאת קברי צדיקים, ושחז"ל גילו שהמשיח יבוא מטבריה. שאלתי אותה על הקשר למשה רבנו והיא אמרה שנשמת משה חוזרת בחמשת צדיקי הדורות, שאלו הצדיקים שהורידו תורה לעולם והם: משה רבנו שהביא את התורה, רבי שמעון בר יוחאי שגילה את הזוהר הקדוש, האר"י הקדוש שגילה את תורת הקבלה, הבעל שם טוב הקדוש שגילה את תורת החסידות ורבי נחמן שגילה את הסוד של שיר חדש ואמר: "האש שלי תוקד עד ביאת המשיח". ובפתק הזה מגלה לרבי ישראל שהוא הוא שחזר: "ועליך אמרתי האש שלי תוקד עד ביאת המשיח". והוא ערב לקב"ה שיתקן העולם. רבי ישראל לא רצה שיקראו לו רבי לכן הוא מכונה בפי כול "הסבא". היא אמרה שהסבא אמר: רק להגיד בפה השם הזה: נ נח נחמ נחמן מאומן זה ממתיק כל הצרות וכל הדינים וכל העוונות וכל הכפירות, הכול!..נ נח אז הכול טוב... זהו הכול, כל התורה וכל ישראל וכל הרפואות וכל הישועות הכול בדיבור אחד... היא סיפרה לי שרבי יונתן בן עוזיאל כותב בהקדמה לשיר השירים על התגלות עשרה שירים מבריאת העולם עד ימות המשיח. ובזוהר הקדוש פרשת פנחס, אומר רבי שמעון: "... יתעורר בעולם, שיר פשוט, כפול, משולש, מרובע, שהוא מעלה אותיות שלו י, י"ה, יה"ו, יהו"ה"... (מרמז על השיר נ נח נחמ נחמן מאומן שהוא שם השם מלובש בשם הצדיק שעל ידו נפתחין עיני ישראל).

שאלתי אותה אם יודעים מה הם השירים! והיא מנתה בפניי: 1. שירת הים 2. שירת הבאר 3. שירת האזינו 4. שירת יהושע 5. שירת דבורה 6. שירת חנה 7. שירת דוד 8. שירת שלמה 9. שירת חזקיה (יש אומרים כי שיר השירים הוא התשיעי)ו-10. שירה שלעתיד, הוא כמו שרבי נתן תלמידו המובהק של רבי נחמן כותב: "..ולעתיד לבוא הכל יהיה נכלל בהניגון הזה כל מה שעבר על כל אחד". ורבי נחמן אמר על עצמו: "אני אשיר שיר לעתיד שזה יהיה העולם הבא של כל הצדיקים והחסידים", ובתורה ח' בליקוטי תנינא, שהיא

התורה האחרונה שאמר בראש השנה לפני הסתלקותו וגילה שם שעל ידי השיר הזה יהיה חידוש העולם לעתיד.

נתמלאתי התרגשות לנוכח דבריה, ביקשתי לדעת יותר. והיא הראתה לי בספר את כל מה שאמרה ואת התורה הזו: "לעתיד יתער שיר חדש של בחינת נפלאות, בחינת השגחה, כי אז יהיה ההנהגה על יד השגחה לבד".

ניסיתי לדמיין איך זה לחיות על השגחה לבד... עם כל דיבור ששמעתי כבר הרגשתי בעתיד.

הסבא אמר: "אני אודיע לכם פה עכשיו מי אני! אני נ נח נחמ נחמן מאומן, זה אני! אתם יודעים כבר מי אני". חשבתי, איך עד ירושלים הגעתי ללמוד יהדות במדרשה, ואת הדבר החשוב ביותר לא לימדו אותי?! בראשי כבר החלטתי שאינני רוצה להמשיך את הלימודים במדרשה. איך יכלו שלא להזכיר, אפילו לא ברמז את רבי נחמן ואת הנס של הפתק הזה?!. הרגשתי בלבי שכל מה שעברתי בחיים היה כדי להגיע לרגע הזה, הכול התגמד לעומת מה שהרגשתי באותו רגע. רציתי לדעת הכול על הפתק ועל בעל הפתק, וללמוד את כל ספרי רבנו רבי נחמן, להגיע לכל אדם בעולם ולהפיץ את הפתק הזה שהוא ספר של דף אחד, שורש התורה, וכפי שאמר רבי נתן: "דף אחד מספרי רבנו יהיה התיקון על הכול!" וגם: "דף אחד מספרי רבנו יעקור את כל הרע מן העולם". היא אמרה שהסבא אמר להודיע שיש פתק, ושיש בעל הפתק, ביקשתי לבוא אליה ללמוד עוד. היא התקשרה לבית קצרות, וחזרה אליי. "אנחנו משפחה מיוחדת", אמרה בחיוך, "חמש נשים עם אותו איש", מגניב חשבתי. בכל אופן, אפשר לבוא?! הייתי להוטה ללמוד מרבי נחמן על הפלא, על הנ-נח! הלכנו ברגל כרבע שעה, בדרך דיברנו כל אחת על עצמה, היה לי נחמד לדבר אתה, הרגשתי שאנחנו מכירות, היה בה משהו יפה בפשטות שלו, לא מתאמץ. לא הכרתי עד אותו זמן אישה דתייה באופן אישי, כלומר, לא משיעור או הרצאה. ועם המשפחה של חצב, ההיכרות הייתה לא עמוקה ובתקופה אחרת לגמרי שבה לא התעניינתי באותם הנושאים. בכל אופן, כשהגענו לבית, פתחה לנו את הדלת אילנה בחיוך רחב והרבה לב. אימא לעשרה ילדים ואשת אשכולות. היה נראה שזו אישה שאוהבת את החיים שלה. התרגשתי לנוכח מדפי הספרים. במדרשה הייתי מבלה את הלילות בספרייה, ולדאבוני לא הצלחתי למצוא שם ספרים שאני יכולה ללמוד מהם, רציתי ללמוד ולקיים. כשראיתי את דניאל, רציתי לדבר אתו. ישבנו ליד שולחן האוכל בסלון ודיברנו. זה מצחיק, אבל הרגשתי שאנחנו דומים. לא יכולתי לשער שהחבר הכי טוב שלי, שחיפשתי משך חיים שלמים, אמצא אותו בדמות רקדן בלט מפורסם שחזר בתשובה; נשוי, עם זקן ופאות ג'ינג'יות וכיפה כחולה שמכסה את כל הראש עד המצח ועליה רקום בצהוב נ נח נחמ נחמן מאומן בירושלים. הוא חשב כמוני, והזכיר לי את עצמי. שיחות רבות שישבתי עם אנשים מכל המינים, בדרך כלל היו מגיבים אליי שאני "חיה בסרט", ושיש לי רעיונות בלתי אפשריים ושאי-אפשר לחיות איך שאני חושבת שאפשר לחיות... בגלל זה תמיד בסופו של יום, אפילו כשהייתי מוקפת "חברים", הרגשתי לבד. כי אף אחד לא באמת הלך אתי "עד הסוף", וכולם חזרו לשגרת שעמום החיים של רדיפה אחרי כסף. חיפשתי תמיד מישהו שחושב כמוני. שמחתי שגם הוא הרגיש בנוח אתי, ודיברנו על החיים שלפני, כלומר, על הזמנים שהובילו אותנו לתשובה, ומצאנו שהסיפור שלנו במרקם הטעמים, התחושות המחשבות והרגשות היה כמעט זהה. דיברנו על הפתק ועל בעל הפתק, כשצילה נכנסה, היא הציעה להראות לי ב-DVD את הסבא מספר בעצמו את סיפור ההתקרבות שלו לברסלב, ואיך הגיע אליו עד הבית רבי ישראל קרדונר, שהיה מל"ו צדיקים נסתרים ועד סיפור נס הפתק. לפני שיצאתי, ביקשתי מדניאל שיבחר עבורי אחד מהספרים שלו, וישאיל לי עד הפעם הבאה שאבוא. דניאל בחר את אחד הכרכים של "ליקוטי הלכות" שכתב רבי נתן, תלמידו המובהק של רבי נחמן, שאחראי על כתיבת כל ספרי רבי נחמן ותורותיו. רבי נתן מסביר כל הלכה לעומק: פשט, דרש וסוד, דבר מתוך דבר, ואפשר להבין את העומק הגשמי והרוחני של הלכות שולחן ערוך מה שמקל מאוד לדעתי, את קיום ההלכה.

הבנים הקטנים חזרו מבית המדרש, ונכנסו לבית כמו רכבת, אחד אחרי השני; הציציות השתלשלו ממכנסיהם השחורים מתחת לחולצות המשבצות המכופתרות, וכיפות נ-נח צבעוניות עם פונפון, פאות ארוכות בצדי פניהם – הם היו נראים כל כך יפים. חשבתי לעצמי, הלוואי שכאלו יהיו ילדי לעולם. צילה הראתה לי את אלבום המוזיקה של הלהקה המשפחתית "הבעטלירס", שבו הבנים הקטנים והגדולים שרים ומנגנים עם דניאל. אלבום כפול של דיסק מוזיקה ודיסק סרטים, חוברת שירים עם כל המילים, תמונות וספר שמסביר על הנ-נח מהמקורות, שיחות חברים וחידושים. קניתי את האלבום, וחזרתי לדירה במדרשה. למחרת בבוקר מצאתי את עצמי לבד בדירה. זה היה נדיר שחמשת השותפות שלי לא היו. אחרי מקלחת ותפילת שחרית ארוכה, ישבתי עם הקפה ליד שולחן המטבח, והשקפתי למרפסת בשכונה החרדית הצפופה. הבניינים היו בנויים כמו אחד בתוך השני, צמודים, כשכל מרפסת צופה לחלון או למרפסת של בית אחר. והכול מסורג בסורגים גסים וארוכים. לקחתי את אלבום "הבעטלירס" לידיי והוצאתי את חוברת המילים. וואו מי כתב את המילים האלה חשבתי, קפצתי ממקומי והכנסתי את הדיסק המוזיקלי. לא יכולתי להמשיך לשבת והתחלתי לרקוד בהתלהבות לאורך כל הדיסק! בכיתי, צחקתי ובעיקר

התחזקתי. החלפתי לדיסק הסרטים, וצפיתי בסרטים על הסבא ובסרטים של הפצות ושל הופעות שאף פעם לא ראיתי, בסרטונים קצרים; אחד של ילד מספר מיסיפורי מעשיותי בעל-פה בניגון נעים ונפלא מאוד (https://youtu.be/nNB3fTT5OzM), סרט פרודיה קצר בשחור-לבן, בכיתי מהתרגשות. פתחתי את הספר המצורף לאלבום וקראתי בשקיקה. התקשרתי לאדרת וסיפרתי לה מה עשיתי בכל אותו הבוקר, ורעדתי מהתרגשות, רציתי לדבר על זה, ולדעת הכול על רבי נחמן, שהוא רבי ישראל. שאלתי אותה מה היא עושה. היא אמרה שהיא מחפשת מורה להעשרת הלימודים של הבנות. אמרתי לה שאני יכולה לתלות מודעות על קירות הבניין ובמדרשה... היא שמחה. פתאום צץ במוחי רעיון... אני יכולה לעשות את זה! כל החיים עבדתי עם ילדים, אני שחקנית, אני קוראת, אני כותבת... ביקשתי ממנה לפגוש את הבנות ולחשוב איך לבנות חוג לימוד והעשרה. היא הסכימה! התלבשתי כמו מורה... והלכתי מרחק עשר דקות ברגל לביתם. כשנכנסתי, הבנות קיבלו את פניי, וחשבתי שמעולם לא ראיתי ולא הכרתי יופי כזה, אור של תמימות ושל מתיקות. הן שאלו אותי שאלות, ואני – אותן. לא יכולתי להוריד את החיוך מהפנים... קבענו שאגיע למחרת ב 30: 07.

הגעתי, והבנות כולן ישבו סביב שולחן אחד. צמה הדוקה קלועה לראשן, לבושות חולצות מכופתרות וחצאיות ארוכות, בפנים רעננות ועיניים סקרניות... התיישבתי אתן. אילנה הגישה לכולן ארוחת בוקר ושתייה חמה. אכלנו, שתינו ובירכנו על המזון. לאחר מכן קיפלנו את שולחן האוכל, כולן ישבו בשולחנות בית ספר, ואני עמדתי מולן והלוח הלבן מאחורי גבי. כדי שאוכל לזכור את השמות שלהן חילקתי לכל אחת מלבן חתוך מבריסטול צבעוני, וביקשתי שכל אחת תכתוב את שמה, תקפל את הבריסטול ותעמיד על שולחנה. לאחר שעשו זאת כל אחת לפי הסדר סיפרה את הסיפור שמאחורי השם שלה, וכך גם למדתי על הנשים בתורה, כי כולן קרויות בשמות מהתנ״ך. כשתורי הגיע לספר על שמי, אמרתי ששירן זה שם טיפשי עם סיפור סתמי, אימא שלי סיפרה לי על שירן ומורן, ילדות שבנעוריה הייתה השמרטפית שלהן, ואני בתה הראשונה, לכן קראה לי על שמן. אמרתי שאני לא אוהבת את השם הזה ושאין לו שום משמעות. שוש קפצה ואמרה: ״זה לא סתם שם! זה **שיר נון שיר נ**-נח״ זה השיר של רבנו, בטח שיש לו משמעות! יפה! חשבתי, ומאז התחלתי לאהוב את השם שלי.

בכל יום הייתי מגיעה ב-30 :7 בבוקר ומלמדת חוגי ספרות, הבנת הנקרא ולשון. כשהבנות היו בחוגים או בשיעורים אחרים, הייתי יושבת בחדר העבודה שביחידה ומכינה את השיעורים הבאים. תמיד הייתי משלבת אלמנטים של משחק ודרמה, כי זה היה חלק בלתי נפרד ממני, ותמיד היינו גולשות לשיחות אישיות, ועל כל דבר. בעקבות כך שוחחתי עם דניאל, וסיפרתי לו על החוויה שלי עם הבנות שלו. כיוון שהגעתי מאורח חיים מתירני, כשהן שאלו אותי שאלות אישיות, גמגמתי, כי לא ידעתי אם זה בסדר לספר להן שגרתי עם בן זוג במשך כמה שנים, ושלא רציתי להתחתן, ועל הצבא, ובכלל כל סיפור החיים שלי הוא מופרע לגמרי לאוזניים של מי שאורח חייו דתי או שמרני. דניאל אמר שאהיה עצמי. אהבתי את הדרך שבה הוא חושב, את הדרך שבה הוא מדבר, את הדרך שהוא זורם עם מצבים, ועם זאת, אכפתי ודואג, ומנסה להבין את המורכבות של כל אחד. בימי הולדת נהגנו לקנות מתנות לכולם, וכולנו ראינו סרט טוב ביחד שהקרנו על מסך ענק אחרי ארוחת ערב חגיגית, ברכות, ריקודים לצלילי הנגינה של הבנים ושירה במיקרופון. הרגשתי אחת מהמשפחה. הייתי נשארת עם הבנות, וכשהבנים הקטנים היו חוזרים מהלימודים, היינו עושים סדנאות אוכל ומבשלים ביחד. הם ראו בתיק שלי ספרים של ש״י עגנון ואת ״יומנה של אנה פרנק״, וביקשו שאקריא להם. היינו יושבים שעות, אני בכיסא המורה, והם מולי, בריכוז יוצא מן הכלל, ואני מקריאה להם, תוך כדי המחזה של הסיפורים. הם היו מרותקים, ולאחר שעות, היינו שואלים שאלות בהבנת הנקרא. הם הדהימו אותי בחדות החשיבה שלהם, בקליטה, בזיכרון, בעניין שהם מביעים ובאהבה לדעת. נהניתי מהם כמו שלא נהניתי משום דבר לפני כן. הזמן אתם היה עבורי עונג צרוף. למדתי מהם המון: תורות, הלכות, מדרשים, סיפורי צדיקים והנהגות אמת ומוסר של חסידים. הרבה פעמים הבנים הקטנים היו חוזרים מבית המדרש ומספרים לי מה שלמדו באותו היום עם המלמד. פעם אחת יהונתן בן התשע הכתיב לי ממחברת הלימודים שלו, ובחן אותי כדי לראות כמה זכרתי. כשהייתי מתאפרת, ידידיה בן השמונה היה אומר לי שאני מכוערת, והבנות היו אומרות שאני נראית כמו אישה מצוירת. עשינו שבתות וחגים יחד, וגם כשהיו בהקלטות עם דניאל באולפן בגבעת שאול, הייתי אתם. כשאדרת ערכה הגהות של הספרים, ישבתי לצדה; וכשאנסטסיה רצתה שאחווה דעה על התלבושות שתפרה, גלשנו לשיחות נפש ארוכות. כל אחד בבית הזה היה כל כך רגיש ומיוחד, מוכשר ולהב. בסעודה, לאורך שולחנות ארוכים, מצד אחד הנשים והבנות ומצד שני הגברים והבנים, הילדים אהבו להגיד בעל-פה דברי תורה ומדרשים, פותחים ספרי ״ליקוטי מוהר״ן״, ולומדים יחד כל המשפחה, כל אחד אומר את דעתו ומנתח כפי הבנתו. הייתי מרגישה כחלק מהמשפחה, אבל גם כצופה מהצד, מדמיינת איך הכול מצולם לסדרת ריאלטי בין-לאומית, שמעוררת את כל העולם לראות את הפלא, שניתן לחיות בעקבות האהבה לרבי נחמן ולהשתדלות היומיומית לחיות את עצותיו... ככל שהתאהבתי בילדים והערצתי את הגדולים, התאהבתי במי שהביא אותם לעולם: השם, האימהות והאבא.

מצחיק איך החיים מובילים אותנו לפי הרצון שבוער בנו. אחרי שקראתי את הסיפורי מעשיות של רבי נחמן, עוד כשהייתי בקיבוץ, היה לי חלום: למצוא חבורה של שחקנים, שביחד נפקיר את עצמנו לחיי הפצה עם תיאטרון נודד שיופיע בכל הארץ, ונעלה הצגות על פי המעשיות של רבי נחמן. ראיתי בזה דרך חיים, שהעיקר הוא המטרה המשותפת, שחזקה הרבה יותר מהצלחה אישית בקריירה טיפשית וממלחמות על מעמד חברתי, על כסף שנובעות מתחרותיות אגוצנטרית. המטרה היא ההצלחה הכללית; איחוד לבבות שמסוגל להפוך את כל הרוע של העולם, את כל השנאה והאיבה לשלום ואהבה.

ועכשיו, הבו לי את מי שאמר שיותר מעשרים נפשות יחד זה לא פשוט. מניסיון גיליתי שזה זורם הרבה יותר מחיי זוגיות טריוויאליים, שבהם בני הזוג כמו סוסים טרויאנים, מאיימים להתפוצץ בכל רגע; או מחיי משפחה בנאליים, שכל יום דומה מדי למשנהו, והשגרה קוצצת כנפיים.

בתום אחד השיעורים שלי עם הבנות, ציפי, שהיה לה גבס על היד, התלוננה שקשה לה לכתוב ויוצא לה כתב מכוער. ישבתי לידה כדי לעזור לה והיא זרקה לי את העיפרון ואמרה: "למה שנסמוך עלייך בכלל?! היו פה מורות שלימדו אותנו ואחר כך עזבו ודיברו על המשפחה שלנו לשון הרע!" אמרתי לה שאני מצטערת, וזה לא אותו דבר, אני כבר חלק מהמשפחה, ואני אוהבת אותם כמו הם היו הילדים שלי. ציפי התפרצה לדבריי ואמרה: "אם את כל כך אוהבת אותנו למה שלא תתחתני עם אבא שלי?!" עצרתי בתדהמה מסוימת, היא הסתכלה עליי, רצינית וקשוחה, ואז חייכה...

הבתים של המשפחה התנהלו כבמות בתיאטרון. אין קביעות מגורים, השחקנים מחליפים במות ותפקידים. התפאורה והחדרים זזים לפי סצנה ולפי צורכי הנפשות הפועלות. גיליתי שזה נוח יותר מכל ריהוט יוקרתי. ערמת כיסאות פלסטיק שערוכים לקבל אורחים בכל רגע, וחברים רבים שמגיעים. שולחנות פלסטיק ארוכים, שלובשים לבן לשבת ולחג או מפות ניילון חד-פעמיות לימי החול. רגליים מברזל, שמתקפלות ביעילות, ועליהם סדורות סעודות ונערכות שיחות... לא פעם, כשהתיישבנו כולנו לסעודת בוקר, מרגע נטילת ידיים, וברכה על הלחם וחלוקתו, היינו מתחילים לדבר שיחה ערה, עד שכבר כמעט הגיעה שעת שקיעה. תפילת מנחה קראה לבנים לעזוב את השולחן, והם היו מתקבצים יחד למניין בבית המדרש. כשחזרו, לא היה שולחן ולא אוכל. קיפלנו הכול הצדה, והסטודיו הפך לרחבת ריקודים. כלי נגינה למנגנים, והשאר קופצים, רוקדים וגם שרים, עד שמתעייפים.

הנשים היו פעילות ואנרגטיות, מלאות שמחת חיים והתלהבות. היו להן רעיונות משלהן להפצה, והן היו מקיימות ישיבות ומפיקות אירועים והופעות ללהקת 'הבעטלירס'.

**2010**. ביום בהיר אחד – עצרו את דניאל במפתיע.

כולנו היינו המומים.

פתחתי את מגרת המטפחות בחדר נשים, והוצאתי מטפחת לכסות את שערות ראשי. רציתי להראות להשם יתברך שגם אם הוא עוזב אותי, אני לא עוזבת אותו,! היה לי חשוב שדניאל ידע שאני אתו, ומחכה לו, העברתי לו מסר דרך עורך דינו...

המשטרה טענה שאנס את בתו החורגת אנסטסיה.

זו הייתה מהלומה קשה.

האכזריות חסרת הרחמים של אלו שמעזים להוציא דיבה רעה, להמציא עלילה, להרוס בן אדם ואת בני ביתו, על סמך מה? ולמה?

שנאת חינם ולא יותר. רצח בדם קר לאור יום. שפיכות דמים.

אחרי ארבעה ימים – שבהם היינו במתח נורא, והילדים לא רצו לעשות כלום חוץ מלהתפלל ולקיים את העצות שכתובות בספרים של רבי נחמן ל"המתקת דינים" ול"ישועה" – שיחררו את דניאל. התיק נסגר מחוסר ראיות.

השופט נזף בחוקרי המשטרה.

לא היה כתב אישום.

אנסטסיה בחקירה המשטרתית הקשה סיפרה בגילוי לב את האמת שלה; היה לה סטוץ עם בחור שהפסיק לענות לה לטלפונים. אנסטסיה השתגעה מזה שהוא לא עונה לה, כמו כל בת 17 שמתגפפת עם בחורים

שבסופו של דבר מזלזלים בה ומתחמקים ממנה, וחשבה על תחבולה איך להשיג אותו בחזרה. העצה שלה הייתה להגיע לקופת החולים ולעשות הצגה שהיא בהיריון, וכך לפי דעתה המשובשת – יזמנו את מי שהכניס אותה להיריון, וכך תפגוש שוב את הבחור, שיהיה מוכרח להינשא לה בעל כורחו. כך חשבה לפי דעתה המשובשת.

מובן שהתכנית שלה כשלה, אנסטסיה הייתה אז בת פחות מ-18, וזירזה את אילנה ללוות אותה לקופת החולים הקרובה, ולא לחכות לאמה קארי, שביקשה שתיאזר בסבלנות עד שתחזור הביתה ותיקח אותה היא. בקופת החולים קרה דבר מוזר: עובדת סוציאלית שנכחה בקופה כתבה דו״ח סוציאלי, ושלחה אותו למשטרה, על נערה בת 17 שהגיעה בחשש להיריון, עם אישה, שהיא לא אמה. למה זה דבר מוזר? בכל מקום בעולם, אלפי ומיליוני בנות 17 חוששות שנכנסו להיריון, ומגיעות להיבדק בקופת חולים, עם אמן או שלא עם אמן. כלל לא חשוב! הדו״ח הסוציאלי גרם למעצר אביה החורג כקשור להיריונה?! נראה שמישהו רוקח פה תבשיל רעלים. אבל מי? במשטרה הוסיפו תוספות חמות ותבלינים, כגון האשמות באינוס הבת של האישה השנייה! נשמע כמו סקופ לחדשות, ותוספת כבוד למשטרת ישראל, שתפסה עבריין מין שנשוי לשש נשים! איך הוא מעז? היו בטוחים במשטרה שכך יגרמו לשמחה ולששון ברחובות העיר: זרקו אותו לגוב האריות, ונראה מה יהיו השאריות... אם אנחנו לא חיים ככה, למה שהוא יחיה כך? כולם עסוקים בגנבות, בפריצות, ברמאויות בהתנכלויות, בבגידות, במעילות, בכזבים ובהטעיות, כולם שקועים, יתר על המידה בסרטי אימה ובטלנובלות. לכן הם בוודאי לא מסוגלים להבין שלא מוכרחים לחיות כנוכלים. אבל מסתבר שהשכנים, צופי הטלוויזיה, השוטרים, החוקרים, עורכי הדין, השופטים, מערכת הרווחה ושאר הרשויות מאותו המין, מוכרחים. תוהו ובוהו וחושך על פני תהום. אני היום כבר הבנתי שכל אלו שמאמינים ללשון הרע או מפיצים אותו, הם הם אלו שיש להם שק של עקרבים ונחשים שהם ממש לא היו רוצים שמישהו ידע עליו. אז מצאו להם פתרון, ישירות מהיצר הרע – ללכלך את שמו של חף מפשע – וכך להתחמק מההתגלות כרשע. אין עוררין על כך שמי שפועל מתוך לשון הרע – הוא רע בעצמו.

אנסטסיה אהבה לדבר אתי ולספר לי סיפורים בלי סוף, שהרבה פעמים הכבידו עליי ועייפו אותי. למרות זאת, הפכתי להיות עבורה חברה טובה. היא אפילו נסעה אתי מירושלים עד כפר חטים לביקור אצל הוריי. כנראה שנוצרו אצלה מיני תסביכים כתוצאה ממסכת הגירושין של אימא שלה, ומהאבא הביולוגי שלה שהתחתן שוב ואשתו החדשה לא רצתה את אנסטסיה בקרבתה, והוא מצדו לא השתדל לשמור אתה על קשר והיא חשבה שהוא לא אוהב אותה. האחים מהאבות האחרים שהתנכרו לה, מחלת השרירים של אמה, וגרמה לה להיות בתשישות תמידית ובעיסוק בכאביה יותר מתשומת הלב שאנסטסיה, לדבריה, הייתה זקוקה לה. כמו גם ניבולי הפה של אמה על כל גרושיה, על הקהילה שנידתה אותה ועוד ועוד סיפורים מסוג זה. לא האמנתי לכל מה שיצא לה מהפה, רציתי לעזור לה, להבין למה יש לה צורך להמציא סיפורים כל הזמן. בין היתר היא סיפרה לי שבעצם היא מאוהבת מגיל צעיר בבועז, והראתה לי קלסרים שלמים עם מכתבי אהבה אליו. מאחר שבועז לא החזיר לה אהבה, שבורת לב היא חשבה להתנחם בזלמן אחיו הגדול, בכך שיתחתן אתה. זה לא קרה. זלמן התחתן עם צילה – אחותה הגדולה. באחד הימים היא גם סיפרה לי שניסתה לפתות את דניאל, אך הוא עצר בעדה, וניסה לעזור לה למצוא פתרונות לסיבוכים הנפשיים שלה מילדות; אימא שלה הייתה מפרסמת בקול גדול שבעלה הראשון עשה מעשים מגונים בצילה וביאן. צילה ויאן היו מופרעים ולמדו בבית ספר מיוחד לילדים בעייתיים, אנסטסיה לעומת זאת הייתה ילדה מנומסת ומסודרת ואהבה ללמוד, ולכן גם קיבלה ציונים גבוהים מהמורים. כיוון שהיו אחיה גדולים ממנה ולא הכניסו אותה לסודות חברותם, וגם הרבו לצחוק ממנה, והיא הרגישה דחויה. היא רצתה שאימא שלה תרחם עליה. אחרי ששמעה את עליזה מספרת שאח שלה אנס אותה מילדות, אנסטסיה התחילה לספר שרב הקהילה של אביה הביולוגי אנס אותה. וגם הבן שלו. והשכן והבן של המפיץ מטבריה, והבנים של המפיץ מבית שמש, וההוא וההוא וההיא (סיפרה שעליזה אנסה אותה ושהיא מתכוונת לתבוע אותה). בעדותה במשטרה, הסנגור של דניאל דאז, העיד שבחקירתה החזיקה טלפון פתוח ואפשרה לו לשמוע איך החוקרים עוברים על החוק ומנסים להדיח אותה מעדות ולהלביש לה התעסקות מינית עם אביה החורג – דניאל. היא לא התבלבלה, והסבירה להם שדניאל בחיים לא נגע בה וגם לא משהו שקרוב לכך. והמשיכה וסיפרה לחוקרי המשטרה את סיפורי ההוללות שלה עם בחורים בני גילה, שחלקם אמתיים, וחלקם – פרי דמיונה.

אחרי ארבעה ימים במעצר, שדניאל שב הביתה, והשמחה חזרה, הייתה התרגשות גדולה! כשרצה לנוח מעט, כל הילדים, מקטן ועד גדול טיפסו עליו במיטה ושיחקו ביחד עד שנרדמו בתפזורת.

היחסים שלי עם הנשים התהדקו והתחזקתי מהפתיחות בינינו. דיברנו על הכול וחיפשנו פתרונות לבעיות של כל אחת. הצטרפתי לסדנאות האלתור עם הנשים, ובכל פעם גילינו על עצמנו, ואחת על השנייה, דברים חדשים. המחזנו רגשות והקצנו מצבים, שיחקנו ״דרמה״. עליזה הייתה ללא ספק מלכת הדרמה. היו לה פנטזיות לא רגילות, והיא ידעה לבטא את עצמה במלוא העצמה. הרבה פעמים גם צילמנו את האלתורים כי חשבנו ברצינות להפוך אותם לסרט. הצטערתי שאין צוות צילום מסביב לשעון שמתעד כל פינה. הגענו

לשורשם של דברים, והשתחררנו מהכחשות עצמיות ומתפיסות שקריות. התובנות שאליהן הגענו, חשבתי, יכלו לעזור לכל מי שהיה צופה בנו.

תמנע הכירה את המשפחה קצת לפני שאני הגעתי. היא הייתה אחת מבין האורחים הרבים שהזדמנו לביתנו. תמנע גדלה בלי אבא, ולצד אימא סכיזופרנית (כפי שהעידה בבית המשפט), והתגלגלה בין פנימיות, עד שלבסוף נשרה מהלימודים. תמנע הגיעה לביתנו לשבתות וחגים, ופיתחה אובססיה להתחתן עם דניאל. כשניסתה לארוב לו ולהיות אתו לבד, היא ביקשה שיבתק את בתוליה. הוא נבהל, וביקש מהנשים שידאגו לכך שהיא לא תבוא יותר. איכשהו, היא כל פעם חזרה. כשניסתה שוב ושוב ללכוד אותו ברשתה, דניאל נאלץ להבהיר לה באופן חד-משמעי שהוא לא מתכוון להתחתן שוב. תמנע לא חדלה מחיזוריה, שהפכו כפייתיים. כשאני הגעתי, זיהיתי שתמנע מתנהגת בצורה מוזרה וחולנית, ועלולה להוות סכנה לדניאל ולילדים, אמרתי לה שלא תבוא יותר. תמנע הסתכלה עליי בעיניה השחורות, מגדילה את עפעפיה ומקטינה אותם לסירוגין, לא הבנתי מה היא מנסה לעשות. אחר, הלכה בכעס וכמה חודשים לא ראינו אותה ולא שמענו ממנה. עד שהגיעה שוב לביקור, וכמעט שיצאה מדעתה כשהתחוור לה שמהיום שראתה אותי לראשונה, לא עזבתי את דניאל ואת המשפחה, והמטפחת שלראשי העידה שהכתרתי את עצמי רשמית לאישה שישית לדניאל. היא התאפקה, ושאפה מהסיגריות שלה ארוכות והיה אפילו נדמה שאולי השתנתה, התעלתה על עצמה והשתדלה. כיום, לפי התוצאה... קנאתה החולנית שרפה באכזריות כל רגע שעשו עמה חסד בני המשפחה, ובשעת מחסור האכילו והשקו אותה.

מה צריך ללמוד מזה? שצריך להיזהר בהכנסת אורחים? מה היינו צריכים לעשות? ואיך היה אפשר לצפות לזה או למנוע השתלשלות שכזאת?!

יותר משנה אחרי אותו מעצר מצער שאנסטסיה היוותה תירוץ לכלוא את דניאל, התברר לנו שכבר כמה שנים המשטרה והרווחה תכננו לפרק את המשפחה שלנו, והסיבה היחידה שלא עשו זאת הייתה כי לא הצליחו למצוא עילה מספקת לכך. מהמקרה של אנסטסיה הגיעו למסקנה, שיש לאיים אך לא רק על אחת מבני המשפחה – יש ללכוד את כולם, להפריד בין אימהות לילדים, להפריד אחים, לבודד כל אחד מול חוקר מיומן, שיאיים וילחץ, יצעק וינבח, ואם יהיה צורך להכות – יש להם מענה גם בשביל זה, מהלומות חזקות. ואז החוקר יאמר לכל אחד שהוא עשוי להיכלא מאחורי הברזלים, לעשרות שנים, כי כבר יש להם את החומר הדרוש והוכחות מוצקות, שלא ניתן עליהם לערער, והאפשרות היחידה להינצל ממאסר בטוח היא לאשר את דברי החוקר, ולא כל דבר אחר. עכברים במעבדת הימ"ר סגרו אותנו בצנצנות אטומות – **מעצר 2011**.

ההוכחות והראיות הברורות באשר לקרבן האמתי שאליו כוונו כל כלי הנשק למטרה ברורה אחת ויחידה להרשעה וכליאה עד מוות הוא ללא ספק – נאשם 1 – דניאל אמבש. קרבן של מערכת בלי חוק, בלי אמת ובלי צדק.

בבית המשפט תמנע הצהירה לפני השופטים:

"בחיים אני לא אוהב גבר כמו שאהבתי את דניאל".

מה הולך פה?! הבחורה מצהירה על אהבתה, כביכול האין-סופית לאיש, מסור ונאמן לאלוהיו, אדם יציב, הנשוי לשש נשים, שאתן ועם ילדיהם הוא גר. איך ייתכן שהיא זאת שגורמת למעצרו ולפירוק משפחתו?!

לא עלה על דעתה של תמנע, שכבחורה צעירה, גבוהה, בעלת חזה נפוח (תרתי-משמע), אף משופץ, והליכה פרובוקטיבית, היא תיתקל בהפתעה מרה ולא צפויה, סירוב נחרץ של דניאל.

זה הטריף אותה. היא פצחה במסע נקמה, פרי קנאה טיפשית והרסנית!

ייתכן ששלושה שופטים התייחסו למסע הנקמה של תמנע בת העשרים ברצינות?

תמנע הייתה זרוקה ברחובות, מכורה לסמים, וגם סחרה בהם. היא הגיעה אלינו כשרצתה להיגמל, להתחזק ולחזור בתשובה. היא עבדה לפחות בארבע עבודות שונות במקביל (בבני ברק ובהרצליה), וגרה בדירה שכורה עם שותפים בגבעת שמואל. היא דיברה בלחץ רב על החובות הכלכליים שאליהם נקלעה, ועל חובות לאנשים גם בשוק הסמים.

תמנע מעידה לפני בית המשפט שהיא הגיעה למרכז הישראלי לנפגעי כתות אחרי שראתה את הכתבה על המשפחה בערוץ 2, בתכנית "360", ולא הייתה יכולה לסבול את העובדה שרינו צרור, מנחה התכנית אמר שכנראה יצטרפו נשים נוספות. היא אמרה בבית המשפט שהכתבה גרמה לה להבין שמשפחת אמבש היא

כת. בכתבה, רינו צרור עורך השוואה לגואל רצון שמייחס לעצמו אי-אלו כוחות, ואומר על עצמו שהוא ה"גואל". הוא חי עם עשרות נשים שקעקעו את שמו ואת דיוקנו על זרועותיהן, הוא הוגדר כראש כת ונעצר. רוב הנשים עזבו אותו בעקבות המעצר והכריזו שהיו שפחות וקרבנות, והוא הודה בחלק מהמיוחס לו. חשוב להדגיש שאין לנו שום דבר משותף לא אתו ולא עם נשותיו או סגנון חייהם. תמנע אמרה לפני בית המשפט שהיא חשבה שהמרכז הישראלי לנפגעי כתות ייתן לה מענה פסיכולוגי למצוקתה, ולא ציפתה שיגישו תלונה בשמה למשטרה.

"המרכז הישראלי לנפגעי כתות" השתתף בתכנית של רינו צרור, ושלח אישה שמעידה על עצמה שהייתה השפחה של גואל רצון, וגם עו"ד מתחזה, כמצג "המומחים" של התכנית, וזאת כדי לקבוע שאנחנו "קבוצה תאומה", וכך יוכלו להקל את עבודת המשטרה, כשדעת הקהל כבר תהא גורפת, וכשכל המדינה תדבר על האיש עם שש הנשים, שהוכרז בתכנית התחקירים בערוץ הפרסומי של ישראל כראש כת מסוכנת. או-אז, שום שופט לא יעז לתת פחות ממאסר עולם למי שהתקשורת הפכה לעבריין מסוכן. המרכז הישראלי לנפגעי כתות, השנוי כשלעצמו במחלוקת, מורכב משלושה אנשים. תחקיר "ידיעות אחרונות" מאותה שנה גילה שהמרכז הוא גוף שהוקם לשם סחיטת מיליוני כספים, והם גם קיבלו תביעות עתק מגופים גדולים שבפניהם נאלצו להתנצל. למרות כל זאת, זכו לתהילה במדינת ישראל, והודות למעצרנו, הצליחו להתברג בכנסת וברווחה, כשהם למעשה גוף עצמאי פוגעני. ולאחר רוע גזר דיננו, גם קיבלו תעודת הוקרה ותודה מהמשטרה...

המפגש הראשון של תמנע עם ראש חוקרי הימ"ר אשר ליזמי ולילך רנן התנהל ללא תיעוד (ללא הקלטה וללא צילום, ללא זיכרון-דברים וללא מזכר. כלום) על בבית מלון על חוף הים בתל אביב.

לא היה דבר שמנע מחוקרי המשטרה להשתמש בתמנע, שהייתה נכונה להגיד הכול כדי לנקום על כבודה שנפגע; לא היה דבר שמנע מחוקרי המשטרה לסגור לה את החובות ואת התיקים שהיו לה עוד קודם במשטרה; ולא היה דבר שמנע מראשי צוות החקירה אשר ליזמי ולילך רנן להדריך את תמנע ולהכין אותה איך לדבר, מה בדיוק לומר ובאיזה טון.

רק לאחר שניהלו משא ומתן שהשתלם גם לה וגם להם, והסכימו ביניהם, היא הגיעה לפרוס את עדותה במשך שלושה ימים, שלא כולם מתועדים בעין המצלמה.

תמנע הייתה העילה. היא היא העדה המרכזית, הראשית, והכול התחיל ונגמר בעדותה.

ראוי לציין כי תמנע לא נחקרה על ידי עוה"ד של דניאל בבית המשפט, וגם גילינו את הסיבה לרשלנות מכוונת זו: למעשה, עוה"ד של דניאל ייצג במקביל גם תיק שבו היה זקוק לשירותי המרכז הישראלי לנפגעי כתות, בניגוד אינטרסים לתיק שלנו, ולכן אם היה מבצע חקירה נגדית, הייתה אז מוכחת התרמית של המרכז, ששלח את תמנע, ואז עדותה הייתה קורסת).

ואין שום הוכחה או ראיה לסצנות האימה שהיא מתארת כרשימת מכולת מבולבלת. לעומת זאת, ישנם מזכרים רבים על מזומנים שהועברו לידה מאותם חוקרי הימ"ר, ומזכר מפורט שבו אותה חוקרת (לילך רנן) מתארת איך תמנע התקשרה בוכה וצועקת שאין לה דירה, ואיך זה שמותירים אותה זרוקה ברחובות. לילך רנן החוקרת מציינת שהרגיעה אותה ואמרה שידאגו לה לכך...

השופטים הכתירו אותה "קוהרנטית ואמינה", על אף שתיאוריה לא הגיוניים ולא מעוגנים בשום דבר, לא בזמן, ולא במקום. כמו כן, היא לא נשאלה, לא על ידי השופטים ולא על ידי הפרקליט, שום שאלה שתוכל לאשש את עדותה הדמיונית, ולתת אחיזה מציאותית להרשעת חף מפשע ל-26 שנה.

עדי התביעה שאותם הצליחו לגייס במשטרה – על ידי סחיטה באיומים, שוחד, מצג שווא ומכות קשות – בחקירותיהם הראשונות לא הבינו מה רוצים מהם, והשופטים אף ציינו בהכרעת הדין כי כל בני המשפחה נתנו גרסה אחידה, המכחישה את כל המעללים שניסו לייחס לדניאל. עדי התביעה שנבראו כתוצאה ממסכת התעללות נפשית ופיזית מחוקרי משטרה, התגלו כ"לא אמינים" בעיני השופטים, שקבעו שכל דיבור שלהם זקוק ל"סיוע" על מנת שיתקבל כעדות, כיוון שהסתירות רבות מדי, ו"זיהום העדויות" של החוקרים עצום עד כדי כך שהשופטים הגדירו אותם "מחדלי חקירה רבים", דבר ששופטים לא נוהגים לציין, אלא אם כן מחדלי החקירה הם חמורים עד לכדי שחרור הנאשם לחופשי, וביטול כתב אישום בשל חקירה בניגוד לחוק, אי-לכך, יש לפסול את כל החקירה והמעצר מלכתחילה, ולשחרר את דניאל לאלתר.

מעניין לראות בהכרעת הדין שהשופטים מכנים את כל מי שהעיד על עובדות פשוטות בחייה של תמנע, שבקלות מוכיחות את גודל השקרים שהיא מספרת, ומבטלות באחת את כל העדות הזדונית שלה, כ"משחירים את פניה"...

משחק מכור?! רולטה רוסית?! גיליוטינה?! רצח לאור יום תחת הכותרת "משפט"?! שמישהו יירה בי, כי אני לא מצליחה להתעורר מהסיוט הזה?!

אפרט מעט, כגרגר אבק, מהעובדות המזעזעות שבתיק הזה. תיק שתויג כתפ"ח, תיק פלילי חמור. נכון מאוד, חמורים מאוד הם מעשיהם של חוקרי ימ"ר ירושלים, שנטלו לעצמם את החירות לעבור על החוק ולהתעלל התעללות של ממש, מבחינה פיזית, נפשית ומנטלית, בנשים, בגברים ובילדים, ולא בחלו בכל האמצעים על מנת להכריז מוות על בן אדם שחף מכל עוון. למה?! כנראה שלגורמים מדיניים כמו המשטרה והרווחה יש מה להסתיר...

עליזה הותירה אותי מזועזעת כשגילתי שהצליחו לשבור אותה ולהפוך אותה ל"עדת מדינה". היא היחידה מהנשים שלא חיבבתי במיוחד, אני זוכרת את השבת הראשונה שהתארחתי בבית המשפחה. משהו בי לא יכול היה לסבול את הנוכחות שלה. מורחת על פניה חיוכים אימתניים החושפים שורות שיניים עצומות. השתדלתי להביט קדימה למדפי הספרים, ולא לסובב את הראש לכיוונה, להתעלם מהתכנים שלחשה באוזני ללא הרף ודי בחוצפה, כיוון שבהחלט היה אפשר להבין שאינני מעוניינת בחברתה. היא המשיכה וסיפרה שגם היא הייתה חילונית, והתפארה ברשימת 300 הגברים שאתם שכבה. סיפרה שאפילו עסקה בזנות. על חוויות של סמים קשים. כשיחסינו היו קצת יותר חבריים, היא סיפרה לי שסבלה בבית הוריה, ושאמה עשתה ממנה שפחת ניקיון ועליזה כינתה אותה "מכשפה", על אחיה הגדול, שלדבריה אנס אותה והפך אותה לשפחת מין של חבריו העבריינים... סיפרה כמה שהיא מרגישה היום חזקה, ושיש תקווה. היא גרמה לי להרגשות לא נינוחות ולמבוכות. האווירה שיצרה הייתה איומה. הילדים התחננו אליי שלא אשאיר אותם לבד אתה. שאלתי: "למה?" הם אמרו שהיא רעה, מכשפה. אני ניסיתי להגיד מילים שיחבבו אותה עליהם. היא הייתה אדם אחד בנוכחותו של דניאל: מתחשבת בזולת, אכפתית, עדינת נפש ובעלת חסד. ושלא בנוכחותו, התגלה אדם אחר, כמו הייתה אדם בעל שתי ישויות: אז התנהגה בצורה המונית, דיברה בשפה זולה והתנהגה בטיפשות, מחפשת בין מי למי לסכסך, והכל בלוויית צחוק נבזי ולעג מרושע.

היה קשה מאוד להגיע לדניאל כשהיא הייתה משוחחת אתו לבד, ומבהירה לנו במבט קשה, בלי למצמץ: "אני צריכה את הזמן הזה, מצטערת" ולא הייתה ברירה. אמרתי לדניאל שלא כדאי לו להאמין לשום מילה שלה, מולה. עברתי הרבה בחיים לפני שהכרתי את משפחת אמבש, ולמדתי לזהות אנשים. מה שזיהיתי בעליזה לא התאים לבית הזה, שבו אין מקום למשחקים מניפולטיביים. זה בית של אנשים שלא מתחפשים. כולנו התקרבנו, התקבצנו והתחברנו כדי לקיים את התורה באמת.

עליזה התעקשה, חרף התנגדותו של דניאל, להמשיך לעבוד ב"חברה קדישא", ברחיצת גופות. באחת הפעמים שחזרה משם סיפרה שהעבודה הזו גורמת לה "תחושת עליונות והתנשאות על הנפטרות". דניאל חשש שזה עלול להזיק גם לה וגם להם, והיא בכל זאת המשיכה.

אני מאמינה באמונה שלמה, שהתורה חיה וקיימת בשבילנו כדי שנזכה לקיימה באמת. וזה מה שרצינו וזה מה שניסינו. לדאבוני הרב, היו הרבה אנשים שניצלו את התמימות של המשפחה הזאת, בפרט של דניאל. וכואב לי, כואב מאוד, לגלות שלא רק שלא התבדיתי במה שהרגשתי כלפי האישה הזאת – עליזה, אלא גרוע מכך, שהיא הרחיקה לכת, והחליטה לצאת למבצע חיסול. מבצע לחיסול משפחת אמבש. עכשיו אני מבינה שמה שהילדים ניסו להגיד לי ולא רציתי לשמוע היה אמתי.

במהלך המעבר של עליזה לשיתוף פעולה עם המשטרה ולמתן עדות השקר שנתנה לפני בית המשפט, נתפסה על ידי חוקרים פרטיים ששכרו ילדיו הבוגרים של דניאל מזייפת את חתימתו של דניאל בציקים שלו שלקחה מהבית, ומשכה למעלה מ-250,000 ₪ בגנבה!! בעזרת בן-זוגה החדש ואחיה הגדול ממנה (כן, אותו אחד שאהבה לספר ששנים היה אונס אותה, והעריצה אותו, וחיפשה תמיד דומה לו, ושום דבר לא סיפק אותה כי הזדקקה לכוח ולאלימות. מה שאף אחד לא יכול היה לספק לה...); כשבאותו הזמן, דניאל נמצא בחקירת המשטרה, מוקף השפלות, סופג מכות קשות: משיכות בזקן, בעיטות, דחיפות, ומטיחים בו האשמות חמורות על עברות שלא ביצע! ומאיימים עליו שיירקב בכלא הרבה לפני שיגיע לשלושים שנות מאסר כי הם הולכים לשלוח לו עבריינים סמויים שיפוצצו אותו למוות אם לא יתאבד לפני כן.

זלמן, בועז, צילה וגיא-נועם לא נחו לרגע, ועברו מעו"ד אחד למשנהו כדי למצוא פתרונות למצב הבלתי אפשרי שאליו נקלעו. בצו משטרה נאסר עליהם לגור בבתים שעדיין שילמנו עליהם שכירות, ולכן הם העבירו את הלילות בשינה ברכב ששכרו. יום אחד, עליזה ביקשה ללוות מהם את הרכב, "כדי לנסוע לאירוע משפחתי". מאותו יום נעלמו עקבותיו של הרכב הזה, והיא מצדה, כשנשאלה על כך בבית המשפט מול השופטים של דניאל, טענה בלי בושה שהחזירה אותו. עד עצם היום הזה הרכב מוכרז במשטרה כ"גנוב"... שמישהו ידליק את האור בחושך הזה! כמה שקר! לשקר אין רגליים, והוא עומד ליפול. תחזיקו חזק.

לדבריה של עליזה היא לא יכלה להתאפק, ולא עמדה בניסיון, היא בגדה בדניאל בעודה נשואה לו, גם עם כמה מחוקרי המשטרה שאחד מהם מעיד במשפט הזוטא ("מחדלי חקירה"): "נכון, הייתי אתה בקשר ולא רשמתי מזכרים על השיחות והפגישות שהיו לנו, אז?"

החוקרים לקחו את עליזה לבית ברוממה, כי "ביקשה לקחת כמה דברים". היא לקחה בין היתר, מכונות כביסה, אלבומים של תמונות של כל המשפחה וגם את המחשב הנייד הפרטי שלי שקניתי לעצמי. אולי כי ידעה שהיו לי שם ראיות מפלילות נגדה, על ההתנסות המינית שלה עם לא אחרת מאשר... תמנע! הייתי מוכרחה לתעד, כי ידעתי ששתיהן יכחישו. זה נותן הסבר נוסף למתח ששרר בין השתיים ולתחרות "הסמויה" ביניהן, שעליה העידה עליזה בחדרי החקירה. בכל אופן, עד היום, אפילו שציינתי לפני בית המשפט כי המחשב האישי שלי הגיע אליה בעזרתה "האדיבה" של חוקרת המשטרה רויטל צרף, לא זכיתי לתגובה. וכשהגעתי לתחנת המשטרה לדרוש את קנייני הפרטי, שלחו אותי כלעומת שבאתי.

זלמן, בועז, גיא נועם, צילה, מארי ויאן דיברו ביניהם על כך שמוכרחים לשמור על אבא, והחליטו שזלמן יהיה הנציג שלהם בביקור אצל דניאל בכלא, ושיספר לו על הפנים האמתיות של עליזה, ושכדאי לו להתגרש ממנה, כי היא נוכלת והם אפילו לא יכולים לספר לו הכול.

בבית המשפט המחוזי שאליו הגעתי כעדת הגנה, התחייבתי להגיד את האמת ורק את האמת. את השופטים האמת עניינה הרבה פחות. אחד השופטים צרח עליי במלוא הגרון כשהתעקשתי להגיד את האמת, והפסיק רק שעוה"ד של דניאל מצאה הוכחה לאמירתי, והפרקליטות הוצרכה להתנצל בפניי. זה קרה שלוש פעמים באותו הדיון; הם התעקשו על שקר, ואני התעקשתי על האמת. ניצחתי אותם. אבל זה לא עזר, כי השקרים הגסים עסיסיים יותר, מרגשים אותם ומשפיעים עליהם כנראה הרבה יותר מהאמת, והם אלו שמכריעים בניסוח הכרעת הדין.

**<u>"אישה מוכה" – בחזרה לחדרי החקירות 2011</u>**

פחות מ-24 שעות שאנחנו עצורות, תחת הכינוי "חשודות", ביציאה מאולם הדיונים, בדיון בנוגע אלינו הנשים, כשהחוקר עידן ניסה לדחוף אותי להתקדם מהר יותר, הזזתי את ידי כדי שלא ייגע בי. בקפיצה מהירה חבטה את ראשי בקיר הבלשית מעיין צור, לפתה סביב צווארי את שתי ידיה בסגירה חזקה והדוקה עד לחניקה. בפנים רעות ובכוח, על מנת להכאיב, אזקה את ידיי, וזרקה אותי בכל המדרגות, תוך שהיא מקללת את דניאל ואת איבר מינו באכזריות יוצאת דופן. כשגרבוני ניילון וכפכפי עץ הולנדיות לרגליי, החלקתי ועפתי על הרצפה בחזקה, היא בעטה בי ומשכה אותי מאזיקי הידיים, גוררת אותי בהמשך מורד המדרגות. חבולה ומבועתת משנאת החינם של הבלשית שנראתה בגילי, דאגה להבהיר לי שבכל מחיר הם הולכים "לגמור" אותנו. אחרי שגררה אותי במסדרונות הימ"ר, היא הטיחה אותי בחזקה על כיסא, בחדר קטן, במחלקת תשאול. לא התנגדתי, הייתה לי הרגשה שזה יהיה יותר גרוע, וכלל לא בטוח שאצא מפה חיה. אך גם את זה הם יכסו בקלות ובשלווה, ואף אחד לא ידע על הרצח בחדרי החקירות, ואת האשמה לבטח ייחסו לדניאל. אלא מה?!.

היא פוצצה לי את הפנים בסטירות. מהר מאוד הגיעה לילך רנן לחזק את מעיין צור, ויחד תוך שהן מקללות את דניאל (!!!), שימוש בסרקזם ודם בעיניים, המשיכו להכות אותי כפליים! מדי פעם נכנסו שוטרים בלבוש אזרחי, שאלו משהו בטון יבש וקר, זרקו כל אחד קללה משלו, ודיברו ביניהם כבדרך אגב מה עושים לדניאל, ומה עוד הולכים לעשות לו, תוך שימוש בביטויים של רוצחים מנוסים, ויצאו. הדלת נשארה פתוחה, כנראה שזה מראה נורמלי במחלקת תשאול ימ"ר ירושלים. ראשי היה שמוט לאחור, והנחמה היחידה שלי הייתה, שלמעלה יש עין שצופה, מצלמת ומקליטה...

אחרי זמן, שקשה לי להעריך את משכו, כיוון שהייתי תחת הלם המהלומות, הותירו אותי לבדי. כשהתאוששתי, צעקתי שאני רוצה להגיש תלונה. השוטרים עברו וחזרו במסדרון, ולעגו לי. בשלב כלשהו, חוקר בשם עודד שמעא העביר אותי לחדר אחר, והגיש לי דף ועט, כדי לצחוק ממני, שאני יכולה לכתוב איזו תלונה שאני רוצה, להם אין ממה לפחד, הם "המשטרה". תוך חצי שעה לכל היותר הגיעה עובדת סוציאלית בשם יעל שוחט, שליוותה אותי למונית שתסיע אותי למקלט לנשים מוכות באשדוד. מה?! התרעמתי והתנגדתי, אני מעדיפה להיות בתא מעצר, אני רוצה לעמוד מול שופט ולהסביר לו מה הולך פה! התחלתי לספר לה בשצף את כל שעבר עליי, ושאינני אישה מוכה אלא על ידי המשטרה!! היא נשארה אדישה, ובמהלך הנסיעה בכיתי בהיסטריה וללא הפסקה, תוך שניסיתי לספר לנהג המונית, שיוכל להיות עד ולספר למישהו שיזעיק עזרה. העובדת הסוציאלית דיברה בטלפון עם עובדת סוציאלית אחרת, על הסלט שהיא מתכננת לצהריים... חשבתי שאני משתגעת. כשהגענו למקלט לנשים מוכות, מאחורי גדרות

ברזל חשמליים וחוטי תיל ניסיתי לשפוך את לבי לפני רונית, מנהלת המקלט, ולהסביר לה את המצב האמתי. על המכות שבפניי – השוטרות היכו אותי ולא בעלי! היא ישבה מולי זקופה, רגל על רגל, וקבעה: "תסמונת האישה המוכה – היא מכחישה, וממשיכה להגן עליו, אל דאגה יש לנו את כל הכלים לטפל בה...".

זה לא אמתי זה לא אמתי.

נ נח נחמ נחמן מאומן.

אחרי חודשיים לא פשוטים, של סיוטים ועוד (בהרחבה – בבלוג האישי) הצלחתי לברוח מהמקלט. לא ידעתי לאן ללכת, לא יכולתי לסמוך על אף אחד, הייתה לי הרגשה שכל העולם תחת השפעה של סם מטשטש, ואיש אינו ער למה שבאמת קורה... הגעתי להר המנוחות, להתפלל לעצה אצל הסבא, ולצעוק בלי קול למקיץ נרדמים. לכיווני רץ ילד מבוהל בחליפה שחורה. סמי?! מעולם לא ראיתי אותו לבוש בצורה כזו. הוא היה כולו נסער, רועד ומלוכלך, בפנים חיוורות, ועיגולים שחורים סביב לעיניו, מבטו מרצד מימין לשמאל ומשמאל לימין במהירות, כפרנואיד. הוא נראה לא טוב, ופחדתי לדעת מה עבר עליו בימים האלה מאז שעצרו את כולנו והעבירו אותנו עינויים ממשיים... הוא דיבר במשפטים לא ברורים ומהירים בגבות קפוצות וכמו שהוא על גחלים לוהטות:

"אני פה כבר שלושה ימים. ישנתי ליד הקבר של הסבא... לא היה לי לאן ללכת... הם הרסו את הבית... לא אכלתי כמה ימים... בבקשה שירן קחי אותי אתך אין לי איפה להיות! תהיי אימא שלי, קחי אותי לאן שאת הולכת...".

נאלמתי. לא ידעתי מה להגיד ואיך לעזור לו. ניסיתי להסביר לו: "גם אני ברחתי, ממקלט לנשים מוכות, כלאו אותי בתנאי מאסר ולקחו לי את הטלפונים והכסף והכול. נשארתי בלי כלום". התחלתי לצעוד בצעדים מהירים במעלה הכביש המתפתל חזרה לחניה, ביקשתי בתפילה חרישית שיראו לי את הדרך... סמי, בצעדים מהירים ובקופצנות בלתי פוסקת לא חדל לומר משפטים מהירים ומבולבלים על כל מה שעבר עליו... הוא היה נראה על סף התמוטטות עצבים... הגיע אוטובוס, עליתי. הוא קפץ במעלה המדרגות ועקף אותי. לנהג הוא אמר: "אימא שלי משלמת עליי", והתיישב במושב הראשון. כשהתיישבתי על ידו הוא ביקש כמעט בדמעות שלא אעזוב אותו. הוא חזר ואמר שהוא מפחד להיות לבד. הוא הגיע אתי לדירתה של חברתי בתל אביב, ולא הצליח להירגע מסיפורי חוקרים וחקירות, והיה מסויט כולו. התקשרתי לאחיו הגדולים צילה וזלמן, בועז וגיא-נועם שיגידו לי מה לעשות אתו, הם אמרו שהוא מוכרח לחזור לפנימייה, כי אם לא הוא יסבך את כולנו, והם לא יכולים לקחת אותו כי הם ישנים ברכב שכור, וביום הם עמוסים בפעילות. ליוויתי אותו לתחנה המרכזית, והחברה שלי שילמה על כרטיס הנסיעה שלו לירושלים, ונתנה לו עוד כסף להגיע לפנימייה. הוא היה כמו גור כלבים נטוש, מסכן ומעורר רחמים, ואי-אפשר להשאיר אותו בבית מחשש לכלבת... אחרי שנסע, הרגשתי קצת הקלה. עם זאת, הייתי אחוזת דאגה, ולא ידעתי אם עשיתי את הדבר הנכון. הוא מצא את האחים הגדולים בירושלים, הם צלצלו אליי בפאניקה שסמי לא מוכן לחזור לפנימייה שבה סגרו אותו השוטרים, ושאם אני רוצה לעזור, שאקח אותו ואדאג לו. הם עמדו בלחץ עצום כי הם היו המבוגרים היחידים שנשארו לטפל בכל הצד הפלילי מול עוה"ד. מאותו היום, לקחתי על עצמי את המשימה לדאוג לסמי כמו היה התינוק שמעולם לא היה לי. הוא סיפר לי שסבל מאוד בפנימייה, שהמדריכים והנערים כיבו עליו סיגריות, השפילו אותו ואיימו עליו שיחתכו לו את הפנים. סגרו אותו שם אחרי חקירות, השוטרים הפעילו עליו את משחק התפקידים: "השוטר הרע והשוטר הטוב", אחד איים עליו במכות ושיסגור אותו בכלא לעבריינים, והשני ניסה להפוך אותו לאחד משלהם ואמר לו שהוא יכול לעבוד אתם אם הוא רוצה בתור שוטר סמוי. לקחו אותו למסעדות ושיחדו אותו במתנות יקרות. הוא אמר שהיו עליו לפעמים ארבעה חמישה חוקרים שביחד התקיפו אותו וצעקו עליו והפעילו עליו לחץ אדיר. מאז הוא בחרדות, וכל שוטר או ניידת מקפיצים אותו להתחבא ולרעוד מפחד ומהיסטריה דקות ארוכות. הוא אמר שהכניסו את אנסטסיה (אחותו למחצה) לחדר החקירות, והיא החלה לצרוח עליו שאין יותר משפחה, אין יותר בית, אין יותר אבא, ושבין כה וכה הוא לא האבא הביולוגי שלהם, שסוגרים אותו לשלושים שנה, ואם הוא רוצה להסתדר, שלא יהיה טיפש, יעשה מה שהיא עשתה ויגיד מה שהחוקרים יגידו לו, והם יסדרו לו הכול, ויקנו לו מה שירצה, אם לא, יסגרו אותו בכלא ל-14 שנה... הוא שנא אותה על זה. (https://youtu.be/_aK4udkcN1E).

סמי היה בטראומה מכל מה שעבר עם השוטרים. הוא היה מתעורר בבהלה ומתחנן שלא אזוז מהמיטה שלו. חלם חלומות שהעירו אותו באמצע הלילה והקפיצו אותו מהמיטה. לילה אחד התעורר מחלום מרגש: "אבא חזר הביתה וכולם ביחד", סיפר לי פרטים בהתלהבות, וביקש שאכתוב והוא יחתום עם תאריך, כי זו סגולה מרבי נחמן שהחלום יתקיים. ישנו אצל חברות שלי ובבתי חולים. הוא היה תמיד בלחץ. אני הייתי תמיד צריכה לתת לו ביטחון שהכול בשליטה. כלום לא היה בשליטתי, ולא היה לי מושג מה יקרה

מרגע אחד למשנהו. רק השתדלתי לשמוע אותו, כי היה לו צורך לדבר על כל מה שקרה בחדרי החקירות, והוא בכה והצטער מאוד שדיבר רעות על דניאל בהשפעת החוקרים שהדריכו אותו מה להגיד, על מנת להגן על עצמו אם הוא לא רוצה שיתפרו לו תיק על אונס אחותו בת השש. הוא רצה לנקום במשטרה, באחותו אנסטסיה, בעליזה ובכל מי שגרם לפירוק המשפחה. ניסיתי להרגיע אותו שכתוב בתורה שאסור לנקום ושהשם בכל מקרה ישלם לאיש כמעשהו. הוא החליט שמעכשיו נעשה פעולות לשחרר את אבא. בשיתוף עם אחיו הגדולים הכנו פליירים שמסבירים את המצב, וסמי רץ לחלק אותם בכל מקום. הוא רצה שנצא למסע בקברי צדיקים, שנעסוק בלימוד הספרים הקדושים ושנעשה מצוות.

סמי חי בחוסר יציבות מאז שפירקו לנו את הבית, לקחו ממנו הכול, את כל נקודות הביטחון והאהבה, בלי אבא, בלי אימא, שאותה סגרו ב׳מקלט לנשים מוכות׳ בבאר שבע, ולא נתנו לה להתקשר אלינו, היא גם לא ידעה לאן. הבריחה שלו מהפנימייה, הפרנויה מהמשטרה. חיינו במנוסה, כל יום לא ידענו איפה נישן בלילה, דיברתי עם בעלי מסעדות שייתנו לנו לאכול אצלם, וניסיתי לתת לו תקווה שזה רק זמני, ושהדברים עומדים להסתדר. כשמישהו נתן לנו דירה לכמה שבועות, סמי התמלא שמחה ורצה שנעשה תכנית לחטוף את כל הילדים מהפנימיות, שנתאחד כדי להוציא את אבא. בתום השבועות האלו הוא שוב התפרק ובכה כל הלילה שהוא נתן יד למאסר של אבא, והוא לא מסוגל לחיות עם עצמו. ארבעה חודשים הוא ייסר את עצמו והאשים את אנסטסיה שהשפיעה עליו בצרחות שלה ומתוך הלחץ דיבר שטויות בחקירות. הוא פרק את התסכול בהתפרצויות אלימות כלפיי, לא ידעתי איך להגיב ומה לעשות כדי לעזור לו. מצאתי את עצמי רצה ברחובות, בורחת מפניו כשנבהלתי שהרביץ לי וניסה לשרוף אותי, הוא רץ אחריי וצעק ששיקרתי לו כשאמרתי לו שאני אימא שלו, שלא אכפת לי ממנו ושאני לא אוהבת אותו. זה הכאיב לי. היינו במצב מסובך. לילה אחד נסענו לישון אצל זוג חברים שלי שהיו להם שני ילדים. ישבתי אצלם, על כיסא גדול מול המחשב, הוא בא מאחוריי עם צעיף, קשר על פניי והפיל אותי עם הכיסא לאחור. צלצלתי לאחיו הגדולים שיבואו לקחת אותו.

כחצי שנה אחר כך, בזמן שאילנה, אדרת ואזמרה כלואות, ואני וקארי מתניידות בין דירות, הגעתי למגרש הרוסים. ידעתי שדניאל אמור להגיע לשם בפוסטה לפני דיון, וחשבתי שהוא יוכל לראות אותי ושאוכל להעביר לו מסרים של אהבה בפנטומימה. חשבתי שאם אתלבש בסגנון שאני לא מזוהה אתו ואפרע את שערי, לא יזהו אותי. זה לא היה חכם. החוקר שהיכה את דניאל ואת אזמרה, אשר לזמי, הופיע מולי והכריז שאני עצורה, ואם לא אבוא אתו מיד לתחנה – ישתמש באלימות. ארבעה חודשים באגף בידוד על ״שיבוש הליכי חקירה״ ו״הדחת עד״. סמי היה אחראי גם על זה. בתמיכתה של עליזה, שאת הלב החליפה באבן, ושל תמנע, שהמשיכה להתעקש לספר הכול חוץ מאת האמת. בעדותה נגדי אמרה שרדפתי אחריה, הטרדתי אותה ונתתי לה כסף, ועוד שקרים בלי סוף כהרגלה הנבזה, כפי שגם דיברה נגד דניאל, מאש הקנאה שבערה בה, וכל קשר בין דבריה למציאות אינו קיים, אפילו לא במקרה.

יש לי עוד הרבה מה לספר, כי כשלא הייתי בתא של 2 מטר על 2 מטר וחצי, העבירו אותי כמעט בכל התאים, כשבכל פעם נועלים אותי עם אסירה אחרת שמנסה להרוג אותי או את עצמה או את שתינו. מה שכן אוסיף ואומר, שעוה״ד שלי מטעם המדינה הזהיר אותי שאם לא אודה במיוחס לי, אשב 9-11 שנה במאסר, וכששאלתי אותו מה הם רוצים ממני, אמר שהפרקליטות רוצה שאתגרש מדניאל ואצא נגדו. התחזקתי ואמרתי: ״אם כך, מצדי להישאר פה!״

חצי שנה קודם, תמנע ראתה אותי בתל אביב ליד כיכר רבין, אחרי שברחתי מהמקלט לנשים מוכות, והתקדמה לכיווני בהתלהבות:

> ״וואי שירן! איזה קטע, אני בדיוק באה מפרישמן, וראיתי שם בחור שמזיה הזכיר לי אותך, ובדיוק חשבתי עליך איך היית בתור חילונית בתל אביב. ואת לא מבינה! חלמתי הלילה שכל המשפחה סביב שולחן גדול עם דניאל ויש שמחה כזאת נעימה כמו שיש תמיד אתכם...״.

שתקתי. לא ידעתי באיזה צד היא. תמיד היא נראתה חשודה בעיניי. היא המשיכה: ״מה, איפה את? מה שלום כולם?״ כשהסברתי לה איפה כולם ומה המצב, היא הזילה דמעות ואמרה שהמרכז הישראלי לנפגעי כתות ניצל אותה, היא אמרה שהיא רוצה לעשות משהו כדי לבטל את התלונה שבמרכז הגישו בשמה ללא ידיעתה, היא התקשרה לעוה״ד שלה לראות מה אפשר לעשות, ואז ביקשה שניפגש עם בועז והבנים באיזה מקום לעשות תכנית. נפגשנו עם כל מי שביקשה אצל חברה שלי. עליזה גם באה וישבה עם תמנע לשיחת לחישות בחדר המדרגות. ממצלמה נסתרת שהייתה במקום ניתן היה לשמוע שעליזה מספרת לתמנע, איך בכל רגע היא מנסה להתחזק כדי להתגבר על הניסיונות שמכל כיוון באים כדי להפריד אותה מהבן אדם שהיא אוהבת ומהחיים שבחרה, ואיך שאפילו אימא שלה שלחה לה בחור שצעיר ממנה כשליח להפריד אותה מבעלה ולפתות אותה לשכב אתו, כדי שלא תהיה לה דרך חזרה. בעקבות הפגישה הזאת נרקמה התכנית הסודית של מקום המחבוא עבור עדי התביעה.

סמי פוצץ את התכנית כשכבר הכול היה מוכן, אחרי שהילדים הגדולים לקחו הלוואות של מאות אלפי שקלים למימוש החזון. וכשבועז לא נתן לו סיגריה מיד כשביקש, התקשר למשטרה, וכך גרם למעצר של בועז, זלמן, גיא-נועם, אזמרה, אדרת ואילנה.

לבסוף, אני ושאר הנשים חתמנו על עסקה שבה הודנו שנפגשנו בינינו, ושאר האשמות נגדנו התבטלו באחת. השתחררנו מהכלא. אילנה אדרת ואזמרה אחרי שנה! ואני אחרי ארבעה חודשים.

לסיכום,

נשים חופשיות, עצמאיות וחזקות, שמאמינות בכם קוראים יקרים, שאתם, כן רוצים לדעת את האמת. אחרת את מי יעניין לקרוא ספר על נשים סוררות שנשברו בחדרי חקירות!! ושיהיה ברור לכולם; אנחנו כמו כל הנשים – בנויות אותו הדבר; רק שבחרנו לחיות יחד באהבה אחת.

שירן אמבש.

*כעת, חודשיים לפני הערעור בבית המשפט העליון, בתקווה להוכיח את חפותו של דניאל ולהחזיר אותו אלינו.*

*ערב חג סוכות תשע"ו, עוד חג שאנחנו בלעדיו.*

*הלב דופק מהר, בהתרגשות ובפחד לקראת החלטת השופטים.*

*האם לדעתכם למדינה יש את הזכות לגזור על פירוד לכל החיים בין אנשים אוהבים שרוצים להיות ביחד?*

*האם זה אנושי שהם לא נותנים לאנשים שאוהבים אחד את השני לראות זה את זה לשארית חייהם?*

*האם מותר לאסור על קשר בין אנשים רק בגלל שהמדינה החליטה שצורת החיים שלהם לא מקובלת ב"חברה מתוקנת".*

**הצטרפו גם אתם לדף ה facebook דניאל אמבש חף מפשע וסמנו 'אהבתי'**

**www.danielambash.info**

תמצאו אותנו גם ב youtube נשות אמבש.

# Philosophie
# aux éditions L'Harmattan

## *Dernières parutions*

**ALAIN BADIOU**
**Vivre en immortel**
*Vinolo Stéphane*
À la différence de penseurs comme Deleuze ou Derrida, Alain Badiou est un philosophe classique, cherchant à apporter des réponses aux questions les plus anciennes de la philosophie. Pour Badiou, la philosophie n'est plus au coeur du processus de production des vérités. Toute la pensée de Badiou nous enjoint donc à cesser d'être des animaux humains pour devenir des sujets, à ne plus survivre à l'aune de nos seuls intérêts, pour vivre pleinement, c'est-à-dire, vivre enfin comme des immortels.
*(Coll. Ouverture Philosophique, 20.00 euros, 196 p.)*
*ISBN : 978-2-343-05087-4, ISBN EBOOK : 978-2-336-36612-8*

**CENT MILLIONS D'ORGASMES**
**Essai sur la pornographie**
*Rubino Francesco*
La pornographie sera l'un des objets les plus invasifs des réglementations morales à venir. Aux positions naïves (M. Marzano) et aux reconstructions puristes (C. MacKinnon) et relativistes (M. C. Nussbaum, L. Williams), ce «pornouvrage» oppose le sens authentique de cette anomie érotique : le sens d'un corps opprimé qui, pourtant, pornographiquement écrit (A. J. Magliacane) et se resymbolise dans un cri (P. Pat Califia) ou se désymbolise dans un fantasme (Ch. Ackerman, E. Lemoine-Luccioni).
*(Coll. Ouverture Philosophique, série Arts vivants, 24.00 euros, 240 p.)*
*ISBN : 978-2-343-05144-4, ISBN EBOOK : 978-2-336-36662-3*

**COURT TRAITÉ D'ONTOLOGIE**
*Bouvier Pascal*
Pourquoi existons-nous ? Est-ce que nous existerons après la mort ? Autant d'interrogations profondément humaines qui sont prises en charge par la philosophie. Au sein de celle-ci, une discipline spécifique se consacre à la question de l'être : l'ontologie. Elle semblait tombée en désuétude et dans l'oubli depuis les critiques sévères de certains courants philosophiques. Ce traité tente de saisir les grandes lignes de cette histoire de l'être.
*(Coll. Ouverture Philosophique, 14.50 euros, 148 p.)*
*ISBN : 978-2-343-04094-3, ISBN EBOOK : 978-2-336-36722-4*

**CRITIQUE (LA) RADICALE DE L'ARGENT ET DU CAPITAL CHEZ LE DERNIER-MARX**
**Matériaux pour une refondation du marxisme**
*Bayer Philippe*
Ce livre s'inscrit dans une réflexion sur la Critique radicale associée à ce qu'on peut appeler le Dernier-Marx. Ce Dernier-Marx, on peut le lire dans l'édition française du *Capital* en un repositionnement de Marx, venant problématiser sa pensée objective précédente, qui réceptionnait un donné du mode de production capitaliste pour l'interpréter comme un donné de l'histoire. À

cette entreprise ruineuse pour le mouvement ouvrier, le Dernier-Marx substitue une problématique radicalement subjective à partir d'une ontologie de l'identité vitale.
*(Coll. Ouverture Philosophique, 25.00 euros, 248 p.)*
*ISBN : 978-2-343-04705-8, ISBN EBOOK : 978-2-336-36730-9*

**DÉCONSTRUCTION PHÉNOMÉNOLOGIQUE ET THÉOLOGIQUE DE LA MODERNITÉ OCCIDENTALE**
*Awazi Mbambi Kungua Benoît*
Le puissant travail de déconstruction phénoménologique et théologique de la modernité occidentale fait apparaître l'autisme épistémologique qui caractérise son horizon de la Mathesis Universalis à la base de ses productions scientifiques, techniques, athées, consuméristes et médiatiques. À travers cet ouvrage, l'auteur opère un puissant tournant prophétique, mystique et thérapeutique de la théologie négro-africaine de la libération holistique, échappant ainsi aux schèmes idéologiques et politiques des théologies occidentales frappées d'obsolescence.
*(33.00 euros, 320 p.)*
*ISBN : 978-2-343-03719-6, ISBN EBOOK : 978-2-336-36791-0*

**ÉVEIL BOUDDHIQUE ET CORPORÉITÉ**
*Marcel Antoine*
«Voir dans sa propre nature», dans le bouddhisme zen, est une expression convenue qui désigne l'éveil. Pourquoi, et comment ? Observant l'importance première donnée au corps dans la pratique méditative, la mise à l'écart de la noèse, l'auteur, s'appuyant sur les développements de la pensée phénoménologique à la suite de Maurice Merleau-Ponty, tente une investigation de l'éveil bouddhique.
*(Coll. Ouverture Philosophique, 12.00 euros, 108 p.)*
*ISBN : 978-2-343-05191-8, ISBN EBOOK : 978-2-336-36785-9*

**PROBLÈME (LE) KANTIEN DE L'ÉTHIQUE**
**Habiter le monde**
*Gaudet Pascal*
La philosophie critique de Kant peut être interprétée comme une éthique, qui signifie non pas seulement l'impératif de la vertu, mais l'exigence d'une réalisation du souverain Bien en l'homme et dans le monde. Ce livre montre comment la recherche d'un passage de la liberté à la nature fonde le projet d'une « habitation » du monde et permet de penser le sens éthique de la philosophie en ses domaines théorique et pratique.
*(Coll. Ouverture Philosophique, 12.00 euros, 110 p.)*
*ISBN : 978-2-343-05328-8, ISBN EBOOK : 978-2-336-36702-6*

**RACINE (LA ) DE LA LIBERTÉ**
*Urvoy François*
À l'issue d'un siècle qui a vu le plus grand écrasement des hommes et des peuples et en ce début qui en prend bien le relais, les préoccupations de liberté ont pris une urgence plus grande et plus sensible. Les investigations obtiennent jusqu'ici des résultats très décevants car elles s'attachent aux moyens externes sans jamais chercher qui et surtout comment on sera en mesure de les produire et de les mettre en œuvre. Il s'agit, ici, de remonter à la racine de la question : ce qui dépend de nous, ce que nous pouvons par nous-mêmes dans un monde qui nous produit et nous conduit.
*(Coll. Ouverture Philosophique, 27.00 euros, 258 p.)*
*ISBN : 978-2-343-03005-0, ISBN EBOOK : 978-2-336-36731-6*

**SYMBOLIQUE (LE) ET LE TRANSCENDANTAL**
*Verley Xavier*
Ce livre part du différend qui a opposé Frege et Husserl à propos du psychologisme. Comment ces deux pensées tournées vers une réflexion sur l'arithmétique ont-elles pu parvenir à deux conceptions si différentes de la logique ? Il est apparu qu'il s'agissait d'évaluer l'idée de représentation qui est au cœur du problème. Ainsi, faut-il se (re)présenter pour penser ou y a-t-il la place pour une pensée symbolique et aveugle ?
*(Coll. Ouverture Philosophique, 30.00 euros, 294 p.)*
*ISBN : 978-2-343-02833-0, ISBN EBOOK : 978-2-336-36557-2*

**CRITIQUE ET ÉMANCIPATION**
**Recherches foucaldiennes sur la culture arabe contemporaine**
*Beghoura Zouaoui - Préface de Jacques Poulain*
Cet ouvrage utilise les pensées de Michel Foucault dans la culture arabe. Il joint à une histoire socio-politique de cette culture une critique qui vise à y établir les conditions d'une émancipation réelle, indépendante de l'actualité brûlante qui semble la rendre aujourd'hui impossible. Cette expérience de critique socio-politique développe en effet les critères d'une émancipation intellectuelle qui conditionne toute émancipation sociale.
*(Coll. La philosophie en commun, 17.00 euros, 176 p.)*
*ISBN : 978-2-343-04092-9, ISBN EBOOK : 978-2-336-36304-2*

**DU FÉMINISME DANS L'ŒUVRE DE MICHEL FOUCAULT**
**A demain le bon sexe**
**Essai**
*Sastre Danièle*
«Le sexe, disait Foucault, ça s'administre, la sexualité, ça se subit ; quant à la sensualité, elle est chaque jour à inventer.» L'auteur a voulu rouvrir le dossier, emprunter les chemins qu'il a tracés en 1976 en écrivant son Histoire de la sexualité, qui est l'histoire des discours sur la sexualité, eux-mêmes histoire des corps investis par le pouvoir.
*(27.00 euros, 268 p.)*
*ISBN : 978-2-343-04763-8, ISBN EBOOK : 978-2-336-36305-9*

**GASTON BACHELARD, UNE POÉTIQUE DE LA LECTURE**
*Buse Ionel*
L'éthique bachelardienne est une éthique simple, mais pas du tout simpliste : l'homme du théorème est complété par l'homme du poème. Mais, si l'éthique est une direction de la pensée qui doit maîtriser notre avenir, la poétique est la source ontologique de cette pensée. C'est-à-dire la liberté de rêver doit être à l'origine de la liberté créatrice de la pensée ou de l'homme des théorèmes. En fait, il ne s'agit pas d'une éthique fermée dans les modèles artificiels d'une pensée techniciste, mais toujours d'une éthique soutenue, à l'origine, par une poétique de la pensée ouverte.
*(Coll. Ouverture Philosophique, 16.50 euros, 160 p.)*
*ISBN : 978-2-343-04292-3, ISBN EBOOK : 978-2-336-36292-2*

**HOMME (L') EST-IL UN ANIMAL POLITIQUE ?**
**Physique de la misanthropie, entre littérature et philosophie**
*Ainseba Tayeb*
Le compartimentage disciplinaire hérité du XIXe siècle pousse à opposer les intentions esthétiques de la littérature au chemin vers la vérité que serait la philosophie. Cette opposition nie la possibilité d'une philosophie littéraire tant que, réduite à un dogme, elle n'est pas critiquée. Ce livre, plutôt que d'opposer la littérature et la philosophie, raconte ce qui les rapproche en prenant un thème qui leur est commun, celui de la misanthropie.
*(30.00 euros, 298 p.)*
*ISBN : 978-2-343-04870-3, ISBN EBOOK : 978-2-336-36346-2*

**LOGIQUE ET RHÉTORIQUE SELON CHAÏM PERELMAN**
**ou le jugement partagé**
**L'éloquence de la raison**
*Melcer Jean-François*
Des trois volets de l'oeuvre de Chaïm Perelman – la philosophie du droit, l'éthique et la logique – le troisième est le moins connu. Les précédents tomes de *L'éloquence de la raison* ont mis l'accent sur les deux premiers. Il s'agit, à présent, d'expliciter les conditions épistémologiques de possibilité de la nouvelle rhétorique, conçue comme logique argumentative, non comme technologie persuasive.
*(Coll. Ouverture Philosophique, 31.00 euros, 304 p.)*
*ISBN : 978-2-343-04209-1, ISBN EBOOK : 978-2-336-36286-1*

**MERLEAU-PONTY - FREUD ET LES PSYCHANALYSTES**
*Le Baut Hervé*
Le parcours de Maurice Merleau-Ponty ne peut se comprendre sans le fil rouge de la Psychanalyse : dès sa thèse, il restaure le primat de la perception et du corps sexué à la lumière de Freud et de Binswanger. A la Sorbonne, il renouvelle la Psychologie de l'enfant en y intégrant M. Klein, J. Lacan et F. Dolto. Au Collège de France plusieurs cours font des rêves et de la libido une dimension inéluctable de l'humain. De nombreux psychanalystes et psychiatres se sont « laissés interroger par lui « : citons : H. Ey, A. Hesnard, P. Fédida, A. Green, J. Laplanche, J.-B. Pontalis, Luce Irigaray...
*(Coll. Ouverture Philosophique, 24.00 euros, 296 p.)*
*ISBN : 978-2-343-04080-6, ISBN EBOOK : 978-2-336-36381-3*

**NAÎTRE MÈRE**
**Essai philosophique d'une sage-femme**
*de Gunzbourg Hélène*
Cet essai est la réflexion d'une sage-femme qui, depuis trente ans, a accompagné des femmes pendant leur grossesse et après la naissance de leur enfant, écoutant leur questionnement sur l'arrivée au monde d'un enfant désormais « désiré ». La révolution dans la procréation et la transformation de la famille concerne chacun d'entre nous. Faut-il redouter que les forces aveugles de la nature ou du destin soient remplacées par la rigueur glaciale et anonyme de la technoscience et de son « expertise » ?
*(Coll. Ouverture Philosophique, 28.00 euros, 274 p.)*
*ISBN : 978-2-343-04437-8, ISBN EBOOK : 978-2-336-36405-6*

**PENSÉE DIALOGIQUE, LANGAGE ET INTERSUBJECTIVITÉ DANS LA PHILOSOPHIE DE FRANZ ROSENZWEIG**
*Muller Alain - Préface de Bernard Forthomme*
L'originalité de cet ouvrage, c'est de tenter d'éclairer le « retour » de Franz Rosenzweig au judaïsme, - et le concept de « révélation » qui s'y rattache -, à partir de l'itinéraire intellectuel et de la philosophie de celui-ci, et en s'appuyant sur les philosophies d'Hermann Cohen et d'Eugen Rosenstock, et cela en plaçant le premier dans le contexte historique de la « symbiose judéo-allemande », le second dans le cadre du dialogue interreligieux entre le christianisme et le judaïsme.
*(Coll. Ouverture Philosophique, 28.00 euros, 270 p.)*
*ISBN : 978-2-336-00746-5, ISBN EBOOK : 978-2-336-36432-2*

**PENSÉE (LA) POSITIVISTE SOUS LE SECOND EMPIRE**
*Charlton Donald Geoffrey - Traduction : René Boissel*
Le Second Empire fut l'époque charnière dans la construction de la France moderne : développement exponentiel de la science qui repousse les frontières de l'inconnaissable, culte du 'Progrès' sans limite qui atteindra son apogée à la veille de la Première Guerre mondiale. Parallèlement, une nouvelle philosophie se construit avec pour base la science et remet en cause les profondes certitudes préalablement acquises : le positivisme, esquissé par Saint-Simon et structuré par Auguste Comte. Le professeur Donald Geoffrey Charlton (1925 – 1995) présenta sa thèse à l'Université de Londres.
*(Coll. Ouverture Philosophique, 26.00 euros, 260 p.)*
*ISBN : 978-2-343-01340-4, ISBN EBOOK : 978-2-336-36430-8*

**PHILOSOPHIE ET SPÉCIFICITÉ AFRICAINE DANS LA REVUE PHILOSOPHIQUE DE KINSHASA**
*Massamba-Makoumbou Jean-Serge*
La revendication d'une rationalité purement africaine par les milieux scientifiques ou universitaires africains, depuis des décennies, dérive de la minorisation de l'Afrique. Cette étude s'interroge sur le sens et la signification de la notion d'africanité attachée à sa philosophie. Elle tente de répondre à la question de l'identité africaine de cette philosophie et partant de celle du philosophe africain, telle qu'elle se donne à lire dans la Revue philosophique de Kinshasa.
*(Coll. Ouverture Philosophique, 16.50 euros, 168 p.)*
*ISBN : 978-2-343-05119-2, ISBN EBOOK : 978-2-336-36416-2*

**L'HARMATTAN ITALIA**
Via Degli Artisti 15; 10124 Torino

**L'HARMATTAN HONGRIE**
Könyvesbolt ; Kossuth L. u. 14-16
1053 Budapest

**L'HARMATTAN KINSHASA**
185, avenue Nyangwe
Commune de Lingwala
Kinshasa, R.D. Congo
(00243) 998697603 ou (00243) 999229662

**L'HARMATTAN CONGO**
67, av. E. P. Lumumba
Bât. – Congo Pharmacie (Bib. Nat.)
BP2874 Brazzaville
harmattan.congo@yahoo.fr

**L'HARMATTAN GUINÉE**
Almamya Rue KA 028, en face
du restaurant Le Cèdre
OKB agency BP 3470 Conakry
(00224) 657 20 85 08 / 664 28 91 96
harmattanguinee@yahoo.fr

**L'HARMATTAN MALI**
Rue 73, Porte 536, Niamakoro,
Cité Unicef, Bamako
Tél. 00 (223) 20205724 / +(223) 76378082
poudiougopaul@yahoo.fr
pp.harmattan@gmail.com

**L'HARMATTAN CAMEROUN**
BP 11486
Face à la SNI, immeuble Don Bosco
Yaoundé
(00237) 99 76 61 66
harmattancam@yahoo.fr

**L'HARMATTAN CÔTE D'IVOIRE**
Résidence Karl / cité des arts
Abidjan-Cocody 03 BP 1588 Abidjan 03
(00225) 05 77 87 31
etien_nda@yahoo.fr

**L'HARMATTAN BURKINA**
Penou Achille Some
Ouagadougou
(+226) 70 26 88 27

**L'HARMATTAN SÉNÉGAL**
10 VDN en face Mermoz, après le pont de Fann
BP 45034 Dakar Fann
33 825 98 58 / 33 860 9858
senharmattan@gmail.com / senlibraire@gmail.com
www.harmattansenegal.com

**L'HARMATTAN BÉNIN**
ISOR-BENIN
01 BP 359 COTONOU-RP
Quartier Gbèdjromèdé,
Rue Agbélenco, Lot 1247 I
Tél : 00 229 21 32 53 79
christian_dablaka123@yahoo.fr

Achevé d'imprimer par Corlet Numérique - 14110 Condé-sur-Noireau
N° d'Imprimeur : 123371 - Dépôt légal : novembre 2015 - *Imprimé en France*

www.ingramcontent.com/pod-product-compliance
Lightning Source LLC
LaVergne TN
LVHW010929061026
849535LV00007B/2304